END-TIME VISIONS

VISIONS

THE ROAD TO ARMAGEDDON?

Other books by Richard Abanes

Cults, New Religious Movements, and Your Family

American Militias: Rebellion, Racism and Religion

Defending the Faith: A Beginner's Guide to Cults
and New Religions

Journey into the Light: Exploring Near Death Experiences

END-TIME VISIONS

THE ROAD TO ARMAGEDDON?

BY RICHARD ABANES

FOUR WALLS EIGHT WINDOWS
NEW YORK / LONDON

Published in the United States by:
Four Walls Eight Windows
39 West 14th Street, room 503
New York, N.Y., 10011

U.K. offices:
Four Walls Eight Windows/Turnaround
Unit 3, Olympia Trading Estate
Coburg Road, Wood Green
London N22 6TZ, England

Visit our website at http://www.fourwallseightwindows.com

First printing April 1998.

Library of Congress Cataloging-in-Publication Data:
Abanes, Richard.
End-Time Visions: The Road to Armageddon?/ by Richard Abanes.
p.   cm.
Includes index.
ISBN 1-56858-104-1
1. End of the world--History of doctrines. 2. Christian sects--History. 3. Cults--History. 4. End of the world--Controversial literature. I. Title.
BT876.A22   1998
291.2'3--dc21   97-44524
                                                                                      CIP

10 9 8 7 6 5 4 3 2 1

Printed in the United States

Contents

Introduction

There is no common denominator in the world today except religion.

Billy Graham
American Evangelist[1]

RELIGION HAS FASCINATED ME for most of my life. I was raised a Roman Catholic, dabbled in occultism as an adolescent (e.g., Edgar Cayce and ouija boards), and became an evangelical Christian at the age of seventeen. Then, in my twenties, I found myself involved with a cult known as The Way International. Upon leaving this group, I continued my search for spiritual fulfillment among hyper-Pentecostals who writhed on the floor during church services and wailed their praises to God in "tongues." Now, after more than thirty years of involvement with religion, it seems only natural that I would earn my living as an investigative reporter specializing in cults, the occult, world religions, and new religious movements.

There is no lack of work for someone in my field of interest. Since the 1980s a wave of spirituality has been steadily engulfing numerous countries, especially the United States. According to scholars in American religious thought, we are "witnessing a spiritual awakening unprecedented in modern times."[2] Church historian and University of Chicago professor Martin Marty observes, "spirituality is back, almost with a vengeance. . . . I find myself treating the concern for spirituality as an event of our era."[3]

One need only glance through a few periodicals to see the validity of Marty's comment. Articles bearing titles such as "Desperately Seeking Spirituality," "The New Spin Is Spirituality," "The Power of Faith," "In Search of the Sacred," and "Exploring Spiritual Approach to Business-World Challenges" are now common.[4] Early indications of this renewed interest in religion appeared in a 1987 *Better Homes and Gardens* survey of more than 80,000 readers. Sixty-two percent of those polled said that in recent years they had "begun or intensified personal spiritual study and activities."[5]

Even more telling are figures from a 1994 *Newsweek* poll, which found that fifty-eight percent of Americans feel a need to experience spiritual growth.[6] The data further revealed that a third of all adults had recently had a mystical or religious experience. Furthermore, twenty percent said that they had received a revelation from God within the year, and thirteen percent claimed to have seen or sensed the presence of an angel.[7] More recent surveys from 1996 and 1997 show that almost ninety percent of American adults believe in God, eighty-seven percent say that God answers prayers, and eighty-one percent believe in a heaven "where people live forever after they die."[8]

These statistics confirm the obvious: religion and spirituality are "in." As a result, Christianity and Judaism are again flourishing. Hinduism, Buddhism, and numerous meditative arts "have become permanently embedded in the American scene."[9] Shamanic practices from various cultures are being used as "tools for inducing healing trances."[10] Native American spirituality is gaining popularity, and New Age instructional courses on "out-of-body" travel annually attract thousands.[11]

Interestingly, many of the faiths now experiencing rapid growth throughout the world promote a common doctrine: at some point in the near future, our world will be destroyed. An understandable by-product of this belief has been an increase in the number of people who think that Armageddon (i.e., the final battle between the forces of good and evil that, according to many Christians, will occur just prior to the world's end) is fast approaching. As far back as 1994, fifty-nine percent of American adults believed doomsday to be very near. Of these individuals, sixteen percent saw it happening within several hundred years, twenty-one percent gave earth just decades, and twelve percent placed the terminus of humanity some-where within a few years.[12]

A veritable epidemic of end-time visions is now sweeping across the globe, infecting the hearts of millions of people. John "Running Dear" Eleazer — a Native American from New Jersey — says his spirit guides told him that the next few years will bring increased earthquake activity, intense hurricanes, and massive tidal waves; one of which will engulf all of

New York City. Roman Catholic Jerrie Castro from Santa Maria, California claims that she is regularly visited by the Virgin Mary, who imparts a message that is plain and simple: humanity must change *now*, or humanity is doomed. There is also Jim Singer of Toronto, Canada, a 37-year-old Croatian who says that he went through 100 days of visions in 1989. His spiritual visitors include the Virgin Mary, St. Peter and Jesus. Singer, too, has seen terrible earth changes and global disasters in the near future. He was also told by God that evil spiritual forces are presently creating two new diseases to unleash against mankind, each of which will be worse than AIDS.[13]

Predictably, the entertainment industry has picked up on our culture's newest "hot button" and has released scores of made-for-TV movies, blockbuster films, and television specials built on a single subject: dooms-day. The May 1, 1996 CBS special *Mysteries of the Millennium*, for example, opened with the following lines: "Are you going to witness the end of the world? The Bible, Nostradamus, the Mayan Calendar, and ancient Hopi Indians all predicted that doomsday will be sometime in the next few years. . . . [N]ow modern science seems to support them."[14]

Thanks to the magic of Hollywood, the final world event has been depicted with shocking clarity for all to see and savor. Since the early 1990s, fans of riveting special effects have beheld global devastation by way of Earth-impacting asteroids, lethal microbes, and hostile UFOs. Consider the story line of the February 7, 1997 episode of the sci-fi/occult series *Millennium*: "Frank believes an apocalyptic force is driving a serial killer."[15] Even TV sit-coms have capitalized on the millennial fever infecting society; one character on NBC's *Boston Commons* fearfully shouted: "God's coming back again in the year 2000 and we're all gonna die!"[16]

But to a significant percentage of the population, the new millennium's arrival is not merely an innocuous source of entertainment. Many people seriously believe that the world may indeed end by 2000/2001.[17] These same individuals seem completely unaware of the fact that similar pro-nouncements have been made in centuries past about various years: 1033, 1260, 1533, 1844, and 1914, to name but a few. Meanwhile, the apocalyptic dogmatists continue to proclaim: "We are the final generation. Never before has humanity been faced with such definitive signs of the end."[18]

The current fascination with doomsday is so widespread that scholars
have inaugurated a new field of research called millennial studies, sometimes referred to as simply "end-times." It has produced "a wave of books,
papers, courses and conferences."[19] History professor Richard Landes of
Boston University has even created a Center for Millennial Studies to serve
as a clearinghouse for scholars.[20] Several discoveries have already been
made through the research being conducted in connection to Landes'
organization. For example, according to professor Stephen O'Leary (co-
founder of the Center), end-time prophets and their followers are often far
different from stereotypical images of doomsday fanatics:

> Millennial prophets today bear little resemblance to the cartoon caricature of
> the bearded, white-robed figure with the picket sign proclaiming, "The End
> is Near." They can be found in business suits, at church, at work, on television
> and on the Internet. Their followers are too easily dismissed as hypnotized
> cultists. They are our children, our parents, our brothers, our sisters and
> potentially ourselves.[21]

Is our generation the last generation? Does the Bible foretell Armageddon near A.D. 2000? *End-Time Visions* seeks to answer these and other
relevant questions by tracing the history of end-time prophecies through
the many religious cults, sects, and movements that have been built on
doomsday declarations. Some of these date back as far back as the first
century after Christ and have long since died out. Others of more recent
origin continue to draw followers at an impressive rate of thousands per
year. This volume also examines the many "signs" consistently cited by
today's prognosticators as proof of Earth's imminent destruction. It additionally catalogues many of the predictions that have been voiced by end-
time speculators from widely divergent socio-economic and religious
circles.

Finally, *End-Time Visions* takes a penetrating look at the source of
apocalyptic obsession: the human mind. It reveals: 1) how people become
convinced that the end is near; 2) how persons can continue believing in a
particular religious leader even after that individual's predictions have been
proven wrong by the passage of time; and 3) how false prophecies have been

rationalized and/or covered-up by leading doomsayers and their followers in an effort to preserve their overall belief system.

I invite you to go for a walk with me on the road to Armageddon. According to some modern-day prophets, it could well be the last journey you ever take.

PART ONE

Apocalypse Now

Cover page to a 1997 issue of *Endtime*, one of many Fundamentalist
Christian magazines now proclaiming the imminent end of the world.

ONE

1990s: Decade of Death

I'm glad it's over. Hurry, hurry my children, hurry. . . . [L]et us not fall in the hands of the enemy. Hurry my children, hurry. . . . Now quickly, quickly, quickly, quickly, quickly. . . . No more pain. . . . No more pain. . . . All we're doing is laying down our life, we're not letting them take our life, we're laying down our life. All it is is taking a drink . . . to go to sleep. That's what death is, sleep. [SCREAMS IN BACKGROUND]. . . . I'm tired of it all. . . . [A]ssure these kids, can some people assure these children of the relaxation of stepping over to the next plane. We'll set an example for others. . . . [O]ne thousand people who've said we don't like the way the world is. . . . [K]eep your emotions down, keep your emotions down. . . . [It] will not hurt if you will keep your emotions down, if you will be quiet [SCREAMS IN BACK-GROUND]. . . . Death is a million times preferable to ten more days of this life. If you knew what was ahead of you, if you knew what was ahead of you you'd be glad to be stepping over tonight. . . . This is a revolutionary suicide. It's not a self-destructive suicide. . . . [SCREAMS IN BACKGROUND]. . . . [T]he best thing you can do is relax and you will have no problem. You will have no problem with the thing if you just relax. . . .

— Reverend Jim Jones (November 18, 1978)
excerpted recording of Jones' final address
to followers as they committed suicide[1]

NOT SINCE THE 1978 mass murder-suicide of more than 900 people at Jonestown, Guyana has the world been so keenly aware of end-time religious cults and their deadly power. The term "cult" was coined by German theologian Ernst Troeltsch (1865–1923) in his classic work, *The Social Teaching of the Christian Churches* (1912). He applied the designation to any spiritually-oriented group or movement that was neither a church nor a sect.[2] Eventually, however, the word *cult* evolved into a disparaging label for any group advocating "curious and unconventional belief and behavior."[3]

Jonestown not only reinforced this latter definition, but added an element of danger to it. Most people today continue to think of a cult with the stereotypical picture in mind of a socially odd and destructive religious body led by a crazed, authoritarian, messiah figure. Some groups *should* indeed be viewed in this a manner. Their practices radically depart from societal norms and are quite harmful. But many other "cults" (e.g., Mormonism, Jehovah's Witnesses) bear little resemblance to Jones' organization. Why do some scholars still classify these more socially acceptable groups as cults?

The answer to this question depends on whom you ask. Religion researchers classify religious groups and movements as cultic from three main perspectives: 1) sociological; 2) psychological; and 3) theological. Each perspective focuses on a different aspect of a group's complex composition and includes numerous "red flags," indicating whether the organization is cultic from that particular perspective.[4] If one or more psychological, sociological, or theological red flags are present, then the group can properly be considered a cult.

Interestingly, a significant number of cults manifesting red flags from all three perspectives commonly espouse doctrines involving an imminent doomsday. Throughout the 1990s, several countries (Canada, Switzerland, Korea, Japan, France, America, and Russia) played host to these types of cults. The various tragedies they spawned can only be compared to Jonestown. Consider a few of the news headlines from recent years:

"Korean Sect Stunned As 'Rapture' Doesn't Come"
"4 Federal Agents Killed in Shootout with Cult in Texas"
"Kiev Cult's Doomsday Prediction Draws Parents Searching for Children"
"Swiss Cult's Bizarre Last Act Leaves 'Wax Museum' of Death"
"Secretive Japanese Cult Linked to Germ Weapons Plan"
" ' Follow Me': Inside the Heaven's Gate Mass Suicide"[5]

One might easily jump to the conclusion that the misguided zealots whose actions gave rise to these stories were foolish losers with a glazed look in their eyes. But nothing could be further from the truth. The roster of cultists involved in such incidents include doctors, lawyers, engineers, politicians, university students, and most tragically, innocent children. We must never overlook, or forget, this fact. As the Spanish philosopher George Santayana (1863–1952) famously noted: "Those who cannot remember the past are condemned to repeat it."[6]

In this chapter, therefore, we will begin our stroll down the road to Armageddon with a brief recap of the many doomsday-inspired episodes of sorrow that may still be fresh in all of our minds. Perhaps such reflection will in some way help to avert similar events in the future.

THE RAPTURE DISASTER

It was already 11:30 P.M. when I arrived at the Maranatha Mission Church located in downtown Los Angeles. According to the Korean worshipers gathered inside the old building, Christ's "second coming" and their departure to heaven (i.e., the "rapture") would occur within thirty minutes. This cataclysmic event would mark the beginning of the end of the world. As I approached the door of the run-down structure, two security guards blocked my path. They had been instructed to prevent all non-members from entering the facility. Consequently, I was forced to wait out in the cold evening air for Jesus' midnight arrival.

The apocalypse, however, never materialized. Only a few relatives of sect members showed up to console loved ones who might exit the prayer vigil after realizing that their miraculous transportation to heaven was not going to transpire. As I drove home at 1:30 A.M., I could not help but reflect on the two years of misguided hopes that finally had been brought to a close for members of the Korean *Hyoo-go* movement. It was a sad tale that first gained national attention through a full-page ad appearing in the October 20, 1991 issue of *USA Today*. The message was simple and straightforward:

RAPTURE
OCTOBER 28, 1992
JESUS IS COMING IN
THE AIR

This was only one of many warnings given by several Bible-based groups associated with the *Hyoo-go* (Korean for "rapture") movement, which had a membership that reportedly fluctuated between twenty thousand and one hundred thousand.[7] Affiliated groups included Korea's Dami Church (known in America as Mission for the Coming Days), Taberah World Mission, Shalom Church, and Maranatha Mission Church. One *Hyoo-go* group predicted that beginning on October 28, 1992, 50 million people would "die in earthquakes, 50 million from collapsed buildings, 1.4 billion from World War III and 1.4 billion from a separate Armageddon."[8]

Predictions such as this one were instigated by Lee Jang Rim's Korean bestseller *Getting Close to the End*, which promised an October 28, 1992 date for the supernatural departure of all Christians from Earth. In addition to Rim's book, *Hyoo-go* followers substantiated their rapture deadline with appeals to a variety of sources that they considered authoritative. One *Hyoo-go* pamphlet, for instance, borrowed a twisted time calculation from American prophecy pundit Jack Van Impe.

According to the brochure, Van Impe had calculated a biblical "generation" to be approximately fifty-one years. He further taught that the establishment of Israel as a nation in 1948 signified the end of the Gentile times spoken of in Luke 21:24. The year 1948 + 51 years ("the generation" that would see the end) came out to 1999. From this figure, seven years were subtracted for "the tribulation," a period of unparalleled destruction that many Christians believe will occur just prior to the world's end (Matt. 24:34). *Hyoo-go* followers thus arrived at their 1992 date for the rapture. This view's corollary was that the year 1999 would see the end of the world as we know it.[9]

Divine revelations given to a twelve year old boy named Bang-Ik Ha were also used to confirm the October date.[10] God allegedly called young Bang-Ik into a prophetic ministry in July 1987, telling him: "Therefore, just as I have prepared John [the Baptist] before the Son of Man came to earth [i.e., Jesus Christ], again I am preparing Ha Bang-Ik!"[11] A 1992 Taberah World Missions pamphlet announced that Jesus himself had actually spoken through the boy, saying: "I will be there in Oct. 1992. Prepare!"[12] Another publication explained that the child's mother had her son's calling confirmed to her in a dream.[13]

Adding to the tension was the antagonism of *Hyoo-go* followers towards those who disagreed with the movement's beliefs. Individuals who

A *Hyoo-go* movement brochure featuring end-time prophet Bang-Ik Ha
(published by Taberah World Missions, c. 1992).

did not accept the 1992 prophecy were labeled heretics and told that God
would punish them after Jesus' return.[14] A far more dangerous doctrine,
however, was also being promoted: i.e., only a select group of *Hyoo-go*
believers would be taken in the rapture. These would have to prove
themselves worthy of transportation to heaven.[15] All others would face the
post-rapture tribulation, a seven-year era marked by unspeakable terrors
perpetrated by the dreaded Antichrist. Moreover, persons not taken in the
rapture would have to be martyred in order to go to heaven. Their only
alternative would be eternal damnation.

At the Los Angeles Maranatha Mission Church (MMC), members
demonstrated their worthiness by praying loudly throughout each night,
often until their throats bled from vocal straining. Spitting blood soon
became a sign of salvation and devotees who expelled blood frequently were
seen as the most likely candidates for the rapture. This phenomenon was

viewed as a way of purging oneself of sin.[16] According to former members of MMC, children unable to accomplish such a feat — some as young as six years old — were forced to participate in the church's "martyr training program":

> [T]hey were forced to kneel down and pray until morning. If they fell asleep, they were hit on their calves with a stick, or they had to raise their hands for an extended period of time. One former child member claimed he was forbidden to use the restroom or sleep during the all night prayer meetings.[17]

Meanwhile back in South Korea, social disruption mounted. The city of Wonju saw one fanatical *Hyoo-go* group burn their furniture in the street while waiting for the rapture. In Seoul, five thousand *Hyoo-go* believers quit their jobs. Many of them sold their homes, abandoned their families, and amassed huge debts. Countless young people stopped attending college, high school, and even elementary school. Several pregnant women reportedly had abortions "so they would not be too heavy to be lifted to Heaven" and at least four followers committed suicide before October 28.[18]

On the predicted date, thousands of *Hyoo-go* adherents gathered in churches around the world to await their glorious departure. The South Korean government responded by dispatching 1,500 riot police to Mission for the Coming Days, one of Seoul's largest *Hyoo-go* churches. Police agencies, fire companies and ambulances were also placed on alert by officials seeking to prevent a second Jonestown.

Fifteen minutes after the deadline passed, Rev. Chang Man-Ho — senior pastor of Mission for the Coming Days — took the pulpit and simply said, "Nothing has happened. Sorry. Let's go home."[19] Loyal followers were not only outraged, but broken-hearted. Many began weeping uncontrollably. Some physically attacked the preachers who had misled them. One distraught member tearfully lamented, "God lied to us."[20] Months after the disappointment, some parents were still searching for their children who were kidnapped and taken to mountain hideouts by more radical rapture sects.[21]

What happened to 46-year-old cult leader Lee Jang Rim? He was sentenced by a Korean court to two years in prison for defrauding believers out of $4.4 million dollars and illegally possessing United States currency. It was also discovered that Rim had invested a significant portion of his ill-gotten cash in bonds scheduled to mature in May 1993, more than six months *after* his predicted rapture date![22]

Rim's conviction, his failed prophecy, and the many lives shattered by the *Hyoo-go* movement left the Korean community wondering how such a terrible thing could have happened. But four months later, their tale of suffering was pushed aside as the attention of the world's media was grabbed by another band of religious zealots obsessed with end-time prophecies: the Branch Davidians.

ARMAGEDDON IN WACO

Few traces remain of what occurred on the outskirts of Waco, Texas between February 28 and April 19, 1993. Time, bulldozers and the dusty winds that blow across those lonely flatlands have erased virtually all visual reminders of the Branch Davidian tragedy. Although the black smoke that once filled the Texas skies has long since cleared, the fiery images of more than seventy-five men, women and children dying at the hands of the U.S. government have been irrevocably burned into millions of American minds.

The bloody saga began when one hundred heavily armed agents from the Bureau of Alcohol, Tobacco, and Firearms (BATF) raided the group's isolated compound in an effort to serve a search and arrest warrant on David Koresh, the cult's self-proclaimed "Son of God" leader. According to federal authorities, the Davidians had stockpiled an enormous cache of weapons, many of them illegal.[23]

To the Davidians, however, the arrival of evil intruders signaled the beginning of Armageddon. Koresh and his followers responded with a brutal greeting of heavy and sustained gunfire from all directions. One journalist on the scene said that the compound "sounded like a war zone," recalling how he could hear people screaming in agony. Another eyewitness to the explosive confrontation recounted how "there were people dropping left and right." After a forty-five minute war, four BATF agents were dead and twenty others wounded. Six Davidians had also been killed.

Photo courtesy of David Bunds

David Koresh with his first wife, Rachel Jones, and their first child, Cyrus.
Rachel and Cyrus perished with Koresh in the Davidian fire.

The ensuing standoff under FBI jurisdiction lasted fifty-one days, ending on April 19 when the FBI attempted to drive the Davidians out into the open by demolishing the compound in which they had barricaded themselves. The plan called for using several tank-like Combat Engineering Vehicles (CEVs) to punch huge holes into the walls of the Davidians' poorly constructed domicile. Tear gas would then be injected through the gaps in hopes of forcing the cultists from their stronghold. Tragically, government officials failed to adequately consider the Davidians' religious fervor and its influence on the situation's outcome.

Six hours into the operation, tiny puffs of white smoke began to escape from one of the many second-story windows in the Davidian home. Minutes later, the entire structure was engulfed in flames and the world watched in horror as the building burst into a city-block-sized funeral pyre. Coroner reports indicated that although many Davidians perished from smoke inhalation and fire, a significant number of them, including Koresh, died from a single gunshot wound to the head.

Photo courtesy of David Bunds

An extremely rare photograph of several Davidians. On the top row (l. to r.) are Perry Jones (father of Koresh's first wife and third wife), Michelle Jones (Koresh's third wife), Rachel Jones (Koresh's first wife), Cyrus (Koresh's son by Rachel), Robyn Bunds (another of Koresh's wives), Jeff Little, and Paul Fatta. On the bottom row (l. to r.) are Karen Doyle (Koresh's second wife), Star (Koresh's second child by Rachel), and Sheri Jewell (yet another wife of Koresh). All of these Davidians, except Bunds and Fatta, died in the April 19, 1994 Davidian blaze.

Only nine cult members escaped. Five of them — along with six other cult members arrested during and after the siege — stood trial on a variety of charges, including murder, conspiracy and weapons violations. Three of the eleven were acquitted of all charges. Four of the defendants, however, were given forty years. The four remaining Davidians received sentences ranging from three to twenty years. One of the most disturbing questions that continues to be asked is: How did the fire start? Some people believe FBI agents deliberately began the conflagration to eliminate troublesome cultists.[24] Others think FBI tanks accidentally ignited the flames by knocking over kerosene lanterns.[25] The U.S. Justice Department officials say the Branch Davidians set the fire themselves. This latter theory is based in part on FBI listening devices placed inside the cult's wooden structure. These recorded several Davidians making comments about pouring fuel, spreading it around, and lighting a fire.[26]

Even more significant is the major role fire played in Davidian eschatology (i.e., beliefs about the "last things," or, more specifically, the end of the world). I learned about their fire-related doomsday doctrines from a Bible owned by Robyn Bunds, one of Koresh's many wives. She had defected from the cult approximately one year before the BATF raid. Her Bible contains notes she wrote during the years she studied with the group. One comment in the Bible's margin links Armageddon, which Koresh believed would be a confrontation with the government, to the sixth seal of Revelation 6:12, 17.[27] Noteworthy are the verses involving fire that she had cross-referenced:

- "[T]he day of the LORD is at hand. . . . every man's heart shall melt. . . . their faces shall be as flames" (Is. 13:6–9, King James Version).
- "[H]is throne was like the fiery flame, and his wheels as burning fire. A fiery stream issued and came forth before him" (Dan. 7:9–10, KJV).
- "Who can stand before His indignation? and who can abide in the fierceness of His anger? His fury is poured out like fire and the rocks are thrown down by him" (Nahum 1:6, KJV).

Robyn had also referenced Jeremiah 50 to the sixth seal passage. This is noteworthy in that Koresh quoted Jeremiah 50:22 to the FBI in a letter sent from the compound.[28] Verses 24 and 32 of that prophetic section reads as follows:

I have laid a snare for thee. . . . thou hast striven against the LORD. The LORD hath opened his armoury. . . . I will kindle a fire to his cities, and it shall devour all round about him. (KJV)

In an April 13 interview, FBI agent Bob Ricks revealed that Koresh had warned the authorities that they might be "devoured by fire."[29] Could Koresh have thought that fire would somehow act as a defensive weapon against the unholy invaders? Yes, according to several other highlighted passages in Robyn's Bible. Consider Amos 1:2-7: "The Lord will roar from Zion . . . and the top of Carmel shall wither. . . . I will send fire" (KJV). Next to verse 7, Robyn had scribbled: "The fire that will cleanse." Coincidentally, the Davidians called their home Mt. Carmel. Even more significant is a cross-reference Robyn made from the Amos passage to Isaiah 4:4–5, which says:

> When the Lord shall have washed away the filth of the daughters of Zion, and shall have purged the blood of Jerusalem. . . by the spirit of judgment, and by the spirit of burning. And the LORD will create upon every dwelling place of mount Zion. . . a cloud and smoke by day, and a shining of flaming fire by night: for upon all the glory shall be a defence. (KJV)

Next to "washed away the filth of the daughters of Zion," Robyn had penned a fascinating message: "CHANGE THE DNA." Beside the phrase, "a cloud and smoke by day, and the shining of a flaming fire by night," she had written an even more cryptic reminder: "FACES OF FLAME." These notes, when compared with information contained in teaching tapes by Koresh, indicate that he and his followers expected some type of genetic mutation to occur in them. As God's representative on earth, Koresh would loose fire upon his faithful followers, thereby killing off their old nature and transforming them into flaming entities of divine judgment who would smite the enemy.

Adding support to this theory are seven words in Robyn's Bible that are written next to Isaiah 34:2. The passage reads: "For the indignation of the LORD is upon all the nations, and his fury upon all their armies: he hath utterly destroyed them, he hath delivered them to the slaughter." Here, Robyn had scrawled: "Because we're hot cloven tongues of fire." Another relevant passage is Nahum 2:3–4. It explains exactly what might have prompted the Davidians to light the fires on April 19:

> The shield of his mighty men is made red . . . the chariots shall be with flaming torches in the day of his preparation . . . . The chariots shall rage in the streets . . .they shall seem like torches, they shall run like lightnings. (KJV)

Above this verse's reference to "chariots," Robyn had written the word "TANKS." The implication is clear. When the government's "tanks" (i.e., "chariots") attacked the compound, the Davidians believed that Nahum's prophecy was unfolding before their eyes. It was time to unleash the fire, as Nahum 2:13 instructs: "Behold, I am against thee, saith the LORD of Hosts, and I will burn her chariots in the smoke" (KJV).[30]

The adults at "Ranch Apocalypse" were not the only ones who understood prophecy. Eleven-year-old Scott Mabb and his 9-year-old brother Jake knew the future, too. They sat unmoved in front of the television on April 19 and watched their former home go up in flames. The boys had been among twenty-one children released midway through the siege. After the fire subsided, the boys looked up at their father, and with an eerie calm remarked: "Mom said a year ago they might have to burn it down."[31]

The Davidians were apparently willing to follow Koresh into a blaze of glory because they believed that he was God in the flesh. Dana Okimoto (Koresh's sixth wife), who left the group prior to the siege, says that she begain having doubts about Koresh when he "started implying that he was Jesus Christ."[32] His growing delusions of grandeur convinced Okimoto that it was time for her to depart.

Former Davidian Poia Viega, who lost several relatives in the Waco fire, maintains that when she visited the compound in 1990, the group was clearly acknowledging that Koresh "was God, and that whatever God wanted, that was the best for them."[33] Koresh himself, in an October 1989 recorded teaching titled "The Foundation," thunders out exactly who he believed himself to be:

> God in the flesh. Do you know who I am? God in the flesh! The Word of God
> in the Book has been shown to you . . . I will be exalted amongst the heathen.
> Stand in awe and know that I am God.[34]

As horrible as the Waco tragedy was, it at least served to dispel the dangerous myth that end-time fanaticism only affects societal outcasts and the psychologically unstable. Koresh's gun-toting followers included an attorney, a nurse, an engineer, a teacher, and an ex-police officer. But even before Americans could come to grips with this disturbing reality, a third doomsday sect was already causing concern in another part of the world.

RUSSIA'S GREAT WHITE BROTHERHOOD

A momentous turning point in Russian history occurred in A.D. 988 when Vladimir (956–1015), Prince of Russia, made Christianity the official religion of his realm. It continued to be the state religion until the 1917 Bolshevik Revolution, which marked yet another decisive moment in Russia's history as atheistic communism declared a separation of church from state. This, of course, was only the beginning of what would quickly evolve into brutal religious repression.[35]

Things began to change in the late 1980s, however, when Russian president Mikhail Gorbachev's policies of *glasnost* (openness) and *perestroika* (restructuring) were initiated. In 1988, Gorbachev actually set aside a national holiday for the celebration of the millennial anniversary of Christianity's arrival in Russia. The Russian people were warmly receptive to the officially sanctioned return of religions; spiritual fervor swept over the land. One survey conducted by the International Research Institute on Values Changes, Inc. found that between April 1990 and April 1991 the number of Moscow residents who said they believed in God jumped dramatically from twelve percent to thirty-four percent.[36]

With this renewed sense of spirituality came an influx of every imaginable belief system. Mainstream religions (Islam, Judaism, and Christianity) were first to emerge. Next came less conventional belief systems (i.e., "cults") including: Hare Krishnas, Moonies, The Family, Jehovah's Witnesses, Scientology, Mormonism, and New Agers. After the Soviet Union dissolved in the early 1990s, home-grown prophets began to spring up like weeds all over the land, attracting young people "searching for a new identity to fill the void left by the collapse of communist ideology."[37]

For example, the former Soviet empire has seen the emergence of a mystical, long-haired, Rasputin-like "prophet" named Serghei Torpo (a.k.a. Vissarion). This former traffic cop, who was fired for excessive drinking, dresses in a red tunic, claims to be the reincarnation of Christ, and seeks to establish his own kingdom in Siberia. He has declared his intentions through speaking engagements to large crowds at Moscow sporting arenas as well as on broadcasts aired by Radio Moscow. As of 1997,

Vissarion had attracted about 5,000 followers to his "City of the Sun" located near the isolated town of Minusinsk.[38] He threatens that if mankind does not believe in him, nuclear plants will explode along with the release of a new virus, destroying all but those devoted to him.[39]

"Vissarion Christ" (a.k.a. Serghei Torpo)

The most disruptive cult leader to emerge in the former Soviet Union was Maria Tsvygun, cofounder of The Great White Brotherhood, which began forming in the Ukrainian city of Kiev in 1990. It was in the town's quiet southern section known as Rybny Pereulok that 52-year-old ex-scientist Yuri Krivonogov moved into a house with thirty teenagers. The youths and their leader proceeded to surround the place with a thirteen-foot-high brick wall that was reinforced by an electrified barbed-wire fence. Krivonogov usually billed himself as John the Baptist or Swami Ioann, the prophet of the Living God: i.e., his 33-year-old wife, Maria Tsvygun, a former Communist Youth League worker and graduate of Kiev University's school of journalism.

According to Krivonogov, Tsvygun became the physical embodiment of Jesus Christ after dying on April 11, 1990. Her soul was supposedly taken to heaven where it was united with the essence of Jesus Christ and the Virgin Mary. After three and a half hours in heaven, Jesus' body of pure light re-entered Tsvygun's lifeless corpse, which was in turn resurrected. Afterward, Marina was called Maria Devi Khristos.[40]

As for Swami Ioann (also spelled Yuoann), his role was to direct the world to worship Maria, also known as the Mother of the World, Maria Devi Christ, Messiah and Savior, and YUSMALOS (YUS - Yuoann Swami, MA - Maria, LOS - Logos [i.e., Jesus]). Krivonogov, too, assumed various titles. He appointed himself Pope Peter II and further claimed to be the reincarnation of Adam (i.e., the first man), Russian Prince Vladimir, Shakespeare's Romeo (even though no actual "Romeo" ever existed), Tsar Nicholas II (last of the Russian emperors), and the Greek god Apollo.[41]

Even more troubling was the group's doctrinal hodge-podge of Hinduism, occultism, and Christian end-time prophecy based on the book of Revelation. In this mish-mash of beliefs the ultimate fate of all members of the group, including Krivonogov and Tsvygun, would be death. Tsvygun taught that the day she became the embodiment of Jesus marked a three-and-a-half year period of evangelism that would conclude with a terrible day of judgment on November 23, 1993. "In commemoration of this she was supposed to commit self-immolation on the ancient square [in Kiev]. Then arise. And then in the form of Christ to pronounce judgment on the world. Whoever did not believe this was supposed to go to the fires of Gehenna (hell)."[42] Reporter Nikolai Porublev wrote the following explanation in the counter-cult periodical *Take A Closer Look*:

> After that day the Golden Age will dawn with 144,000 people forming the government of that Age. Sixty million people who will respond will be saved. The rest will be annihilated. . . . [N]ow is the time of the Great Tribulation. They say that many of the followers of the Great White Brotherhood will be killed before Judgment Day. Their deaths are necessary for the salvation of

the earth. Maria Devi and her prophet Swami Ioann will themselves be killed. Her own death will apparently serve as a redemptive act for the earth.[43]

Maria Devi Khristos, self-proclaimed "Living God."

Not content with their crew of thirty, Krivonogov and Tsvygun sent some of their followers to neighboring towns to make more converts. The devotees then traveled on to Moscow and St. Petersburg. It was not long before dozens of young people were heading for Kiev to join The Great White Brotherhood. Among these new converts were scores of single mothers who had been caught unprepared for life in a non-Soviet world. The Brotherhood, they thought, would be a safe haven. Youths approximately fifteen to sixteen years old, however, were clearly the main targets for recruitment. Krivonogov and Tsvygun convinced many teens that only by joining The Brotherhood could they save themselves from their "demonic parents."[44]

Government authorities began to investigate the group when reports of children and teens running away from home to join The Brotherhood began pouring in not only from Russia, but from the Ukraine, Belarus, various Baltic states, and Moldova. Then, in late 1992, police finally stormed the Kiev house and took a number of children into custody. The drastic action had come as a result of information leaked to officials from disenchanted followers.[45] But the move came too late. Krivonogov, along with Tsvygun, had gone into hiding and thousands of their dedicated disciples were fanning out across the land seeking more converts.

Within weeks, posters of Tsvygun wearing a long white robe and carrying a shepherd's crook started showing up on the walls of prominent buildings located in various city centers throughout Russia, the Ukraine, and Baltic states. The message beneath her photo was bold and uncompromising: "I am the Living God and through me alone can you receive redemption against Judgment Day."

By early 1993, parents throughout the former Soviet Union had grown extremely alarmed. Children and teens were disappearing from numerous towns, only to show up in a far-off city with The Brotherhood. Many of the children/teens had absconded with their parents' money or jewels. These were apparently given over to Krivonogov and Tsvygun.[46] Worried and angry citizens then began to fear the unthinkable: a mass suicide. It was not hard to read the warning signs. A newspaper printed by The Brotherhood stated: "Yusmalosites! Twelve thousand souls must die as sacrifices in witness to Mother of the World, and they will await their hour. Prepare for this, my children! This is your duty — to wash away the sins of unfortunate mankind with your blood!" A memo from the Ukrainian Ministry of Internal Affairs confirmed the obvious:

From the words of the "White Brotherhood" preachers, it has been established that this fanatical religious community is planning to conduct an action in Kiev in November 1993 in connection with the belief that our planet is to enter into another dimension, which will cause universal cataclysms. In connection with this, the "White Brotherhood" will "free themselves from their material bodies," i.e., they will commit suicide. According to YUSMALOS doctrine, on November 24, 1993, Kiev will be assigned the role of Jerusalem.[47]

As the November martyrdom drew closer, zealous members of The Brotherhood invaded various countries to declare Tsvygun's identity as the Living God and proclaim her apocalyptic prophecies. Their tactics were often less than socially acceptable. In the middle of revivals held by foreign evangelists, young members of The Brotherhood would spring from the crowd and grab the microphones. They would be carried away screaming and waving pictures of their savior. At subway entrances in metropolitan areas, white-robed believers in Tsvygun fervently preached to all who would listen. "Leave your families and come with us," they would yell. "The end of the world has arrived and you must follow the Living God or die an agonizing death."

October 1993 found The Brotherhood claiming that its membership had ballooned to a staggering 150,000 — and all of them were headed for Kiev's St. Sophia Square to await the public appearance of Maria Devi and the fulfillment of her predictions. The general populace and government authorities started to panic, especially when the group moved their date with death up to November 14. Police subsequently contacted Interpol (the international police group) for help. Deputy Interior Minister Valentyn Nedreyhaylo admitted, "We know what to do with 15,000 people at a demonstration or a soccer game, but here we're talking about 150,000 people."[48]

In a desperate attempt to avert death on a massive scale, security forces began rounding up known members of The Brotherhood. By early November almost two hundred cultists, including about fifty adolescents, had been detained in Ukrainian hospitals and jails. Most refused to eat or drink. Many would not even give their names. One boy, for instance, would only say: "I am 87,000 years old."[49] The majority of followers shunned all questions from journalists, police, and doctors, repeatedly shaking fists and chanting: "I curse you in the name of Maria Devi Khristos!"[50] But the detainees needed to say little to confirm officials' fears. A flyer found in the possession of many of the members read: "Do not be afraid to die. You will have died for our God, Maria Devi Khristos."[51]

Five days before "the end," Tsvygun's devotees were sporadically bursting into Russian Orthodox Church services and urging everyone to renounce Christianity and worship Maria Devi.[52] Ultimately, seven hundred members of The Brotherhood were taken into protective custody. Both

Krivonogov and Tsvygun were apprehended just days before the doomsday deadline. They and about sixty followers were arrested after they used chemicals and fire extinguishers to desecrate the inside of Kiev's St. Sophia Cathedral. During the brawl between cult followers and police, Tsvygun actually went unrecognized. Her identity became apparent only when authorities noticed that she was being treated with great deference by the others. Vadin Kurchenko of Russia's Internal Affairs Ministry related that the arrestees "were kissing her feet."[53]

The next day a videotape was made of Tsvygun being interrogated. All through the questioning she kept waving her arms wildly and maintaining that she was the second coming of Christ. "I am Maria Devi Khristos," she shouted. "You are all servants of Satan and the devil." In a reference to Jesus' crucifixion, she stated: "Just like 2,000 years ago, I am 33 years old."[54] Police ended up charging her and Krivonogov with hooliganism, which was an effective enough way of keeping them behind bars until the prophesied date of Tsvygun's martyrdom had passed. Officials eventually learned that the whole series of wild events started back in 1990 when Tsvygun overdosed on drugs. Her first husband, whom she left for Krivonogov, revealed that after recovering from the overdose she told him: "I'm not Maria. I've been to the cosmos and I have a mission."[55]

In the end, there were no suicides and both cult leaders were sentenced to several years in prison. Most of their followers were either sent home to other countries or banished from the Ukraine. Nevertheless, as of 1995, Russian police estimated that the cult still had 12,000 adherents. Remaining members of the White Brotherhood are still seeking converts in the former Soviet Union. They have been especially active since August 13, 1997, when Tsvygun was released from Denprodzerzhinsk women's correctional labor colony. She and her followers are now declaring that the end of the world will take place at the end of the century.[56]

FLAMES OF THE SOLAR TEMPLE

Russian officials were understandably relieved in 1994 when the alarming declarations of Tsvygun failed to materialize. Unfortunately, things did not go as well a year later for French, Swiss, and Canadian police seeking to piece together the macabre deeds of the Order of the Solar Temple. "Gruesome," "shocking" and "bizarre" is how public officials referred to the series of murder-suicides that began just after midnight on October 5, 1994, when villagers in the tiny Swiss farm community of Cheiry "saw the moonless sky lit by flames over the farmhouse of Albert Giacobino, a wealthy retired farmer who had bought the place four years ago."[57]

By the time fire engines from Fribourg arrived on the scene, the secluded dwelling was fully engulfed in flames. Three hours later, when firefighters were finally able to enter the burned-out ruins, they found Giacobino lying dead in his bed. A plastic bag tied around his head concealed a bullet wound.[58] Further exploration of the property yielded an underground garage leading to a door. This opened into a meeting room containing, among other things, a trail of blood that stopped at the room's wooden paneling. A secret entranceway in the wall gave access to a small inner sanctuary decorated entirely in red. Investigators entering it were horrified by the sight of eighteen bodies — men, women, and a boy about ten years old — arranged in a circle, face up, beneath the portrait of a robed Christ-like figure holding a rose. Another corpse was found in an adjacent room and three more bodies were discovered in an adjoining chapel.

Many of the victims wore either red and black, or white and gold, ceremonial robes. Some of them had their hands tied behind their backs; ten had plastic bags over their heads. Most of the dead had been drugged with a substance described by Swiss investigating magistrate André Piller as "a powerful, violent substance."[59] Twenty of the victims had been shot in the head at close range. According to a forensics expert at the University of Lausanne's Institute for Legal Medicine, some of the victims had as many as eight bullet wounds in their head.[60]

At approximately 3:00 A.M., as police officials were still trying to piece to together what had happened in Cheiry, another fire broke out one hundred miles south at three neighboring ski chalets in the small city of Granges-sur-Salvan. Firefighters sifting through the rubble of these chalets uncovered another macabre sight: "25 bodies, all of them badly burned, including the remains of at least five children."[61]

Within twenty-four hours, Canadian authorities halfway around the world were confronted with their own grisly discoveries at Morin Heights, Quebec. Fire had broken out at another isolated retreat, where authorities found the badly burned bodies of a man and a woman wearing red-and-gold medallions engraved with the letters TS. In a nearby villa, police found three more bodies: those of Tony and Nikki Dutoit and their three-month-old son, Christopher.[61] The couple in their mid-thirties had been stabbed perhaps fifty times and then rolled in carpet. Christopher had been suffocated and "stuffed behind a water heater with a bag over his head.[63]

All of the deceased were members of a highly secretive end-time cult known as the Order of the Solar Temple, which blended elements of astrology, freemasonry, New Age spiritualism, occultism, and quasi-Christian beliefs focusing on doomsday. The group was led by 46-year-old Luc Jouret and 70-year-old Joseph di Mambro. Jouret, a Belgian homeopathic doctor, founded the group in 1987 and served as its spiritual leader. Di Mambro, a shadowy figure who had served six months in a French jail in 1972 for posing as a psychologist, was the group's financial director. The bodies of both men were found in the Salvan chalets.[64]

One victim carried a note in her clothing, which she had addressed to surviving relatives. It stated that she had come to Switzerland to die. Three other letters with similar messages were sent by cult members to Jean-Francois Mayer, a Swiss authority. One read: "We leave this Earth in full freedom and lucidity in order to find a dimension of Truth and Absolute, far from the hypocrisies and oppression of this world."[65] Cassette tapes and documents found with the bodies indicated that the killings were indeed linked to a belief that the end of the world was imminent.

Jouret had convinced his followers that the world's destruction would result from humanity's degradation of the environment.[66] "The present world chaos is not just by chance," Jouret taught his followers. "We have arrived at the hour of Apocalypse."[67] According to former members, Jouret also taught that only those who joined him would escape perdition because he, as the "new Christ," had been chosen to save them.[68]

Even after the fifty-three deaths, faithful members of the Temple who had not been part of the suicide-murders remained faithful to Jouret's teachings. Then, fourteen months later, some of these surviving members decided that their time had come to enter the spiritual realm and join their master. The method of departure was a second wave of grisly suicide-murders. Their bodies were discovered after Swiss and French authorities launched a massive hunt for Solar Temple members in December 1995.

Law enforcement officials began the search when sixteen cultists — half from France and half from Canada — were reported missing.[69] Within days a helicopter spotted burned corpses on a remote forest plateau in the Alps of southeastern France. Fourteen of the sixteen bodies were arranged in a star pattern. The victims had used shooting, poisoning, stabbing, and asphyxiation to complete their elaborate deaths. Most of the corpses had plastic bags over their heads.

The two cultists not found in the star pattern had acted as executioners, methodically shooting fellow believers in the head before killing themselves with bullets delivered under the chin. Among those murdered with a .357 magnum were two sisters aged two and four, daughters of policeman Jean-Pierre Lardanchet, who had acted as one of the executioners.[70] A note retrieved from a victim's apartment read: "Death does not exist, it is pure illusion. May we, by our inner life, find each other forever."[71]

Investigators have since learned that the 1994 ritual was intended to take sect members through fire to a new world near the star Sirius.[72] Cultists who did not participate in the first ceremony may have believed that their deaths in 1995 would lead them to a similar destination. This is not to say that all of the victims died willingly. A final Swiss report noted that only fifteen of the dead — a fanatical inner circle known as the "awakened" — committed suicide. Another thirty, called the "immortals," who shared the apocalyptic beliefs of their leaders, were forced to kill themselves. The rest of the victims, classified as "traitors," were murdered.

After the 1995 suicide-murders, French authorities remained apprehensive about surviving Solar Temple believers, fearing that devotees might make new converts and instigate more suicide-murders.[73] Their apprehension proved to be well-founded in March 1997, when five more Solar Temple members — Didier Queze and Chantel Goupillot (husband and wife), Goupillot's mother, Suzanne Druau, and two friends, Bruno Klaus, and Pauline Rioux — killed themselves in Quebec. As before, they made their exit for Sirius via asphyxiation and self-immolation.[74]

Members of the Solar Temple were well-respected citizens of the European and Canadian communities, who often dined in expensive restaurants and contributed millions to Jouret's twisted religion. Victims of his deception included two police officers, a psychotherapist, an architect, an official in the Quebec finance ministry and the mayor of Richelieu, Quebec. The most famous cultist to die was 27-year-old Patrick Vuarnet, son of skier Jean Vuarnet, the 1960 Winter Olympics gold medalist who became widely known for his line of designer sunglasses. Patrick's companion, Ute Vérona, and their 6-year-old daughter, Tania, also were among the dead.[75]

According to Alain Vuarnet, his brother Patrick felt guilty for not being in the first group of Temple members to die. During one confrontation, Alain remembers Patrick saying, "Alain, you are the one deluding yourself. You just don't understand."[76]

ASAHARA'S AUM

Japan is among the most technologically nations. Its crime rate is one of the lowest on record; its citizens habitually rank among the best-educated; its economy is one of the world's most prosperous. But none of these factors counted on March 20, 1995, when a sociopathic end-time cult known as Aum Shinrikyo ("Supreme Truth") unleashed a lethal tool of mass destruction into the Tokyo subway system: sarin, a nerve gas invented by the Nazis.[77] Twelve persons died and more than 5,500 people were sickened with nausea, blurred vision, and breathing problems. Some would be permanently blinded. The cult's actions were linked to its view that Armageddon would begin around the year 2000.

Police immediately began searching for Aum's leader, 40-year-old Shoko Asahara, who had disappeared a day after the attack. He had made his first doomsday warning in 1987. "Between 1999 and 2003, a nuclear war is sure to break out," he stated. "We have only fifteen years before it."[78] According to his book *Day of Annihilation*, the world's end would start in 1999 after Japan sinks into the ocean. Russia, China, America, and Europe would then collapse, paving the way for a civilization-destroying nuclear exchange between October 30 and November 29, 2003. From the rubble of this post-apocalyptic world would rise "a race of 'superhumans' " (i.e., Asahara's followers).[79]

But Asahara was not content to wait. In his 1995 book *Rising Sun Country: Disaster Is Getting Close*, he additionally prophesied that nerve gas would be the weapon of choice used during the last battle between good and evil. The volume detailed the chemical characteristics of sarin: how to mix it, and how to treat symptoms if exposed to it.[80] He apparently wanted World War III to begin immediately:

> [P]lans called for cult attacks on government buildings . . . to spark what Asahara saw as a world war. . . . To triumph in that war, the cult built a series of munitions factories . . . Aum researchers were trying to develop germ weapons — including the Ebola virus — and an assembly line was about to produce automatic rifles. Behind one building's false walls was a $700,000 lab able to turn out 132 to 176 lbs. a month of the nerve gas sarin — enough to kill 6 million to 8 million people.[81]

Fifty-seven days after the subway attack, Asahara (who had declared himself "the Christ"),[82] was finally tracked down. He was found lying face down and meditating inside a coffin-like chamber located between two floors of a building at the cult's Kamikuishiki compound. The ten-foot-long by three-foot-high hiding space also contained a cassette player, some medicine, and the equivalent of about $100,000 in cash. When police officers attempted to climb in and get Asahara, the half-blind guru said: "I'll come out myself. No one, not even my followers, is allowed to touch me."[83]

It was not Asahara's first run-in with the law. In 1982 he was taken into custody and fined for selling fake medicinal cures.[84] This minor brush with police, however, did not dissuade Asahara from marketing miracles. By 1986 he had started his own religion. An advertisement for his first book promised converts that they would receive extraordinary benefits from following its tenets:

> The Venerable Master [Shoko Asahara] will show you the secrets of his amazing mystic powers. See the future, read people's minds, make your wishes

come true, X-ray vision, levitation, trips to the fourth dimension, hear the voice of God and more. It will change your life![85]

Asahara, of course, claimed to already have these powers. "[T]he length of time I can levitate is about three seconds, but this period of time is gradually lengthening," he told the occult magazine *Twilight Zone*. "In about a year, I should be able to fly freely through the sky."[86] He also said that he could see through objects and meditate underwater for six hours. A year after this interview, Asahara christened his group Aum Shinrikyo.

Less than a decade later, Aum had solidified into a vast empire of "over 40,000 followers in over 30 branches in at least six countries, and a global network which had acquired sophisticated lasers, chemical reactors and a Russian military helicopter."[87] Asahara cleverly used his new religion to fund numerous businesses ranging from computer stores to noodle shops, some of which had holdings as high as $1.1 million."[88] Most of Aum's financing came from wealthy members who were instructed to donate their monetary resources to the cult if they wanted to obtain salvation. The response to this teaching was so great that Aum's total assets eventually rose above $1 billion.[89]

Each passing year found Asahara's belief system (a blend of Buddhism, Hinduism, and Christian apocalypticism) growing stranger. In their efforts to find enlightenment, some Aum followers allowed themselves to be hung upside down or lowered into scalding water.[90] For $600, members were given the privilege of drinking Asahara's bath water; a loyal follower could drink a cup of their guru's blood for $8,000–$12,000.[91] Approximately $100,000 bought Aum believers their own "Perfect Salvation" skull cap — i.e., a battery-operated piece of headgear made of leather straps and electrodes designed to synchronize the brainwaves of members with those of their Venerated Master.[92] One especially odd initiation rite of the group was examined in the January 1995 issue of *Focus*, a popular news and lifestyle magazine:

First, one drinks some liquid. For 20 hours they see hallucinations. One who experienced it said he could see colorful objects, or things collapsing, and that he had no hearing. If during this hallucination one gets a fever, they pour ethyl alcohol on the person's body to reduce the fever. After 20 hours, diuretics and purgatives are given to get the substance out of the body. During this initiation, they have to wear diapers.[93]

Unusual forms of physical, mental and emotional abuse soon became a standard practice in Aum. When police raided its Kamikuishiki compound, they found approximately fifty cultists in a state of malnutrition. Many suffered from dehydration. Some were on the verge of starvation. Six members in critical condition had to be hospitalized. A 23-year-old woman found hiding in a toilet stall pleaded with police for protection. She had been confined inside a small container for many days.[94]

Torture and intimidation were commonly used against members. Persons trying to leave were bound with handcuffs and imprisoned inside small cargo containers so they could atone for their sins.[95] Other cultists were given electric shocks: "During one three-month period beginning in October 1994, Dr. Hayashi [a high-ranking Aum doctor] administered more than six hundred electric shocks to 130 followers. Afterward, some of them forgot which cult they were in, their guru's name, even their own names."[96] Children in the group also suffered. Many of them "were so dirty with matted hair, lice and fleas that [officials] could not immediately tell which were boys and which were girls. . . . Their living quarters were cramped and dirty. All of the children wore long-sleeved garments even in the summer because 'there was poison outside.' "[97]

Aum leaders also conducted biological experiments on less important followers.[98] Medical tests done on seven cultists rescued from Aum's Satian No. 10 site revealed highly unusual blood characteristics. One had been poisoned by sarin. Another had blood level readings that registered a particular enzyme at forty times its normal level. This latter patient told police: "Every day I was forced to take water mixed with white powder, and also I was supposed to get injections."[99] The victim's symptoms included memory loss and severe muscle stiffness.

Only after Asahara's arrest did the full extent of Aum's criminal activity come to light. One case involved 68-year-old Kiyoshi Kariya, who in February 1995 tried to keep his sister from giving her wealth to Aum. The sister disappeared and Kariya was abducted by four men. Mystery surrounded the event until after the subway attack, when a senior cult member who had been arrested confessed that Kariya was murdered at one of Aum's compounds. The body was burned in an industrial-scale microwave incinerator that was widely reported to have been used for "reducing human bodies to powder — thus disposing of the remains of some thirty people who allegedly died or were murdered within the complex."[100]

Another kidnap-murder dated back to June 1989, just after attorney Tsutsumi Sakamoto began representing a family trying to locate their child in Aum. On November 4, 1989, Sakamoto, his wife and their infant son disappeared. Although friends found an Aum lapel badge in Sakamoto's disheveled apartment, no substantial evidence linking the cult to the crime scene could be found. Police suspicions were confirmed in 1996, however, when Tomomasa Nakagawa — a former Aum leader — pled guilty to murdering Sakamoto and his family at the request of Asahara.[101]

At the outset of his trial on April 24, 1996, Asahara faced seventeen charges, including murder and attempted murder, either of which can draw a sentence of death by hanging under Japanese law.[102] Not long after the hearings started, the guru's peculiar personality and ideas began to surface. He often interrupted the proceedings whenever someone began testifying against him. During one outburst he declared that "fear of his own death had forced him to plot the nerve gas attack."[103] He became extremely agitated when former aide, Yoshihiro Inoue, began telling the court about Asahara's teachings concerning salvation through terrorism. Inoue also stated that the Aum leader had personally plotted attacks against "anything that challenged (his) teachings." Asahara reacted to these charges by proclaiming that "the gods told him that they did not want Inoue taking the stand."[104]

Inoue was not the only Aum member to reveal information about Asahara's dark world of murder and madness. Kiyohide Hayakawa — Aum's former "construction minister" who functioned as the cult's de facto second-in-command — testified that Asahara ordered his devotees to murder the Sakamoto family as well as a former cult member named Shuji Taguchi. Hayakawa testified that "there was no person other than Asahara who could order 'poa' (Sanskrit for 'murder'), for he was thought of as the Buddha [i.e., enlightened one]." Hayakawa explained: "At that time, murder was considered a good deed to enlighten the spirit."[105]

Aum itself was forced to declare bankruptcy due to a court's seizure of its assets (worth approximately $300 million). The group's sprawling main compound near Mount Fuji was also confiscated. But this did not put an end to Aum. Under the direction of five senior members, the cult continues to survive by operating "profitable businesses selling computers, bread and other items."[106] In fact, Asahara has retained a sizable number of followers and has even made some new converts. Japan's Public Securities Investigation Agency announced in August 1997 that Aum had actually established ten new "departments" and now has twenty-six facilities with about five hundred live-in devotees and another 5,000 believers living on their own.[107] Police authorities report that "of the 427 Aum members arrested following the gas attack, 138 have rejoined the cult, many after serving prison terms."[108]

One of the group's newest members, 32-year-old Chizuru, first learned of Aum through television news conferences after the subway gas attack. As she watched Asahara's followers defending themselves against verbal attacks, she felt herself becoming more and more impressed by their answers. Chizuru's story was recounted in a 1997 interview she granted to journalists:

> Chizuru said she was a former bookshop employee who, like so many of the people who have joined Aum, was feeling spiritually unfulfilled and unsatisfied with life. "I felt like I really wanted to serve something and to be of help," she said, sitting cross-legged and barefoot on the floor of the Yokohama apartment. She joined Aum in August 1995, and now she is an Aum "nun" who counsels other followers on their religious questions. She works on the assembly line in an electronics factory and cleans office buildings, and she gives most of her wages to Aum. "I understand that people wonder why we don't just completely disappear, but that would not solve anything," Araki said. "All our members joined for a reason; they decided that their present life was not enough, and there must be something more."[109]

By early 1998, more than one hundred of Asahara's followers had been convicted of crimes committed on behalf of the cult; crimes that included manufacturing nerve gas and murder. Of the more than forty Aum members still missing, most are presumed dead, probably as a result of their participation in some of Aum's more peculiar rituals. It is believed that their corpses were disposed of by Aum leaders. What of Asahara? His fate may not be known for another ten years, due to Japan's complex legal system.

One of the most mystifying aspects of Aum was its membership, which consisted of some of Japan's most promising minds.[110] Converts included lawyers, doctors, and scientists from Japan's top universities, as well as several policemen and thirty members of the Self-Defense Forces (Japan's army).[111] According to a 1995 *Newsweek* article, Japanese citizens were puzzled that "bright young men with impressive university credentials would join the cult, when they could have had fine careers."[112]

In October 1997, the Office of the Coordinator for Counterterrorism, U.S. Department of State, officially designated Aum Shinrikyo as a foreign terrorist organization, along with such groups as Japan's Red Army, the Khmer Rouge of Cambodia, Hamas (Islamic Resistance Movement), and Hezbollah (Party of God).[113]

WEB OF DEATH: WWW.HEAVENSGATE.COM

It was approximately 1:30 P.M. on March 26, 1997 when former Heaven's Gate cult member Richard Ford (a.k.a. Rio DiAngelo) placed an emergency call to police:

> *911 dispatcher:* Hello?
>
> *DiAngelo:* Yes, uhm. I need to, ah, report, ah, an anonymous tip. Who do I talk to?
>
> *911 dispatcher:* Okay. This is regarding what?
>
> *DiAngelo:* This is regarding a mass suicide. And I can give you the address.
>
> *911 dispatcher:* Okay. What happened there?
>
> *DiAngelo:* Well, ah. I think there was a religious group that committed suicide.
>
> *911 dispatcher:* How long ago? Do you know about how long ago?
>
> *DiAngelo:* I'm not really sure.
>
> *911 dispatcher:* Okay. And how did you hear about this?
>
> *DiAngelo:* I was notified by mail. I just thought I'd pass it on to you. Just so you can know.

911 dispatcher: Okay. Can I get your name?

DiAngelo: No. I'd rather remain anonymous.

Because authorities did not take the call seriously, no one was dispatched to the Rancho Santa Fe, California address that DiAngelo had given them. Only when Ron Matzorkis — DiAngelo's Beverly Hills employer — made a follow-up call to police two hours later were San Diego Sheriff's Deputies sent to the location. Officer Robert Brunk was the first to arrive at the sprawling mansion. The first thing he noticed upon entering the home was the pungent odor of death.[114] It permeated the entire residence. He immediately backed out of the house and called his partner, Deputy Laura Gacek.

When Gacek entered the home, she, too, smelled death. Both officers decided to investigate further. As they moved through the mansion, the two deputies found one body after another. Each person was dressed in black and lying on a mattress with hands at his or her sides. The head and upper torso of each corpse was covered by a triangular, purple shroud. The two officers stopped counting at ten bodies, realizing that they were dealing with something far different from anything they had ever encountered. They left the home and called for back-up units.[115] Eventually, thirty-nine suicide victims would be discovered. Brunk would later comment: "[It was] one of the most bizarre things you'd ever see. . . . almost like it wasn't real."[116]

The dead were members of Heaven's Gate, a UFO cult that doubled as an Internet web page design company known as Higher Source. Their beliefs were a warped tapestry woven out of doctrinal threads borrowed from occultism, the Bible, Christian apocalypticism, ancient Gnosticism, UFOlogy, science-fiction, and contemporary conspiracy theories about a coming "one-world government." According to a homemade videotape left behind by the group, the world was teetering on the brink of annihilation and they were simply making their exit before Armageddon arrived.

Their leader, 65-year-old Marshall Applewhite, believed that the group's sign to leave was the 1997 arrival of the Hale-Bopp comet. Its magnificently brilliant tail was allegedly shielding a giant spaceship that had come to take them all to heaven. But to get to the craft they had to shed their earthly "containers" (i.e., bodies). This they did without hesitation. As purposeless as their final act may have seemed to everyone else, it fit perfectly into their religious belief system, which they explained in *How and When Heaven's Gate May Be Entered*, their self-published book.

Their sci-fi tale of doomsday delusion dates back to a chance meeting in 1972 between Applewhite and a 44-year-old nurse named Bonnie Lu Nettles. A talented opera singer known for his fifteen lead roles with the Houston Grand Opera and the son of a Presbyterian minister, Applewhite had been admitted to Houston's Bellaire Hospital for treatment of a heart blockage. He was put in the care of Nurse Nettles, an amateur astrologer who did people's "charts" under the spiritual guidance of a monk named Brother Francis who had died in 1818.[117]

The two new acquaintances immediately hit it off and soon found themselves inexplicably drawn into a platonic relationship cemented by their shared affinity for occult phenomena, UFOs, and apocalypticism. By 1975, Nettles and Applewhite had arrived at some rather odd conclusions about themselves and the world around them. They came to believe that they were each possessed by a space being from The Evolutionary Level Above Human (T.E.L.A.H.). Applewhite claimed that the entity inhabiting his body was the same one that had dwelled in the body of Jesus Christ 2,000 years ago.[118] Nettles maintained that the entity possessing her was that of Jesus' Heavenly Father, who had came back to Earth with his son to help spread a glorious message: the doorway to T.E.L.A.H. (i.e., the "Next Level") was now open to humans interested in taking an evolutionary step forward to T.E.L.A.H., that distant galaxy more commonly known as Heaven.[119]

The only thing humans had to do was to allow themselves to be possessed by other T.E.L.A.H. representatives who would in turn help each human host bring their mammalian "vehicles" (bodies) under control, which amounted to utterly rejecting everything human (e.g., names, identity, family ties, individualistic thinking, sexual feelings, human affection, gender recognition, personal likes and dislikes). When the time was right, a spaceship would come and pick up the humans who had overcome their humanness and whisk them away to T.E.L.A.H., where they would receive new bodies — genderless, perfected bodies — suited for life in God's Kingdom.

Nettles abandoned her four small children and husband of twenty-three years in order to trek through America with Applewhite and spread their extraterrestrial gospel. The first thing they did was cast away their identities and adopt various pseudonyms: "Bo" and "Peep," "Guinea" and "Pig," "Nincom" and "Poop," and "Do" and "Ti." They would often identify themselves simply as "The Two," as in the two witnesses mentioned in chapter eleven of the Bible's book of Revelation. Do and Ti claimed that they, like the two biblical witnesses, would be murdered after they finished their testimony. Then, after three-and-a-half days, they would be resurrected.

Unlike the Revelation witnesses, however, Do and Ti would be picked up by a spaceship. As Do said in one interview: "We're gonna wake up, just get right up and you're gonna watch us."[120] Interestingly, a former traveler with The Two — Joan Culpepper — remembers that Do and Ti were rather inconsistent on this last point of doctrine: "They armed some of the followers so that they could protect them from being killed even though being killed was what this was all about."[121]

The Two made a surprising number of converts as they toured the country. Their speaking engagements in Florida, New England, California and several other states often drew crowds numbering well into the hundreds.[122] People by the dozens were joining their flock, sometimes after hearing The Two speak only once. Aaron Greenberg, a former follower, remembers: "They had some hold on the audience. They could weave some sort of enchantment spell over the people."[123] Culpepper makes a similar comment: "I didn't buy a lot of the things they said. But an extraordinary thing happened when I was listening to Bo. It was as if a strong force came down over my mind and shut off my critical sense."[124]

Do and Ti soon had a following of at least 1,000 believers, all of whom abandoned their families, friends, and lives in order to wander through the country in pairs or small groups. Like their leaders, converts took on new names in an effort to erase all that reminded them of their human lives.[125] Their aliases ranged from "the biblical to the whimsical": John, Joshua, Peter, Joy, Wink, Moneybags, Fanta.[126] Everything human had to be rejected, as one memo stated: "[Y]ou must leave all your past behind. This means that you walk out the door of your human life, taking with you only those things that will be necessary while you are still on this planet."[127]

This new mode of living (known as "The Process"/"The Classroom") was designed to help members overcome all human attachments, especially family attachments, in preparation for their journey to T.E.L.A.H. The group's beliefs also may have served as little more than an excuse to flee unwanted responsibilities. One Oregon couple set off with Do and Ti after turning over their two small children to some friends.[128] A successful Colorado businessman abandoned his wife and six children to join the group. Converts also included a 39-year-old Cincinnati woman who followed Do and Ti after leaving her five small children to fend for themselves.[129] Children and adolescents were not eligible for the space flight because they could not make the kind of calculated decision necessary to enter the classroom. Youngsters, therefore, were merely attachments to the human level that had to be overcome in order to evolve.[130]

Eventually, though, a significant number of followers became disillusioned with Do and Ti when the expected arrival of their mothership did not occur within a year of the summer of 1975, as Do had promised.[131] The derisive press coverage that followed brought great frustration to the group, and hundreds fell away. Several hard-core believers, however, refused to abandon their teachers. These faithful followers, along with Do and Ti, went underground for the next seventeen years. They would occasionally resurface to make a few new converts, but for the most part lived in isolation from society in a continuing effort to overcome their human qualities.[132]

Procreation, child-rearing, love, human affection, sexual activity, sexual identity, or even the notion of "family" were aspects of humanness that seemed particularly offensive to Heaven's Gate members. An acquaintance of the group who works for Arrowhead General — a company for which the cult did freelance computer work — remembers how Applewhite's followers would actually recoil whenever physical contact was made with them. "To touch or hug them was almost offensive to them," he said. "They did not like to be touched."[133] The response is not surprising when one considers Applewhite's teachings on love, sex, and human relationships:

> [S]ex is the strongest drug — there's not a drug, there's not a morphine, or anything that is produced by chemicals, or plants of this world as strong as that drug. . . . [A]s long as you participate in that drug your capacity for recognizing the Truth (the facts) is just about as good as it is for someone who's had a half a dozen martinis, and you say to them, "Are you clear-headed?"[134]

For a while in our classroom . . . if I was gone from them [cult members] for a period of time and I returned, I would hug them and try to show my affection for them. And after a while, I began to feel, "This is inappropriate. We need to get past this. This is less than right. It may not have done any harm for a period of time, but it's inappropriate. . . . That doesn't mean that we don't love each other. . . . . But we don't love each other certainly in any physical nature where we need to touch or we need to hold hands or we need to hug or we need to kiss. We don't need those things. And it's certainly safer to avoid them during this more advanced position of overcoming, because in some we might innocently retrigger something. If they were permitted to engage in touching or hugging or even kissing on the cheek, it would re-engage something that they have worked very hard to overcome. So, we certainly don't want to re-engage an old addiction. And withdrawing from the drug of sensuality and sexuality is as difficult a withdrawal, if not more difficult, than any other withdrawal. It's tough. And Satan keeps sending it back again and again and again, to test you.[135]

Since we're moving into a world that is genderless, then we try to not be associated with the gender of our vehicles. Females are not trying to look like males. Males are not trying to look like females. They're trying to be neither. . . . We are trying to have no masculine characteristics, no feminine characteristics, but in a sense, still sensitive and soft, but neither male nor female — genderless. . . . . [Members] do have a haircut that is pretty much neither male nor female and one that they can handle and is easy to care for. . . . As far as the clothing they wear, they wear pretty much unisex-type clothes, that certainly aren't tight fitting, and they wear a loose shirt. . . . [T]hey want loose-fitting things that do not accentuate the waist or the hips or any shape of the vehicle. They don't need to color themselves. They don't need lipstick or rouge. . . . [Y]ou have to say - "Do I need to cling to my femininity? Do I need to cling to my masculinity?" Because if you do, then you're not really ready to make this transition from the human kingdom into our Father's Kingdom.[136]

Do and Ti's students made similar comments regarding how they utterly abhorred sex or anything remotely suggestive of sexuality:

[The Next Level] finds any sensuality offensive. . . . From the Next Level's point of view, being sexual at all is primitive, and eventually must be outgrown by anyone hoping to move up. Therefore, neither heterosexual nor homosexual is acceptable. In fact, the original meaning of "fornication" seems to have been "any sexual activity," but the aliens have reprogrammed people to interpret it as only "any sexual activity outside of holy matrimony."[137]

Everything from ads for toothpaste to clothing elevates human sexuality. Being from a genderless world, this behavior is extremely hideous to us.[138]

LOVE: In the human kingdom it is a literally a four-letter word between two individuals doing an act they would be embarrassed to do in front of their Heavenly Father.[139]

To eradicate their humanity, Do and Ti's followers resorted to behavior modification and psychological conditioning techniques that obliterated their individuality. Some practices were extreme, to say the least:

- six male members, including Applewhite, castrated themselves to avoid sexual feelings;
- members wore unisex, uniform-like clothing that included shirts buttoned to the neck;
- women adopted an androgynous look, complete with shortly-cropped haircuts;
- members would eat the same foods, at the same time, and in the same place;
- members sought to eradicate individual thinking, varying opinions, and personal desires in favor of the thoughts and opinions of Applewhite who was their "Older Member."[140]

Eventually, all Heaven's Gate members took names with the same suffix in an apparent sign of oneness: Glnody, Lvvody, Nrrody, Wknody, Smmody, Yrsody, Drrody, Qstody, Chkody, Jwnody, Srrody, Slvody, etc. According to Brnody, persons wanting to grow toward the Next Level would have to continue living in a very specific way, which Brnody explained in a document uploaded to the Internet:[141]

- Your prime directive would be: "My relationship with my Older Member is my #1 priority — NOTHING else matters."

- You'll ask Ti and Do at least once a day, "Am I displeasing you in anyway?" And know that you will be shown if you are — so be ready to correct quickly.

- You'll hate coasting, despise the days that don't have hurdles, and love the days that turn into steeple chases.

- You'll know that you must state frequently to Ti and Do that you request and desire maximum growth if it is appropriate for you.

- You'll learn that being consistently positive using your Next Level mind is fun — that negatives using the human mind are no fun.

- You'll apply the axiom that desire is synonymous with a sustained well-disciplined effort, and that you must learn discipline to be of service. Puny effort does not take you far.

- You'll ask, "What would Ti and Do do in this circumstance? How would they handle it?" — when you face every type of situation - in order to learn how they would do it.

- You'll examine often, "How does my thinking or behavior differ from Ti and Do's?"

- You'll frequently ask yourself, "Do I still respect or value anything of this world? From my past? Any type of special diet? Sensuality? What are my weaknesses, what am I still clinging to of the human kingdom?"

- You'll learn how to negotiate in Next Level ways so that all involved participate in decisions, to not be aggressive or take the lead lobbying for your position, carefully considering the value in others' positions, and to check with others before taking any action, so you all are in agreement.

- You'll come to know that you are NOTHING without your Older Member, and that NOTHING originates with you.

It was also during their reclusive period that Nettles/Ti died of cancer (1985). Applewhite told followers that because the physical body inhabited by Ti had ceased to function, Ti was forced to return to Heaven. They had nothing to fear, however. Ti would henceforth communicate to them from

T.E.L.A.H. via a telepathic link with Do.[142] Consequently, Do would be able to keep preaching their sci-fi gospel and leading humans in the group (i.e., "classroom") on toward total control over their bodies.

Obviously, Ti's unexpected departure forced a change to the group's original message regarding Do and Ti's death and resurrection. But this posed no problem for loyal followers. According to Dick Joslyn, a fifteen year member (1975–1990), The Two "didn't have any problem with updating or altering what they taught."[143] Core believers took false predictions in stride, especially those dealing with the mothership's arrival time. They were constantly looking for a sign. Josyln remembers:

> When Mount St. Helens blew, when the different earthquakes occurred, we were always wondering: "O.K., is this it? Is this the signal? Are they gonna come for us now because are things gonna hit the fan so bad that they'll come and take us away?" We were really anticipating that.[144]

Heaven's Gate resurfaced in 1992 in order to make a "Final Offer" to all humans who would listen to them. They took out advertisements in many magazines, alternative newspapers, weekly periodicals, and daily publications around the country as well as overseas.[145] They even took out a one third page advertisement in both the national and international editions of *USA Today* that read: " 'UFO Cult' Resurfaces with Final Offer." The cult subsequently embarked on another nationwide tour in hopes of finding more interested persons. In September 1995, the cult issued another statement over the Internet: "Undercover 'Jesus' Surfaces Before Departure."[146] But the world's reaction to this final plea for converts was less than positive. Heaven's Gate members interpreted the response to their truths as yet another sign of our planet's imminent destruction.[147]

Then, an even more spectacular indication of approaching doom caught their attention: the Hale-Bopp comet. Months prior to their mass suicide, the Internet had been buzzing with rumors about a UFO supposedly hiding behind the celestial wonder. When astronomers posted a few course corrections to the comet's predicted trajectory, UFOites feverishly spread a fantastic explanation: intelligent beings were actually altering the course of Hale-Bopp.[148] More speculation resulted when amateur astronomer Chuck

Shramek of Houston took a photo of Hale-Bopp that included a luminous object, several times larger than Earth, hovering just behind the comet.

On November 14, 1996, Shramek posted the picture on his Internet site, commenting that the object was "so bright and strange" that he began to pray.[149] He then announced his discovery on the talk-radio program *Coast to Coast*, hosted by Art Bell. The nationally-aired show spawned so much UFO hysteria that Alan Hale (co-discoverer of the comet) was forced to get involved in the controversy. News reporters actually contacted him for a comment about the "mysterious spacecraft" following his comet. After doing his own investigation of the photograph, Hale concluded that the unidentified object was actually a star called SAO141894.[150]

Hale proceeded to post his findings on the Internet and, like Shramek, appeared on the Art Bell show. UFOlogists swiftly responded sending "large amounts of surprisingly vicious 'hate mail' to www.halebopp.com."[151] Hale was also accused of being part of a massive government conspiracy to cover-up the truth about Hale-Bopp. What truth? Shramek explains: "The big picture, the true story of what's really going on includes alien artifacts and races, space travel and outrageous technology.[152]

Heaven's Gate meanwhile had picked up on the rumors and worked it into their belief system. To them, Hale-Bopp was leading the way for Ti's spaceship that had finally come to pick them up and take them home to T.E.L.A.H. Between March 21 and March 26, 1997, each member of Heaven's Gate dropped his or her container/body and left with the T.E.L.A.H. emissary/representative allegedly inhabiting it. A final statement written by one Heaven's Gate member remained as a sober warning:

> The climax of this civilization has begun . . . . A war in the literal heavens is underway as the alien races battle for the spoils of this planet. Their campaign is escalating. They are actively engaged in recruiting, experimenting, and mining elements both mineral and biological (genetic) — in their efforts toward survival. They know their time is short. The Physical Evolutionary Level Above Human is about to surface from their undercover, behind-the-scenes involvements, ready to make their counter. There is not, and never has been, any contest. The only question that remains unanswered is how long the Next Level will permit the alien forces to present their agenda — how

long is long enough for all souls to pledge their allegiance for or against — to one side or the other. Every soul must be put to the final test. And as we warned you at the outset, consider your options thoroughly. Hasty judgments are ill-advised.[153]

Ironically, it was Marshall Applewhite, who, referring to the various forms of religious expression in the world, stated: "Some people are like lemmings, who rush in a pack into the sea and drown themselves. . . . They join any movement. . . . Some people will try anything."[154]

TWO

Seers, Sages, and Soothsayers

The world as we know it will cease to exist . . . on August 18, 1999. . . . [W]e will cease to exist before the year 2000! . . . And if you and I meet each other on the street that fateful day, August 18, 1999, and we chat about what we will do on the morrow, we will open our mouths to speak and no words will come out, for we have no future.

The Amazing Criswell[1]
psychic (1968)

ONLY THE "HOW ARE YOU TODAY?" greeting of the supermarket check-out girl could pull my attention away from the dramatic headline embla-zoned across the front page of the *Weekly World News,* a tabloid newspaper displayed by the cash register: "Star Over Bethlehem Signals the End of the World." The story was especially appropriate since Christmas 1996 was only a few weeks away. After the holidays had ended, I noticed that the same publication ran an equally alarming article: "4 Horsemen of the Apocalypse Photographed in Arizona — Just Days to Go." Within one month, yet another sensational announcement appeared in its pages: "1997: Beginning of the End of the World — World's Religions All Agree the Apocalypse Is Near!" This latest news flash revealed that "planet earth will undergo swift cataclysmic changes beginning in 1997 followed by the end of the world on January 6, 2000."

Although stories like these merely amuse most people, a vast number of suggestible individuals find them genuinely disconcerting. Such persons may not believe *every* doomsday yarn that is spun, but they cannot help but be affected by them (see Chapter 11). This chapter examines some of the various prophetic sources that many people, especially those involved in the occult, look to in hopes of getting a glimpse of that dreaded event looming ever so near: the end of the world. Our journey along the road to Armageddon continues with those perennial seers of the future — psychics.

1-900-SEER-4ME

Psychics. They are everywhere these days. Turn on any one of a dozen television talk shows and see them predicting the world's future. Dial a celebrity-endorsed "Hotline" for $1.95 a minute and hear one of them tell you about your need for more romance. Stand in a grocery store check-out line and browse through their tabloid predictions regarding next year's Hollywood divorces and/or political scandals. Their prophecies can also be perused in bookstores, where psychic volumes fill shelf after shelf. They even have their own nationally distributed newspaper: *Psychic News*.

The definition of a psychic is quite broad. According to the *Dictionary of Mysticism and the Occult*, a psychic is someone who "possesses paranormal powers or extrasensory perception: precognition, clairvoyance, mental telepathy, ability to see and diagnose the aura [i.e., an invisible cloud of colored light that allegedly surrounds plants, animals, and humans]."[2] *The Encyclopedia of the Occult* defines a psychic as "a sensitive, one susceptible to psychic influences. . . . anyone who is in any degree sensitive."[3]

Most psychics are especially "sensitive" to information about the earth's last days. This otherwise unobtainable knowledge is received by them through a variety of paranormal phenomena: meetings with dead relatives, angelic encounters, disembodied voices, and color visions of Armageddon. A slew of end-time predictions have resulted:[4]

- 1908: Lee T. Spangler — a grocery store owner in York, Pennsylvania — announced a prediction that he remembered making after coming out of a trance when he was twelve years old: the world would end by fire in October 1908. Spangler's followers were heartily disappointed. The only extraordinary October event was a light rain on the month's last day.

- 1925: A young Los Angeles girl named Margaret Rowan had a vision wherein the angel Gabriel appeared and informed her that the end of the world would occur at midnight on February 13, 1925 (Friday the 13th). Believers of Rowan's story included house painter Robert Reidt of Freeport, Long Island who took out "large advertisements in New York newspapers summoning the faithful to join him on a hilltop at the hour of doom." Many people — all wearing white muslin gowns — showed up with Reidt to await doomsday. At the appointed hour they all threw up their hands and shouted, "Gabriel! Gabriel! Gabriel!" When nothing happened, Reidt claimed that "the end" would strike at midnight *Pacific Time* rather than Eastern Standard Time. Three hours went by and still nothing happened. As befuddled followers left, Reidt blamed Gabriel's no-show on the reporters who used flashbulbs to take pictures of the event. Apparently, the flashes had somehow scared away God's holy messenger.

- 1954: Charles Laughead — a respected physician at Michigan State College — shocked friends and relatives by proclaiming that doomsday would occur on December 20, 1954. Laughead, 44, had gotten involved with psychic-medium Dorothy Martin, who had taught him how to communicate psychically with beings from a cosmic civilization located somewhere in the "Great Beyond." These entities told Laughead that in December a global calamity would leave America's east coast, France, England, and Russia underwater. As for Laughead, Mrs. Martin, and those who believed in them, a spaceship was supposed to come and whisk them all away to safety. When December came and went uneventfully, Laughead claimed that "God had stopped it all." Laughead's relatives then tried to have him committed to a mental institution. But the judge ruled that although Laughead held unusual ideas, he was not clinically insane.

- 1996: According to California psychic Sheldon Nidle, the end of the world was to occur on December 17, 1996 with the arrival of "millions of spaceships" and accompanying angels. The event was supposed to bring sixteen years of 24-hour-a-day light. Nidle claims that his prophecy did indeed come to pass, but nobody noticed it because the angels placed all of us in a special holographic projection in order to give us "another chance to make good."

Despite the many inaccurate pronouncements that have come from psychics, people continue to look to them as reliable prognosticators. The twentieth century has seen at least three psychics whose end-time prophecies have enjoyed immense popularity: Charles "Criswell" King, Gordon-Michael Scallion, and the famous Edgar Cayce. Scallion and Cayce were even featured on "Ancient Prophecies," a 1996/1997 four-part television documentary about the coming apocalypse. This program's host — actor David McCallum — gave audiences an ominous warning:

> The signs may surround us even now — doomsday, Armageddon, visions of the end of time — signs that prophesy the final chapter of future history. Those deciphering the secrets of the future . . . . all speak of time that may soon come to pass: the end of history, the final judgment. The clock is ticking and time may be running out.[5]

Do modern-day psychics *really* possess some supernatural gift that has allowed them to foresee Earth's imminent destruction? To answer this question, one need only take a look at their prophetic track record.

Criswell

Charles Criswell King (1907–1982) began speaking to large audiences not as a psychic, but as a television newscaster in New York. He made his transition from reporter to end-time prophet quite by accident one evening when, after running out of news with fifteen minutes of air time left, he decided to tell the viewers what he thought would happen the next day. To the delight of station employees, his impromptu effort to save the broadcast worked. He filled the news void with an entertaining series of ad-libs until the credits began rolling down the screen as scheduled. Everyone enjoyed King's prophetic antics so much that network executives gave him a small segment of time at the end of each newscast so he could make a few predictions. It was all fun and games, a lighthearted joke that studio personnel and the audience enjoyed.

As fate would have it, though, one of King's off-the-cuff predictions came true one day when a local politician died. The public was astounded and almost overnight turned newscaster Charles King into the "Amazing Criswell."[6] King's new title would be borne well. By his own admission he was a natural actor, who as a child could not get enough of performing on stage.

Criswell understandably went into newscasting. But after his on-air prediction awed the masses, he could not resist the potentially lucrative opportunity that had presented itself. Criswell subsequently used his media contacts to carve himself a niche in the entertainment industry as America's newest psychic sensation. He not only appeared on many national television programs including Johnny Carson's *Tonight Show* (December 31, 1965), but made a record album entitled *Someone Walked Over My Grave* and landed his own syndicated newspaper column called "Criswell Predicts."

Although Criswell had several eccentricities (e.g., he slept in a "satin-lined coffin, studded and flounced with white silk trimmings"),[7] these only helped solidify his image as a man who could see into the future. After all, a true seer is bound to be a little odd given the amount of psychological pressure that no doubt accompanies visions of the future.

By 1968 Criswell was able to release a bestseller: *Criswell Predicts: From Now to the Year 2000*. This 141-page volume was chock full of predictions that not only seemed possible, but probable in light of that era's social unrest. Many of Criswell's prophecies were also bizarre. For example, he predicted that a new sex drug (i.e., a love gas) would accidentally be invented and released by a scientist who was innocently trying to create a new antiseptic spray. The resulting cloud of "aphrodesian fragrance" was to float across America between May 1, 1988 and March 30, 1989, resulting in widespread incest, rape, unrestrained perversion, and uncontrolled sex in the streets (specifically, in Hollywood). The power of the "gaseous drug" would bring about some unbelievable effects. Criswell psychically foresaw one especially odd event in connection with the love gas: "[A] young man in Arkansas will ask to be legally wed to his cat."[8]

Criswell Predicts is brimming with similarly explicit predictions, most of which have proven to be inaccurate as well as strange:

- 1975: On April 7 the "strongest earthquake in the history of the U.S." will wipe out San Francisco, killing more than 25,000 people (p. 25). Also, all metal coins will be withdrawn from the market and only paper money will be used (p. 69).
- 1977: It will not rain for ten months. The Great Lakes will become "beds of sand." Niagara Falls will dry up. The English Channel "will be so shallow that people will walk from the British Isles to the shores of France." Millions will migrate to the North and South Poles, where water will be available from snow and ice. One third of the Far East will die (pp. 41–44).
- 1977–1980: Shifting ocean currents and earthquakes will gradually submerge New York City.
- 1980: People will give themselves a facelift at home by using a $5 chemical cream (p. 67). A terrible accident at an experimental laboratory in Pittsburgh, Pennsylvania will result in the release of a gas that makes people insane and hungry for raw flesh. From November 28–December 21 "over one thousand flesh mad and blood crazed men will wander through the streets suddenly attacking unsuspecting victims. . . . Each and every day more bodies will be found. . . . Many others will be found stripped of their clothing, bound and gagged in cellars and attics meeting a most horrible death." (p. 116)
- 1988: A meteor will destroy London (p. 79).
- 1989: Denver, Colorado will be destroyed after being hit by a strange and invisible "pressure" from outer space that will "cause all solids to turn into a jellylike mass. . . . [A]s rescue units approach the city they will lose all semblance of solidity and will be rendered helpless. The people who attempt to escape in wild panic will be unable to move through the gummy streets. . . . The citizenry of this Colorado city will find themselves enveloped in a jellylike substance that was once brick, concrete, steel, and lumber. . . . Gradually, as conditions

ease survivors will be evacuated but this will become a dead city and will never again be reborn." (pp. 29–30)

Some individuals have noted that many of Criswell's prophecies sound strikingly similar to low-budget horror film plots. This may be more than coincidence, since Criswell was a close friend of Ed Wood Jr., a well-known Hollywood producer/director and writer of sci fi films and B-grade productions. Criswell even appeared in a few of Wood's films. He delivered a short monologue in the sixty-nine-minute classic, *Night of the Ghouls* (1958), and had a significant role in *Orgy of the Dead* (1965). In the latter picture, he played the omniscient supernatural ruler of "an underworld colony of topless, undead go-go dancers." The Internet's Edward D. Wood, Jr. Home Page explains the film this way: "A young, middle class couple gets lost and winds up at judgment day. Here, with Criswell presiding, a whole bunch of strippers do their acts one after another. . . . A werewolf and mummy show up too. This is amazing."[9]

Criswell's greatest role, however, was that of the narrator in Wood's 1959 cult classic *Plan 9 From Outer Space*, which also starred Bela Lugosi.[10] The movie opens with Criswell sitting at a desk. "My friend," he says while staring into the camera, "we are all interested in the future — for that is where you and I are going to spend the rest of our lives." His monologue serves as the film's introduction and ends with a classic sci fi/horror line: "[W]e cannot keep this secret any longer. My friend, can your heart stand the shocking facts of *GRAVE ROBBERS FROM OUTER SPACE?*"

Although an occasional actor, Criswell was best known for his predictions, the most famous of which concerned "the end of our civilization" via nuclear holocaust on August 18, 1999. According to this prophecy, Earth will be utterly destroyed on that date and remain uninhabitable for four hundred years. The only human survivors will be the human "space colonists" fortunate enough to be living on the two hundred space stations that supposedly will be orbiting the planet by then.[11] Criswell did not live to see his predicted doomsday date. He died in 1982, the same year that he said "a full medical education will require six months of study [because]. . . . everything in medicine will be automated, and a course to qualify one as a medical doctor will require only knowledge of how to operate the proper computers and other equipment."[12]

Gordon-Michael Scallion

Gordon-Michael Scallion (often referred to as simply GMS) is the newest star on this century's prophetic horizon. He has been a featured "futurist and spiritual visionary" on CNBC, *Borderlines* (UPN), *Sightings* (Fox), *Encounters* (Fox), and *Ancient Prophecies* (NBC). Scallion has even been written about in *Rolling Stone Magazine*. He is "considered by many to be one of the most accurate intuitives of our times."[13] Most of his prognostications deal with one thing: doomsday.

GMS's career as a self-proclaimed "futurist" began in 1979 when he was working in the field of communications. One day, as the story goes, he lost his voice for no apparent reason. "I thought I was having a mid-life crisis or a stroke," Scallion remembers. "I ended up in the hospital for tests and observations."[14] That evening, while in the hospital, the eleven o'clock hour brought his first of many visions. According to GMS, "the room lit up and a series of colors and lights danced about the room."[15] After about thirty minutes these lights turned into three-dimensional scenes of the future. Suddenly, a woman who materialized out of nowhere "floated" into the room. She explained the images to GMS and also told him what would take place in the future.[16]

By the next day Scallion's voice had mysteriously returned, much to the surprise of concerned and baffled doctors who had gone so far as to hook GMS to an I.V. all night long. (Exactly why GMS needed treatment as drastic as an I.V. simply because of losing his voice he has never explained.) In an interview on Art Bell's sensationalistic *Coast to Coast* talk-radio show, Scallion recounted what happened to him next:

> The visions continued and within days, literally, events that I had seen in those visions began to occur. . . . [But] I took three years before I was even willing to deal with the fact that this might be a natural thing rather than some form of a crisis that I was going through, or some kind of a mental disorder, or disease. And I found that throughout the 80's I was able to use these visions, which would come spontaneously, to help people. . . . I conducted

thousands of sessions in the 80's, mostly on health issues and finding missing people . . . . And then back in 1989 . . . the only visions I began to see was the Earth. Now I had seen, as early as 1982, visions of the Earth as viewed from space. And I look[ed] at the Earth and what I saw was much different than the Earth that we know. Everything had changed, the land masses had changed, even the colors, that we now take for granted, had changed.[17]

GMS predicts that imminent Earth changes will be drastic enough to alter the entire face of North America. A horrific quake will rock California, sending most of the western U.S. into the Pacific. Nearly all of New York will also be inundated along with about one third of Maine, most of Rhode Island, and approximately half of Connecticut.[18] The Great Lakes will expand into one giant inland sea connecting to the Mississippi, which will swell to a giant inland waterway. Other nations will face devastation as well. Japan, for instance, will be completely swallowed by the ocean. Scallion's 1998-2001 doomsday scenarios sound like a bad dream:[19]

- Seven plagues will run rampant on the planet within the next seven years: metastatic melanomas; a new virulent form of TB; a new strain of AIDS, which can be transmitted through the air; "optic system failure"; "thymus failure"; "pancreatic failure"; and "a disorder of the Astral and Etheric bodies, wherein they meld, making the victim susceptible to interference from the 'border-land' beyond death (which would create psychic disturbances)."
- Erratic weather patterns will hit the world. Dry areas will become wet and wet areas will become dry. Extended droughts, wide-spread flooding, and unusually powerful storms will also plague humanity. In America, summer and spring will merge into one long season.
- Water will become as valuable as gold in the next five years.
- There will be one year of darkness due to volcanic ash from volcanoes erupting in the Pacific.

All these tragedies will allegedly culminate with the ultimate disaster: a shifting of the earth's poles. This will completely restructure life on our planet. Scallion has gone so far as to print a new 1998–2001 map of the U.S. (60 x 46) that he sells in three configurations: 1) on folded paper for $22 plus shipping and handling; 2) on rolled paper in a map tube for $25 plus S&H; and 3) on laminated/rolled paper in a map tube for $35 plus S&H. Scallion's visions are nothing short of cataclysmic, as he readily admits:

> In '98 to 2001, the earth becomes very quiet. The animals are quiet. Then a wind picked up from the east. It was hurricane velocity. I then watched the sun reverse its direction in the sky. The oceans themselves buckled, and land masses were thrust up. I can't even begin to tell you how many sleepless nights I've had and nights where I've just emotionally totally lost it.[20]

Like many supposed psychics, Scallion sometimes induces visions by entering an altered state of consciousness (ASC). An ASC is induced when anything interrupts or brings to halt "the normal patterns of conceptual thought without extinguishing or diminishing consciousness itself."[21] In other words, an ASC occurs when normal everyday awareness (or consciousness) is replaced by an alternate (or altered) awareness. A hypnotic trance, for instance, is an ASC. A person in an ASC is functioning under an extremely confused sense of reality. Consequently, separating fact from fiction during such a state is very difficult, if not impossible.

But this has not stopped Scallion from using ASCs to receive visions from his "Higher Self,"[22] which according to occultists, is the "most spiritual and knowing part of oneself, said to lie beyond the ego, the day-to-day personality or self, and beyond the personal unconscious, and which can be channeled for wisdom and guidance"; variations include the *oversoul, superconscious, Atmen, Christ* (or *Krishna* or *Buddha*) *Consciousness, God within*, or *God Self.*[23]

Scallion describes the visions themselves as scenes that appear on what he calls his three psychic "news channels." One channel transmits only in gray. These visions are the ones least likely transpire. Other visions appear in "muted colors." These scenarios have a far better chance of coming true. Then there are the sights and sounds that come over his full color channel. These images present a "probable outcome." GMS comments: "The kind of details that I see are the actual collapsing of the buildings. The people running in panic — the actual people. Watching the water actually come in and covering communities. I see cargo planes coming in with red cross symbols on the side."[24]

Scallion is easily this decade's premier psychic visionary. In addition to his many speaking engagements and public interviews, he publishes *The Earth Changes Report* (since 1991), a monthly newsletter that lists up-to-the-minute prophecies ($36 a year subscriptions). He also runs New Hampshire's Matrix Institute, an organization dedicated to disseminating "newsworthy information, including future trends and thought provoking articles, relative to geophysical, atmospheric, economic, and/or spiritual changes taking place on the earth."[25] The Institute alleges that reading today's headlines "is like reading early editions" of *The Earth Changes Report (ECR)*.[26] Scallion himself claims to have an accuracy rate of about 89%.[27] The Internet publication *Karinya*, which is published by two of GMS's fans, bumps this figure up to 90%.[28]

This is an impressive percentage. But is it accurate? The claim is easy enough to investigate since most of Scallion's prophecies have appeared in issues of *ECR*. In fact, each January edition of *ECR* includes a long list of GMS's prognostications for the coming year. Scallion also used to include a "hit and miss" list in each February issue in order to detail how accurate he had been about the previous year. This list, however, suddenly disappeared from the *ECR* as of February 1997. It may have vanished because too many people were noticing that Scallion's accuracy rate is hardly 89%-90%.

Moreover, GMS has misrepresented his predictions in an apparent effort to make himself appear more accurate than the average "seer." In the February 1996 issue of *ECR*, for instance, he claimed a phenomenal accuracy percentage for his sixty-six 1995 predictions: 82% (fifty-four "hits" and only twelve "misses"). But a careful review of Scallion's predictions reveal that many of his "hits" are not really hits and that "many of Scallion's most trumpeted predictions for 1995 not only didn't come true, *but were scarcely mentioned, or not mentioned at all.*"[29]

GMS admitted to the following failed predictions: 1) a 7.2 quake to hit Portland; 2) a 7.3 quake to hit Utah; 3) Nevada hit by a 6.7 quake; 4) Northwest New York hit by a 5.0 quake; 5) Southwest Florida hit by a 5.2 quake; 6) Southwest Illinois hit by a 5.0 quake; 7) the southern part of North Carolina gets hit by a 5.0 quake; 8) Massachusetts hit by a 5.0 quake; 9) Vermont-New York State region hit by a 5.0 quake; 10) Palm

Springs, California area hit by a 9.0 quake; 11) Northeast hit by fifteen or more snowstorms; and 12) the Northeast — along the Connecticut River and its tributaries — is hit by destructive flooding due to a very early melt-off.[30]

But GMS did not even mention five more failed predictions that he had made in the January 1995 *ECR*: 1) Sonoma County and San Francisco Bay area hit by a 8.5 quake; 2) area southwest of Mt. Rainier in Washington state hit by a 7.5 quake; 3) Colorado — west of the Rockies — hit by a 7.0 quake; 4) average annual wind velocities will increase to speeds of 200, 250 and 300 or more m.p.h.; and 5) twelve volcanic eruptions will cause ash to cover the planet between 1995-1997 with a minimum of 30% coverage. Sunlight reduction will decrease global temperatures at least a half degree.

Scallion's alleged "hits" leave much to be desired. In seeking to find a world event that fulfilled his prophecies, he was forced to draw upon events that were hardly fulfillments right on the money (see table 2.1) :[31]

1995 PREDICTIONS	ALLEGED FULFILLMENTS
1. An *8.5 (+ or −.5)* quake will hit the Indian Ocean area and unleash 100-foot tidal waves.	1. A *7.8* quake (not in GMS's range) hit Indonesia on 10/30/95. No tidal waves.
2. Pictures of alien spaceships will be broadcast live on national television.	2. No similar event was recorded anywhere, but GMS still claimed a "hit."
3. New York, Los Angeles and other U.S. cities hit by widespread terrorist attacks.	3. Oklahoma City Bombing. No widespread terrorism or attacks in New York or Los Angeles.
4. "War spreads in Europe — the Holy War begins in Middle East — watch Turkey."	4. "At least 15 people were killed when riots broke out in a suburb near Istanbul in March."

Table 2.1

What about Scallion's other "hits"? Most of them were so vague and/
or based on commonplace events, that it would have been difficult for them
not to have been hits:

- UFO sightings will increase.
- Mary and angelic sightings will occur in over 100 countries.
- Herb sales will soar as more people seek alternative methods of
  healing.
- Media programming on metaphysics, the world of spirit, and
  phenomena will expand.
- Cottage industries and home industries flourish, especially writing
  — books, publications, journals, reports — "How To" will do very
  well.

Despite Scallion's dismal prophetic record, his devotees remain faithful. One follower explained this "support-your-psychic-regardless-of-his-
accuracy" mindset thusly:

Late last year Sheldon Nidle [another psychic] predicted that 15.5 million
spaceships would physically descend upon Earth in December '96. It would
seem that this did not happen. . . . As expected, it didn't take long for people
to start trashing Sheldon and his work in various Internet newsgroups and
mailing lists. It sounds a lot like the situation with Gordon Michael Scallion
when people started to lose faith in him when he began to have more misses
than hits. I will not be one who is quick to judge. . . . Was Sheldon wrong about
last month? Yes. Does that make him wrong now? No. . . . It is important that
we support those who are willing to step forward and share information. It is
not a question of being right or wrong, but a question of manifesting our
future. Their value and contributions are in projecting possible futures. . . . I
for one enjoy reading all the prophecy and predictions.[32]

The most recent end-time information from GMS is rather depress-
ing. As previously mentioned, he has for many years sold a 1998–2001
map of the U.S. that prophesies and illustrates Earth's complete geological

overhaul by the year 2002.[33] As of 1997, however, Scallion had replaced this map with a 2012 chart that gives humanity an extra decade of turmoil and tribulation until the planet is restored to harmonic balance after a series of cataclysms. GMS has thus far given no plausible reason for adding another ten years to his original timetable.

Edgar Cayce

Edgar Cayce (1877-1945) was one of the world's most famous psychic/healer-mediums. He reportedly had many visions even while still a young boy. By the time he reached his sixteenth birthday, he allegedly possessed an "uncanny ability to prescribe remedies for illnesses."[34] Cayce's journey into the world of occultism began in 1900 when he mysteriously lost his voice (note the similarity to Scallion's story), "but regained it temporarily under hypnotic trance. When speaking under hypnosis, he diagnosed his own trouble and cured himself by posthypnotic suggestion."[35]

He eventually used this "gift" to diagnose and cure others. His patients did not even need to be present for him to discern their problem. Cayce would simply enter a trance and be able to see them wherever they were residing. The only thing Cayce needed to have from a patient was their name and address. He would then fall "asleep," spiritually "travel" to their location, examine them, and prescribe a remedy for their malady. Thus he earned his famous title: "The Sleeping Prophet." Cayce could supposedly also read auras, describe a person's past life, and see into the future.

Most of Cayce's trance-induced "readings" were not only transcribed and preserved, but catalogued and stored at his Association for Research and Enlightenment (A.R.E.) in Virginia Beach, Virginia (founded, 1931). Included among these readings are a number of statements that foretell devastating global disasters. Although numerous psychics since Cayce (e.g., Scallion) have made similar predictions about cataclysmic earth changes involving widespread natural disasters, Cayce was the first to make such prognostications. They are very much like those of today's major psychic prophets, all of whom are familiar with Cayce's works:[36]

READING #1

"The earth will be broken up in the western portion of America. The greater portion of Japan must go into the sea. The upper portion of Europe will be changed as in the twinkling of an eye. Land will appear off the east coast of America. There will be the upheavals in the Arctic and in the Antarctic that will make for the eruption of volcanoes in the torrid areas, and there will be the shifting then of the poles — so that where there has been those of a frigid or the semi-tropical will become the more tropical, and moss and fern will grow."

READING #2

Portions of the now east coast of New York, or New York City itself, will in the main disappear. . . . [T]he southern portions of Carolina, Georgia — these will disappear. . . . Los Angeles, San Francisco, most of all these will be among those that will be destroyed before New York even."

READING #3

Observer: "What great change or the beginning of what change, if any, is to take place in the earth in the year 2000 to 2001 A.D.?" *Cayce:* "When there is the shifting of the poles, or a new cycle begins."

Many contemporary occultists believe that Cayce's predictions clearly confirm the prophecies of more recent prophets who have predicted imminent global disaster. John Van Auken, an A.R.E. lecturer, teaches his students that a seven-year period of cataclysmic cleansing of the earth will most likely be completed by 2002.[37] But what seems to be consistently and conveniently overlooked is Cayce's timetable.

Reading #1's prophecies were supposed to have occurred "in those periods" between 1958–1998.[38] The disasters foretold in Reading #2 were scheduled to happen within "one generation" of 1941. In this same reading Cayce stated, "*In the next few years* land will appear in the Atlantic as well as in the Pacific. And what is the coast line now of many a land will be the bed of the ocean. Even many battle fields of the present will be ocean, will be the seas" (emphasis mine). He also prophesied that the mythical continent of Atlantis would rise from its ocean grave in 1968/1969.[39] Reading #3 obviously names 2001 as the terrible "Pole Shift" year.

Other interesting bits of information cast an even greater shadow of doubt on Cayce's psychic abilities. On one occasion, for instance, he gave a reading for a little girl who had died the previous day from leukemia. The letter he received about her had been written while she was still alive. But Cayce had no idea while in his trance that she was already dead, and proceeded to give a cure![40] For another patient who had passed away without Cayce's knowledge, the Sleeping Prophet prescribed this noxious concoction as a remedy: boiled cherry bark, sarsaparilla root, wild ginger, tolu balsam, buchu leaves, prickly ash bark, ginseng, Indian turnip, mandrake root, and alcohol.[41]

His cures for cancer were even more unconventional. He often prescribed a serum "made from the blood of rabbits for patients with 'glandular,' breast, and thyroid cancers."[42] In 1926, Cayce took this remedy even further by directing a New York patient to place the raw side of a pelt from a freshly skinned rabbit — "still warm with blood, fur side out" — on her breast for cancer in that area.[43]

It is also not widely known that Cayce attempted to use his psychic powers to find buried treasure. He even went on an expedition along the seashore with Henry Goss, the famed "dowser" (i.e., one who uses a forked stick to locate underground water). The two men hoped to find millions of dollars worth of jewels and coins, but after weeks of searching they only succeeded in digging up tons of mud, sand and gravel.[44] James Randi — the internationally known magician/escape artist who has investigated and debunked countless psychics — makes the following observation in his book *Flim-Flam*:

> The matter of Edgar Cayce boils down to a vague mass of garbled data, interpreted by true believers who have a very heavy stake in the acceptance of the claims. Put to the test, Cayce is found to be bereft of real powers. His reputation today rests on poor and deceptive reporting of the claims made by him and his followers, and such claims do not stand up to examination.[45]

Psychics have clearly shown themselves to be unreliable when it comes to forecasting the date for our world's destruction. Their prophetic track record, however, is not the worst among occult prognosticators. That distinction goes to astrologers.

THE STARGAZERS

Divination is defined in occult literature as "[t]he act of foretelling the future by apparently irrational and unscientific means, often by interpreting omens."[46] One of the oldest forms of divination is astrology, which rests on the foundational assumption that the movement and position of celestial bodies (i.e., the Sun, the Moon, stars, and planets) not only affect individual lives, but nations and even humanity as a whole.[47] It is an extremely popular belief system, especially in countries such as Sri Lanka, Indochina and India. This is not to say that astrology has failed to flourish in other countries. On the contrary, astrology is widely accepted as a legitimate form of religious expression that many people look to for guidance. A recent poll found that forty-eight percent of Americans think astrology is "probably or definitely valid."[48]

According to astrologers, a number of celestial events can spell disaster. For example, a severely "afflicted" Mercury in a person's chart indicates that he or she may be prone to insanity.[49] On a much wider scale, a planet passing through the wrong constellation during a war campaign might mean utter defeat for an entire nation. One of the most ominous heavenly omens has been the comet. A medieval prayer reads: "God protect us from the Comet. And from the fury of the Norsemen."[50]

In the twentieth century, the 1910 appearance of Halley's Comet sparked widespread panic, especially after astronomers voiced the possibility that earth might actually pass through a portion of the comet's tail. Several entrepreneurs sold "comet pills" designed to guard people against the comet's gaseous emissions. An Oklahoma religious sect known as the Select Followers actually tried to sacrifice a virgin![51] Police fortunately stopped them before the deed was done. More recently, the Hale-Bopp comet played a significant role in the deadly beliefs of the Heaven's Gate cult (see Chapter 1).

Even more dreaded than a comet, however, is a planetary alignment (or conjunction). Such incidents have regularly brought predictions of global cataclysm. In ancient Babylon (c. 1830–1025 B.C.) — astrology's birthplace — the seer Berossus declared that "all terrestrial things will be consumed when the planets, which now are traversing their different courses, shall all coincide in the sign of Cancer, and be so placed that a straight line could pass directly through all their orbs."[52]

In 1179, an astrologer named John of Toledo "predicted a terrible catastrophe for the year 1186" because an alignment of the planets would take place at that time.[53] This conjunction would form in the "stormy" sign of Libra, which left no doubt in John's mind that tragedy lay ahead. His warning was widely heeded. In Germany, people dug shelters. Persons in Mesopotamia and Persia "readied their cellars for occupation." The Byzantine emperor boarded up his palace's windows, and England's Archbishop of Canterbury declared a national fast of atonement. When 1186 and its planetary alignment passed uneventfully, John refused to admit his error, maintaining instead that his prophecy was meant as merely a symbolic reference to the invasion of barbarian Huns. Faithful followers believed John, apparently disregarding the fact that such invasions had been regularly occurring for hundreds of years.[54]

German astrologer Johannes Stoeffler claimed in 1499 that a conjunction of the Sun, Mercury, Venus, Mars, Jupiter, and Saturn world bring doomsday via a giant flood on February 20, 1524 (even though the conjunction actually took place on February 23).[55] Stoeffler was regarded as a fairly credible source of information since he was not only a faculty member at Tübingen University, but an advisor to royalty. The years 1499–1524 saw countless people building boats in preparation for the deluge. Among them was a Count von Iggleheim, who ordered a three-story ark to be built for his family. When it started raining on February 20, 1524, bedlam broke out and huge crowds rushed to the docks in hopes of boarding von Iggleheim's ship. The count bravely drew his sword, but all efforts to protect the ark were in vain. He was trampled/stoned to death by the mob. Hundreds of people died while "fighting to reach the supposed safety of the craft."[56]

The twentieth century, too, has had its share of astrologically-related disaster predictions involving planetary alignments. In the early 1900s, a widely respected seismologist/meteorologist named Albert Porta predicted that December 17, 1919 would see a conjunction of six planets. This was supposed to create a magnetic current that would "pierce the sun, cause great explosions of flaming gas, and eventually engulf the earth."[57] His prediction set off a worldwide panic. Suicides and hysteria were reported in several countries. The conjunction did indeed take place, but that was all. Porta spent the rest of his life working as a newspaper weatherman.

Less than fifty years later, another planetary conjunction — this time of all five planets visible to the naked eye (Mercury, Venus, Mars, Jupiter, Saturn) — set off numerous speculations about what might happen. Although much more cautious than prior interpreters of celestial events, our modern-day astrologers unanimously declared that "something" would happen during the February 4, 1962 alignment. Others went a step further, believing that the "something" would be calamitous. In India, for instance, millions of Hindus held a vigil of non-stop prayer to avert the wrath of the gods.[58]

Many Americans were also worried about the possible effects of five planets lining up within a 17° span of each other. Making the event even more threatening was the eclipse of the sun scheduled to occur at the same moment. Consider the following report filed by astronomer Robert Richardson of Los Angeles's Griffith Observatory. He had some rather interesting encounters with the general public:

> [On] Sunday, February 4 . . . [the crowd at the Observatory] must have been the largest since it was opened to the public in 1935. By two o'clock . . . the road leading to and from the observatory was a solid mass of cars lined up bumper-to-bumper for half a mile. . . . [One] woman was weeping so badly it was hard to understand her. She was practically on the verge of collapse. "I know it's silly to carry on this way," she gasped between sobs, "but I can't help myself." . . . In talking to these "alarmed" individuals, one gets the impression very strongly of an insecure personality, torn this way and that by vague doubts and fears. When confronted by a problem, they seem incapable of forming an independent opinion concerning it, but tend to rely on the judgment of others. They are so highly susceptible to suggestion that it would be very easy for anyone who has gained their confidence to take advantage of them. The barest hint that there might be something wrong could drive them to suicide or hysterics.[59]

Like other alignments, the 1962 astronomical rarity passed without a corresponding change in the course of human events. But devout believers came up with an ingenious explanation for what had transpired. The "something" that they were awaiting had indeed taken place, but its results would only be seen after many years. The "something" that had occurred, however, remained unidentified.[60]

Widespread apprehension throughout the 1970s and early 1980s was caused by yet another alignment of planets. This time, all nine planets in the solar system were slated to form a heliocentric conjunction on March 10, 1982. In other words, as seen from the sun, the planets would span a 95° arc (about a quarter of the sky), which is a fairly tight grouping. Personalities from widely divergent points on the apocalyptic spectrum (e.g., Christians, occultists, New Agers) felt that it would, at the very least, cause a devastating earthquake on the San Andreas Fault, thus destroying California.

This episode of doomsday paranoia began with the 1974 publication of *The Jupiter Effect*, written by astrophysicists John Gribbin and Stephen Plagemann. The two men hypothesized that the imbalance of planets in our solar system could create tidal effects on the sun, which might then cause an increase in sunspots. These sunspots in turn could intensify the release of solar particles toward Earth. The subsequent "Jupiter Effect" — named after Jupiter's gravitational pull — might then disturb our atmosphere so dramatically that the planet's rotation rate would change, putting a tremendous strain on Earth's tectonic plates. It was further theorized that the geological strain could make unusually large quakes, especially in California, a real possibility.[61]

The volume was written as a lengthy hypothesis based on an endless list of astronomical "ifs." It was not intended to be taken as a dogmatic assertion about cataclysmic earthquakes in 1982. Unfortunately, the authors failed to emphasize "the enormous uncertainties at each link of their complicated chain of hypothetical connections."[62] As a result, the general public read the work as more of a "this-is-definitely-going-to-happen" book than as a frivolous essay born out of the intellectual musings of two academicians.

As 1982 drew nearer, more people began to panic. The sheer fact that Gribbin was a recognized scientist — although well-known in scientific circles as a highly speculative writer — was enough to push his hypothesis deep into the secular community's psyche. Throughout the Christian community, though, increasing fear resulted more from the prophetic ramblings of various prophecy pundits; most notably, Bible teacher Hal Lindsey, author of the 1970 doomsday bestseller *The Late Great Planet Earth* (see Chapter 3). In his 1980 book *The 1980s: Countdown to Armageddon*, Lindsey gave this warning:

> [A]uthors of *The Jupiter Effect*, have predicted that history's greatest outbreak of earthquakes will occur around 1982. They make this claim because of an unusual astronomical phenomenon that occurs every 179 years. That phenomenon has been dubbed the "Jupiter Effect". . . . The term describes a situation in which all of the planets of our solar system become aligned in a straight line perpendicular to the sun. This alignment causes great storms on the sun's surface, which in turn affect each of the planets. The sun storms will not only affect our atmosphere, as was previously mentioned, but they will slow down the Earth's axis slightly. . . . [T]his slowing puts a tremendous strain on the Earth's faults, touching off earthquakes.[63]

Lindsey, of course, got it all wrong. As previously explained, the destruction envisioned by Gribbin and Plagemann was "based on a series of hypothesized geophysical connections," each of which was considered "highly speculative with little confirming evidence."[64] Furthermore, the planets were *not* scheduled to "become aligned in a straight line." They were to gather in a 95° arc across the sky. Lindsey's book — originally published by Westgate Press in Pennsylvania —went on to become a *New York Times Bestseller* and was reprinted by Bantam Books in 1981.

Oddly, the 1981 Bantam edition was released with its Jupiter Effect warning *after* Gribbin had publicly repudiated the entire theory. In a number of articles and interviews with magazines, Gribbin completely renounced the possibility of a Jupiter Effect occurring in 1982. One can only wonder why Lindsey and others would continue to propagate the discredited theory, especially after Gribbin wrote a highly publicized article in the June 1980 issue of *Omni* entitled "Jupiter's Noneffect":

> I have bad news for doomsayers. The book has now been proved wrong; the whole basis of the 1982 prediction is gone. . . . Because of the way the book

has been misused by cultists who must never have read it, I want to make it clear that there is no reason now to expect any unusual seismic disturbance in 1982 from the causes given in the book. . . . In retrospect, some of the accusations that our book was alarmist seem justified. I am older now and, I hope, wiser. I would certainly not present the same material in the same way if the idea had just occurred to me. . . . [T]here is every prospect that 1982 will be quieter in seismic terms than 1979 or 1980. . . . There's an important lesson here, which may be what our academic critics were trying to tell us. Don't open the door for half-baked cults to latch on to your ideas. The key words *earthquake*, *planetary alignment*, and *1982* were all that the weirdos needed and all they ever knew about the Jupiter effect. Don't believe anything you hear about "scientific" forecasts of doom without reading the original. If anyone tries to warn you about the Apocalypse coming in 1982, just tell him that that old theory has long since been disproved.[65]

The world has certainly not seen the last of planetary-alignment jitters. A series of planetary conjunctions are scheduled for the year 2000. The most spectacular one will happen on May 5, when the Moon, the Sun, Mercury, Venus, Earth, Mars, Jupiter, and Saturn will all line up within a span of approximately twenty-six geocentric degrees of each other (see figure 2.1). An even tighter alignment of these same celestial bodies (minus Earth and the Moon.) of 19.5° will take place on May 17, 2000.

Foremost among the many alarmists who are predicting that this conjunction may bring worldwide catastrophe is Richard Noone, author of *5/5/2000 — Ice: The Ultimate Disaster.* According to John Mosley, astronomer at Los Angeles's famous Griffith Observatory, the book is nothing but "an unorganized mish-mash" containing dramatic predictions "that some people will find scary."[66] Mosley additionally points out a rather peculiar aspect to the book: it devotes barely *half a page* to the 5/5/2000 conjunction. Noone spends the remaining three hundred fifty pages trying to convince readers of Earth's imminent demise by linking together a array of topics that would otherwise be completely unrelated: the *Book of Mormon*, Inca fortresses, dinosaurs, the Old Testament's Ark of the Covenant, and the mythical continent of Atlantis.

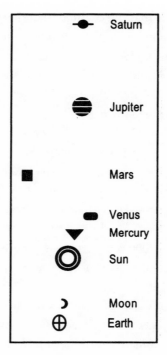

The May 5, 2000 alignment as seen from a view above the sun.

Fig. 2.1

The main tenet of *5/5/2000* is that the earth will be destroyed when the coming alignment *somehow* dislodges the South Pole's ice, thereby throwing our planet off its axis (i.e., a "pole shift"). Noone provided the following explanation in the related videotape *Enter Darkness/Enter Light*:

> On May 5th in the year 2000, our Moon, the planets Mercury, Venus, our Sun, Mars, Jupiter and Saturn will be aligned with the earth, significantly increasing the centrifugal momentum exerted on the earth's crust. On that day, the ever growing ice build up at the South Pole will upset the earth's axis — sending trillions of tons of ice and water sweeping over the surface of our planet.[67]

Noone further claims that the coming calamity is hinted at in several ancient texts, which he obligingly pieces together for us in his book. Most compelling to him are the hidden messages contained in the Great Pyramid of Giza. He spends so much time delving into the pyramid's complex measurements that a better title for his book might have been *The Pyramid Speaks*. Mosley observes the following:

> The alignments seem to be a definite afterthought in a book that is really about secrets of the Ancients. The alignments give the book a dramatic cover illustration and they provide a date in the alarmingly near future to focus on, but they are entirely incidental to the book.[68]

Noone uses the **A.D.** 2000 conjunction as a mere time reference point for the more important underlying theory that he tries to prove, which is that Earth gets destroyed about every 6,000 years. What does the alignment have to do with this lengthy span of time? According to Noone, May 5, 2000 will mark *exactly* 6,000 years since the last time "all the planets of our solar system" were arrayed in "practically a straight line."[69]

But Noone is simply wrong. The planets will *not* be in "practically a straight line" (as the cover of his book suggests) and only the five "naked-eye" planets plus the earth, the Sun, and the Moon will be involved in the alignment. Furthermore, conjunctions such as the one scheduled for May 2000 have happened many times in recorded history. The years 1821, 1953, and 1962, for example, saw such an alignment. There have even been years when all of the planets (minus Pluto) aligned: 1128, 1666, and 1817. On February 1, 949 *all* nine planets moved into a 90° conjunction.[70]

Moreover, Noone's assertion that the extra gravitational pull from the alignment could possibly trigger earthquakes is nothing less than absurd. First, similar conjunctions in the past have never resulted in natural disasters. Second, the extra pull from the coming alignment will barely be measurable: .01 percent of normal tidal forces. As a point of reference, the tidal force exerted by Mars (when closest to Earth) is one billion times *less* than the amount of force being exerted by this book against your hands.[71]

5/5/2000 has a foreword by Richard Kieninger, himself a rather interesting fellow. In addition to sharing Noone's "pole shift" theory,

TIDAL FORCES MEASURED[72]

Moon	2.21
Sun	1.00
Mercury	0.000113
Venus	0.0000131
Mars	0.0000023
Jupiter	0.0000007
Saturn	0.0000005
Uranus	0.000000001
Neptune	0.000000002
Pluto	0.0000000000001

Kieninger holds a unique worldview that combines occultism, New Age spirituality, Christian apocalypticism, and pyramidology. Kieninger seems truly an alarmist:

> After Armageddon and Doom's Day [sic] less than a tenth of the world's population will be alive to see the year 2001 A.D. The intensity of the earthquakes will be greater than has ever been measured by scientists. All the volcanoes of the world will burst forth, and a host of new ones will join them. . . . The skies will be filled with dust and choking fumes so that even the sun will not be seen directly for months. Walls of water a thousand feet high will roar across the submerging land and sweep away everything before them. Sea and land animals, vegetation, silt, and sand will be shredded into jumbled muck. . . . The stench of decay and the bleak destruction everywhere will drive many human survivors hopelessly insane. Those who have the strength of their convictions will retain their civilization and rebuild the world. Those people, of course, will comprise the Kingdom of God, and they will be brought through the awful destruction soon to be visited upon the world. Doom's Day will not be without advantages, for it ushers in the Golden Age. After October, 2001 A.D. the Kingdom of God shall be formed.[73]

In 1963, Kieninger started the Illinois-based Stelle Group commune in an effort to build the "Kingdom of God." He founded the organization based on ancient "truths" he allegedly learned as a boy. His teacher was a mysterious "Dr. White," who claimed to be a member of a secret society called The Brotherhoods. Kieninger was told numerous things about humanity, its *true* history, apocalyptic prophecies, and his own pivotal role in future world events. One of the most important pieces of information Kieninger discovered was that he had lived nearly 3,000 past lives, often as an engineer or a manufacturer in the advanced civilization of Atlantis before it sunk into the ocean 10,500 years ago.[74] The following additional information appears in Kieninger's 1963 book, *The Ultimate Frontier*:

- Humanity will soon receive "all of the secrets of God" and be assisted in doing so by none other than Kieninger, whose Brotherhood name is *Eklal Kueshana*, which in a long-forgotten language means "Harbinger of Aquarius, the Judge of Israel, the Builder of Lemuria, and the Fountainhead of Christ." His initiation into The Brotherhoods included a ceremony during which *Eklal Kueshana* was "inscribed into his flesh in a private area of his body."

- Armageddon, as described in the Book of Revelation, has already begun and will culminate in November 1999 with "wholesale obliteration." By the time the "pole-shift" occurs in 2000, only one-tenth of the world's population will still be alive. "Those not driven insane by the inevitable death, destruction and decay will rebuild the world, and embody the Kingdom of God."

- Kieninger's current job is to set up a proto-Kingdom of God commune in Illinois and await Doomsday, after which he and his followers will move to an island he believes will rise out of the Pacific Ocean when the poles shift.[75]

Although Kieninger is still trying to build his mini-Kingdom/commune, he is doing it apart from the organization that he himself started. According to Tim Wilhelm — the Stelle Group's current Executive Director, Corporate Secretary, and Registered Agent — Kieninger was expelled after "it came out that [he] was sexually involved with a number of women in the group."[76] He was subsequently banned from entering the community's premises for a year. Kieninger is now seeking to establish

God's Kingdom near Dallas through his new group: "The Builders of the Nation." He continues to propagate both the 5/5/2000 alignment, Noone's teachings, and measurements of the Great Pyramid, which to many people remains one of the most accurate of all oracles.

PROPHECIES IN STONE

Three miles southwest of Cairo, on the banks of the Nile, rests the Great Pyramid of Giza. The architectural wonder was built around 2650 **B.C.** as a monument to the Pharaoh Cheops (founder of the Fourth Dynasty). Without benefit of the wheel, "some 100,000 workers hewed, hauled, and mortared 2.3 million stone blocks, averaging 2.5 tons each, into a pyramid standing 481 feet high and covering 13 acres."[77] The monument's internal passageways that lead to royal burial chambers and various other kinds of rooms are equally impressive; so impressive, in fact, that they have given birth to an entire prophetic belief system known as pyramidology.

The four propositions about the Great Pyramid upon which pyramidology rests are as follows: 1) it was built as an expression of the mathematical irrational pi (π), which is used to designate the ratio of the circumference of a circle to its diameter; 2) its proportions embody astronomical and geodesic knowledge; 3) its measurements "form prophecies relating to the events that would later form the body of the Old Testament, as well as the complete future history of Christendom up to and including the Second Coming of Christ"; and 4) it was constructed by a non-Egyptian Caucasian race believed to be the ancestors of the ancient Israelites, whose modern-day descendants are Anglo-Saxons.[78] This final proposition is closely linked to Christian Identity, a white supremacist/anti-Semitic religious belief system (see Chapter 4).

The origins of modern pyramidology date back to the concepts expressed in *The Great Pyramid; Why Was It Built? And Who Built it?* (1859) written by British mathematician John Taylor (1781–1864). Although he never traveled to Egypt, Taylor's thirty-year obsession with the pyramid prompted him to relentlessly study its previously published measurements. He discovered that "when he divided the perimeter of the pyramid by twice its height, the result was a number nearly identical to the value of pi (3.14159+), the constant that is multiplied by the diameter of a circle to give its circumference."[79] He also found that the perimeter of the pyramid measured nearly 36,524 inches, which just happens to be the same number of days in one century.[80] Taylor could not help but see a divine hand of guidance in these and other measurements, eventually concluding that God had inspired the pyramid's builders by giving them an increased level of intellectual prowess.[81]

Although it was Taylor who first attempted to impart some greater significance to the pyramid, Scottish astronomer Charles Piazzi Smyth (1819–1900) would be the pyramidologist to widely popularize Taylor's ideas. Smyth came up with what he called the "pyramid inch" based on the dimensions on an original casing stone that he found near the pyramid. Much to his amazement, he found that its sides were equal to just slightly more than twenty-five British inches (i.e., 25 x 1.0001 British inches). Smyth, who believed that the Israelites mentioned in the Bible's Old Testament were actually Anglo-Saxons rather than Jews, concluded that the similarity of measure was no mere coincidence. The builders of the Great Pyramid *must* have been ancient Israelites, God's chosen people — i.e., Anglo-Saxons.

He further asserted that the "cubit" unit of measure mentioned in the Bible was that of the casing stone which he had found: twenty-five inches. This notion is still propagated by some twentieth century "Anglo-Israelite" pyramidologists. Adam Rutherford, in his 1961 book *Pyramidology*, dogmatically declared: "What was the origin of the Sacred Cubit? . . . Moses used the Sacred Cubit of 25 inches, the same unit as revealed in the design of the Great Pyramid . . . . The Israelites used the 25-inch cubit during their long sojourn in Egypt prior to the Exodus."[82]

But neither history nor archeology supports this conclusion about the biblical cubit. It is a commonly known fact that the common cubit used in ancient Israel was about 17.5 to 18 inches.[83] Smyth also failed to take into account the fact that in the Bible there are *two* kinds of cubits mentioned: the "common" cubit (Deut. 3:11); and the "long" cubit (Ez. 40:5), which added a handbreadth to the common cubit's measure. It seems that Smyth believed in his twenty-five-inch cubit for no reason other than because he wanted to believe in it. This is especially apparent given the fact that soon after he had announced his pyramid inch, other casing stones of widely varying lengths were recovered. This rendered Smyth's "pyramid inch" meaningless since he built his whole theory on the presupposition that *all* of the casing stones were 25 inches x 25 inches.

Smyth ignored the conflicting evidence and continued to preach his new ideas about the cubit and the pyramid inch. In *Our Inheritance in the Great Pyramid* (1864), he additionally alleged that the pyramid was a storehouse of divine revelations and prophecies leading up to the second coming of Christ had been cleverly encoded by the same great race of Caucasians that had built the pyramid. He felt that the colossal edifice was "the highest and holiest subject that can ever occupy a scientific society."[84]

Then, in 1865, pyramidologist Robert Menzies refined Smyth's view by theorizing that the proportions and measurements of the pyramid's chambers and passages could be deciphered using a one-pyramid-inch-equals-one-year-ratio mode of measuring time. By employing this method of calculation, Menzies "proved" that the earth's creation took place in 4004 B.C. This date had previously been popularized by Bishop Ussher (1581–1656) who, by calculating the genealogies listed in Genesis, determined the world's age. All subsequent "readings" of the pyramid have used this measurement.[85]

Many of today's pyramidologists maintain that the world as we know it will end on September 17, 2001 with the second coming of Jesus. But this date is only the latest in a series of dates that pyramidologists have previously declared as "the end." In February 1928, just prior to the outbreak of World War II, Basil Stewart — famous interpreter of the Great Pyramid — made the following proclamation: "[T]he present prevailing unrest will ultimately lead, in the abnormally disturbed period between May 29, 1928 and September 16, 1936, as to cause and effect, the war of Armageddon. . . . [T]he symbolism of the Great Pyramid clearly reveals that that 'time of trouble' is within the period of eight years ending in September 1936."[86]

The various pyramid-related dates for doomsday have resulted from a lack of consensus among pyramidologists about where measurements should start, and which world event should mark each particular starting point. Does the beginning of the First Ascending Passage mark Jesus' birth? His death? His resurrection? No one seems to know. Only after a "prophecy" proves untrue are the calculations and measurements re-invented so as to find yet another future termination date for humanity's destruction.

Even when they can agree on where to start measuring, pyramidologists often arrive at different measurements. John and Morton Edgar, for instance, in their 1924 book *The Great Pyramid Passages and Chambers* (vol. 3) admitted the following:

> The length of the Horizontal Passage leading to the Queen's Chamber, measuring from the north wall of the Grand Gallery southward to the line of the north wall of the Queen's Chamber, is, according to Professor Smyth, 1517.8806 inches with a possible variation of .3 of an inch, while according to Professor Petrie it is 1522.3761, or nearly 4 ½ inches longer, which difference, as Professor Petrie says, seems difficult to account for. We therefore measured this passage with special care and got a result which lies between these two, namely, 1520.9775 inches. . . . [I]n nearly every measurement noticed so far the figures we have adopted lie between those of Professor Smyth and Petrie.[87]

Anyone taking a cursory look at pyramidology soon discovers that there is a highly manipulative way in which pyramidologists *make* the pyramid foretell world events, both past and present. For example, pyramidologists agree that the one-pyramid-inch-equals-one-year-ratio is of primary importance when interpreting the predictions of the pyramid's corridors and chambers. Nevertheless, this standard of measure is simply discarded if it no longer proves useful. Consider how the 2001 date is discovered.

Beginning at the entrance corridor (see figure 2.2), if one measures down to a point that corresponds to 1486 B.C — approximately the time of Israelites' exodus from Egypt under Moses — there is a sharp upward corridor that eventually forks, which corresponds (according to the one-pyramid-per-inch measuring system) to the time of Christ. The fork's left path goes to the Queen's Chamber. The right path leads to the King's Chamber (or the return of Christ). On the way to the King's Chamber, one must walk through the Grand Gallery which allegedly represents the 1900 years of enlightenment

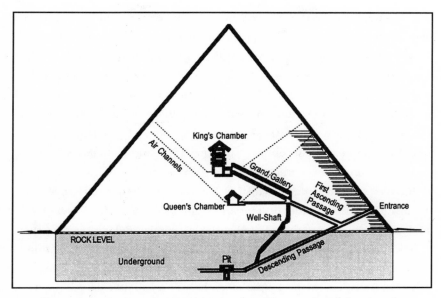

Cross section of the Great Pyramid, showing the major tunnels and chambers that pyramidologists most often refer to in their attempts to decipher the monument's "secret" prophecies.

Fig. 2.2

after Christ. Inch by inch, year by year, century by century, the passage ascends to the King's Chamber. The years/inches pass one by one.

Suddenly, though, the "one-pyramid-inch-equals-one-year" mode of measuring is replaced by a one-pyramid-inch-stands-for-*thirty-days*-ratio.[88] Pyramidologists are *forced* to make the change so that such landmark events as World War I, the Great Depression, and World War II can fit into their prophecy timeline. Even more significant is the poor accuracy record haunting those who have sought to tell the future by measuring the Great Pyramid's passageways:

- The earth's "Great Tribulation" starts: 1881
- Jesus Christ begins reigning on the earth for 1,000 years: 1914
- The second coming of Jesus Christ: 1936
- The second coming of Jesus Christ: 1953
- Jesus Christ begins reigning on the earth for 1,000 years: 1979.[89]

What about all of those *past* events that seem to indeed be marked within the Great Pyramid? Martin Gardner — prolific book author and longtime mathematics columnist for *Scientific American* — explains: "It is not difficult to see how Smyth achieved these astonishing scientific and historical correspondences. If you set about measuring a complicated structure like the Pyramid, you will quickly have on hand a great abundance of lengths to play with . . . since you are bound by no rules."[90]

Any architecturally complex structure (ancient or modern) — e.g., a building, monument, statue, or tomb — can be measured is such a way as to produce significant dates in history. For example, French scholar Maurice Bouisson took the number of steps and landings in the Eiffel Tower (1,927) and subtracted the number of men at the last supper and got the date 1914: the beginning of World War I![91] But if the Great Pyramid of Giza is not a "Bible in Stone" or a divine oracle by which the future can be plotted, then what is it? A comment by nineteenth century writer H. G. Wells is applicable: "[The pyramids are] unmeaning sepulchral piles."[92]

VISIONS FROM BEYOND THE GRAVE

Another group of individuals who claim to have the inside scoop on the timing of the world's demise are those persons unfortunate enough to have endured a near death experience (NDE). This term — coined by psychiatrist Raymond A. Moody in his 1975 bestseller *Life After Life* — applies to the testimony of persons who, after being revived from apparent death, have related that while unconscious they continued to experience sights, sounds and sensations. Many NDE survivors, often called "experiencers" (NDErs), claim that during their brush with mortality they have spiritually left their bodies and journeyed to a realm of existence so unlike our physical environment that it defies description. An endless stream of colorful narratives from NDErs have flooded bookstores. *National Review* dubbed some these popular tomes "The Light Brigade" in honor of their titles: *Embraced by the Light*; *Transformed by the Light*; *Saved by the Light*; *Closer to the Light*; *Beyond the Light*; and *The Light Beyond*.[93]

The basic elements that comprise an NDE are commonly known: a feeling of peace, a brilliant light at the end of a dark tunnel, interaction with deceased relatives, meetings with angels, conversations with "God," and a life-review. One important, though lesser known, feature of NDEs that began to be studied in the 1970s was end-time "prophetic visions." According to renowned NDE researcher Dr. Kenneth Ring, some NDErs claimed that their brief look at the imminent future revealed global catastrophe, "often in association with an encounter with guides or a being of light."[94]

The end-time scenario outlined by NDErs is highly reminiscent of Cayce's readings, even down to his "pole shift" prediction and the appearance of new land masses:[95]

> Because of this pole shift [there is] a kind of magnetic pull [causing] the continents to move toward each other. . . . Along the East Coast [of the United States], there will be a significant rise in the tide because of the polar melt.

> There may be a pole shift . . . there are going to be polar changes . . . it's not going to kill all the races off, but we're going to have to start again from square one. . . . There's going to be a larger land mass.

> The weather is going to go crazy. We're just as likely to have snow in the middle of the summer as one hundred degree weather. . . . I see droughts in other countries.

Such forecasts quickly drew a considerable amount of attention from persons maintaining that NDErs actually leave their bodies for a brief visit to "The Other Side." But as time went on, these catastrophic visions proved to be false alarms; their target date for Earth's destruction was 1988/1989.[96] It has since been documented that NDEs are nothing more than subjective, physiological/neurobiological hallucinations that take place in the brain in response to trauma (see Appendix A).

Anyone's brain can produce an NDE-like experience, even when death is *not* an immediate threat. NDE elements are created from one's thoughts, religious beliefs, past experiences, emotions, knowledge about current events, and personal fears. Obviously, the brains of some NDErs have manufactured doomsday images by drawing upon familiar end-time predictions made by the likes of Cayce and Scallion.

The NDE phenomenon has recently been expanded upon by the man who began the whole NDE craze: Dr. Raymond Moody. While investigating altered states of consciousness (ASCs), he discovered that throughout history different cultures employed occult techniques "by which apparitions of the dead were made to appear to living persons."[97] Moody concluded that conjuring up apparitions might be a way for persons to alleviate grief over losing a relative or friend. He subsequently established a "psychomanteum" at his home in Alabama, where visitors can talk to departed loved ones.

Moody's psychomanteum uses a variety of elements to create an environment conducive to ASCs: "art, music, play, relaxation, creative activity, physical exercise, nature, hypnogogic states, perceptual illusions, intellectual stimulation, and humor." He describes his refuge for necromancers as being "at once a theater, a temple, a fortune teller's parlor, a spiritual retreat center, an art museum, a school, a library, and a funhouse."[98] Visitors summon forth spirits of the dead in the "apparition chamber," a small room located on the second floor of Moody's Theater of the Mind.

Many of Moody's clients claim to have seen life-sized, realistic-looking, three-dimensional "apparitions of departed persons."[99] Predictably, it did not take long for people to start having vivid end-time visions as well. These ASC-induced images all center around the newest and most widely-disseminated date for Armageddon — 2000. Consider this revelation received by Darlene Brunson:

> I could see a scene coming up and it looked like a portal looking down into planet earth. However, there were no trees, there were no houses, there were no buildings, there was no nothing. What I continued to see was atomic explosion, after atomic explosion, after atomic explosion, As I kept watching that, I saw on the right, at the top [of the vision] — '2 - 0 - 0 - 0.' At first, I wasn't sure what that was. I finally decided it had to be the year 2000. It stayed, and it stayed, and it stayed, and I saw many, many, many, explosions.[100]

Others have had similar experiences in Moody's psychomanteum. They all reflect the many "earth changes" predictions that have been circulating within the occult community for years with constantly varying dates for their fulfillment:[101]

> *Joi Thomas:* "I think perhaps the only reason that I saw this dome city was to indicate that there was an energy source coming underneath. Perhaps the earth changes, the violent earthquakes and the uprising of the land uncovered this source of energy. . . . There were people in the laboratory wearing lab coats and they had test tubes full of a clear liquid with plants starting to germinate inside. I asked for a year for that particular vision that I saw and the year 2021 came to mind."

> *Lydia Bough:* "I asked what had happened that caused this [dark and deserted cities]. And it was an asteroid. I could see it hit the earth and cause a lot of destruction . . . . There was a lot of grayness, just gray and dark. I asked also for some places where it would be safe for people to live at that time, around 2011? And I got that it would be in Western Canada, Northern Colorado, Chile, and part of Egypt. Those places will be safe."

These people, like so many others, have created scenes of the end with their own minds based on cultural symbolism coupled with personal fears and frustrations. Of course, they are not alone. As the millennium draws closer, more and more end-time prophecies from a wide variety of areas are being disseminated.

AN ARMAGEDDON GRAB BAG

According to many apprehensive date-watchers, the world will end on 2012 because that is the last day of the ancient Mayan calendar, a timekeeper that reads somewhat like an odometer with a starting point of 13.0.0.0.0 (i.e., August 13, 3114 **B.C.**). The odometer's beginning date marked the fourth creation of the cosmos. Earth's destruction will occur on December 21-23, 2012 when the calendar clicks back to 13.0.0.0.0. On that date, those things that humanity has created and/or subjugated will attack us. In other words, our loving pets — from parakeets to puppy dogs — will turn vicious. The wind, oceans, and land will also use their powers against us. Even inanimate objects that we ourselves have created (e.g., waffle irons, vacuums, computers, fax machines, automobiles, etc.) will suddenly become sentient with a collective mind bent on one thing: punishing humanity for its evil deeds.[102]

What Mayan-obsessed prognosticators do not seem to realize, however, is that Mayan texts deciphered by archeologists explain that the end of the ancient calendar's cycle actually marks a *reinforcement* of the universal order, not its destruction! Linda Schele, a Mayan expert at Austin's University of Texas, comments: "The ancient Maya would be celebrating it [i.e., 13.0.0.0.0] if they were here to see it. The real 'end' of the Mayan calendar runs out somewhere in the fiftieth century."[103]

The year 2000 is also the termination point of humanity for many Kabbalists, i.e., Jewish occultists whose worldview and theological beliefs are based on a combination of medieval mysticism, pseudo-science, and various coded texts from the thirteenth century (e.g., the Zohar). In 1994, Kabbalist Rabbi Philip Berg — leader of New York's Kabbalah learning Center — declared: "A ball of fire will descend upon all of mankind. There will be periods whereby mankind will forget that the sun even appears. World War II will be so finite, so minuscule, as compared to the ultimate destruction that will take place within the next six years."[104]

Rabbi Ariel Tzadok, another Kabbalist, echoes the oft-repeated "earth changes" prophecies: "Certain types of earth changes — hurricanes, volcanoes, earthquakes — can be caused by the unleashing of certain yet unknown technologies. And I believe that during World War III these unknown technologies will be the cause of the majority of horrible storms."[105] Rabbi Berg adds the following:

> If we don't get our act together by the year 2000 . . . [I]f mankind does not take control of their actions, preventing the forces of evil from growing, expanding, then this ball of fire is what will be inevitable; a holocaust of a nature that the world has never seen is going to take place, destroying almost all of mankind, all vegetation, all forms of life. And only those who have studied and learned how to preserve their own physical bodies will live beyond Armageddon.[106]

There is certainly no lack of end-time vision in the world of the occult. But the number of prophecies about Armageddon from occultists pales in comparison to the volume of literature about the end of the world that has been produced by Christian doomsayers. These prophets of the end will be the subject of Chapter 3.

THREE

"Thus Saith The Lord"

*Behold, I am coming quickly, and My reward is with me, to render to
every man according to what he has done. I am the Alpha and the Omega,
the first and the last, the beginning and the end.*

Jesus of Nazareth

(Revelation 22:12–13)

*This is it! We are living in the final era of earth's history. Soon will come
the visible, manifest Kingdom of God. This thousand year time period,
called the Millennium is the inauguration of eternity, at which time the
Creator will make a new earth and heaven.*

David Allen Lewis

Christian prophecy teacher[1]

THE BIBLE'S BOOK OF REVELATION is named after the Greek word
apokalypsis, which appears in its first verse: "The revelation [*apokalypsis*]
of Jesus Christ, which God gave Him to show to His bond-servants, the
things which must shortly take place." The term, which simply denotes an
"uncovering" or "revealing" of something, is used in various ways throughout Scripture. Its most familiar usage, however, is in reference to the return
of Jesus Christ, who promised that he would come back to Earth in order to
receive his followers (John 14:2–3; Cf. 1 Cor. 1:7 and 1 Peter 1:7).

Christians have always looked forward with great anticipation to Jesus'
"second coming" since it will mark not only their savior's reappearance
(Titus 2:13), but the resurrection of the dead, the final judgment of every
soul, and the establishment of a "new heaven and a new earth" (Rev. 21).
Christians further believe that at the *apokalypsis* every follower of Jesus will
receive a "glorified" (i.e., perfected) body designed for immortality (1 Cor.
15:50–53). Christ's second advent will also cause the world as we know it to

end. In reference to this event, the apostle Peter said that the heavens will pass away "with a roar" and that the elements will be "destroyed with intense heat" (2 Peter 3:10–13).

Exactly when will all of these things take place? The Bible leaves that question unanswered. Scripture only states that Jesus' second coming will be like a thief in the night; in other words, when it is least expected (1 Thess. 5:1–2; 2 Peter 3:10). The biblical reason for this lack of information regarding doomsday is found in Jesus' response to questions about the establishment of God's kingdom: "It is not for you to know times or epochs which the Father has fixed by His own authority" (Acts 1:7).

Despite an absence of biblical timetables relating to Jesus' return, end-time predictions have plagued the Christian community since the first century (see Chapter 5). The last one hundred years have seen an especially high number of dates presented for Christ's second coming. Most of these doomsday deadlines have been set by persons subscribing to a view known as premillennialism, which is currently the most popular Christian eschatology (i.e., view of the end-times). Although there are different kinds of premillennialism, the two most popular are *pretribulational-dispensational* and *historic*. Both forms teach that just before Jesus' second coming seven years of unparalleled turmoil (i.e., the tribulation) will occur under a satanic, world dictator: the Antichrist. These two eschatologies, however, differ on some key issues.

According to *pretribulational-dispensational* premillennialism, the tribulation follows what is known as "the rapture," an event wherein Christians will be transformed into glorified physical beings and transported to heaven.[2] According to prophecy teacher David Allen Lewis, this event will bring the instantaneous disappearance of about 500,000,000 born-again Christian. Lewis says it will be a "spiritual shock-quake producing almost unimaginable trauma in the terrified minds of those who are left on earth. The fear of the great unwashed masses [i.e., non-Christians who are left behind] will drive many to insanity, and many more to suicide."[3]

After the rapture and the seven year tribulation, Christians will return to Earth with Jesus in order to overthrow the Antichrist at the Battle of Armageddon. This event will be followed by the establishment of God's "Millennium Kingdom" (a 1,000-year era during which Jesus will physically rule Earth from Jerusalem).[4] When Christ's golden age of global peace and prosperity ends, a final battle between the forces of good and evil will take place, after which time Jesus will once and for all defeat Satan, judge humanity, and inaugurate eternity. The righteous will dwell with God forever, and the unrighteous will be consigned to eternal separation from God (i.e., hell).

Historic premillennialists promote a slightly different scenario. Like pretribulational-dispensationalists, historic premillennialists believe that during the tribulation the Antichrist (also called "the beast") will halt all normal means of purchasing food, acquiring housing, and obtaining employment. Only by receiving the mark of the beast (666) will anyone be able to continue functioning in society (Rev. 13:15–18).[5] But unlike pretribulational-dispensational premillennialists, historic premillennialists believe that Christians will *not* be rescued from the tribulation. There is no rapture. Christians will instead be forced to endure the Antichrist's reign.

It is this particular view of the earth's "last days" which has prompted some people to form survivalist sects and retreat to isolated regions of America with large quantities of food and weapons.[6] Their hope is to live as inconspicuously as possible during the seven year reign of the Antichrist, a tyrannical despot who will govern humanity via a one-world government called the New World Order (see Chapter 4). This era will culminate with the Battle of Armageddon just before Christ's return.

Of course, not all Christians are obsessed with the end-times. On the contrary, most of them are much more concerned with improving society, helping the less fortunate, and living a life that reflects the Bible's two greatest commandments: "You shall love the Lord your God with all your heart, soul, mind, and strength" and "You shall love your neighbor as yourself (Matt. 22:37–40). Unfortunately, however, numerous evangelicals, charismatics, and Pentecostals insist that the end of the world is near. Some of them have actually made a lucrative career out of selling doomsday.

In reference to these individuals, church historian Tim Weber observes: "Whenever history takes one of its unexpected turns, the doomsayers end up with prophetic egg on their faces. But when their schemes don't fit any more, you never see these folks owning up to it. They merely reshuffle [their dates] and come out with another edition [of predictions]."[7] The following pages explore just a few of today's many prophecy pundits and the methods they use to peddle their prognostications.

LINDSEY'S LOOKING GLASS

The undisputed father of today's Christian prophecy movement is Hal Lindsey. His 1970 book *The Late Great Planet Earth* is recognized as the most popular religious volume of the 1970s–1990s.[8] The *New York Times Book Review* crowned it the bestselling nonfiction work of the 1970s. It has gone through more than one hundred printings totaling thirty-five million copies in fifty-two languages. It was even made into a 1978 documentary-like film narrated by Orson Welles.

Lindsey has since produced one bestselling doomsday book after another, including *Satan is Alive and Well on Planet Earth* (1972); *The 1980s: Countdown to Armageddon* (1981); and *The Rapture* (1983). Russell Chandler, award-winning journalist and former reporter for the *Los Angeles Times*, believes that Lindsey's success has a lot to do with packaging:

> Lindsey speaks and writes with authority and clarity in a popular style. He links biblical prophecies to current events and scientific technology — giving many the feeling of assurance that "it's all happening just as the Good Book says it would." And he sets forth uncomplicated arguments that the lives of ordinary human beings fit into God's grand plan of history.[9]

The road to Armageddon paved by *The Late Great Planet Earth* begins with Jesus' words in Matthew 24:32–33: "Now learn the parable from the fig tree: when its branch has already become tender, and puts forth its leaves, you know that summer is near; even so you too, when you see all these things, recognize that He [the Messiah] is near, right at the door." Jesus goes on to say: "[T]his generation will not pass away until all these things take place" (v. 34). This passage serves as the biblical key to all of Lindsey's prophetic speculations. He and other premillennialists claim that the "fig tree" symbolizes Israel, and that its 1948 reestablishment as a state fulfills Jesus' prophecy about the fig tree putting forth leaves. It is alleged that Christ's remark about "this generation" specifically applies to those persons alive during Israel's restoration — i.e., *our generation.*

The Late Great Planet Earth additionally declared: "A generation in the Bible is something like forty years."[10] This assertion left room for a not-so-subtle prediction: "[W]ithin forty years or so of 1948, all these things could take place."[11] In other words, the year 1988 (1948 + 40 years) would bring the end of the world. For dispensationalists, however, the end would come in 1981 with the rapture (1988 minus the seven year tribulation).

Lindsey relentlessly peddled this calculation during speaking engagements and media interviews throughout the years immediately following the release of the book. In 1976, he told journalist Russell Chandler that Christ's return could occur "by the end of the decade."[12] Such speculations caused nothing less than a celebratory uproar in evangelical circles. Countless Christians rejoiced at the prospect of having to endure only nine more years of life on Earth before being raptured.

Included in Lindsey's arguments for a 1981 rapture were several references to the Jupiter Effect (see Chapter 2), which he seemed to think would be a perfect way to start the tribulation. In 1980, he suggested that the planetary alignment would cause five or six nuclear power plant meltdowns as well as other horrifying disasters:

> It [Jupiter Effect] will slow the rotation of the earth down where the crust will go through great stress and there will be great earthquakes and a reaction of dormant volcanoes. . . . If these scientists are right, then what we can expect in 1982 — we'll have the largest outbreak of killer quakes ever seen in the history of planet earth along with radical changes in climate and most climatologists believe that the shift is already taking place.[13]

In 1981, he built upon this theme by publishing The 1980s: Countdown to Armageddon. Page one declared: "The decade of the 1980s could very well be the last decade of history as we know it."[14] The book's back cover announced: "WE ARE THE GENERATION THAT WILL SEE THE END TIMES . . . AND THE RETURN OF JESUS" (caps in original). A former follower of Lindsey's remembers how the popular prophecy teacher convinced listeners of a 1981 rapture without even having to name the year:

> The most salient point Hal Lindsey brought home to all of us in the audience . . .
> was the Bible prophecy that Jesus would return within one generation of the Jews
> being restored to the promised land in Palestine. When I saw that in the Bible, I
> hyperventilated! I couldn't believe it! Jesus is coming back in my lifetime. . . . He
> revealed from the scriptures that a generation in the Bible was almost always 40
> years duration. Israel became a nation in 1948, and 1948 plus 40 years meant that
> Jesus would come again in 1988. . . . [S]ubtract 7 from 1988 and you have the
> rapture of the Church occurring in 1981. This was 1972. We were thinking we
> only had 9 years left to win as many souls to Christ as we could . . . . Lindsey was
> always very careful at that time to state that he was not setting dates for the return
> of the Lord. But he gave Biblical data and definitions very cogently and emphat-
> ically so as to make it very clear what he understood the scriptures to imply. Then
> he always finished with, "You figure it out."[15]

But Lindsey's timetable proved to be fallacious, as were his speculations about the Jupiter Effect. This, however, did not slow him down, nor did it hurt his credibility (or book sales). In fact, he and his devotees became even more convinced that "the end" lay just around the corner. Consequently, Lindsey gave his fans another book in 1983: *The Rapture*. It continued to promise Christians that they would more than likely see the end of the world in their lifetime. "[A]ll the predicted signs that set up the final fateful period immediately preceding the second coming of Christ are now before us," promised Lindsey. Discussing the in-house premillennial debate over whether or not Christians will go through the tribulation, he commented: "In all probability, most of the people reading this book will live to experience the answer."[16]

But after the decade of the 1980s passed uneventfully, Lindsey wisely began to revise his obviously flawed timetables. His 1994 volume, *Planet Earth: 2000 A.D.*, substituted 1967 (the year Israel took back Jerusalem via the Six Day War) for 1948 (the year he labeled as pivotal in *The Late Great Planet Earth*). Lindsey wrote: "My recent study of Daniel 9:24–27 has convinced me that the capture of Jerusalem in 1967 may be a more prophetically significant event than the rebirth of the nation."[17]

This rearrangement of prophetically significant dates gave Lindsey another nineteen years to preach his forty-year biblical generation theory which, now that it was starting in 1967, would take him to at least the year 2007. Even before this change, however, he was leaving room for error. During a 1992 radio interview, Lindsey was asked: "At what point would you say you are wrong?" He replied, "One hundred years leeway from 1948."[18] Put another way, Lindsey — now in his mid-sixties — will have to make an embarrassing admission of inaccuracy only if he lives to be 120 years old!

Critics of Lindsey (both secular and Christian) accuse him not only of backpedaling from his predictions, but of using "a mix of bad scholarship and false history" to force his preconceived ideas about the world's end into biblical texts.[19] For instance, he claims that Bible passages concerning *Rosh*, *Meshech* and *Tubal* (i.e., Ez. 38, 39) point to Russia, Moscow and Tobolsk.[20] These identifications play a major role in Lindsey's end-time scenario. He claims that they are terms describing the ethnic background of the people who will invade Israel just before the rapture.

How does Lindsey come to his conclusion about Israel's imminent invaders? He basis his belief on decidedly shaky ground: *Rosh* sounds like Russia, *Meshech* sounds like Moscow, and *Tubal* sounds like the Tobolsk province of Russia. Edwin Yamauchi — history professor at Ohio's Miami University — finds Lindsey's contention "indefensible." *Rosh* simply means chief, or head. *Meshech* and *Tubal* were areas in what is now Turkey.[21] *The Expositors Bible Commentary* agrees:

> Some would understand *Rosh* as modern Russia. Proponents of this view usually appeal to etymology based on similar sounds (to the hearing) between two words. Such etymological procedures are not linguistically sound, nor is etymology alone a sound hermeneutical basis on which to interpret a word. The word Russia is a late eleventh century A.D. term. Therefore, the data does not seem to support an interpretation of rosh as a proper name of a geographical region or country.[22]

Even more problematic for Lindsey was the dissolution of the Soviet Union. Back in 1970s and 1980s few people could have foreseen the disintegration of the U.S.S.R. Consequently, Lindsey felt confident in identifying "Gog and Magog" (Ez. 38:2, 17; 39:1) — Israel's invading enemy from the "uttermost north" (Ez. 38:6, 15; 39:2) — as the Soviet Union: "You need only take a globe to verify this exact geographical fix. There is only one nation to the 'uttermost north' of Israel — the U.S.S.R."[23]

This Soviet attack force also was to have included communist East Germany in fulfillment of Ezekiel 38:6, which mentions the name "Gomer." Lindsey stated: "Gomer . . . [was] the father of Ashkenaz, Riphath, and Togarmah. These people make up an extremely important part of the future Russian invasion. . . . Gomer and its hordes are a part of he vast area of modern Eastern Europe which is totally behind the iron curtain. This includes East Germany and the Slovak countries."[24]

When these particular pieces of Lindsey's prophetic puzzle began to disintegrate in the early 1990s, he tried in vain to salvage his teachings by asserting that the splintering of Eastern Europe was just "a smoke and mirrors game." He further commented: "We've got this idea that the Cold War is over. Don't you believe it."[25] But even Lindsey could not stop communism's defeat, and he eventually had to edit erroneous conclusions out of subsequent editions of *The Late Great Planet Earth*. His "updated" version, along with several newer books he has written, promote an altogether different scenario. Now, instead of the U.S.S.R. attacking Israel, the southern former Soviet republics (predominantly Muslim) "will soon unite with 'their Islamic brethren' in the Middle East to attack Israel."[26] At times, Lindsey has completely reversed himself, as theologians C. Marvin Pate and Calvin B. Haines explain in *Doomsday Delusions*:

> [H]ow does Lindsey deal with the collapse of a major player in his predictions regarding the last days? He simply changes the story and the roles of the players. For instance, in 1970 Lindsey portrayed Iran as the pawn of the powerful Soviets, who force the "Persians" to ally with them to gain easy military access to the Middle East. In Lindsey's latest interpretation, however, the roles are reversed. Here the Russians crawl to Iran to make an alliance in search of financial help and fearing the Islamic presence in Russia. It is then the Russians who are dragged into a war with Israel because of Iran's power.[27]

The gloomiest shadow to darken Lindsey's prophetic reputation fell in 1992 when he and coauthor Chuck Missler (another influential prophecy teacher) were caught plagiarizing *Foes From the Northern Frontier* (1982) by Professor Edwin Yamauchi. As much as twenty-five percent of *The Magog Factor* (authored by Missler and Lindsey) was lifted word for word and without attribution from Yamauchi's work, which by 1992 was out of print. Ironically, *Foes From the Northern Frontier* was written to show how Lindsey and others had "mistakenly identified Russia in biblical prophecies."[28]

Lindsey and Missler's seventy-page report (available *in manuscript form only* for $14.95) argued that Russia did indeed fit the seemingly mysterious names mentioned in Ezekiel. To prove their point, they not only plagiarized Yamauchi's words, but took them out of context and made them fit into their arguments. A 1992 *Los Angeles Times* article noted that even the manuscript's footnotes were "identical to those in Yamauchi's book, again without attribution."[29] Consider this comparison of just one of the many plagiarized passages cited in the *Times:*

FOES FROM THE NORTHERN FRONTIER (1982) by Edwin Yamauchi	*THE MAGOG FACTOR* (1992) by Hal Lindsey and Chuck Missler
Inasmuch, however, as the kingdom of Gyges did not extend to the areas of Meshech and Tubal, as is implied by Ezekiel 38:2 with respect to the kingdom of Gog, there is a problem with assuming that Gog is identical with Gyges, the similarity of the names notwithstanding.	However, since the kingdom of Gyges did not extend to the areas of Meshech and Tubal, as implied by Ezekiel 38:2 with respect to the kingdom of Gog, there is a significant problem in assuming that Gog is related to Gyges.

The Magog Factor was slated for a 1992 release in book form, but never reached that stage because Yamauchi informed his publisher of the problem, who in turn demanded that the work no longer be distributed. Lindsey and Missler complied, promising that they had ceased all "publishing, promoting, selling and distributing" of *The Magog Factor* and would not resume doing so in the future.[30]

But the two authors failed to make good on their promise. Instead, Missler proceeded to repackage *The Magog Factor* and release it as his own book *The Magog Invasion* (1995), for which Lindsey penned a foreword. The new title and cover, however, could not hide the fact that it still contained substantial amounts of apparently plagiarized text from Yamauchi's book. Most surprising was the continued use of the very same quote that the *Los Angeles Times* had reproduced (except for a few words deleted in the middle of the text).[31]

. *The Magog Invasion* was eventually pulled from Missler's list of available resources, but only after concerned Christians began to publicly voice complaints about its unauthorized use of Yamauchi's text. Their criticisms drew so much attention that Missler also was forced to release a letter of explanation to the public. His statement, lightheartedly entitled "Whoops! Our Slip is Showing," claimed that the apparent plagiarism was a simple oversight:

> This unfortunate result was caused by carelessness in drawing from speaking notes assimilated from over 25 years of public presentations on these and related subjects. . . . we are embarrassed to discover that substantial portions of Chapter 4 clearly appear to have been excerpted from *Foes of the Northern Frontier* . . . (What compounds our embarrassment is that this was called to our attention in an earlier draft, and in our haste to make a publication deadline remedies were overlooked.) There was no intent to harm or defraud either Dr. Yamauchi or Baker Book House. Our error was due to inexcusable carelessness and oversight.[32]

Meanwhile, Lindsey continues to make a hefty profit writing books and lecturing on how "we are the generation that will see the coming of the Lord."[33] "[Y]ou cannot miss it," he recently declared. "We're that generation, and I believe we're rapidly moving toward the coming of Christ."[34] In apparent disregard of his track record, countless Christians continue to believe him. Two of Lindsey's most recent books, *Planet Earth—2000 A.D.* and *The Final Battle*, held the number one and two spots, respectively, on the October 1995 *Bookstore Journal's* list of bestselling nonfiction Christian paperbacks.[35]

CLARK'S CANADIAN CAPERS

In 1976, Canadian prophecy teacher Doug Clark etched his name into history's list of doomsayers by warning Christians about the feared Jupiter Effect:

> The prediction is that San Francisco, Los Angeles and surrounding areas will be lost in the coming earthquakes triggered by celestial phenomena in 1982. Is it possible that several million people will die in the fires or in the watery graves predicted to transpire that year? . . . Could millions in New York City perish should that city be affected like San Francisco was in 1906?[36]

Clark encouraged his followers to "[f]lee from the coastlands, store food, sell your homes and stocks, and don't place your savings in banks located in the earthquake or low-lying belts."[37] He additionally warned, "By 1985, we are going to have a food war."[38] Such wild predictions quickly turned Clark into one of the most popular prophecy teachers within the evangelical community. No one seemed to notice that his admonitions to "flee" civilization were inconsistent with his parallel teaching that Jesus would return in 1982 to rescue Christians from the tribulation and "elevate man to a higher level of being."[39]

Although none of Clark's predictions came to pass, he was still able to make a good living thanks to Jan and Paul Crouch, owners of the multimillion dollar Trinity Broadcasting Network (TBN) based in California. The Crouches gave Clark his own television show: *Shockwaves to Armageddon*. It was such a smashing success that Clark soon went into the secondary business of selling trips to the Holy Land to his viewers. He also published another book entitled *Final Shockwaves to Armageddon*, complete with a foreword by Paul Crouch. This volume, using Lindsey's forty-year generation theory, suggested that the rapture would occur in 1988.[40]

In 1989, however, Clark apparently saw the error of his ways and openly recanted his statements regarding the Jupiter Effect:

[T]hat was a mistake on my part, an honest mistake because I did feel the alignment of the planets could tie in to some sort of cataclysmic type event. Number two, I was wrong. Number three, I don't pick dates on anything anymore, and I don't look into these physical things as having direct imminency on the coming of the Lord. . . . I'm a lot more careful. I think we all make one or two major mistakes.[41]

But only two weeks after making this contrite confession, Clark appeared on TBN's *Praise the Lord* talk show (April 26, 1989) and proceeded to announce that World War III would probably begin within three years. When asked by talk show host Paul Crouch whether the tribulation would begin before the year 2000, Clark unhesitatingly replied: "You bet!"[42]

In 1990, though, Clark was forced to discontinue his profession as a prophet when the U.S. Postal Inspector issued a warrant for his arrest for mail fraud involving bogus Holy Land tours. Clark fled from authorities and was not apprehended until 1995, when Canada's Immigration and Naturalization Service caught up with him in Toronto. He was subsequently extradited to the U.S., tried, convicted of mail fraud, and sentenced to prison. Clark was released from a federal penitentiary in Texas on November 11, 1997 after serving twenty-four months.[43] His whereabouts are currently unknown.

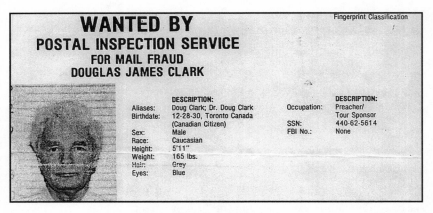

Wanted poster for Trinity Broadcasting Network prophecy teacher Doug Clark. The poster also included a caution: "If arrested, will likely feign a heart attack or other illness."

THE END IN '88

For many years, retired NASA engineer Edgar C. Whisenant was just an average, hardworking, American citizen who enjoyed going to church. Then in 1988, he wrote two books that catapulted him into the evangelical spotlight: *88 Reasons Why the Rapture Could Be in 1988* and *On Borrowed Time*. Although both volumes presented a mind-boggling assortment of interlocking date and number calculations, the basic thrust of Whisenant's message came through loud and clear: sometime between September 11, 1988 and September 13, 1988 — the Jewish New Year, or Rosh Hashanah — Jesus was going to rapture his church out of the world. It would be the beginning of the tribulation; the beginning of the end![44]

Whisenant had no doubts about his date, stating: "Only if the Bible is in error am I wrong, and I say that unequivocally. There is no way biblically that I can be wrong; and I say that to every preacher in town."[45] During one interview he made a declaration that dramatically demonstrated his level of confidence: "[I]f there were a king in this country and I could gamble with my life, I would stake my life on Rosh Hashanah 88.' "[46]

Some Christians dismissed his prognostication as ludicrous. But others stood behind Whisenant. Hart Armstrong — president of Christian Communications of Wichita, Kansas — repeatedly pointed to the Feast of Trumpets 1988 (September 29, 30, 1989) "as possible times for His coming." Armstrong even issued a "RAPTURE ALERT."[47] Equally supportive of Whisenant were Trinity Broadcasting Network (TBN) founders Jan and Paul Crouch. They went so far as to alter regular programming on September 11–13. Instead of airing their nightly *Praise the Lord* television talk show, they ran videotapes of prerecorded shows dealing with the rapture. For non-Christians who might be watching, the revised programming included specific instructions on what to do in case Christian family members or friends suddenly disappeared and the world was thrust into the tribulation.[48]

Despite warnings from various church leaders from moderate segments of the Christian community, believers nationwide flocked to local bookstores to get Whisenant's books. In fact, Christian booksellers had a hard time keeping his volumes in stock.[49] By the time the predicted date arrived, more than 4.5 million copies of *88 Reasons* had been sold, and 300,000 had been sent out *free* to ministers in America.[50]

Nothing cataclysmic happened on Rosh Hashanah 1988. This, however, did not deter Whisenant in the least. Immediately after the scheduled time of Christ's return, the *Atlanta Journal & Constitution* reported that the Arkansas prophet had "revised his prediction, saying that the Rapture could possibly occur by 10:55 A.M. Wednesday [September 15]."[51] As September drew to a close, Whisenant still had not lost confidence. He revised his date again; this time to October 3. Even when that date passed, Whisenant remained undaunted: "The evidence is all over the place that it is going to be in a few weeks anyway," he told *Christianity Today.*[52]

After his "few weeks" had transpired, Whisenant finally saw his error. He claimed that he had made a slight miscalculation of one year because of a fluke in the Gregorian calendar. Jesus was actually going to return during Rosh Hashanah of 1989! Whisenant published his discovery in *The Final Shout — Rapture Report 1989*. "The time is short," he said. "Everything points to it."[53] This publication was subsequently retitled *The Final Shout — Rapture Report 1990* and has since been retitled yearly as *The Final Shout — Rapture Report 1991*, 1992, 1993, 1994, and so on.[54] He continues to revise his date annually.

1994: THIS TIME FOR SURE!

While Whisenant was a relatively obscure individual until he made his false prophecy, the year 1992 saw a more well-known Christian personality — Harold Camping, founder of Family Radio and Open Forum — make his debut as an end-time date-setter. In his bestselling 562-page book *1994?*, he wrote: "When September 6, 1994, arrives, no one else can become saved, the end has come."[55] Camping clearly declared his position: "No book ever written is as audacious or bold as one that claims to predict the timing of the end of the world, and that is precisely what this book presumes to do."[56] Within a year he released *Are You Ready?*, which also pointed to 1994.

In an interview with the *New York Times*, Camping promised that his calculations were beyond correction: "I keep checking and checking and listening to everyone that wants to speak to the issue. Is there anything I've missed? Is there anything I've overlooked? Is there anything that [my debate opponents] could offer that I've missed? . . . [F]rankly, I didn't hear [any good rebuttals]."[57] In another interview, he declared: "Sometimes, I've thought, 'Wow, I wish September was not the month.' But I doubt it. I doubt it. I doubt it. I'm more convinced than I've ever been the world is about to end."[58]

What made Camping so sure? In a 1993 interview with the *Christian Research Journal*, he revealed the source of his confidence: "I'm methodical. And when I began studying the Bible over 30 years ago, I started seeing things others had missed. I discovered that God had a timeline running from Genesis to Revelation, and with precise calculation the end of the world can accurately be determined."[59] Many people seemed to agree with Camping, whose books quickly became huge successes. *1994?* rose almost immediately to the number four spot on the Christian Booksellers Association's bestselling prophecy book chart, selling more than 50,000 copies.

September 7, the day after the end was supposed to have come, Camping acknowledged that he had made an ever-so-slight miscalculation and revised his date toward the middle of the month. A few weeks later he pinpointed September 29. Then he named October 2. This date was followed by yet another date: March 31, 1995, which Camping claimed still counted as 1994 *per the Jewish calendar.* Eventually, Camping ran out of dates and went back to running his Family Radio Network. During an interview with the *San Francisco Chronicle*, he took a remarkably cavalier attitude about the whole incident:

> You know, I'm like the boy who cried wolf again and again and the wolf didn't come. This doesn't bother me in the slightest. The interesting thing is that when we tried to search the scriptures for more information, another date came up. . . . [F]or those who are believers, it is a no-lose, win-win situation. A lot of people have looked at their lives and how they stand up before God and have shaped up their lives. A few people did stupid things — like thinking they didn't have to go to work because Christ was going to come. But if the Lord doesn't come, fine. We'll just keep living our lives for him.[60]

Camping made no comment about the man who had sent him $5,000 after selling his house because he wanted to help Camping get the gospel to as many people as possible before the end of the world in 1994.[61] As of 1995, Camping's Family Radio network was still functioning on an annual budget of $12 million.[62]

A SEVEN YEAR VISION

In addition to the Camping debacle, 1994 witnessed the release of *Seven Years of Shaking: A Vision* by popular Pentecostal preacher Michael D. Evans. "You are about to read the seven year vision that God gave me," writes Evans. "This book will expose the sadistic plot of the new Hitler to exterminate millions. It will show how great numbers can escape the fiery judgment to come. . . . Are you ready to see uncontrollable teen gangs terrorize your neighborhood? Christians jailed, beaten and murdered? GET READY!"[63]

Unlike most prophecy books, Evans's end-time tome is written with a decidedly political edge to it. Disparaging references to President Bill Clinton and his wife are sprinkled throughout the text. In fact, Evans names Clinton's 1993 inauguration as marking a new era of end-time depravity, decadence, and destruction.[64] Using sensationalistic language that is reflective of tabloid talk shows, Evans makes charge after charge against Clinton:

[He] was reportedly involved in a long-term, adulterous affair with a woman who claims to have aborted his love-child! . . . The newly elected commander in chief has never served in the military, and bitterly protested against the Vietnam War.[65]

Clinton supposedly will play a major role in fulfilling Evans' end-time vision from God: "He will drag America down the dead-end road to complete and moral decay. America will no longer be a Christian nation on any shape or form by the end of the seventh year [i.e., A.D. 2000]."[66] Even worse than Clinton and his influence on America are the horrors that will hit humanity within the next few years: 1) a dictator-led Russia that will point its military arsenal toward Washington before the year 2000; 2) new, worldwide plagues that will "MAKE THE BLACK PLAGUE LOOK LIKE

A COMMON COLD" (caps in original); 3) famines that will produce worldwide hunger "LIKE THE WORLD HAS NEVER KNOWN" (caps in original); and 4) a bankrupt America.[67]

Evans' fear-inspiring volume is a masterpiece of prophetic propaganda, complete with contradicting statements that disorient readers to the point where all they can remember is that the world is soon going to be destroyed. For example, Evans states that his vision began to be fulfilled "in the fall of 1993."[68] He also writes: "[T]he SEVEN YEARS OF SHAKING have already begun in America and the entire world."[69] Logically, complete fulfillment of his seven year prophecy will occur by the year 2000. This point emerges again and again from the text:

- page 13: "In this book are shocking prophecies about the next seven years and how you can escape the calamities about to take place on planet Earth."
- page 22: "God has revealed to me that the next seven years will have major prophetic significance."
- page 27: "[W]ithin a seven year period of time, before the year 2,000."
- page 185: "The next seven years will produce unprecedented plagues as well as weather changes around the globe."
- page 192: "Rather than fewer wars in the next seven years, my vision revealed there will be an enormous acceleration of wars."

Opposing these crystal-clear time references are a pair of qualifiers buried in the book's dedication (a portion of text that many readers ignore): "The events you read about in this book will not all take place within the next seven years." In another paragraph he adds: "I emphasize that I have incorporated prophetic information into this vision that will take place at a future time and is not limited to happening within the next seven years."[70] Using these contradictory messages not only serves to disorient readers, but provides an "out" for Evans should his prophecies fail. He can always appeal to the statements in his dedication that say the vision was *not* for the next seven years, and claim that all of the other statements were misunderstood.

Evans even gives his followers an alternate date for "the end" by using Lindsey's 1967/40-year-generation timetable: A.D. 2028.[71] Like Lindsey, Evans erroneously believes that "[t]hroughout Scripture, Israel is referred to as a fig tree that will blossom and bud in the last days" (see Chapter 10).[72] He concludes from his assumption that "we are the generation of the last days. You and I are living in the last-day generation when 'all' will 'be fulfilled.' "[73]

He then asks: "How long is a biblical generation?" His answer is based on Psalm 90:10, which says that the average human life span is threescore years and ten (i.e., seventy years) and often fourscore years (i.e., eighty years). Evans calculates: "If you add eighty years to 1948 — the birthdate of Israel — you arrive at 2028."[74] But again, he presents a qualifier: "I am not claiming Jesus must come back in precisely the year 2028." An obvious question arises: What exactly *is* Evans claiming by pointing out that 1948+80=2028? Interestingly, he does not reveal his purpose for inserting the calculation, but instead makes another statement (written in bold type for emphasis) that further reinforces in the minds of his readers that the end will occur in 2000 and that his vision is a prelude to Jesus' second advent: "[B]iblical prophecy indicates that our generation will not pass away before all things are fulfilled. **Jesus will return to this earth sometime before the end of our generation, and Israel is the key to the prophetic events which will unfold in the next seven years.**"[75]

Although Evans' predictions are very similar to those that have been made by other end-time prophets within the Christian community, he is much bolder in his proclamations since he does not hesitate to declare that his predictions come directly from God and are backed by nothing less than divine authority. In *Seven Years of Shaking*, he writes: "This book describes a seven year vision God birthed in my spirit," he reveals. Based on the accuracy of what God has shown me in the past, I can confidently declare, 'Thus saith the Lord.' "[76]

AMERICA'S DATE-SUGGESTERS

Lindsey, Clark, Whisenant, Camping, and Evans, represent only a small sampling of the thousands of Christian prophecy pushers who market their end-time predictions with a zeal and fervor that stands defiant in the face of all criticism and failure.[77] The number of charismatics, Pentecostals, and evangelicals declaring the world's impending destruction continues to grow exponentially despite contrary opinions voiced by knowledgeable historians, theologians, and sociologists. In fact, scholarship is consistently derided in apocalyptic literature as something that just gets in the way of being able to discern the signs of the times. In *The Mark of the Beast*, for instance, Peter and Paul LaLonde use the following comment to bolster their case for preaching an imminent doomsday:

> [T]he return of Christ is very near. . . . This faith and this great hope are not built on a few random and isolated prophecies. . . . It is built simply on reading the Word of God and then looking at all of the major news events of our day. You don't need a handful of Ph.D.s to do that.[78]

Some prophecy teachers continue unchecked for so long that they end up spiraling into a kind of date-setting free-fall. In his 1987 book *I Predict 2000 A.D.*, Pentecostal preacher Lester Sumrall unabashedly proclaimed: "I predict the absolute fullness of man's operation on planet Earth by the year 2000 A.D. Then Jesus shall reign from Jerusalem for 1000 years."[79] Only three years earlier Sumrall had written *I Predict 1985*.[80] Charles Taylor, however, may hold the evangelical record for rapture predictions: 1975, 1976, 1980, 1981, 1982, 1983, 1985, 1986, 1987, 1988, 1989, 1992, 1994.[81] But no matter how many failed prophecies he has made, Taylor's level of urgency and certainty has remained constant. Consider his warning from 1986:

> [W]e now are standing at the very end of the Church Age. That which you and I desire to do for the cause of Christ we must do it NOW. Any souls we want to win or any service we hope to do, WE MUST DO IT NOW, FOR JESUS IS COMING SOON. And I do not mean in a few years: it now is a matter of months or only of weeks![82]

Not all Christian prophecy leaders are as bold as Taylor or Sumrall. Most of them are more cautious due to a Bible verse regarding false prophets: "When a prophet speaks in the name of the Lord, if the thing does not come about or come true, that is the thing which the Lord has not spoken. The prophet has spoken it presumptuously; you shall not be afraid of him" (Deut. 18:21). To safeguard themselves from being labeled a false prophet per this verse, many prophecy teachers have resorted to using a new date-setting method that might best described as date-*suggesting*.

Date-*suggesting* — which is done by attaching predictions to open-ended qualifiers such as "near," "close to," "just beyond," "not long after," "possibly by," or "very soon" — protects Christian prophecy teachers from being condemned under Deuteronomy 18:21 because the verse only targets individuals who attribute their predictions *directly* to God. It says nothing about persons making predictions based on feelings, time calculations, or faulty biblical interpretation. The evangelical community is filled with even more date-suggesters than date-setters. All of them, however, are virtually indistinguishable from each other, except of course to the date-suggesters themselves, who adamantly maintain their innocence when charged with setting a date for the end of the world, Armageddon, or the rapture. They typically respond with: "I've never set a date, or said that God revealed this teaching to me! It was just my Bible-based opinion."

Some of these soothsayers of the second advent are surprisingly well-known and respected members of the Christian community. Their books have sold millions of copies, and many of them pastor large churches. A few of them even host their own shows on Christian television and radio. Not one of them, however, has ever said that God specifically told them that the world was going to end on this date or that date. Nevertheless, each one regularly gives the distinct impression that we may confidently expect Jesus' return at any moment due to various "signs" of the end.

Prophecy on the Air

David Webber, Noah Hutchings, and Emil Gaverluk of the Southwest Radio Church (SRC) are easily the most sensational of all end-time prophecy teachers operating within Christian circles. Like so many other prophecy-based "ministries," SRC exploits one of strongest of human emotions: fear. In reference to the 1982 Jupiter Effect, for example, Gaverluk suggested that Mars might actually be thrown out of orbit and sent plummeting toward Earth![83] But this assertion is hardly SRC's most outlandish claim. According to cult-watcher William Alnor, whose 1989 book *Soothsayers of the Second Advent* catalogued many of the important evangelical doomsayers, SRC might best be described as the Christian radio equivalent of the *National Enquirer.*

Alnor's assessment is highly appropriate since a source of "news" that is often cited by SRC is none other than the ultimate tabloid: the *National Enquirer.*[84] From page 26 of that newspaper's March 18, 1973 edition, Webber pulled information about scientists trying to decode mysterious radio signals emanating from the Big Dipper. In *Satan's Kingdom and the Second Coming*, he theorized that these transmissions might be coming from Heaven itself. "Certainly, we are witnessing many strange signs from heaven in these last days," wrote Webber.[85]

End of the world dates set by SRC are plentiful. In *Is This the Last Century?* (1979), Webber and Hutchings said that the tribulation *might* start in 1981.[86] By 1987, they were declaring that the rapture and beginning of the tribulation would occur "possibly in 1987 or 1988."[87] Neither men feel that these end-time speculations are worthy of criticism because they placed a question mark after each date. This practice of using a qualifying "?" has become a classic technique used by date-suggesters. It effectively absolves them from all responsibility for failed "predictions" and/or any harmful ramifications that their words might have on followers. In an interview with Alnor, Webber explained his position:

> I never said that the Lord *had* to come in 1981 and any timetables that we suggest that have to do with Israel are *suggested timetables.* I don't think we ever said dogmatically that this timetable is rigid and *will* come to pass. It's not all right to set projected dates. We've never done that; we may have suggested that *perhaps* '81 was a good time for the Lord to come. We hoped that maybe He would, but we didn't establish it or say, "Hey, the Lord *has* to come on Rosh Hashanah, 1981 or '88."[88]

As it turns out, SRC inherited its doomsday philosophy from David Webber's father, Dr. Edward F. Webber, who founded SRC. The elder Webber gained his own reputation as an end-time prophet in the 1940s by suggesting that Hitler was the Antichrist.[89]

Church's Hidden Prophecies

J. R. Church — host of the nationally-syndicated television show *Prophecy in the News* and publisher of a monthly newsletter by that same name — reached evangelical star status after the publication of his 1986 end-time bestseller *Hidden Prophecies in the Psalms*, which claims that the Bible's book of Psalms is actually an encoded guide to the twentieth century.[90] Among Church's many fans are Edgar Whisenant and Charles Taylor, both of whom have cited Church's teachings.

According to Church, each Psalm corresponds to a year in the twentieth century (e.g., Psalm 1 = 1901, Psalm 14 = 1914, Psalm 48 = 1948, etc.). The corollary to this theory is that the Psalms prophetically describe events divinely scheduled for the years corresponding to each psalm's numerical designation. For example, Psalms 39 to 45 supposedly outline the plight of Jews during World War II. Psalm 48 allegedly describes the 1948 reestablishment of Israel as a state.

In reference to Psalm 91:5 ("Thou shalt not be afraid of the terror by night, nor of the arrow that flyeth by day"), Church alleges: "[I]t describes in some detail the events of 1991 and the Gulf War. . . . There was the fear that those scud missiles contained chemical warheads."[91] Regarding Psalm 93:3 ("The floods have lifted up, O Lord. The floods have lifted up their voice"), he says: "In 1993, there were floods unprecedented in history, all over the world not only in the upper Mississippi, but in Europe, in the far east, in Africa. These floods all over the world seemed to be a fulfillment of this prophecy."[92] What about those Psalms that correspond to future years? These, Church claims, undoubtedly give readers a peek at the future.

Although he was at first reluctant to share his miraculous discovery with the public "for fear of being labeled as a date setter," Church eventually decided that he would be remiss in his prophetic calling unless he brought out "the uncanny twentieth century chronology apparent in the Psalms."[93] But in order to protect his standing as a reliable prophet of God, Church was careful to litter his 1986 book with assorted disclaimers, qualifiers, contradicting messages, and the all-purpose "?".

Even a cursory look at Church's work reveals him to be a date-suggester *par excellence*. For instance, after commenting that Psalm 88:10 pointed to a possible rapture in 1988, Church absolved himself from responsibility for the speculation by stating: "It was not I who put a reference to the resurrection [i.e., rapture] in Psalm 88:10, nor would I dare to suggest that the resurrection must occur in 1988.[94] But he then goes on to describe the seven year tribulation period as being outlined in Psalms 88 to 94 (1988–1994). Throughout the book he suggested a 1988 rapture six times, implied that the Antichrist would set a trap for the Jews as early as 1988, described the "dreadful battle of Armageddon" in Psalm 94 (1994), and said that Psalm 95 (1995) described a world celebration over "the appearance of Christ to save the day."[95]

After these interpretations proved to be false, Church released a 1990 "Revised Edition" of *Hidden Prophecies in the Psalms* that effectively updated any errors contained in the 1986 version. He even used this second edition to justify his prior remarks, going so far as to claim that Psalm 88 was actually prophesying the many *incorrect* statements that would be made about a 1988 rapture: "With a verse in Psalm 88 about the resurrection, is it any wonder that some called for the rapture of Christians in 1988? And though the rapture did not occur in that year, *the prediction of the date-setters for the event may have been a fulfillment of the passage*" (emphasis mine).[96]

It is no surprise that Church would find himself holding a handful of false prognostications. His method of interpreting the Psalms is not only unscholarly and without historical support, but is so arbitrary that no principles of biblical interpretation are applicable. Church can make the Psalms say just about anything he wants them to say. In Psalm 13, for instance, he connects the phrase "How Long wilt thou forget me, O LORD? For ever? How long wilt thou hide thy face from me?" with the 1913 passage in America of the Federal Reserve Act and establishment of the Federal Reserve System.[97] This is only one of Church's many odd interpretations:

- The phrase "Keep me as the apple of the eye, hide me under the shadow of thy wings" in Psalm 17 is a description of the wings of British planes as they flew over Jerusalem in 1917.[98]

- "Shew me thy ways, O LORD; teach me thy paths. Lead me in thy truth, and teach me" (Psalm 25) refers to the opening in 1925 of Hebrew University on Jerusalem's Mount Scopus.[99]

Since his 1988 suggestion for the rapture fell through, Church appears to have jumped on the year 2000 bandwagon, claiming that the new millennium may herald the return of Christ. "Once we come to Psalms 101-107 [2001–2007], we have what appears to be a period of tribulation," postulates Church. "Psalm 101, for example, indicates that God will 'early' destroy the wicked out of the land. This word 'early' means at daybreak, at the crack of dawn. And of course, if Psalm 101 represents the year 2001, it would indeed be the dawning of the new millennium."[100] Church has presented this theory several times through his *Prophecy in the News* publication:

- "Around the year A.D. 2000 should also mark the introduction of the seventh millennium [allegedly the 7th 1000-year period since the world's beginning and Adam's creation] — entering the predicted Messianic times!"[101]
- "Since we are approaching the conclusion of this sixth millennium of human history and the introduction of the seventh with the year 2001, we would do well to observe what the prophets were trying to tell us. . . . I am convinced that we are just a few years away from the beginning of Israel's affliction and repentance [the tribulation]. . . . We have noted how each of the Psalms seem to describe events . . . in each year of this century, as numbered by each Psalm, beginning with Psalm 1 and 1901. If Psalm 101 represents the year 2001, then we may note that the year 2001 does indeed represent the dawning of the new millennium."[102]
- "According to Bible prophets, this seventh millennium, which could begin in 2001 and last for a thousand years, should be the time when Christ will reign over the earth."[103]

Although Church has been criticized by several conservative Christian scholars and counter-cult organizations, he has not relented in presenting his groundless theory about the Psalms. In the 1990 edition of *Hidden Prophecies in the Psalms,* he would only admit that some of his past conjectures "did not come about as we had originally anticipated." At the same time, however, he boldly declared: "Since publishing the first edition of this book in 1986, I have carefully followed the progress of Psalms 86–90 and am even more convinced today that the concept which we first espoused is indeed confirmed!" (emphasis in original).[104]

Jeffrey's Jubilees

One of the newest stars in today's parade of date-suggesters is Grant Jeffrey, a former financial planner/tax consultant/insurance broker turned prophecy teacher. His first book — *Armageddon: Appointment with Destiny* (1988) — sold 140,000 copies within two years. Even as Whisenant's 1989 debacle was occurring, he was quickly making a name for himself by suggesting that the year 2000 would be the "probable termination point for the 'last days' " when Christ "may commence His Kingdom." In fact, Jeffrey suggested that this glorious event could fall on October 9, 2000.[105]

He arrived at his date by using a Jubilee cycle timetable, which is based on the Old Testament's book of Leviticus 25:2–9. In this particular Bible passage, God commands all Israelites to observe every seventh year as a Sabbath year (i.e., a year of rest). God additionally commanded that after seven Sabbath years (i.e., forty-nine years), there would be a "Jubilee Year" wherein all Israelites would be forgiven their debts. According to some Christian prognosticators, one can discern the time of the end by simply figuring out the year of the *first* Jubilee, then counting forward using "biblical years" and matching these years up with "calendar years."

Each prophecy teacher usually makes several arbitrary time decisions that succeed in placing Armageddon precisely where they want it placed. Both Harold Camping and Edgar Whisenant used this method to reach their dates. Camping started counting at Israel's entrance into Canaan (c. 1407 or 1357 B.C.) and stopped with sixty-eight Jubilees in 1994. Whisenant, however, began counting at Abraham's covenant with God (c. 1872 B.C.), proceeded forward a full seventy Jubilees, then subtracted 430 years for Israel's captivity in Babylon. The resulting date was 1988.

Discovering doomsday's deadline by counting Jubilees often takes readers through a maze of dizzying calculations that are rife with historical
inaccuracies. Jeffrey, being an ex-accountant, seems especially fond of num-
ber-crunching, as the following passage from *Armageddon* clearly illustrates:

> [T]he Sabbatical–Jubilee system of years began when Israel crossed the Jordan River
> in 1451 B.C. Thus, Jesus Christ [in Luke 4:18–21] precisely fulfilled "**the acceptable
> year of the Lord**" [in A.D. 28 by starting his ministry] on the exact year of Jubilee
> — the year of liberty and release. Please note that He stopped reading [from Isaiah
> 61] at "**the acceptable year of the Lord**" because He knew that the next phrase of
> the prophet's sentence, "**and the day of vengeance of our God**," which refers to
> Armageddon, would be postponed exactly 2,000 biblical years (2,000 biblical years
> times 360 days equals 720,000 days divided by 365.25 equals 1,971.25 calendar years).
> If we add 2,000 biblical years (1,971.25 calendar years) to the beginning of Christ's
> ministry on a Jubilee Year when he read the prophecy about "**the acceptable year
> of the Lord**" in the fall of A.D. 28; we arrive at the year A.D. 2000, forty Jubilee
> Cycles later. The next Jubilee Year will occur in A.D. 2000, completing the Sabbat-
> ical-Jubilee system of years — the seventieth Great Jubilee.[106]

Indispensable to Jeffrey's Jubilee timetable are his 360-day "biblical
year" and his 365.25-day "calendar year." Noteworthy is the fact that
ancient Israelites observed neither measurement.[107] Consequently, all of
Jeffrey's calculations are meaningless. Also problematic is Jeffrey's date for
the crossing of the Jordan River by the Israelites: 1451 B.C. First, it is not
possible to know when the Israelites crossed the Jordan into "the promised
land" (i.e., Canaan) because no date was recorded for either that event or
the departure of the Israelites from Egypt forty years prior to that event.
Second, the most widely accepted possible date given by reputable Christian
scholars for the Israelite migration into Canaan ranges from approximately
1407 B.C. to 1400 B.C.,[108] which means that Jeffrey's date is nearly fifty
years too early. The only other possible date that conservative Christian
scholars accept for the crossing of the Jordan River by the Israelites is 1240
B.C.,[109] which puts Jeffrey's seventieth Jubilee well into the future.

These obvious errors in his method of computing the *possible* date of
Jesus' return has done little to slow sales of his books. Since the publication

of *Armageddon*, he has produced six more bestselling tomes on the end-times, totaling more than two million copies sold. One of his most recent titles, *Final Warning*, blends prophecy with what Jeffrey knows best: finances. In this 1996 volume, Jeffrey claims that humanity is already feeling the first tremors of a worldwide economic collapse, which will in turn pave the way for the Antichrist to take over: "[W]e may have to live through the greatest economic collapse in history. As we who are Christians consider these dangerous economic times in which we live, we may want to obtain information and advice about biblically based financial strategies that will protect our family assets."[110]

What does Jeffrey offer to his confused and frightened readers? Nothing less than his own expertise in financial planning. According to Jeffrey, *Final Warning* represents "over 30 years of economic and prophetic research," all blended with "what his latest research reveals about the exciting events that will culminate in the return of our Lord and Savior Jesus Christ."[111]

Jeffrey does not use his 509-page book to just talk about theology or eschatology. He promises readers that the volume provides biblically-based information relating to "financial strategies that will allow us to survive the economic roller coaster awaiting us in the years ahead."[112] Interestingly, the book begins with a lengthy disclaimer (in small print) from the publisher: "The author and publisher cannot be held responsible for any loss incurred as a result of applying any of the information in this book."[113]

CHRISTIAN OCCULTISTS?

One of the most fascinating aspects of today's Christian prophecy teachers is the obvious similarities between their predictions and those of occultists. Consider *What in the World Will Happen Next?* (1974) and *I Predict* (1970) by prophecy teacher Salem Kirban, who advertised the latter volume of prognostications as "THE BOOK THAT DARES TO REVEAL THE DISASTERS OF THE FUTURE!"[114] These two books were released within just a few years of the bestselling psychic book *Criswell Predicts* (see Chapter 2). Kirban assured readers that his works were "NOT given as occult phenomena, crystal ball gazing or astrology."[115] It cannot be denied, however, that many of his predictions mirror Criswell's, with only a few minor changes (see table 3.1).

SALEM KIRBAN[116]	CRISWELL[117]
"[By 1980] The nation's water supply will be infused with a drug to calm the populace." "Compulsory birth control will be exercised by law. Infants will be conceived on a government controlled 'genetically approved' basis."	"Placed in the water system of the country, every city, regardless of size, will be chemicals which will act as contraceptives on the entire populace."
"In 1975 droughts will curtail farm production. Americans will come face to face with the fact that food is scarce!"	"Rain will not fall [in 1977] for a period of ten months. . . . Farms, fields and homesteads will be covered by mountains of sand and dust."
"Full control of the news media will occur before 1982. The excuse given by the government will be that control is being instituted to 'avoid internal chaos and achieve national security.' "	"[T]here will be no newspapers, as we know them . . . after 1980. . . . [N]ewspapers will be fed into the home via television transmission . . . . And, because television is under government control, every newspaper will be under government control also."
"I predict a U.S. war with China within the next 15 years [i.e., before 1985]."	"[T]he only war to be fought on American soil will be in Alaska in the late 1980's. A combine of Russian, Chinese and Korean forces will try to get a foothold in North America."
"Before 1985 New York City will experience both a devastating hurricane and catastrophic earthquake."	"New York will not exist . . . after January 21, 1980. Shifting ocean currents and earth tremors will begin to remake the Eastern coast of the U.S."

Table 3.1

It is no surprise that most of Kirban's predictions failed to materialize. What *is* surprising, though, is how some Christian prophecy teachers have not only sounded like occultists, but have actually drawn information from occult sources in an effort to support their doomsday pronouncements. This is a major departure from the long-held belief among Christians that occultism is unbiblical and that persons practicing occult forms of divination — e.g., astrology, pyramidology, psychics, witchcraft — are to be condemned (Ex. 22:18; Lev. 19:26, 19:31, 20:6, 27; Deut. 4:19, 18:9–12; 2 Ki. 21:6; Is. 44:25, 47:13–15, Jer. 10:2; Mic. 5:12; Gal. 5:20; Rev. 21:8).

For some prophecy teachers, the desire to peddle doomsday predictions has apparently overridden the tenets of their faith which command an avoidance of occultism. Edgar Whisenant, for instance, favorably quoted psychic Jeane Dixon in reason sixty-five of *88 Reasons Why the Rapture Will Be in 1988*. Whisenant felt that Dixon had been accurate when she psychically saw the February 5, 1962 birth somewhere in the Middle East of a coming world leader.[118] The child, Whisenant ominously declared, is "our Antichrist of the end-time."[119]

Influential prophecy pundit Jack Van Impe (see Chapter 4) has appealed to none other than psychic Gordon-Michael Scallion in an effort to convince his followers that the end is near. In his 1996 book *2001: On the Edge of Eternity*, released by Word (one of the world's largest Christian publishers), Van Impe writes: "Futurist Gordon-Michael Scallion, editor of *Earth Changes Report*, has been suggesting for months that a frightening global killer earthquake pattern is emerging, He [Scallion] is predicting that a series of magnitude 10.0 quakes will rip up America's West Coast in the next few years.[120] Van Impe has also called Nostradamus, the sixteenth century occult seer, "a great Bible student" and has said that the Great Pyramid holds prophetic significance.[121]

Van Impe and Whisenant are not the only Christians who have used occult techniques to foretell the future. J. R. Church's theory about the Psalms is built on two forms of Kabbalistic numerology: Gematria and Notarikon.[122] According to New Age specialist and cult expert Elliot Miller of the Christian Research Institute, Kabbala is an occultic belief system that "must be classified among all other occultic systems as being incompatible with historic Judeo-Christian faiths."[123] Gematria numerology is defined

by the *Encyclopedia of Occultism & Parapsychology* as a "prediction
system deriving from the mystic values ascribed to numbers." In Jewish
mysticism, it is used to discover hidden meanings of words by systematically converting Hebrew letters into numbers. It was "popularized by
palmist and fortune-teller 'Cheiro' [1866–1936]."[124]

End-time prognosticator Colin Deal, in his book *Christ Returns by
1988: 101 Reasons Why*, looked to astrology for confirmation of his
predictions: "As 1982 approaches, the planets will be moving into the sign
of Aquarius. The sign is pictured as 'The Water Bearer.' . . . [Jesus Christ
left Earth] but returned to pour out waters of blessings upon a people
redeemed for the earth. . . . [T]he signs of the heavens are declaring for the
first time in 2,000 years that God's Son is about to be revealed."[125] In
reference to the Great Pyramid of Giza, Deal wrote the following
endorsement in 1981:

> Isaiah said it would be for a sign in the day (last day). . . . It not only reveals
> knowledge of the birth, death, burial and resurrection of our Lord; but prophetic
> timetables based on measurements in the Great Pyramid have been discovered
> which relate to the Twentieth Century.[126]

Prophecy teachers David Webber, Noah Hutchings, and Reginald
Dunlop have also utilized pyramidology. Dunlop went so far as to
dogmatically assert in the mid-1970s that the Great Pyramid definitely
pointed to 1979 as the year when Christ's millennial kingdom would be
established on Earth. He published this doomsday date in *Flee to the
Mountains — God's Message for Survival — No Time to Spare —
Imminent End-Time Destruction*.[127] Webber and Hutchings have made
their own pyramid-based predictions. Their bestseller *Prophecy in Stone*
(250,000 copies sold) contained a chart that slated the beginning of the
tribulation for 1981–1985 and the end of the tribulation (as well as the
Return of Jesus) for 1988–1992.[128] When these dates came and went, the
two men simply reprinted the book with a different cover, changed the
dates on the charts (from 1981/85 and 1988/92 to 1988 and 1996
respectively), and gave the text a new title: *New Light on the Great*

Pyramid.[129] They included in their "new" book an additional chapter concerning pyramids on Mars!

Christians should find these appeals to occultic sources disturbing because they are clearly against the historic teachings of Christianity. But it seems that vast numbers of born-again believers are willing to overlook anything that might hinder their ability to gaze into the future. This tendency has led to an even more disturbing trend: the formation of alliances between non-racist Christians and anti-Semites/white suprema-cists (many of whom are also obsessed with Armageddon). Such alliances have done much to develop the social phenomenon in America known as the patriot/militia movement. This issue will be the focus of Chapter 4.

FOUR

Patriots & Militiamen

[There are] powerful forces at work in America today which have a well-strategized design to move America into a socialist police state and a globalist New World Order. . . to control and subjugate the American people . . . by the year 2000.

Don McAlvany
Christian economist[1]

Document after document of the New World Order plans for the total takeover of this country by the year 2000.

John Trochmann
Militia of Montana[2]

AT 9:02 A.M. ON APRIL 19, 1995, a homemade bomb weighing nearly 5,000 pounds was detonated outside the Alfred P. Murrah Federal Building in Oklahoma City. The resulting blast killed one hundred sixty-eight people and injured six hundred others. Americans were stunned not only by the incident's severity, but by the identity of the terrorists responsible for the carnage: two former U.S. Army soldiers, Timothy McVeigh and Terry Nichols. Both men were involved in the American social phenomenon known as the patriot movement, a loosely-knit network of approximately five to twelve million people.[3]

This movement is one of the most diverse coalitions America has ever seen. Its ranks include farmers, manual laborers, professionals, the unemployed, police officers, and members of the military. On its moderate side are conservative Christians opposed to the liberal establishment. More radical participants include both Christians and non-Christians who deny their U.S. citizenship, drive without licenses, and refuse to pay income taxes in an effort to live outside "the system." Infiltrating these two groups are the most dangerous patriots: Klansmen, neo-Nazis, and Christian Identity believers (i.e., white supremacists who blend pseudo-Christian beliefs with racism and anti-Semitism).

The ideological glue binding together this wide assortment of people is a mixture of four ingredients: a deep-seated mistrust of government officials; an obsessive hatred for federal authority; a belief in far-reaching conspiracy theories; and a feeling that Washington bureaucrats have utterly discarded the U.S. Constitution. To this volatile adhesive can be added a heavy dose of frustration and anger over the ever-increasing chasm between what politicians do and what the general public wants. Consider, for example, the government's approval of GATT and NAFTA — two very unpopular trade agreements — and the 1994 passage of gun control legislation that many Americans did not want enacted (i.e., the Brady Law and Assault Weapons Ban).

All of these elements, combined with unwanted social change, declining economic conditions, the growing imposition of federal authority, rigid environmental restrictions, and federal law enforcement abuses (e.g., the Waco tragedy and the Ruby Ridge shootout), have led persons involved in the patriot movement to conclude that federal officials are waging a cold war against freedom-loving Americans. It is also believed that this cold war will soon give way to a real war between U.S. citizens and global elitists whose ultimate goal is world domination via the establishment by the year 2000 of a one-world government, codenamed the New World Order. Individuals espousing these beliefs, although their political affiliations may differ, are commonly referred to as patriots.

To Christian patriots, the New World Order amounts to nothing less than the long-awaited reign of the Antichrist ("the beast"). Today's politicians, therefore, are viewed as little more than demonically-driven pawns of Satan who are laying the foundation for the soon-to-be-revealed Antichrist and his seven years of terrifying rule (i.e., the Tribulation). The perceived nearness of this final era of human history is most feared by historic premillennialists (see Chapter 3), who believe that they will have to live through the Tribulation. Their only source of hope is the termination of the Antichrist's reign by the triumphant second coming of Jesus and the establishment of his millennial kingdom.

To white supremacist/anti-Semitic patriots, who also see the end of the world approaching, the government is not only demonically energized, but is secretly being run by Satan's chief minions: the Jews. In *this* last days scenario, the federal government is a Jewish tool of oppression that must be destroyed in preparation for an Armageddon-like race war out of which will emerge an army of victorious Anglo-Saxons.[4] White warriors of God will in turn establish an Aryan republic in America (God's Kingdom) by deporting people of color and exterminating all Jews.[5]

Doomsday theories have motivated a large number of patriots to organize themselves into militias. These paramilitary units, most of which function contrary to state laws prohibiting private armies, foreshadow the ultimate implementation of patriot sentiments — an armed resistance to the behind-the-scenes cabal of evil conspirators planning to conquer America. Patriots claim that all of the militias merely serve as a "constitutional safety net."[6] According to Militia of Montana (MOM) leader John Trochmann, they represent nothing but a giant "neighborhood watch, watching out for problems" and alerting proper officials when they perceive "threats to a peaceful society."[7] Michigan Militia spokesperson Ken Adams says that militia members are "totally against violence."[8] But since the early 1990s, several militia-related episodes of violence have shown that not all of these militant groups are benign.[9]

Making the situation even more explosive is the high level of paranoia gripping most patriots. An ocean of pamphlets, newsletters, videotapes, and audiocassettes has flooded their minds with farfetched conspiracy plots the likes of which are usually associated with paperback spy novels. For example, many patriots feel that some of the most infamous random shootings in America have been government actions to facilitate stricter gun control measures. Karen Gentry, representative of the Guardians of American Liberty in southern California, has suggested that Patrick Purdy — the man who murdered five children and wounded twenty-nine others in a 1989 shooting spree in Stockton, California — was set up by the government through mind control.[10]

Similarly, MOM has alleged that the December 1993 New York subway shooting of several commuters was committed by a government-controlled zombie. "He was obviously a CIA preprogrammed asset," declares one of

MOM's many publications. "This was a preplanned agenda to continue their efforts to DISARM THE UNORGANIZED MILITIAS OF THE SEVERAL STATES" (bold in original).[11] A 1997 issue of the patriot newsletter *Unraveling The New World Order* echoed this belief: "We expect, unfortunately, that in the new year, some massacre-type events will be staged as a final push for gun control or gun banning legislation to be enacted."[12]

Professor Phil Agre in the Department of Communication at the University of California, San Diego, has noted that the concepts expressed in the patriot movement are so bizarre that they are "hard to even think about."[13] But think about them we must, as the Oklahoma City bombing has so clearly proven.

SATAN'S SYSTEM

Patriots espouse the radical conspiracy theory that America's ongoing economic and political difficulties are part of a much larger plan to enslave U.S. citizens "by disarming the population and making the currency worthless. The eventual result . . . will be the New World Order — a one-world government administered by the United Nations."[14] This totalitarian regime will allegedly reduce everyone to slaves destined to serve the "international bankers [often a codeword for Jews], wealthy elite, socialists and liberals."[15]

If the term "New World Order" (NWO) sounds familiar, it should. On September 11, 1990, President George Bush popularized the phrase during a speech delivered to Congress. He was speaking of "a reinvigorating of the system of collective security envisioned by the drafters of the United Nations Charter."[16] The ultimate goal of collective security through U.N. peacekeeping operations is the creation of an era wherein "diverse nations are drawn together in common cause [i.e., peace]."[17]

Responsible critics of the NWO fear that U.N. policies may set up the U.S. as "the world's policeman trying to impose a Pax Americana on the rest of the world."[18] Patriots, however, voice a different complaint. According to patriot Jack McLamb, the NWO will be "an oligarchy of the world's richest families who will place ½ of the masses of the earth in servitude under their complete control, administered from behind the false front of the United Nations."[19]

It is additionally claimed that the U. N.'s blue-helmeted troops will one day land on U.S. shores and subjugate citizens. How could such an event happen? Global conspirators are allegedly causing domestic strife and the systematic breakdown of American society 'so that peacekeepers can be summoned to restore law and order.[20] McLamb states, "With just the 'right' manipulation, they [i.e., the globalists] have been successfully conditioning our people to see all our societal problems — government, political, educational, penal, ecological, etc. — as completely out of control."[21] Patriot Linda Thompson, an Indiana attorney who in 1993 proclaimed herself the "Acting Adjutant General of the Unorganized Militia of the United States of America," explains it this way:

> This is the coming of the "New World Order." A one world government where, in order to put the new government in place, we must all be disarmed first. To do that, the government is deliberately creating schizms [sic] in our society, funding both the anti-abortion and pro-choice sides, the anti-gun/pro-gun issues, black-white race riots, gay/anti-gay hysteria, trying to provoke a riot that will allow martial law to be implemented and all the weapons seized, while "dissidents" are put safely away.[22]

Patriots theorize that Americans will soon beg for peacekeepers to restore order. The U.N. — a political body that "ignores God and was founded for the purpose of Global Socialism" — will then invade the country to "eliminate U.S. sovereignty and independence and merge us into a world government."[23] To patriots, calling U.N. forces *peacekeepers* is all part of a master plan by the world's unseen manipulators to dominate humanity. MOM has already announced that "[T]he UN is NOW in CONTROL of America!" (emphasis in original)[24] Of this scenario, patriots have no doubt:

> It is not a matter of conjecture anymore. The plan of the owners of the world is to institute a New World Order — in essence just the consolidation of world control

into fewer hands. When the U.N. has a "peacekeeping" force superior to that of the U.S. military (or perhaps before that) there is no doubt, no argument, that U.N. forces will be used to subjugate the U.S. The forces who intend to implement the New World Order (and they include the politicians who currently rule the roost in the United States) simply will not take no for an answer.[25]

Because a majority of participants in the patriot/militia movement subscribe to some form of Protestantism,[26] a religious spin is often placed on the New World Order conspiracy. *Militia News*, published by the Christian Civil Liberties Association of Tennessee, states: "The time is at hand when men and women must decide whether they are on the side of freedom and justice, the American republic and Almighty God, or if they are on the side of tyranny and oppression, the New World Order and Satan."[27]

The most common element added to this end-time conspiracy involves the totalitarian dictator who will rule the New World Order: the Antichrist. Premillennial patriots posit that "a world dictatorship under the influence of the antichrist . . . will be established — enslaving all nations and destroying individual freedoms."[28] Only by receiving the "mark of the beast" (666) will anyone survive:

> There is a plan to enslave the entire world by forcing them to take an economic mark on their right hand or forehead, and without that mark no one will buy or sell, or own a home, or pay property taxes, or use the freeway, purchase anything anywhere, because the whole world will have been taken cashless. . . . [I]t will be a crime to have any method with which you can circumvent this debit and credit system that's coming.[29]

Christians are especially susceptible to this NWO conspiracy theory because it seems to fit well with selected biblical passages that some evangelicals believe outline the seven-year tribulation, which will allegedly occur just prior to the Battle of Armageddon and Jesus' second coming (see Chapter 3). Although the specifics surrounding minor details of the tribulation vary among premillennialists, nearly all Christian patriots agree on at least one thing: the Antichrist is now alive.[30]

THE BEAST AND HIS MARK

Exactly who, or what, is the Antichrist? This has been a source of debate for many years and has led to an extensive list of candidates. Stalin, Mussolini, Hitler, King Juan Carlos of Spain, Anwar Sadat, Pope John Paul II, Henry Kissinger, Ayatollah Khomeini, Muammar Gadhafi, Saddam Hussein, Jimmy Carter, Ronald Reagan, Mikhail Gorbachev and a host of other religious and political personalities have at various times been identified as the Antichrist.[31]

Virtually no one is immune from being labeled "the beast." In 1985, for instance, a zealous end-time conspiracy-believer named Constance Cumbey pointed an accusatory finger at Pat Robertson, who himself had announced in 1980 that the Antichrist was at that time "approximately 27-years-old . . . [and] being groomed to be the Satanic messiah."[32] When Robertson threatened to sue Cumbey, she dropped the charge.[33]

According to the Militia of Montana, "The Antichrist is not coming — he's here!"[34] Numerous mainstream Christian prophecy teachers have been claiming the same thing for many years. In 1981, Hal Lindsey asserted that the Antichrist "is alive today — alive and waiting to come forth"[35] John Hagee, author of the *New York Times* bestseller *Beginning of the End*, says the Antichrist "is probably alive right now and may even know his predestined demonic assignment."[36] Evangelical speaker Dave Hunt makes a similar statement in his book *Global Peace and the Rise of the Antichrist*:

> Somewhere, at this very moment, on planet Earth, the Antichrist is almost certainly alive—biding his time, awaiting his cue. . . . Already a mature man, he is probably active in politics, perhaps even an admired world leader whose name is on everyone's lips.[37]

Such claims are no different from those voiced by Saint Martin of Tours, who served as Bishop of Gaul, and who believed that the Antichrist existed in his day (c. 316–397). He wrote: "There is no doubt that the Antichrist has already been born. Firmly established already in his early years, he will, after reaching maturity, achieve supreme power."[38] The coming of the Antichrist was also predicted in Western Europe "for the year 1000, and later on for 1184, 1186, 1229, 1345, 1385, 1516, and other dates in between."[39]

All of these erroneous speculations were built on the presupposition that the Antichrist is a real personality. Such a view has not always been so popular. In fact, a large number of conservative Christians disagree with premillennialists and stress that "the modern doctrine of the Antichrist is an amalgamation of biblical concepts and events that either are unrelated or find their fulfillment in past events. . . . Modern Antichrist hunters are pursuing a figure who does not exist."[40]

A close examination of several biblical verses lends support to this latter contention. The word *Antichrist* appears only in two of the Bible's sixty-six books: 1 John and 2 John. The term is used to describe *anyone* who denies that Jesus is the Christ (1 John 2:22), rejects the Father and the Son (1 John 2:23), refuses to profess faith in Jesus (1 John 4:3), and disbelieves that Jesus the Christ came in human flesh (2 John 7). The apostle John was obviously not referring to a particular leader, but rather to individuals who preached a Jesus different from the one represented in Scripture.

Consequently, the term *Antichrist* may simply be a figure of speech applicable to anyone who denies the Christian doctrine that God took on human flesh in the historical person of Jesus. The apostle John plainly stated that during his time "many" antichrists had already risen (1 John 2:18b). Conservative theologian Benjamin Warfield (1851–1921) wrote: "To deny that Jesus is Christ come — or is the coming Christ — in flesh, was again just to refuse to recognize in Jesus Incarnate God. Whosoever, says John, takes up this attitude toward Jesus is Antichrist."[41]

It must be noted, however, that there are a few biblical passages which suggest that biblical writers did indeed have a specific individual in mind that epitomized all antichrist attitudes. This figure is described as *the* "antichrist that is coming" (1 John 2:18a) and *the* "man of lawlessness" who is to be revealed (2 Thess. 2:3). But this does not mean that a future one world government leader is destined to rise to power. Many historians and theologians theorize that these may be references to Nero, one of the cruelest of all Roman emperors. According to conservative theologians C. Marvin Pate and Calvin B. Haines of the Moody Bible Institute, interpreting these passages through a "Neronian backdrop" provides a clearer perspective on what are otherwise baffling Bible verses, especially those found in the thirteenth chapter of the Book of Revelation:

> Nero's infamous character merits the title of "beast" applied to him by the seer of the Apocalypse (v. 1). Revelation 13:1-6 gives the generic background of the beast, which is the Roman Empire of the first century. The seven heads correspond to the seven hills of Rome, while the ten horns allude to the Caesars of the first century, however one may number them (v. 1). The blasphemous worship demanded by the beast distinctly reminds one of the imperial cult of the first century, and the war the beast wages on the saints cannot help but recall the intense persecutions Nero, and later Domitian, inflicted on Christians because they did not worship Caesar. . . . Nero's persecution of Christians from November A.D. 64 to June A.D. 68 could account, in part, for the forty-two months (or three and one-half years) of oppression mentioned in Revelation 13:5. The reference in Revelation 13:10 to those who kill with the sword being killed by the sword reminds one simultaneously of Nero's persecution of Christians and his own apparent suicide by the sword. The reference in Revelation 13:11–15 to the beast of the land securing worship for the beast from the sea (Rome was across the sea from the place of the writing of the Apocalypse, Asia Minor) reminds one of the local priests of the imperial cult in Asia Minor whose task was to compel the people to offer a sacrifice to Caesar and proclaim him Lord. Megalomaniac that he was, Nero had coins minted in which he was called "almighty God" and "Savior." Nero's portrait also appears on coins as the god Apollo playing a lyre. While earlier emperors were proclaimed deities upon their deaths, Nero abandoned all reserve and demanded divine honors while still alive (as did also Caligula before him, A.D. 37-41). Those who worshipped the emperor received a certificate or mark of approval — *charagma*, the same word used in Revelation 13:16. Furthermore, in the reign of Emperor Decius (A.D. 249-251), those who did not possess the certificate of sacrifice to Caesar could not pursue trades, a prohibition that conceivably goes back to Nero, reminding one of Revelation 13:17.[42]

These are but a few of the many ways that Nero fulfills the role of the Antichrist. Perhaps the most fascinating aspect of the Neronian interpretation of Revelation and related passages involves the Roman emperors name. If one takes the name Nero Caesar, translates it into Greek (*Neron Kaisar*), then transliterates the result into Hebrew (*Nrwn Qsr*), and finally, gives each Hebrew letter its numerical equivalent (N=50, R=200, W=6, N=50, Q=100, S=60, R=200), the sum total of all the letters is none other than 666 (Rev. 13:18). Clearly, placing the concept of an Antichrist in the historical and cultural context of the first century makes a great deal of sense. Trying to place the Antichrist in today's culture, however, has consistently led to folly. This is perhaps best illustrated by an incident involving self-styled prophet Colin Deal.

In his 1979 book *Christ Returns by 1988—101 Reasons Why*, Deal discussed a huge computer called "the Beast" that is being housed at the European Economic Community's headquarters in Brussels, Belgium. This high tech brain allegedly contains "all the basic information about every human on earth."[43] The data will supposedly be used to assign "a number to every person on earth in the form of a laser tattoo. Then, through infrared scanners, this invisible tatoo would appear on a screen."[44] As late as 1997, this story was still being spread through prophecy-related books such as Ed Hindson's *Final Signs*, published by Harvest House, a large evangelical publisher.[45]

In reality, there exists no such computer. The rumor grew out of an August 1976 *Christian Life* magazine piece. But the article's author, who had heard about the computer from an unnamed source, did not know that the story was actually part of a fiction novel: *Behold a Pale Horse* by Joe Musser. In a letter to *Christian Life*, Musser expressed his irritation:

> The item referring to a computer "Beast," a confederacy of Common Market nations, and a laser tattooing for a world-wide numbering system (People and Events, August) is based on fictional portrayals of end time events, drawing from my novel, *Behold a Pale Horse* (Zondervan), and a screenplay I wrote for the David Wilkerson film, *The Rapture*. For more than three years I have heard my story ideas circulated as fact. Perhaps, in light of what's happening in the world today, items such as the one printed seem quite plausible. However, for the moment, they are fiction.[46]

Endless speculations have also been expressed regarding the Antichrist's "mark" (666). Revelation 13:16-18 discusses this element of the premillennialist's greatest fear:

He also forced everyone, small and great, rich and poor, free and slave, to receive a mark on his right hand or on his forehead, so that no one could buy or sell unless he had the mark, which is the name of the beast or the number of his name. This calls for wisdom. If anyone has insight let him calculate the number of the beast, for it is man's number. His number is 666.

Many prophecy buffs point to the new Multi-technology Automated Reader Cards (MARC) being used in the military for identification purposes.[47] Others claim that 666 can be found in "the supermarket bar codes now stamped on most products."[48] Some people think that Social Security numbers represent the mark of the beast.[49] End-time extremists David Webber and Noah Hutchings theorize that 666 may refer to one's nine-digit Social Security number *plus* one's nine-digit zip code because $9 + 9 = 18$, which also just happens to be $3 \times 6!$[50] A few individuals contend that the devil's mark may be America's new counterfeit-combating currency. In 1995, sensationalistic end-time preacher Texe Marrs provided an interesting justification for the latter theory:

[T]he U.S. Bureau of Engraving & printing awarded Crane & Co. a $66 million contract to supply this [special] paper to the U.S. mint. . . . [T]o accommodate orders from the U.S. government for the new paper, Crane & Co. has built a 66,000 square foot addition to its mill and is spending $6 million to upgrade its equipment. . . . Pardon me, but does anyone out there recall what the Bible has to say about that very peculiar number 6?[51]

A year later, however, Marrs came up with an even more outlandish scenario involving what he calls the "Beast 666 Universal Human Control System." This end-time fantasy of Marrs' relates to something called Project L.U.C.I.D.©, a new Universal Information Identification System that law enforcement agencies hope to implement in the near future. According to a 1995 article in *The Narc Officer*, which is published by the International Narcotic Enforcement Officers Association, the objective of L.U.C.I.D.© Systems is fourfold:

1. Establish an information clearinghouse which can be used for non-criminal

background checks and tracking of positive identification requests for alias criminals (e.g., employment, immigration status, prosecutorial, firearms purchasing). This will hopefully decrease the number of wanted criminals at large and prevent such criminals from, among other things, obtaining a firearm.

2. Provide a common communications network that can be used by various experts from different locations who may be working on the same criminal cases.

3. Create a universal point where data that is received from various places (e.g., foreign governments, public and private nonprofit organizations, and U.S. federal/state government agencies) can be updated.

4. Link national and international law enforcement agencies seeking to control international terrorism and other criminal activities.[52]

The project is being implemented in order to better manage "the huge increase of criminal justice information requests from developing as well as industrialized countries."[53] But Marrs's explanation of L.U.C.I.D. is vastly different:

Flashpoint has received astonishing evidence of an incredible, new "Beast 666 Universal Human Control System." Officially called L.U.C.I.D., this grotesque system of universal slavery is — even as you read this — being implemented by federal and international intelligence and police agencies. The new Beast 666 system will mandate that every man, woman, and child on planet Earth be issued a high tech, "Smart," I.D. card, called a Universal Biometrics Card. The chilling system is slated to be fully in operation by the year 2000 . . . . This I.D. card allows for the New World Order police state to track and link every man, woman, and child on planet Earth. Our activities are to be monitored 24 hours a day, seven days a week, by federal Gestapo agencies — the FBI, IRS, BATF, CIA, DIA, DEA, NSA, U.S. Treasury Service, and Department of Justice. . . . It is designed so that no one can escape its clutches. No one! . . . Federal and international Gestapo agencies will use the instantaneous information maintained on file at the Beast Universal Computer Center at Fort Meade, Maryland [USA], to trace, investigate, monitor, spy on, arrest, and incarcerate "resisters." Resisters are categorized as: "Any and all persons who protest or oppose the Illuminati's fascist agenda for the New World

Order." . . . [T]he arrest of a targeted Christian or other citizen will take place whether or not that person has actually committed a criminal act. "Thought crimes" alone provide justification for the arrest of dissidents."[54]

Where did Marrs get all of his information? Oddly, from the very same International Narcotic Enforcement Officers Association article previously cited. Marrs' interpretation of the story, however, includes a number of points that appear nowhere in the actual article printed in *The Narc Officer.* For instance, there is no mention made of issuing a high tech "Smart" card to "every man, woman, and child on planet Earth." Nor is there any suggestion that government agencies are going to be monitoring the activities of people "24 hours a day, seven days a week," although these hours are indeed mentioned in passing as being the times that law enforcement agencies will have access to L.U.C.I.D.© Systems. Furthermore, no references whatsoever are made to "resisters" (Christian or non-Christian), "thought crimes," or "dissidents." Nevertheless, Marrs somehow came to the following conclusion:

> *Project L.U.C.I.D.* is Satan's diabolical, end-times system of total and absolute human control. It will put mankind under direct subjection to the Antichrist and his jackbooted, Gestapo-thug storm troopers. Every government on Earth will cooperate to oppress its citizens. *There will be nowhere to hide!*[55]

End-time prophet Jack Van Impe has made some equally stunning assertions about the 666 mark of the beast and computers. In his 1983 book *11:59 . . . and Counting!,* Van Impe revealed that the word computer adds up to 666 when each letter is given a numerical equivalent based on multiples of six.[56] This is not the only calculation that he has used to bolster his contentions about the beast's relationship to computers. The term "VISA" apparently adds up to 666 as well, albeit through the use of a slightly different adding method based on the linking together of three separate languages:

> The number "6" in Roman numerals is made up of the letters "**VI**." The ancient Greek number "6" was taken from the sixth letter of their alphabet, the letter

"sigma" which looks like the English letter "**S**." Returning to the Babylonian empire and their sexagesimal system of numbers, the [computer] programmer considered the possibility that their letter "**A**" equaled 6. Thus, from the three great world empires of history, he found that the composition of the number "666" spells the word VISA" — the exact name of today's most accepted and popular credit card![57]

But such a calculation has several problems. Van Impe's first formula, for instance, only works if one uses multiples of six (A=6, B=12, C=18, etc.) in connection with the English word computer. Adding together the letters of the Spanish word for computer (*máquina calculadora electrónica*) produces a figure nowhere near 666.[58] Of course, this may just mean that the Antichrist will be from either America or England. However, an even more serious drawback is in his second formula. The letter sigma, as any beginning Greek student knows, is not the sixth letter of the Greek alphabet. It is the eighteenth letter. The sixth letter is zeta. Van Impe's equation actually spells VIZA.

Currently, the most popular theory about the mark of the beast involves computer microchips. In the video *Satan's System: 666*, conservative Christian Terry Cook confidently warns that "there is a plan to number every person on the earth by means of injecting under their skin, in either their right hand or their forehead, a microchip."[59] Exactly how this device could be used was explained by radio talk show host Gary Null (WBAI, New York):

> [T]his implanted transponder I.D. chip would replace all currency. It would replace all credit cards. It would be a permanent form of identification. You would then not have to have a driver's license or a health card or a social security card or any form of identification. This implanted microchip alone would be all you would need to conduct all commerce. . . . [E]verywhere in our society there would be scanners which, when you needed to buy something . . . your hand would go through this scanner and it would automatically send [your data] to a local computer. . . . But let's say that you were not allowed to travel. Suppose you were considered to be a political liability. You would then be challenged. You could not purchase things. It would limit your ability to purchase anything. It would limit your ability to go anywhere. You couldn't travel on planes or on trains. You would not be allowed to travel across state highways because the highways would have

these scanners. And so, you would—unless you lived in a very narrow environment and didn't buy anything for yourself, and unless you lived in an underground situation—you would be constantly monitored for your entire life! In effect, you would be controlled.[60]

All of these notions may go hand in hand with patriot beliefs, but nothing in the Bible, either linguistically or grammatically, indicates that the mark of the beast in Revelation 13 is a *literal* mark on, or in, the skin. The Jews of the first century would have understood the reference to a mark in the hand or on the forehead as a *symbolic* identification "of loyalty, ownership, and heart-felt allegiance."[61] This symbolism also appears in Exodus 13:9, which reads: "And it shall serve as a sign to you on your hand, and as a reminder on your forehead, that the law of the LORD may be in your mouth; for with a powerful hand the LORD brought you out of Egypt."

The language used is Exodus is unmistakably similar to the wording used in Revelation. In context, the Old Testament verse is referring to a feast day of unleavened bread as being a symbolic way of showing commitment to God. The sign on the forehead refers to one's thoughts and attitudes. The sign on the hand refers to one's activity. Neither sign has anything to do with a computer microchip. John D. Hanna, professor of Historical Theology at Dallas Theological Seminary, makes an interesting observation concerning this passage:

> Like the Passover ([Exodus] 12:26–27), the Feast of Unleavened Bread had great educational value in the home (13:8-9). The feast was like a sign on their hand or forehead, that is, it was a continual reminder of God's mighty deliverance from Egypt.[62]

When we allow the Bible to interpret itself, it becomes clear that the mark in Revelation 13:16-18 is a *symbolic* representation of people who have turned their minds and actions over to beliefs that are against Christ (i.e., *anti*-Christ). The Revelation passage is addressing where a person's heartfelt allegiance lies. It has nothing to do with a literal mark, but rather a rejection of the Christian concept of God.

Patriots erroneously believe that microchips *must* be Satan's mark because to their minds only these technologically advanced products could accomplish the kind of socioeconomic tracking allegedly described in Revelation.[63] In reality, however, there have always been effective marks that could be placed on the forehead or in the hand (e.g., brands, tattoos). There is no reason to think that today's microchips are the 666 mark. An even more advanced "mark" will likely be discovered in 100 years (e.g., a *super*-chip the size of a human cell rather than a rice grain). Consequently, future generations will probably think that *their* version of our microchip is the beast's mark.

If Christian patriots were to objectively examine the evidence, they might discover that many of their fears are unfounded. There are no official plans to merge the United States into a one-world government, especially under the auspices of the United Nations. Although the U.N. is indeed a multinational organization, it is hardly an ultra-efficient, unstoppable, freedom-destroying machine. Its ineptitude has been well-documented. In fact, U.N. operations have consistently been hampered by poor planning, inadequate and incompetent forces, and complex political problems.[64] Also, the U.N. has for many years been on the brink of insolvency and faces chronic logistical restraints. In 1996, for instance, member nations owed the U.N. more than $2.3 billion, with the U.S. debt alone totaling more than $1 billion.[65]

The overall concept of a "New World Order" is not a revolutionary idea. In the wake of almost every upheaval, "a new generation hoped to be able to create a new international system to obtain everlasting peace and stability."[66] After every major war, people have tried to find a way to prevent further clashes. The end of the Napoleonic Wars saw the major states of that era meet at the Congress of Vienna (1815) in hopes of creating a new balance of power that would preserve the peace.[67] A similar attempt was made after World War I when Woodrow Wilson proposed the ill-fated League of Nations. Wilson based his concept on the phrase, "Every people has a right to choose the sovereignty under which they shall live."[68] This is what the United States and other free countries are trying to achieve through the U.N.

Although *some* secular humanists, New Agers, and globalists might want the U.N. to develop into a world government, they are in no position to compel its member states to surrender their cherished sovereignty. Government and military leaders see a *sovereign* U.S. participating in the NWO as a leader of nations trying to create a peaceful environment. According to a 1992 report by the federally funded RAND Institute, the NWO will be an era "in which the United States, to guarantee *its own stability* and security, must promote international stability and security as well."[69]

A careful study of history might also reveal to Christian patriots that the basic themes underlying their conspiracy theories about the New World Order are traceable "to longstanding anti-Semitic ideologies dating back to the nineteenth century."[70] As Kenneth Stern of the American Jewish Committee says, "The anti-government conspiracy theories that fuel this movement use rewrites of anti-Semitic theories, but with the government replacing 'Jews.' "[71] This fact is easily seen as one explores the origins of today's patriot/militia movement.

FROM RACISM TO PATRIOTISM

The origins of the patriot movement are inseparably interwoven with the violent Christian Identity Movement (CIM), which is not *Christian* at all. It is, in reality, a quasi-underground community of religiously-inclined white supremacists that coalesced as non-Christian racists defected from mainstream Christianity in the early 1940s. Even a cursory look at their violent lifestyle and hate-filled rhetoric reveals that they are far removed from biblical principles (1 John 4:7–8, 20). Furthermore, CIM believers advocate prejudice, which Christianity condemns (Rom. 10:12, Gal 3:28). Religion expert J. Gordon Melton refers to the nationwide collection of 20,000–50,000 bigots as a belief system "by sociopaths, for sociopaths. It turns their sickness into virtue."[72]

Understanding the beliefs of today's religiously inclined white supremacists is important because long before today's militias, CIM followers such as Identity preacher Pete Peters, former KKK Grand Dragon Louis Beam, and Aryan Nations founder Richard Butler were calling themselves "patriots." An Aryan Nations newsletter (c. 1982), for instance, lists Butler along with racist leaders Dan Gaymen and Bob Miles as "Christian patriots." Several racist fundraising letters from the 1980s, such as those produced by KKK Grand Wizard Don Black, were addressed to fellow "White Patriots."[73] By the

1980s, these white "patriots" were even forming paramilitary groups similar to militias.

Identity rests on a misidentification of the Israelites mentioned in the Bible's Old Testament. Contrary to historical fact, which identifies modern-day Jews as descendants of the twelve tribes of Israel mentioned in Scripture, CIM theology claims that the Israelites were actually Anglo-Saxons. The correlative doctrine is that today's Anglo-Saxons are the *real* descendants of Abraham, Isaac and Jacob, and as such, are God's chosen people.

What of the Jews? Most Identity followers believe that Jewish people were the eventual byproduct of a sexual union between Eve and "the serpent" (Gen. 3), which is usually identified as either Satan in human form, or a demonic representative manifested in human flesh. This teaching — known as the "Serpent Seed" doctrine — asserts that Cain and Abel were only half brothers.[74] Cain was conceived by Eve and Satan, while Abel was conceived by Eve and Adam. It is claimed that Cain then sired the Jews by intermarrying with non-white races known as "mud people" or "beasts of the field."

These life forms were created before Adam and Eve, who were allegedly the first white people.[75] Identity leader Bertrand Comparet comments: "God had millions of the pre-Adamic Asiatic and African peoples around. . . . Adam and Eve were supposed NOT to intermingle with these people. . . . [T]he Satanic blood line crept in, definitely, with Cain.[76] As neo-Nazi Richard Butler says, "[T]here are literal children of Satan in the world today . . . the descendants of Cain, who was the result of Eve's original sin."[77]

In the CIM, then, Satan's antagonism toward God began with the seduction of Eve. His second affront was the murder of Abel. The Devil struck a third time when Cain tainted the blood lines of pre-Adamic races, resulting in the creation of the satanic Jew. Satan's fourth diabolical act occurred when the Jewish/Satanic race crucified Christ, who, according to Identity beliefs, was non-Semitic, a "white man."

The latest strategy of the Prince of Darkness is to govern the entire world by corrupting God's holy race of whites with the blood of pre-Adamic "beasts." This plan is supposedly being accomplished through racial integration. A publication from the neo-Nazi Aryan Nations group explains:

> Jews seek to wipe us out as a race. . . . HOW? By mongrelizing us via miscege-

nation [interbreeding] with colored races of the world, especially the Congoloid blacks . . . "beasts of the earth" of Genesis 1:25.[78]

This is one reason why influential Identity preacher Pete Peters teaches that races should never intermarry. The strength of Peters' convictions about "racial treason" is evident in the way he instructs his children about mixed marriages: "I teach them also that if they ever did such a thing — never to come around my house with their mate or their half-breed children because they've been traitors to their own sires."[79]

Louis Beam, one of Identity's most powerful leaders, agrees: "Racial treason is the greatest crime a member of our race can commit, for from its end results there is no recovery." According to white supremacist David Tate, "God loves a sinner but hates a race traitor!"[80] Aryan Nations founder Richard Butler states, "[O]ur greatest enemies are the race traitors in our ranks."[81] These sentiments are echoed in the words of David Lane, who was convicted in 1987 for driving the getaway car used by the murderers of Jewish talk show host Alan Berg:

> Anyone who supports a multi-racial religion, or state, financially, verbally, or even by passive acceptance, commits Race-treason. Such a person could just as well go out and machine gun White children, because the effect on the Race is the same. . . [T]he machine gun would be far more humane than the future that faces White children, if we are not successful.[82]

As previously stated, CIM eschatology holds that the federal government — supposedly under Jewish control — must collapse in order to bring about a race war (Armageddon). Out of this conflict God's Aryan kingdom will emerge. But until the early 1990s, CIM followers had neither the strength nor the funds to destabilize the federal administration. As racist Michael Hansen stated in 1982, "We are both OUTNUMBERED AND OUTGUNNED" (caps in original).[83]

A solution to this dilemma presented itself in the early 1990s when white supremacists realized that public dissatisfaction with the political establishment had created a vast, untapped source of soldiers for their long-desired overthrow of the government: discontented *non*-racists. The plan

credit: Craig Buck

Aryan Nations founder Richard Butler posing at his white supremacist enclave in Hayden Lake, Idaho. Butler, like other influential "Christian Identity" preachers, believes that Armageddon will be the result of a race war through which God's chosen people (i.e., Caucasians) will once and for all destroy Satan's army of Blacks and Jews.

entailed using millions of non-racists to form a unified revolt. To achieve their goal, white supremacists/anti-Semites either joined or formed "patriot" groups and militias, stirred up anti-government sentiments, and spread conspiracy theories about the New World Order.

Montana Human Rights Network president Ken Toole comments, "With the Brady Bill it was like someone poured jet fuel on the movement. Overnight we saw all this militia stuff bleed right out of the white supremacists who had been pushing the idea for years and engulf entire communities."[84] Bruce Hoffman — a former terrorism expert with the RAND Corporation — agrees that there has been an evolution in recruiting efforts of racist/anti-Semitic groups:

> [They began] to bring in militant tax resisters, anti-abortion advocates, the anti-gun control movement, opponents of government intervention . . . . They also

plugged into communities with particular problems, such as the Farm Belt during its economic plight. Since the 1980s, these radical right-wing movements have been constantly reinventing themselves to appeal to new and more diverse constituencies."[85]

Hoping for mass appeal, CIM members avoided public discussion of their more radical beliefs and couched their beliefs in more acceptable terms, hiding their bigotry to "present a sanitized image to the public and attract new recruits."[86] Instead of attacking Jews and Blacks, the federal government and promoters of the New World Order were targeted. Thus began today's patriot movement.

THE NEW MILITIAS

The impetus for many of today's militias can be traced to the August 1992 Ruby Ridge shootings involving Randy Weaver, an Idaho white supremacist charged with selling two sawed-off shotguns to undercover FBI agents. Weaver had failed to show up for a trial, which prompted authorities to conduct surveillance on his property. When the intruding lawmen were discovered, a gun battle ensued, killing Weaver's teenage son and a federal marshal. The eleven-day siege that followed ended with Weaver surrendering after seeing his wife shot and killed by a federal agent. Although Weaver was eventually convicted of failing to appear in court, he was acquitted of the original weapons violation and the marshal's murder.

In late October of that year, between one hundred fifty and one hundred seventy-five men convened in Estes Park, Colorado, to discuss how to respond to the government's actions against the Weaver family. This meeting was reportedly a "Christian" men's conference, but attendees were hardly representative of American churches. Presiding over the event was influential CIM pastor Pete Peters. Other racists present included Louis Beam, Richard Butler, Montana anti-Semitic tax protester M. J. "Red" Beckman, and Kirk Lyons (a renowned attorney for the KKK).[87]

Retired Virginia legislator Larry Pratt (Gun Owners of America director) was also present. He seems to have been one of the first individuals to publicly call for citizens to form armed militias. Although Pratt's racist audience heartily endorsed his idea, it did not catch on with a wider public until after the tragic 1993 raid by the Bureau of Alcohol, Tobacco and Firearms on the Branch Davidian religious commune and the subsequent siege that ended with the tragic deaths of nearly 100 cultists.

White supremacists soon began using both Ruby Ridge and Waco to illustrate why *all* citizens needed to form militias. Private armies, they said, were the only means of protection against America's "tyrannical" government. Many citizens agreed and echoed the call for militias. Missouri State Highway Patrol Superintendent Fred Mills testified before a 1995 Senate Subcommittee hearing that this was how the militant arm of the patriot movement was born.[88]

Although the white supremacists do not openly disclose their views to the general patriot community, they are completely frank with one another. Racist literature consistently refers to the New World Order as the Jew World Order.[89] Neo-Nazi William Pierce bluntly informs Internet surfers at his Web site that "if accuracy were the primary consideration," the coming one-world government "might be given the name Jew World Order instead of the one by which it is commonly known." Pierce believes that in order to achieve Aryan victory, the only feasible strategy is for racists "to develop our own media of mass communication and then use those media to make everyone painfully aware of the true meaning of the New World Order."[90]

According to political science professor Michael Barkun of Syracuse University, the conspiratorial theories upon which the patriot/militia movement is built fit very nicely into the theological framework of the Identity faith:

> Every purported conspiracy and cabal, whether of international bankers, Trilateralists or the U.N., can be brought within Identity's "great conspiracy" — Satan's plot to take over the world and deprive "Aryans" of their birthright, a plot that Identity believes began in the Garden of Eden and will end only at Armageddon. Plot can be nested in plot, in an ascending pyramid of conspiracies that ends with the devil himself.[91]

By propagating and encouraging such conspiracy theories within the movement, Identity adherents have stirred up hatred for the government, which they hope will galvanize discontented masses into a force able to topple the evil Jewish regime. A number of white supremacists have already worked their way in among patriots, and are influencing the thoughts and beliefs of non-racists, including mainstream Christians. In doing so, white supremacists have created an elaborate maze of racists and non-racists who share a similar conspiratorial worldview.[92]

The Christian community had been especially vulnerable to racist-fueled paranoia about the government because a number of evangelical leaders have not taken the time to investigate their sources of information. They are convinced that the end is near, the Antichrist is alive, and that the federal government is somehow linked to the whole end-time prophetic scenario. From such thinking has arisen one of the more disturbing aspects of the patriot movement: some Christians are endorsing, sharing public platforms with, and even quoting neo-Nazis, anti-Semites, and other racists in an effort to support their view of the end-times and their conspiracy theories. Vast numbers of evangelicals have embraced the unsubstantiated NWO conspiracy theory as biblical fact, not realizing that many of their favorite prophecy teachers have gleaned information about the conspiracy from anti-Semites/white supremacists.

INFILTRATION OF HATE

A shared preoccupation with the end-times is but one of several reasons why some Christians have allied themselves, often unknowingly, with racists. Two more prominent reasons for such an odd partnership are as follows: 1) within the evangelical community, strong anti-government rhetoric has become the standard mode of expressing indignation against the liberal establishment; and 2) many Christian leaders are accepting without hesitation anyone who appears to be a like-minded government-basher.

In early 1996, for instance, white supremacist Pete Peters invited church leaders of all faiths to his "Israel Identity" gathering at the YMCA camp near Estes Park, Colorado. According to Peters, the conference featuring various patriot and anti-Semitic speakers was organized by leaders of Baptist, Lutheran, Episcopal and Catholic churches. "There is a teaching spreading from church to church, silently crossing denominational lines," Peters proclaimed in the conference brochure. "It is rapidly being embraced in patriot groups and conservative movements through the land."[93]

Pat Robertson: Fishing in Dirty Waters

One of the most influential Christian personalities is Pat Robertson, founder of the Christian Broadcasting Network (CBN) and host of that network's popular *700 Club* program. The media began associating Robertson with patriots after the release of his 1991 book, *The New World Order*, which successfully introduced patriot conspiracy theories to a wide audience. Unfortunately, the book draws information from some of the same sources used by racists to support their anti-Semitic worldview; namely, Nesta Webster and Eustace Mullins.

On pages 71, 72, and 180 of *The New World Order*, Robertson favorably refers to and quotes Webster's *World Revolution* and *Secret Societies and Subversive Movements*. He even includes the latter volume in his bibliography with no qualifier regarding its content. Both works portray Jews as the evil conspirators behind humanity's woes.[94] *Secret Societies and Subversive Movements*, which includes such chapters such as "The Jewish Cabalists" and "The Real Jewish Peril," is so blatantly anti-Semitic that it is featured in the 1995 resource catalog of the neo-Nazi Sons of Liberty organization as a work exposing the "Jewish founders of secret societies and their inner workings."[95]

Webster believed that Jews were behind all of the revolutionary movements of the eighteenth and nineteenth centuries. She apparently came to this conclusion after discovering her true identity as "the reincarnation of a countess who had been executed in the French Revolution and was convinced it was her duty in this lifetime to expose the secret societies who had plotted the 1789 uprising."[96]

Eustace Mullins, a Christian Identity believer, is even more notorious for racism than Webster. His books also take prominence in the aforementioned neo-Nazi catalog from the Sons of Liberty.[97] He brazenly blames international Jewish bankers for the world's evils and imputes all of

America's troubles, including rising medical costs and its health care system difficulties, to the Jews.[98]

Mullins' beliefs came from the poet Ezra Pound, a staunch anti-Semite who, according to a 1982 *Aryan Nations Newsletter*, was "a great admirer of Adolf Hitler and Mussolini."[99] In fact, Pound worked as a propagandist for the Axis powers during World War II. After the war he was declared criminally insane and imprisoned in St. Elizabeth's Hospital in Washington, D.C. Mullins has boasted on shortwave radio about visiting Pound "every day for three years," saying that Pound lectured him on world history. Mullins admits: "That's how I found out what I know."[100]

Mullins' perspective of the NWO is perhaps most apparent in the epilogue he wrote for the anti-Semitic booklet *The World's Trouble Makers* by Bruce Brown, which viciously attacks Jews and paints Adolf Hitler as a misunderstood hero. Ironically, the epilogue condemns Pat Robertson because he advocates loving the Jews. Mullins actually puts Robertson into the NWO conspiracy! According to Mullins, Robertson is a pawn of the Jews, and CBN is nothing but a Jewish-controlled vehicle through which pro-Jewish sentiments are espoused.[101]

To date, Robertson has not repudiated his use of Webster or Mullins. Nor has he eliminated references to their works from subsequent printings of *The New World Order*, even though the *New York Times* and other notable publications have brought their anti-Semitism to his attention. Jerome R. Chanes, in his book *Anti-Semitism in America Today*, notes that although Robertson may not be an anti-Semite, he "chose to fish in some very dirty waters."[102]

It should also be noted that Robertson, like many other prophecy-obsessed evangelicals, has made one doomsday prediction after another. His earliest prognostications date back to the 1980s when he all but guaranteed that the Tribulation would start by 1982 due to a Russian invasion of Israel: "All available economic and military intelligence pinpoints 1982 as the optimum time for such a Soviet strike."[103] He even tied the event to one of Hal Lindsey's doomsday signs — the Jupiter Effect.[104]

Robertson additionally preaches the forty-year generation theory and, like Hal Lindsey, points to 1967 as the year when God's prophetic clock began ticking. His newest date for earth's destruction, therefore, is 2007. This date was suggested in his 1990 book *The New Millennium*:

> Four hundred years from the beginning of America — ten full biblical generations — takes place on April 29, 2007. . . . Could this be a time of collapse of the Gentile powers? [T]his scenario is fascinating to contemplate.[105]

Coincidentally, 2007 minus seven years (tribulation) equals 2000, which is the same year that patriots believe the New World Order will be established under the Antichrist.

Chuck Missler: From Astrology to UFOs

Idaho Bible teacher Chuck Missler is one of the most eclectic prophecy teachers in the Christian community. He not only appeals to the Bible, but favorably refers to occult forms of divination including a Christianized version of astrology, numerology, and pyramidology.[106] Missler is also a bridge between mainstream Christianity and the patriot/militia movement. His *Personal Update* newsletter has carried several articles promoting the NWO conspiracy theory.

Missler believes that America is no longer in a contest between the Democrats and Republicans, but is in a death struggle between "the Constitutionalists . . . and the global socialists who are pursuing the dream of the New World Order."[107] He even suggested in his July 1995 issue of *Personal Update* that the government blew up the federal building in Oklahoma City.[108] He also asserts that many of "the most knowledgeable" Bible commentators believe the Antichrist may be alive today.[109] This demonic world leader, says Missler, will be even more deceitful "than the politicians who presently dominate the District of Corruption" (i.e., Washington *D. C.*).[110]

Use of such biting references to America's capital city is common among patriots. An article in the popular patriot magazine *Media Bypass* reads: "The mindset in the 'District of Corruption' appears appalled by the resentment of 'we the people' toward the federal government."[111] Of course, Missler draws his information from sources other than patriot magazines. The November 1995 issue of *Personal Update*, for example, not only quotes from, but expresses thanks to and gives the addresses of, the "American Patriot Fax Network . . . and 'The Spotlight.' "[112] Both resources are tied directly to the white supremacist/anti-Semitic community.

The American Patriot Fax Network was co-founded by Gary Hunt, whose name first surfaced during the Branch Davidian siege when he showed up in Waco, claiming to hold Koresh's power of attorney. His network began when he started faxing information around the country to several like-minded patriots. He soon became connected to numerous fax "news" services run by white supremacists and CIM believers. Although the network has since branched out to include non-racist patriots and conservative Christians, it still sends out a steady stream of hate literature.

A 1995 *Los Angeles Times* investigation found that several racist groups belong to the Patriot Fax Network and consistently supply information to it. They include: the Arizona Patriots, a militant CIM group; Guardians of American Liberty, led by Stewart Webb, who made a series of threatening anti-Semitic phone calls from the mid-1980s to the 1990s; and CIM leader James Wickstrom, who in 1984 was convicted on two counts of impersonating a public official and one count of jumping bail.[113]

Missler's use of information from *Spotlight* and his between-the-lines endorsement of it as a reputable news resource is even more disturbing. Besides being factually unreliable, *Spotlight* is notorious for racist articles and advertisements. A survey of its articles from January 1994 – June 1995 reveals that the publication's main purpose is not only to propagate NWO conspiracy theories, but link them to Jews.[114]

Missler is not a racist. Nor is he anti-Semitic. In fact, he is an outspoken supporter of Israel. Nevertheless, he has used white supremacist sources in his attempts to find news that supports his end-time views. Why? Missler's official response to those who criticized him for citing *Spotlight* was given during a February 14, 1997 lecture at Calvary Chapel of Costa Mesa, California. He claimed that it was nothing more than a printing blunder caused by a hurried schedule:

> I was racing for a deadline, I needed a quote from Presidential Directive #25 (PDD #25), and I took it from a newsletter — among several on my desk — called the *Spotlight*. . . . I put *Spotlight* [in *Personal Update*], not being sensitive to the fact

that the *Spotlight* is known in the publication circles as having some anti-Semitic tendencies.[115]

Contrary to this statement, *Spotlight* is not known merely in publication circles as having *some* anti-Semitic *tendencies*. The periodical, produced by the quasi-Nazi Liberty Lobby, is widely known as the major source of rabidly anti-Semitic propaganda in America.[116]

Missler's inaccurate assessment of *Spotlight's* racist reputation is only one example of many erroneous statements he has made over the years. During one lecture, for instance, he implied that the 1994 federal Crime Bill's inclusion of a request to hire former Asian police officers was part of a New World Order conspiracy to turn America into a dictatorial police state.[117] This accusation reflects the charges made in various patriot publications like the *Free American*, which in 1994 asked: "Why Royal Hong Kong Police officers in particular? Could it be because the British control of illegal drugs, through the Royal Institute of International Affairs (the controlling agency for the Council on Foreign Relations), has always been through Hong Kong?"[118]

The truth is not as nefarious as Missler and his patriot following might want to believe. The request for Asian officers in the U.S. is linked to a new form of heroin called China White that is being imported to America by "secret Chinese criminal societies based in Hong Kong."[119] The government faces several difficult problems in its war against this particular drug because the drug dealers do not speak China's national language (Mandarin) when trafficking their contraband. They speak four distinctly different dialects.[120] U.S. law enforcement officials believed that hiring Asian policemen could help them overcome this problem. It had nothing to do with turning America into a police state, the New World Order, or the U.N.[121] All of this is now a moot point, though, since the whole recruitment plan ended up being dropped from the final version of the Crime Bill.[122]

Another inaccuracy by Missler appeared in his 1995 article citing *Spotlight*. He claimed that Presidential Directive #25 (PDD #25) "states that during times of national emergency, complete command and control of the U.S. Military would pass from the President to the U.N."[123] The document, however, says nothing about placing U.S. military personnel under "complete command and control" of the U.N. during a national emergency. In fact, it says the very opposite! PDD #25 deals with *peace-keeping* activities of U.S. forces (no mention is made of a national emergency in America). It also provides for changes to U.S. policy that will bring *more*, not less, stringent criteria for participation in peacekeeping activities. It reads: "The policy directive underscores the fact that the President will never relinquish command of U.S. forces."[124]

Missler misinterprets not only government documents, but statistics regarding world affairs. He is especially prone to do so when the inaccuracies reinforce the perception that either a one-world government and/or Armageddon lies just ahead. During a 1994 Prophecy Update lecture, for example, he told his audience that there are "over thirteen third world countries that have nuclear capability and there's twenty-three of them that are building Intercontinental Ballistic Missiles." Missler added: "There are about 45,000 warheads in the Soviet arsenal, many of which are finding their way to the black market. [Iranian president] Rafsanjani has purchased at least seven of these."[125]

In 1994, however, only eleven countries (Britain, France, Russia, China, India, Israel, Pakistan, the United States, the Ukraine, Belarus, and Kazakhstan) possessed nuclear weapons, and three of these nations (the Ukraine, Belarus, and Kazakhstan) had agreed to destroy their arsenal. One nation remains on the threshold of nuclear capability (North Korea), two more countries (Iran and Iraq) are actively pursuing development of nuclear weapons, and eight nations have the potential for nuclear devices (Germany, Poland, Algeria, Libya, Egypt, South Korea, Taiwan, and Japan).[126]

Regarding Iran and the weapons black market, the U.S. Department of Defense reported in 1994 that "[n]o bombs or other warheads are known to have leaked out of the former Soviet Union."[127] Furthermore, Missler's "45,000 warheads" figure is not only inflated, but impossible to verify. The fact is that no one really knows how many warheads remain in the former Soviet stockpile. In 1994 the official U.S. government estimate was a "ballpark figure" of 19,000. Outside experts, such as Bruce Blair of Washington's Brookings Institution, stated that Russia's tactical nuclear stockpiles "could hold as many as 43,000 warheads."[128] Missler apparently preferred this higher number for its shock value, then rounded it up to 45,000.

A final aspect of Missler's prophetic view of the end-times that must be mentioned is his preoccupation with UFOs. He believes that UFO occupants are actually demonic spirits invading our earthly dimension in hopes of creating a hybrid race via sexual intercourse with women (and possibly men). These inter-dimensional angels of darkness have supposedly committed such despicable acts in the past. Missler contends that Genesis 6:1–4 clearly describes fallen angels ("Sons of God") taking women ("daughters of men") as wives in order to produce a race of giants called *Nephilim* (Hebrew for "mighty ones").[129] Missler comes to a predictable conclusion: "I expect the Antichrist, when he shows up, to be either an alien or connected with one."[130]

Missler says his theory is based on solid biblical interpretation: "[T]he term used for the Sons of God' is $b^e n\hat{e}$ *'Elohîm*, which is a term in the Hebrew that in the Old Testament is consistently used of angels, and is never used otherwise."[131] He additionally asserts that other interpretations of the verse are worthy of immediate dismissal because they come from "liberal theological circles."[132] But once again, Missler does not have his facts straight. The term $b^e n\hat{e}$ *'Elohîm* is not used exclusively of angels in the Old Testament. Similar phraseology appears in Deuteronomy 32:5, Psalm 73:15, 82:6, and Hosea 1:10 to describe righteous humans who follow God.[133] Furthermore, an equivalent phrase in Greek that appears in the New Testament refers not to angels, but to Adam (Luke 3:38).[134]

Regarding his suggestion that only *liberals* adopt alternate views, it was Jesus Christ himself who stated in the New Testament that angels do not marry (Matthew 32:30). Furthermore, numerous conservative Christians reject the "Genesis 6 = angels" theory in favor of more biblically sound interpretations.[135] These arguments, however, do not faze Missler, who continues to declare that the world scene "is rapidly being set for the final climax"[136] and that "we are rapidly being plunged into the climax of all human history,"[137] complete with UFOs and alien encounters.

For devotees who might be tempted to seek out contrary opinions or verify his information, Missler gives an ominous warning: "Our schools, our scientific establishment, our media, and our government are all lying to us."[138]

Don McAlvany: Intelligence Advisor?

Christian economist and New World Order conspiracy-buster Don McAlvany seems to think that the destruction of America has already occurred.

"This is not the America we grew up in," warns McAlvany. "Welcome to the USSA, a branch of the New World Order."[139] Through his monthly *McAlvany Intelligence Advisor* newsletter (*MIA*), McAlvany incessantly focuses on a future when thousands of Christians will be imprisoned under false charges of "hate, environmental, financial, or gun control 'crimes.' "[140] He claims that the Branch Davidian disaster was a declaration of "open season on non-mainstream (non-government approved) religious minorities" and further warns that many small Christian churches, communities, and groups will soon be reclassified as cults so the feds can do away with them.[141]

Like Missler, McAlvany gets his New World Order exposing information from racist as well as non-racist sources. *MIA* has quoted Christian Identity patriot Bo Gritz, *Spotlight*, and Eustace Mullins.[142] McAlvany has even recommended Mullins' book *Murder by Injection* which is featured in neo-Nazi catalogues.[143] *MIA* is full of anti-government propaganda, unsubstantiated rumor, misinformation, and faulty speculation about the NWO. For example, in the newsletter's July 1995 issue, under the subheading "POLICE STATE BRIEFS," a story appeared that probably alarmed many Christians:

> SWAT teams from several Idaho police departments participated in a practice raid on the Community Presbyterian Church in Post Falls. Captain Travis Chaney of the Kootenai County Sheriff's Department said the SWAT teams' goal is "to provide a controlled, measured response to critical incidents . . . to successfully resolve threats to public safety."[144]

The news blurb is followed by an editorial note that seems purposefully constructed to stir up paranoia: "Why would a SWAT team practice a forced armed entry of a church? Are Bible believers a 'threat to public safety'?" The answers to these leading questions are far less insidious than he intimates. During an interview with Jennifer Chapman — secretary of the Community Presbyterian Church of Post Falls — I was informed that the church used by police had become vacant and condemned and was subsequently given to authorities by the congregation. Church members who had been blessed with a new house of worship simply wanted to pass along their good fortune to local law enforcement. "There was nothing anti-Christian about it," Chapman said. "They were just going to tear the [old] building down, so we let them [the police] have it to practice raids in and train their dogs to search for drugs. There's nothing to it."[145]

This story is not the only example of McAlvany's faulty "intelligence" gathering. In reference to the Branch Davidian incident, he announced that "Operation Waco was the beginning of religious persecution of unpopular, non-mainstream religious groups in America.... [T]he attacks will now begin to accelerate."[146] To prove his assertion, McAlvany repeated the patriot claim that there was no child abuse occurring at the commune and that the Davidians were previously cleared of such allegations by Texas authorities. His July 1993 issue of *MIA* reads: "Dr. Bruce Perry, the psychiatrist heading the team treating the 21 children who left the compound, said . . . that '*none of the 21 children had been sexually abused or molested.*" McAlvany concludes: "The facts seem to vary from the Clintonista version."[147]

But the facts vary from McAlvany's version. According to Perry, the youngsters were definitely "being raised in an abusive setting. Ranch Apocalypse, by 1992 and through 1993, was clearly a psychologically destructive environment for children."[148] The testimony of several children confirm that abuse was indeed occurring.[149] Some of the worst child abuse involved harsh corporal punishment inflicted on children as young as eight months old. The beatings occasionally lasted for up to forty-five minutes, or until the child's buttocks bled. Several witnesses have confirmed this abuse.[150]

Regarding the child abuse investigation by Texas authorities, documents and eyewitness testimony reveal that the Branch Davidians were not exonerated of child abuse charges. According to Joyce Sparks, former Children Protection Services investigative supervisor of the Branch Davidian case, officials were *forced* to close the 1992 probe due to uncooperative Davidians and legal red tape.[151]

Like all expert propagandists, McAlvany fails to mention those facts that contradict his assertions. He also makes use of excessively harsh language that fuels the anger of his readers. For example, he has often called the Clinton administration the "Clintonistas."[152] This obvious wordplay refers to the Sandinistas, the Nicaraguan Marxist political party. In response to a relatively benign comment by Senator Newt Gingrich about limited government, McAlvany remarked: "That statement wouldn't have sounded out of place if Hitler, Castro or Stalin had said it."[153] McAlvany is equally sensationalistic in calling law enforcement agencies America's "Gestapo."[154]

As with other end-time teachers, McAlvany routinely hangs imminent doom and destruction over the heads of those who look to him for counsel about the future. At a 1996 "Steeling the Mind of America" conference held in Colorado, McAlvany made several statements that placed catastrophe in the road:

> Watch Red China right now. They are in a new alliance with Russia. They are arming like Japan was and like Nazi Germany were [sic] in the 1930s, and we will fight Red China in the next five, to ten, to fifteen years if Jesus Christ doesn't return before that, or maybe it will all be part of the Armageddon scenario. . . . We're talking about the New World Order. We're talking about the part that the Russians will play in the New World Order. They will end up dominating the New World Order. . . . [The Russians] have seduced America and the West into disarming while massively arming themselves in preparation for war in the latter part of the 1990s, maybe in the early part of the next decade.[155]

McAlvany's answer to safeguarding one's life and family against the tyrannical regime in power, the coming persecution of Christians, the soon-to-emerge Antichrist, the NWO, and imminent wars is conveniently self-serving. In nearly every issue of *MIA*, he strongly urges readers to buy gold and silver from International Collectors Associates (ICA)[156] — his gold, silver, and rare coin brokerage "specializing in precious metals and other conservative investments."[157] Gold and silver, he says, "should be aggressively accumulated up to 35% percent of a total investment portfolio."[158] In one issue he claims that buying precious metals is an "insurance policy against the despotic, socialistic, people controlling New World Order oriented actions."[159]

McAlvany has been ICA's president/owner since 1972. This makes for a lucrative, self-perpetuating cycle that begins with *MIA*:[160] 1) warn readers of the coming New World Order; 2) identify precious metals as the chief, practical hope of survival; 3) sell precious metals to frightened subscribers; 4) use the profits to spread more NWO conspiracy theories and induce more panic; and 5) gain more gold/silver customers.

McAlvany also recommends that people move to towns with less than 15,000 inhabitants, take their children out of the public school system, and store one to two years of freeze-dried food per person, as well as "several hundred (or thousand) pounds of staple grains."[161] He declares, "If one understands the times in which we live . . . one will have at least a one-year supply of dehydrated food reserves for each member of the family."[162] This food storage advice stems from McAlvany's feeling that all Bible-believing Christians "may have to go 'underground' in the next 2 to 5 years."[163]

He made this latter speculation to 1,200 attendees of a 1993 prophecy conference sponsored by Chuck Missler.[164] For the convenience of those present, as well as for readers of *MIA*, McAlvany's ICA "offers several long-term food storage systems" containing "an assortment of easy-to-cook entrees, grains, vegetables, fruits and side dishes."[165] McAlvany's "top of the line" one-year plan, which contains three meals a day for one person, costs $2,513.[166] This means McAlvany can make more than $10,000 from every family of four that follows his counsel.

Texe Marrs: The Conspiracy King

According to Texe Marrs, who may be the conspiracy king of all prophecy teachers, the world is ruled by "ten unseen men" controlling the Council on Foreign Relations, Trilateral Commission, CIA, Russian KGB, British Intelligence, Freemasonry, and most of America's elected government officials.[167] "[T]here *is* a World Conspiracy by a hidden elite," Marrs contends. "All the evidence is there — mountains of evidence. No other conclusion is possible. . . . *It is for real.*"[168]

This is only the tip of Marrs's conspiratorial iceberg. His list of "Devil Companies," "Devil Products," and "Devil Logos" includes: 1) Lucent

Technologies, formerly AT&T's Bell Labs, which Marrs says has occult overtones (the name "Lucent" may even be short for "*Luc*ifer's *Ent*erprises"); 2) Reebok; 3) Honeywell; 4) Microsoft; 5) America Online; 6) Saturn automobiles, which has a logo that Marrs says looks like a "crossed horn"; and 7) Nabisco, which has a logo that looks to Marrs as if it may be the "Masonic phallic symbol of fertility."[169] Even Apple computers has been attacked by Marrs, who suggests that its logo — "an apple that has a bite taken out of it" — may signify Adam and Eve's eating of the forbidden fruit![170]

In the November 1997 issue of *Flashpoint*, Marrs went so far as to build a conspiracy around the tragic death of Princess Diana. He actually drew a parallel between her popularity and how the ancient Ephesians viewed the goddess Diana. According to Marrs, Princess Diana's fame amounts to the widespread worship of a "heavenly Queen right here on planet earth"[171] He then ties her death into a possible murder plot, raising suspicion against American CIA, British Intelligence, Scotland Yard, the Israeli Mossad, the French Secret Service, Interpol, and even the Royals themselves.

Unbelievably, Marrs goes on to link all of these groups to a secret plan by the mysterious Illuminati to kill Diana and crown her son — Prince William — as king. Marrs caps off his tasteless theory by questioning whether William could be the coming Antichrist. He presents all of his data in a $7 audiotape titled *The Cult of Diana: Was There a Plot to Murder the Princess of Wales?*, an ad for which reads as follows:

> What shall become of prince William, heir to the throne? Young, handsome, the future of the Prince is now energized by the charisma of his late mother and the devotion paid to her by her worshippers and admirers around the globe. . . . Could his royal highness, William . . . someday be universally acclaimed as Prince of Wales *and* the entire planet earth, defender and god of all faiths, and protector of the image of his beloved mother? In sum: the Antichrist and Beast?[172]

There seems to be no conspiracy that Marrs does not "expose" through his Texas-based Living Truth Ministries, which supposedly is "100% patriotic and 100% pro-God."[173] He sees nearly all political/religious leaders, as well as almost every major political/religious organization, as part of "the international banking conspiracy" that is rushing us toward the establishment of a New World Order.[174] Those disagreeing with Marrs are summarily dismissed by him as either "ignorant" or "stupid."[176]

He markets his conspiracy materials through a monthly newsletter called *Flashpoint*, which he claims has a yearly budget of $700,000.[179] Marrs' NWO enemy list includes, but is certainly not limited to, the Illuminati, Freemasonry, Catholicism, the Pope, Billy Graham, Pat Robertson, Robert Schuller, Oliver North, Oral Roberts, Democrats and Republicans, the U.N., the Russians, the Germans, the Turks, the Chinese, and the Anti-Defamation League of B'nai B'rith.[177]

In one of his videos, Marrs reveals plans for a 208,000-man "Gestapo brigade" strike force to be used by the federal government "to assault and conquer dissenters."[178] In another tape titled *Concentration Camps in America*, Marrs asserts that there exist NWO-related crematoriums, foreign troops, concentration camps and human tracking systems.[179] This tape also provides information on the government's "top secret, operational plan to identify, arrest, categorize, imprison, and put to death dissenters to the New World Order."[180]

Under the guise of Christianity Marrs claims:

- "Hillary and Bill [Clinton] have surrounded themselves with the most wicked and demon-possessed people imaginable."[181]

- "[Clinton is] a heartless, New Age occultist — an occultist who has relentlessly used the full resources of the White House to slander, defame, persecute, and kill true Christians and American patriots."[182]

- "Is President Bill Clinton a practicing Satan worshipper? . . . [Are the Clintons] demonically charged to perform hideous and barbaric acts unimaginable to decent and trusting Americans? What are the true religious beliefs of Bill and Hillary Clinton? Are they lovers of the Father of Lies—Lucifer himself? Order this exclusive Special Report. . . . [Y]ou may just conclude that Bill and Hillary Clinton are the most wicked, witchcraft-evil couple ever to reside at 1600 Pennsylvania Avenue!"[183]

- "Arrogant and anti-Christian lesbians, homosexuals, and pedophile advocates now hold the reigns of political power, and the 'D.C' in Washington D.C. has become the 'District of Corruption.' "[184]

It is not surprising that he is often recommended by patriots such as Jack McLamb, who in *Operation Vampire Killer 2000*, refers to Marrs's *Flashpoint* as a "very good source" for the religious aspects of the "NWO con-job."[185] Racist preacher Pete Peters featured a large advertisement in his newsletter for Marrs's book, *Big Sister is Watching You*. Peters said the volume "unmasks the coven of brutally correct women who now rule over us. Hillary's regiment of hardened, militant feminists include lesbians, sex perverts, child molester advocates, Christian haters, and the most doctrinaire of communists."[186] This book struck such a positive chord with Identity believers that "Texe was a guest on Pastor Peters's Truth for the Times television program."[187]

Marrs also sells the anti-NWO book *ChequeMate: The Game of Princes* by Christian patriot Jeffrey Baker.[188] It promotes all of the classic patriot conspiracies about a U.N. takeover, concentration camps, and a group of secret elites bent on destroying the U.S. to achieve world domination. Each chapter of the 339-page diatribe is built entirely around excerpts from *The Protocols of the Learned Elders of Zion*,[189] a rabidly anti-Semitic document forged by czarist police just before the Russian Revolution (c. 1898–1904). *The Protocols* allegedly contain the transcripts from a secret meeting of high-ranking Jews and details the Jewish plot to enslave humanity.[190]

Predictably, Marrs's target date for the beginning of "the end" coincides with the same year patriots believe the new World Order will be established: "We don't know if Jesus Christ is coming next month or next year or in the next few minutes, but we do know that these are undoubtedly the last days. . . . It could wrap up by the year 2000, which is, by the way, the year the Devil proposes to bring his plan to fruition."[191]

Jack "I'm not a date-setter" Van Impe [192]

Jack Van Impe — commonly referred to as "The Walking Bible" — is an energetic, charismatic televangelist who can spout scripture verses faster than any preacher on the airwaves. He is billed as one of the world's "foremost experts on Bible prophecy" and his Jack Van Impe Ministries boasts of having "the most comprehensive Prophecy website on the Internet."[193] He adamantly declares that we cannot know the *exact* day or hour of Christ's second coming, but like all date-suggesters, goes on to predict the year, or years, of Jesus' "possible," "likely," or "almost certain" return.[194] In fact, Van Impe, has been churning out non-stop doomsday deadlines ever since publishing an April 1, 1975 newsletter that read: "Messiah 1975? The Tribulation 1976?"[195]

Van Impe was also fairly certain that "the Soviet flag would fly over Independence Hall in Philadelphia by 1976."[196] He then implied a 1988 date for the rapture, which would be followed by the Tribulation until 1996.[197] A subsequent time calculation, however, seemed to zero in on 1992 for the rapture and 1999 for the end of the world.[198] (This timetable, promoted in his 1990 videotape titled *A.D. 2000 . . . The End?*, was used by the Korean *Hyoo-go* movement, see Chapter 2).[199] At the end of 1992, he announced: "Beloved, it is vital that you and I understand end-times Bible prophecy! . . . I believe the President of the U.S.A. during the next eight years may face horrendous decisions concerning World War III and even Armageddon."[200]

Then, Van Impe released his 1995 video *2001: Countdown to Eternity,* which he advertised as a resource that would prepare viewers "for the end of the age — and the beginning of eternity." This $24.95 video revealed "how a Millennial Kingdom is predicted to begin shortly after A.D. 2000." The video was followed in 1996 by *2001: On the Edge of Eternity,* a bestselling volume that placed Jesus' second coming "perhaps as far ahead as the year 2012."[201]

Van Impe has recently raised his prophetic rhetoric several notches. During a July 2, 1997 broadcast he emotionally declared: "The Bible teaches that an Antichrist comes to power (Rev. 13:1) — a world dictator. . . . This world dictator could appear anywhere from now to 2003. . . . It means Jesus is about to return, folks! Oh, the year 2000 is so important. *Are you ready?*"[202] Immediately following this statement, Van Impe's announcer gave a predictable sales pitch to the television audience:

The years 2000 – 2012 will be awesome. Now to completely understand your future you need this month's offer. You can order the Van Impes' videos *666: The United States of Europe* and *The New World Order* by calling 1-800- . . . . For a limited time, you can receive this incredible video for a gift of just $24.95 in the U.S. or $29.95 in Canada, plus $3.00 S&H.[203]

Predictably, Van Impe's prophetic teachings have taken on a patriot-friendly tone. His entrance into the NWO-exposing arena began in 1994 with a warning to television viewers that several military bases were being used by global conspirators to house U.N. soldiers in preparation for a massive invasion. During his national news program *Jack Van Impe Presents,* which is aired on more than 250 stations and several cable networks, he presented militia claims that "motorists had photographed trainloads of military equipment on roads and rail routes, and foreign troops of 'battalion strength' had been confirmed by base spokesmen at Fort Polk, LA and Fort Benning, GA."[204]

This information was drawn directly from patriot/militia sources. The allegations about Ft. Polk and Ft. Benning had previously appeared in an October 1994 issue of the *Patriot Report*, a extremist newsletter out of Arkansas.[205] But when the assertions were investigated by reporters from the *Mobile Press Register,* they found them to be erroneous. "It's simply not true," said Dan Vance, deputy public affairs officer at Fort Polk. Vance explained that Ft. Polk has trained company-sized groups of perhaps 100 foreign soldiers, but has never hosted battalion-sized elements. Ft. Benning spokesman Griff Godwin said essentially the same thing, recalling that his station has trained possibly up to 200 foreign soldiers at any one time.[206]

Van Impe not only refused a one-on-one interview with the *Press Register,* but failed to answer a page of faxed questions, even after Van Impe Ministries executive director John Lang had informed the newspaper's reporters that Van Impe would answer written questions.[207] Ultimately, the televangelist faxed the Press *Register* several mimeographed sheets of paper containing pictures of trucks and other military equipment in an effort to substantiate his assertions. He had mentioned this military equipment during his program, stating: "They've actually taken photographs of these U.N. Army personnel in Saucier, Miss., Gulfport, Miss. in New Orleans, La., and western Texas."[208]

These same photos, however, had already been debunked as fraudulent after they first appeared in the *Spotlight* and Militia of Montana materials.[209] *Soldier of Fortune* magazine's investigation of the photos revealed that the supposedly "chemical and biological warfare" trucks in Saucier

actually have no offensive capabilities whatsoever. Furthermore, the bro-
ken-down vehicles are "being modified and re-exported, and the parts
scrapped-out and sold locally."[210]

During a 1994 television spot, he predicted that the U.N.'s "world army
eventually will play into the hands of the Antichrist spoken of in the Book of
Revelation." He also named the militias "as one possible deterrent to the
rising one-world government, led by the United Nations."[211] These teachings
have terrified some Christians into packing their bags and fleeing civilization,
leaving their friends and relatives dumbfounded. Consider the words of David
and Michele, who wrote a letter to the Christian Research Institute. The
Christian couple asked for advice on how to help some distraught acquaintances who had taken to heart the information in Van Impe's 1990 video *A.D.
2000: The End?*: "Our friend and several of her friends are now trying to
liquidate their assets and buy land in the country, to live on and grow food on,
in the event of a crisis (a form of 'Millennial Madness,' if you will)."[212]

As of January 1998, Van Impe was still preaching the imminent
establishment of a satanic New World Order and the persecution it will
bring to freedom-loving, God-fearing Americans. Despite his many failed
predictions and penchant for inaccurate news reporting, Van Impe has
declared: "We never make a statement unless we can back it. . . . I'm not
some loony guy folks. I study. . . . And we give you the facts."[213]

IT NEVER ENDS

The patriot movement might best be described as an odd mishmash of
evangelicalism, apocalypticism, extreme political conservatism, anti-estab-
lishment rebellion, white supremacy, and anti-Semitic legends.[214] Such an
alliance, of course, is in direct conflict with the biblical mandate for
Christians to separate from strange and demonic doctrines (1 Tim. 1:3; 4:1).
Nevertheless, countless evangelicals seem to have little problem appealing
to racists as long as it serves to undergird their personal beliefs about the
end-times and the New World Order:

- Speakers at the Liberty Lobby's 40th Anniversary National Convention included Militia of Montana leader John Trochmann

(Aryan Nations associate),[215] anti-Semite Eustace Mullins, and Ted Gunderson, who spoke on federal aggression.[216] Gunderson, who claims to be a Christian, is featured in the video *Demons: True Life Evil Forces* produced by His Majesty's Media. On this video, Gunderson voices his anti-government views by claiming that high-ranking politicians regularly have Satanists deliver children to Washington, D.C. for sex orgies.[217]

• Since 1993, Pastor Pete Peters has had his own television show on the influential Keystone Inspiration Network (KIN), a Pennsylvania-based conservative Christian television network.[218] Keystone's Comptroller, Rev. Clyde Campbell, has rebuffed warnings and complaints about Peters, saying: "Peters is a minister of the Gospel and he does a good job. Pete says he loves the Jews."[219] Peters says the new television exposure has brought him nationwide support.[220]

• Beverly LaHaye, leader of Concerned Women for America, endorses *En Route to Global Occupation* by Gary Kah, which is yet another NWO conspiracy-exposing book. LaHaye writes: "The message of Gary Kah is a powerful reminder that we are getting closer and closer to the return of the King of Kings. . . . we are heading swiftly into a One World Government."[221] Unfortunately, *En Route to Global Occupation* leans heavily on information from anti-Semites Nesta Webster and Eustace Mullins.[222] Kah also quotes the 1937 book *Adam Weishaupt*, written by Christian Identity leader Gerald Winrod.[223] Winrod (1900–1957) not only published *The Protocols of the Learned Elders of Zion*, but praised Hitler for ridding Germany of "Jewish communism."[224] His Nazi extremism earned him the title "Jayhawk Nazi."[225] Gerald's son, Gordon, has continued in his father's footsteps by calling for the death of all Jews to solve America's problems.[226] In 1994, LaHaye had Jeffrey Baker on her show to discuss his book *ChequeMate*. Baker's personal copy of *The Protocols of the Learned Elders of Zion* sat on the desk in front of him during the interview.

• Chuck Smith, founder of the Calvary Chapel system of churches, also endorses *En Route to Global Occupation*. He writes: "Gary's book is an insightful look and a great analysis of the direction that the world is moving toward . . . the one-world government."[227]

The irony in all of this is that most of the evangelical leaders who appeal to works that rely on anti-Semitic literature are staunch *supporters* of Israel and the Jews. But because they hold to a premillennial eschatology — which includes the idea that there will someday be a one-world government under the Antichrist — they are vulnerable to anti-Semitic ideas concerning a secret cabal of conspirators seeking world domination. The only difference between the NWO conspiracy being spread by *non-*racist premillennialists and the Jewish conspiracy outlined in anti-Semitic literature is the nature of the enemy.

For racists, the Jews are conspirators. For many premillennialist Christians, a myriad of conspirators — humanists, atheists, Freemasons, the Illuminati, feminists, homosexuals, liberal politicians, "international bankers," etc. — are the Antichrist's henchmen. As a result, many *non-*racist premillennialists have endorsed books *proving* their preconceived ideas about the last days, not knowing that those same volumes are relying on anti-Semitic conspiratorial theories.

A significant amount of blame for the current trend among Christians can also be laid squarely at the feet of Hal Lindsey, whose books have popularized a newspaper-style approach to interpreting prophecy. To Lindsey and his fans, nearly every world event, no matter how insignificant or far afield from theology it may be, can be inserted neatly into Scripture as fulfillment of prophetic verses. Forcing world events into biblical texts has undeniably led to many of the wild speculations about microchips, the New World Order, gun control legislation, and the United Nations. Just about anything can be made to fit into the Bible using this method of interpretation. As one prophecy student declared in *Paranoia* magazine, the third Seal of Revelation 6:6 — which talks about an angel of the Lord not harming "the oil and the wine" — actually refers to George Bush sending troops against Iraq during the Gulf War.[228]

The NWO conspiracy theory, including its correlative notion that Armageddon is near, is rife with logic flaws. Furthermore, patriot information is convoluted, twisted and often impossible to verify. Their "news" is often blended with outright lies, mangled half-truths, and wild extrapolations from relatively simple facts. Craig B. Hulet, a policy analyst with KC

& Associates of Washington, reached a similar conclusion after investigating patriot conspiracy theories for *Soldier of Fortune* magazine:

> Their truth and understanding are, far more often than not, just plain wrong. I could not find one instance of educational material, documentation or evidence that was not without the most egregious errors and outright fabrications. . . . Fact is, there's not one shred of evidence that anything sinister is going on.[229]

Using conspiracy theories to explain world events is not a new phenomenon. Various culprits have been blamed throughout the years for the woes of society: the Freemasons (a non-Christian fraternal men's society that teaches symbols, rituals and doctrines strikingly similar to occultism); the Illuminati (a defunct secretive order founded in 1776 by occultist Adam Weishaupt); and the Catholic Church.

The whole idea that humanity stands on the brink of annihilation is an ancient one. Nearly every culture throughout history has espoused some kind of doomsday theory. And since the first century, each generation has claimed that they were the last generation; the generation that would see the glorious appearing of their God and savior Jesus Christ (Titus 2:10).

PART TWO

The Annals of
Armageddon

The Descent of the Antichrist. On the left, the Antichrist preaches by Satan's inspiration. On the right, the Two Witnesses of Revelation preach against him. In the air, the Antichrist is being supported by demons as the archangel Michael prepares to slay him (Lucas Cranach, *Nuremberg Chronicle*, 1493).

FIVE

A Timeless Obsession

[P]rimitive man conceived of the cosmic process not as something stable, but as a great and continuous battle between the forces of creation and destruction, order and chaos. . . . [There] was always the fear that at some time, to be appointed by the gods, a return to chaos would take place. Natural phenomena — hurricanes, floods, volcanic eruptions, earthquakes — suggested the means: man's ritual and moral shortcomings suggested the motive.

Man, Myth & Magic[1]

Humanity's preoccupation with doomsday may go back as far as our earliest evidence of communal living. Many ancient civilizations (e.g., the Babylonians, Hebrews, Greeks, Romans, Persians, and Teutons, and Vikings) were influenced by end-time visions.[2] Several cultures (e.g., the Guarani of South America, Aztecs of Mexico, Lakali of New Britain and Native Americans of the Pacific Northwest) even created unique rituals linked to a belief that one day the world as we know it would be destroyed by God (or the gods).[3]

Several end-time scenarios from centuries past sound strikingly similar to each other. Consider the Babylonian *Epic of Gilgamesh* (c. 4000 B.C.). According to this narrative poem, Earth has already been destroyed at least once by a flood much like the Noahic deluge described in the Hebrew Old Testament (Gen. 6–8). Both stories share several elements: a righteous man who builds an ark so that he and his family can escape the flood, use of bitumen to make the ark watertight, a gathering of animals into the ark, the release of a dove by the righteous man after the rain stops, and a mountain top as the post-flood resting place for the ark.[4]

This same story, including most of the aforementioned elements, can be found in the religious tradition of numerous cultures: the Sumerians, Persians, Greeks, Arabs, Eskimos, Norsemen, Lithuanians, Irish, Aztecs, Chinese, Mayans, North American Indians (Huron, Mandal, Sioux, Chickasaw, Hopi), South American Indians (Guarani, Inca, Tuscarora), and the Satapatha Brahmana of India.[5] Most of these civilizations also preached about a *future* doomsday.

In ancient Greece, the Stoics — a group of influential philosophers (c. 300–200 B.C.) — taught that the cosmos exists in cyclical stages which periodically end "with a conflagration, a return to the fire from whence it came."[6] According to Zeno (c. 336–264 B.C.), founder of Stoicism, the all-consuming blaze purifies the world, "eliminating all evil and leaving future inhabitants prudent and wise."[7] Earth is then reborn from the flames. The Stoic version of our planet's destruction can be traced to an even earlier Greek philosopher, Heraclitus (c. 500 B.C.). He, too, postulated that there exists a cosmic fire (Gr. *ekpurosis*) "into which the world is periodically dissolved, and from which it is born anew."[8] It is not surprising that the Greeks would formulate such a concept. Their religious mythology contained several cataclysmic confrontations among the gods that, on more than one occasion, nearly obliterated the cosmos.[9]

The end-time belief system of the ancient Persians was remarkably like that of some contemporary eschatologies. Persians maintained that one day increased earthquakes, fires, floods and pestilence would herald a final battle between good and evil called "The War of the Sons of Light with the Sons of Darkness." A subsequent judgment of humanity would seal the fate of the righteous (who would go to heaven) and the unrighteous (who would be consigned to a hell-like realm of eternal existence).[10]

The Teutons and Vikings thought that the end of the world, which the Vikings called *ragna rök* (i.e., "the fatal destiny, the end of the gods"),[11] would occur through increased bickering and betrayal among the gods coupled with the deeds of evil monsters and wicked men. *Ragna rök* is best described as nothing less than a full-scale celestial war that destroys nearly everything, including the gods.[12] But like many end-time myths, the story allows for a rebirth of the planet and a chance to start all over again.

From the wreckage of the ancient world a new world was born. Slowly the earth emerged from the waves. Mountains rose anew and from them sprang cataracts of singing waters. Above the torrent the eagle again began to hover, ready to swoop suddenly down on the fish which played in the waters. . . . Ears of corn grew where no human hand had scattered seed. . . . And a new generation of gods appeared. . . . To them it was reserved to renew the world. . . . Men also reappeared. For all of them had not perished in the great catastrophe.[13]

Given the prevalence of doomsday beliefs in antiquity, it is understandable that today's religions (e.g., Hinduism, Buddhism, Islam, Judaism, and Christianity) all provide their own versions of how history will conclude. Although the end-time visions of modern religions have a number of contradictory elements, all of them share some common themes. The most obvious similarities involve a belief that the annihilation of the cosmos will be followed by a divine renewal of Earth.

Hinduism, for instance, divides time into four ages: Krita, Treta, Dvapara, and Kali. These might best be thought of as seasons of humanity. Krita (spring) is "the beginning of a cycle, the purest of times" when shelter and food are magically provided to humans by trees and meditation is the highest virtue.[14] But this idyllic state gradually degenerates throughout Treta and Dvapara (summer and fall). Next comes Kali, a wintry age wherein "nobility has been replaced by wealth, scholarship by arrogance, virtue by power and marriage by pleasure. Social inequities are divisive, and people die young. Finally there is disease, drought and famine, followed by revolution and war, and the epoch-ending cataclysm. . . . [i.e.,] a total drought that removes all sustenance from the surface of the earth."[15] Then, the cycle starts again. After 1000 of these cycles, an even more spectacular end occurs, after which there is a complete re-creation of life:

[The god Vishnu] drinks all the water on the planet and then dries the entire surface of the earth. He creates seven suns that ignite the world, burning all the vegetation and creating a global desert. Everything is consumed by fire. Then colossal clouds pour down rain, killing the fires and creating one huge ocean. When the storms subside, the seas come to rest. Vishnu, too, comes to rest, in a long meditative sleep from which he will awaken to continue the cycle, to recreate the world.[16]

Buddhism, founded in India by Gautama Siddhartha (c. 560–480 B.C.) partially in response to Hinduism's prejudicial caste system, also presents reality as being cyclical rather than linear. It teaches that humanity's cycles will ultimately lead to a point of global change marking the end of the world as we know it. In this religious tradition, the future will bring a final Buddha ("enlightened one") called Maitreya, who will spread Buddhist teachings throughout the world with unparalleled success. He will allegedly perform many miracles to validate his identity and gradually save humanity.[17]

Islam's version of the world's final days are so much like those expressed by Judaism and Christianity that it is "usually counted among the biblical (or 'biblical type') religions."[18] Like Judaism and Christianity, Islam promotes a future "day of the Lord" that will bring God's judgment on humanity and the beginning of an age ruled by a messiah. Islam, again like Judaism and Christianity, also teaches that God will one day bring righteous persons into heaven and condemn the unrighteous to hell. Muslims call their deliverer the great *Mahdi* (the "rightly guided one"). Jews still await the *Moshiach* and Christians look for the return of Jesus, the Christ ("anointed one").

The end-time beliefs of Hinduism, Buddhism, Islam, and Judaism have certainly had an effect on various cultures. But it is the apocalyptic teachings of Christianity that have had the greatest influence on society in the Western world. This is because adherents to other major religions relegate teachings about "the end" to a secondary, often tertiary, level of importance. In Christianity, however, Earth's destruction via God's final judgment is often considered a main doctrine.

In many ways, an imminent Armageddon marked by Jesus' return is an indispensable part of the Christians' great hope of salvation (Rom. 8:18–23; Titus 2:13; 2 Peter 3:11–13). It serves as a consummation and confirmation of every other belief contained in Christianity. Consequently, a lengthy list of visionaries fixated on Christ's return have left their mark on each generation since Jesus preached his gospel ("good news") of God's Kingdom nearly 2,000 years ago. The following pages explore but a few of the many personalities throughout early Christianity who declared the end of the world.

THREE PROPHETS OF DOOM: A.D. 150-180

By the middle of the second century, Christianity was well on its way to becoming the primary religion of the western world. Believers in Jesus of Nazareth numbered well into the tens of thousands and churches dedicated to their resurrected Son of God were scattered throughout the Roman Empire "in nearly all the provinces between Syria and Rome."[19] But the spread of Christianity came at no small price. Countless believers were martyred because they were viewed as a destabalizing force in the Empire. The new faith, it was soon discovered, did not permit its adherents to worship the emperor as a god. Such obstinance was viewed as nothing less than an act of treason.

Roman authorities responded with a series of persecutions against Christians. These began with Nero's brutal deeds in A.D. 64 and continued through the reigns of Domitian (81–96), who demanded that he be worshipped as *Dominus et Deus* ("Lord and God") and Marcus Aurelius (161–180), who "thoroughly disliked Christians."[20] Some of the worst attacks on Christianity occurred in Rome (c. 165) and in Gaul (c. 177) under Marcus Aurelius. During the Gaul persecution neither age nor sex was taken into consideration by authorities. Men and women as old as ninety and as young as fourteen were slaughtered. Leniency was shown only to Roman citizens who, if they refused to recant their beliefs, were mercifully beheaded rather than tortured to death.

During the worst of Roman persecutions against Jesus' followers (c. 156–172), a number of other troubles affected not only Christians, but the entire Roman Empire. In the year 166, "havoc was wrought by plague, flood, famine, and barbarian invasion from beyond the Danube frontier."[21] The chaos and violence gave birth to a "new variety of Christian life and activity" known as Montanism.[22] This social phenomenon was the first of many doomsday movements to emerge from within Christianity.

Its founder, a convert named Montanus from Phrygia in Asia Minor, began attracting devotees after declaring himself to be God's mouthpiece. "I am the Father and I am the Son and I am the *Paraclete* [Holy Spirit]," uttered Montanus.[23] Also leading the movement were two women, Priscilla and Maximilla, who had forsaken their families to follow Montanus as prophetesses.[24]

Montanists taught that Jesus' return was just about to occur, along with the descent of the New Jerusalem (Rev. 21:2) to Phrygia, and the establishment of God's 1,000-year kingdom of peace on earth (i.e., the Millennium). Priscilla declared: "In the form of a woman arrayed in shining garments, came Christ to me and set wisdom upon me and revealed to me that this place is holy and that Jerusalem will hither from heaven."[25]

Several events fueled their expectations. The civil wars that "ripped through the Roman world at the end of the second century were viewed by Montanists as signs of the coming end."[26] Added confidence in their apocalyptic notions came by way of rumors circulating in A.D. 198 that "many witnesses had actually seen a walled city in the sky over Judea. It had been seen on forty consecutive mornings. . . . [T]o Montanists it could only be the heavenly city descending."[27]

Montanism was "the first example of an earnest and well-meaning, but gloomy and fanatical hyper-Christianity."[28] Followers eschewed marital relations, fasted frequently (sometimes for as long as two weeks), and ate dry foods only. The sect also banned remarriage, forbade ornamental clothing for women, required virgins to be veiled, saw art as incompatible with Christian soberness, and rejected the idea that Christians could be forgiven for serious sins after baptism. Other aspects of the movement that made onlookers uncomfortable were the many visions reported by members and the group's practice of speaking in "tongues" (i.e., unintelligible babbling often prompted by altered states of consciousness).

Moreover, Montanists fostered divisiveness among Christians by referring to themselves as *spiritual*, in distinction from other believers whom they saw as *psychical* (i.e., carnally minded).[29] Even more troubling was the movement's exaltation of Montanus, Priscilla, and Maximilla to a position above that of Jesus' twelve apostles. Montanus argued that as the Holy Spirit's voice, his authority was second only to Christ's.[30] Maximilla made similar claims, stating: "Listen not to me, but listen to Christ [speaking through me]."[31] Such assertions were resoundingly condemned by church leaders, some of whom had known and been taught by the apostles. [32]

There existed a final feature of this sect that non-Montanist Christians found especially disturbing. Montanus, Priscilla, and Maximilla actually urged followers to seek out and relish persecution, rather than flee from it, stating: "Desire not to die in bed, nor in the delivery of children, nor by enervating fevers, but in martyrdom, that He may be glorified who suffered for you."[33] They went so far as to equate escaping death with denying Christ. This resulted in the execution of many believers. Numbered among their martyrs was Tertullian (c. 160/ 170–215/220), one of the most famous and admirable theologians of early Christianity.[34]

Montanists "lived under the vivid expectation of the great final catastrophe and therefore looked with contempt on efforts to change the present order of things."[35] The apocalypse, of course, never came. Instead, believers were excommunicated from the broader church and faced 200 more years of persecution. Maximilla — who outlived both Montanus and Priscilla — eventually placed doomsday after her death, prophesying: "After me there will be no prophecy, but the End will come."[36] In years to come, she complained: "I am driven away like a wolf from the sheep. I am not a wolf; I am the Word and Spirit and Power."[37] She finally died in 179. Montanism itself eventually faded out of existence during the sixth century reign of Justinian (527–565).

Montanus was not alone in thinking that the end of the world was near. During the second century, a bishop of Pontus in northeast Asia Minor told his flock that the Second Coming would happen within two years. Believers responded by not cultivating their fields, and giving away their houses and goods.[38] Clement (c. 30–100), an early leader of the church at Rome, declared: "Soon and suddenly shall his will be accomplished." Ignatius (d. 98/117), Bishop of Antioch, wrote: "The last times are upon us." Cyprian (c. 200–258), Bishop of Carthage, said: "The kingdom of God, beloved brethren, is beginning to be at hand." Even Hippolytus (d. 236) had the world's end foremost in his mind. He actually predicted a year for the consummation of the ages: A.D. 500.

Fortunately, Christian persecution did not continue until 500. It ceased with the conversion to Christianity of the Roman Emperor Constantine (c.

280–337). But emotional, psychological, and spiritual tensions remained as Christians and pagans alike were forced to face the death of the Empire.

THERE'S NO PLACE LIKE ROME: A.D. 200–950

Many elements contributed to Rome's decline. Pestilence, revolution, and war ravaged the land from the second to fourth centuries: "Epidemics of major proportions decimated the population under Aurelius, Gallienus, and Constantine. In the plague of 260–265 almost every family of the Empire was attacked. . . . [In Rome] there were 5,000 deaths every day for many weeks."[39] Furthermore, the mighty Roman legion had been gradually replaced by provincial mercenary armies comprised of criminals, barbarians, and sons of peasants. These problems were accentuated by the Empire's economic instability, which had been fostered by a depletion in precious metal supplies, a collapsed slave trade, and currency depreciated. Finally, Rome's "increasing despotism destroyed the citizen's civic sense and dried up statesmanship at its source. . . . [T]he Roman lost interest in government ."[40]

A final assault on Rome's 800-year reign came in the form of hostile invaders. The Visigoths, with an army of 40,000 men under the leadership of Alaric, were the first to reach Rome in 410. They pillaged the city for three horrifying days: "Hundreds of rich men were slaughtered, their women were raped and killed; it was found almost impossible to bury all the corpses that littered the streets."[41]

After Alaric withdrew southward to conquer Sicily, a door to Rome was left open for the Vandals, from whose destructive exploits we derive our word vandalism. They began their awful campaign by crossing the Alps in 406 and marching through Gaul (later to become France). Sweeping to the south, they entered Spain with a merciless army of 100,000 men and plundered the region for two years. The Vandals then proceeded into Northern Africa, and from there, set sail for Italy with "an invincible armada" in 455. They reached Rome that same year and sacked the city for four days. Rome's imperial government, which had by this time been moved to the northern city of Milan, held on for only another twenty years, finally collapsing in 476.

The ramifications of Rome's fall were numerous. Invading barbarians continued to wage war with one another in an effort to seize a piece of the old Empire. Trade routes that were once safe became dangerous. Organized education ceased and the progress of knowledge stagnated. In Italy, a century of invasion, famine and pestilence left thousands of farms ruined and their acreage untilled. Pope Gelasius (c. 480) described great regions of Northern Italy as "almost denuded of the human species; Rome itself had shrunk from 1,500,000 souls to some 300,000."[42] Art, music, and architecture were understandably no longer a priority. The Dark Ages had fallen upon Europe.[43]

Nevertheless, Christianity continued to flourish. The city of Rome itself, through a series of fortuitous events too complex to explain in a chapter of this size, became the very seat of what had once been the Empire's outlaw religion. Thus was born the Roman Catholic Church under the leadership of a succession of Roman bishops, who were eventually called popes (i.e., "Fathers"). Despite a lack of Christian persecution, the instability of this period in history led to a continuance of apocalyptic movements.

Bishop Gregory of Tours, in his *History of the Franks*, records that in 591 residents of several French districts began following a self-proclaimed "Christ" from Bourges.[44] This particular end-time preacher entered the prophetic arena quite by accident when he, "having gone into the forest, found himself suddenly surrounded by a swarm of flies; as a result of which he went out of his mind for two years."[45] He later became a praying hermit clad only in animal skins. "When he emerged from this ascetic training he claimed to possess supernatural gifts of healing and prophecy."[46]

This "False Christ" soon set himself up to be worshipped along with a female companion whom he called Mary. Church leaders, including Gregory, attributed the man's alleged ability to heal the sick and accurately predict the future to his having Satan's help. Not everyone, however, felt this way. In fact, the French prophet had a sizable following well into the thousands, including some priests, that regularly brought him gold, silver and clothing. He subsequently became sort of a deified Robin Hood, organizing his followers into an armed band "which he led through the countryside, waylaying and robbing the travelers they met on the way."[47] The monetary gain was then redistributed to poor townspeople.

Obviously, financial prosperity was not what the prophet from Bourges wanted. His desire was to be worshipped. In each town that he and his band of merry men (and women) entered, residents would be threatened with death unless they prayed to him. Of course, such conduct could be tolerated for only so long:

> When he arrived at this important episcopal city [Le Puy] he quartered his "army" as Gregory calls it — in the neighbouring basilicas, as though he were about to wage war against the bishop, Aurelius. Then he sent messengers ahead to proclaim his coming; they presented themselves to the bishop stark naked, leaping and somersaulting. The bishop . . . sent a party of his men to meet the messiah on the way. The leader of the party, pretending to bow, grabbed the man [from Bourges] around the knees; after which he was quickly secured and cut to pieces. "And so," comments Gregory, "fell and died that Christ, who should rather be called Antichrist." His companion Mary was also seized, and was tortured until she revealed all the diabolic devices that had given him his power. As for the followers, they dispersed, but still remained under their leader's ban. Those who had believed in him continued to do so; to their dying day they maintained that he was indeed Christ and that the woman Mary, too, was a divine being.[48]

The sixth and seventh centuries also saw sporadic outbreaks of apocalyptic fever in various locations, especially around the year 751, when Childeric III — the last of the Frankish kings descended from the Merovingian line — was deposed and replaced by Pepin the Short of the Carolingian family. This historical milestone resulted in so much turmoil that "it was openly believed that Antichrist's coming was near."[49]

One hundred years later, doomsayers were still proclaiming the imminent arrival of the devil's disciple. The Spanish monk Beatus (d. 798), in his three-part *Commentary on the Apocalypse*, written from 776–786, remarked that there were "only fourteen years left to complete the sixth millennium [since creation], and therefore presumably only fourteen years also until Antichrist's coming."[50] In other words, Beatus felt that he would live to see the Antichrist and the end of the world by the year 800.[51] The heretic Elipandus (c. 718–802), in a letter to the bishops of Gaul, described what he had witnessed regarding Beatus's end-time speculations:

Beatus prophesied the end of the world to Hordonius of Liébana in the presence of the people during the Easter vigil so that they became terrified and crazed. They took no food that night, and are said to have fasted until the ninth hour on Sunday. Then Hordonius, when he felt afflicted with hunger, is said to have addressed the people, "Let's eat and drink, so that if we die at least we'll be fed."[52]

Beatus's end-time views were shared by others. Agobard (c. 779–840), Bishop of Lyons, believed the Antichrist to be so near that he advised Emperor Louis the Pious to "commission someone 'to collect everything which the Church's teachers have understood, explained or signified concerning Antichrist in the sacred Scriptures.' "[53] Not long after Abogard's request, a prophetess named Thiota was able to gather a sizable following by announcing that the end of the world would take place by 848.[54]

By the mid-800s, fear of the Antichrist and apprehension over "the end" thoroughly permeated the Christian community. The doomsday paranoia was intensified, however, when a previously unknown "sign" of the Antichrist's imminent arrival appeared on the scene: Muslims, the "infidels" who had captured the holy city of Jerusalem in 638. According to Bernard McGinn, professor of historical theology at the University of Chicago Divinity School, Islam's effect on Christian apocalypticism was natural:

Because heretics had long been associated with antichrists and Antichrist, it was an easy move to interpret the rise of Islam as a sign of Antichrist's coming and to see its founder, Muhammad, as a type of the Final Enemy.[55]

Christian-Muslim tensions were bound to become violent and did so in the 850s. In Córdoba, Spain "some fifty or more Christians were put to death after deliberately provoking the Muslim authorities by insulting their religion."[56] Church leaders were strongly divided over the legitimacy of Christians provoking Muslims. Eulogius, a monk who supported the actions of the martyrs, "praised those who marched out 'against the angel of Satan [i.e., the Muslim prophet Muhammad] and forerunner of Antichrist.' "[57]

Another end-time watcher was Odo (879–942), abbot of the monastery at Cluny. He felt that the excessive evils of the age were a sure sign that the

Antichrist was just about to make his presence known. In five of Odo's works — *Life of St. Gerald Aurillac*, *Occupation*, and *Collations* (three parts) — references to the nearness of the end can be found.[58] McGinn comments: "The influential Odo indicates that there were probably others who saw the turmoil of the tenth century . . . as proof of the imminence of Antichrist, whom Odo . . . calls *'Vehemoth, rex malorum* [Behemoth, King of the Wicked].' "[59]

Indeed, the turmoil of the 900s was significant. Even more changes to European life were on their way, not the least of which would be the end of the Carolingian dynasty in Germany (911) and in France (987). Moreover, a new barbarian horde — the Magyars — would make their presence known by robbing and burning their way through Hungary, Italy, Bavaria, southern Germany, and France (c. 889–955).[60] Suddenly, the medieval populace found themselves transfixed by a specter looming ever closer on the horizon: the year 1000. It seemed like a perfect time for the end of the world.

A.D. 1000: FACT OR FICTION?

The episodes of last days mania that punctuated the centuries from 500 to 950 climaxed with widespread millennium expectations about 1000/1033. Charles Mackay, in his 1841 work *Extraordinary Popular Delusions and the Madness of Crowds*, gives one of the most oft-quoted descriptions of what happened:

> An epidemic terror of the end of the world has several times spread over the nations. The most remarkable was that which seized Christendom about the middle of the tenth century. . . . The delusion appears to have been discouraged by the Church, but it nevertheless spread rapidly among the people. The scene of the last judgment was expected to be at Jerusalem. In the year 999, the number of pilgrims proceeding eastward, to await the coming of the Lord in that city, was so great that they were compared to a desolating army. Most of them sold their goods and possessions before they quitted Europe, and lived upon the proceeds in the Holy Land. Buildings of every sort were suffered to fall into ruins. It was thought useless to repair them, when the end of the world was so near. Many noble edifices were deliberately pulled down. Even churches, usually so well maintained, shared the general neglect. Knights,

citizens, and serfs, travelled eastwards in company, taking with them their wives
and children, singing psalms as they went, and looking with fearful eyes upon the
sky, which they expected each minute to open, to let the Son of God descend in his
glory. During the thousandth year the number of pilgrims increased. Most of them
were smitten with terror as with a plague. Every phenomenon of nature filled them
with alarm. A thunderstorm sent them all upon their knees in mid-march. It was
the opinion that thunder was the voice of God, announcing the day of judgment.
Numbers expected the earth to open, and give up its dead at the sound. Every meteor
in the sky seen at Jerusalem brought the whole Christian population into the streets
to weep and pray. . . . Fanatic preachers kept up the flame of terror. Every shooting
star furnished occasion for a sermon, in which the sublimity of the approaching
judgment was the principal topic.[61]

Some individuals maintain that all eighteenth and nineteenth century
chronicles of the year 1000, including Mackay's, are fraudulent.[62] Peter
Stearns of Carnegie-Mellon University dogmatically asserts "there is no
reason to expect that unusual attention was paid to the advent of a new
millennium in the 10th century."[63] He goes so far as to condemn all
contrary claims as sloppy, self-serving and inexcusable. Stearns says the
"myth" of the year 1000 was created by eighteenth century Enlightenment
historians and then embellished by nineteenth century anti-Catholic writers. Their alleged motivation was a desire to further the philosophy and
ideals of the Age of Reason by casting aspersions on everything connected
to the Middle Ages, especially medieval Roman Catholicism.

According to Stearns's conspiracy theory, encouraging a negative attitude about medieval Europe was supposed to help direct the eighteenth
century populace toward liberal rationalism and away from religion and
superstition.[64] "The apocalyptic history of the year 1000 turns out to be one
of the most successful, largescale frauds in modern treatments of the past,"
says Stearns. "Some of the best minds in the business dealt with the
millennium myth, particularly from the 1920s to the 1950s — after which
(save in the conceptions of the general public and its exploiters), the case
seemed closed."[65]

But more recent investigations into the year 1000 contradict Stearns's
elaborate theory. Documents written just before and after the new millen-

nium make clear reference to the apocalypse, Antichrist, and end of the world. Richard Landes, medieval history professor at Boston University, has unearthed several relevant manuscripts:[66]

- c. 950: The monk Adso writes his lengthy *Letter on the Antichrist* to Gerberga, sister of Otto I (German ruler from 936–973, who renewed the Western Empire). This letter was extensively copied and recopied, translated into vernaculars, and circulated through-out Europe. Adso declared that the Antichrist would rise when the rule of Frankish kings ended.

- c. 950-80: A letter about the Hungarians from the Bishop of Auxerre to the Bishop of Verdun "speaks of widespread apocalyptic reactions among the population."

- 964: Carlulaire de Saint-Jouin-de-Marnes writes: "As the century passes, the end of the world approaches."

- 968: Soldiers in Otto's army panic at an eclipse, which they see as a sign of the end.

- 987–991: The Carolingian Dynasty ends, and with it, the rule of Frankish kings, which Adso had taught would be the sign of the Antichrist's arrival.

- 989: Halley's comet appears in the sky and is seen by many as yet another sign of the coming apocalypse. Three years later (992), the aged Adso begins a one-way pilgrimage to Jerusalem.

- 990s: Aelfric (c. 955–1020), the Abbot of Eynsham, delivers numer-ous sermons filled with apocalyptic imagery, references to the Last Judgment, the unleashing of the Antichrist, and time links point-ing to the year 1000.

- 994/996: Abbo of Fleury (945–1004), an influential French abbot, in his *Apologetic Work*, relates: "When I was a young man [c. 965] I heard a sermon about the end of the world preached before people in the cathedral of Paris. According to this, as soon as the number of a thousand years was completed, the Antichrist would come and the Last Judgment would follow in a brief time. I opposed this sermon with what force I could from passages in the Gospels, the Apocalypse and the Book of Daniel."

These and other end-time comments in medieval literature present an altogether different picture that the view advocated by Stearns, who seems to have missed what Landes describes as a "wealth of evidence."[67] Landes has also pointed out that after the year 1000 passed, a new date was immediately seized upon: 1033. The former deadline was based on the passage of one millennium from Christ's birth, whereas the latter date measured a millennium from Jesus' crucifixion.

By means of recalculation, which continues to be the typical response of "apocalyptic hopefuls disappointed by the passage of their target date," Christians were given "a second run at the Apocalypse."[68] According to Landes, "we find ourselves confronted with a society-wide period of intense apocalyptic expectations, of a vast double-headed apocalyptic sine curve which, peaking first in 1000, retargeted and peaked again, perhaps still more powerfully, in 1033. . . . [T]he documentation of these millennial generations (965–1035) is immensely rich in material."[69]

As with the year 1000, the 1033 deadline was preceded by several widespread speculation regarding the consummation of the ages:[70]

- 1005-1006: Several texts suggest that a terrible famine raging throughout Europe is a sign of the coming apocalypse. In France, scarcity of food leads to cannibalism.
- 1012–1014: Numerous natural disasters of significant proportions lead some people to believe that the world was "returning to its original chaos."
- 1026–1027: Richard of St. Vaast leads a large pilgrimage to Jerusalem, possibly in connection to beliefs that the year 1033 will bring the end of the world.
- 1033: Another mass pilgrimage is made to Jerusalem.[71]

End-time obsession leading up to the year 1000 brought a number of changes to European life. First, several Peace Councils were formed in an effort to stop the unchecked violence of that era. Peace leagues comprised of cooperative warriors were also created. Second, new parishes and villages were organized, which in turn led to a more prosperous society. Third, the peasant-aristocratic boundary lines faded as the light at the end of the world burned increasingly bright. Fear of doomsday "brought together unimag-inable numbers . . . and encouraged all the most extravagant emotions — joy, forgiveness, brotherly love, self-sacrifice, ecstatic celebration.[72]

But it soon became apparent that the end was not going to transpire. Jesus did not come back on the anniversary of his birth, nor did he return on the anniversary of his crucifixion. The social classes again parted as the powerful "reneged on their oaths and renewed the cycle of violence."[73] The royals retreated to their castles with mounted warriors and began to "enforce their own understanding of the agreements made under the duress of apocalyptic fears and crowd pressures."[74] This division shaped European culture for the next several hundred years, as Landes explains:

> It is in these middle years of the eleventh century that the lordly ban began to take hold of rural society, like lava hardening into a blanket of obligations that defined the status of serfs for centuries to come: . . . forced use of the lord's mills, annual and extraordinary payments, restricted movement and marriage options, etc. . . . [T]he Peace movement began to shift towards a more hierarchical model: commoners were no longer invited and councils became a dialogue between the elites. Clerics and warriors looked more to practical means of enforcing legislation than to the miracles of the saints and the pressure of public opinion.

Out of this mid-eleventh century period came: 1) the codification and obligations taken by warriors known as chivalry; 2) the "Truce of God," which limited the days when "private" warfare could legitimately be pursued (this in turn "strengthened the power of the highest lords — counts, dukes, kings and emperors — by giving them a monopoly of the use of violence during those days of Truce"); 3) enthusiasm for the Crusades, the first of which would began in 1095/1096.[75]

Europe's emergence from apocalyptic fervor also brought about economic prosperity, increased commerce, and agricultural revitalization. Universities were built, churches constructed, new religious orders formed, and illiteracy combated. The Dark Ages were slowly, but surely, fading away. What refused to die, however, was curiosity about Jesus' second coming and the appearance of the Antichrist. Within 100 years, this curiosity would again mushroom into nothing less than widespread obsession.

RENAISSANCE AND REFORMATION: 1200-1600

Europe's religious scene during the 1200s was bloody and violent. It was during this era that the fourth, fifth, sixth, and seventh Crusades (1202–1291) — i.e., military campaigns against Muslims who had taken control of Jerusalem and other parts of the East — were initiated. Moreover, the church at Rome (once the seat of Christianity) had long since degenerated into a corrupt political power that did not hesitate to use fear and intimidation to achieve its goals. These years, for example, saw the popes establishing the infamous inquisition (1230–1600s), which by 1252 was using torture to extract confessions of "heresy" from suspected enemies of Catholicism.

Adding tension to the mid-thirteenth century was the anti-Semitism that had obtained a vice-like grip on Christendom. The horrors perpetrated on Jews during this era began soon after Innocent III — who served as pope from 1198 to 1216 — expressed the need for Jews as "blasphemers of the Christian name," to be "forced into the servitude of which they made themselves deserving when they raised their sacrilegious hands against Him who had come to confer true liberty upon them, thus calling down His blood upon themselves and their children." Pope Innocent III also believed that the Jews "must be preserved as 'wanderers' upon the earth until they acknowledged their crime and called on the name of Jesus Christ as Lord and Saviour."[76]

In 1215, the Fourth Lateran Council enforced segregation of Jews by "requiring them to wear distinguishing dress — a conical hat in the German lands and a 'Jew Badge' (usually a yellow disc sewn into the clothing, whose colour symbolized Judas's betrayal of Christ for gold pieces) in the Latin countries."[77] Jews were subsequently portrayed in literature and art as agents of Satan/ the Antichrist.

Inflammatory hearsay about Jews reached a peak of absurdity when Jews were accused of torturing consecrated wafers of bread used by Roman Catholics during communion services.[78] Roman Catholics, it must be remembered, believe that the bread they consume during communion has been miraculously transformed into the body of Christ, even though it still *appears* to be bread.

Next came the "blood accusations" that flourished between 1144 and the late 1200s. These horrendous stories accused Jews of killing Christian children and draining their blood for use in Passover meals. Other macabre accounts concluded that murders occurred "because Jewish men menstruated and needed to refill their blood, or because Jewish boys lost blood while being circumcised . . . [and] needed to replenish it."[79] Another rumor alleged that "the Jewish faith required the sacrifice of a Christian child annually 'in scorn and contempt of Christ, so that they might avenge their sufferings on Him.' "[80]

During the First Crusade (1095/96) countless Jews were massacred by bands of European crusaders on their way to Jerusalem. Almost one third of all the Jews in Germany and Northern France (about 10,000) were killed in just the first six months of 1096. The massacres continued until the crusaders reached Jerusalem in 1099, at which time they murdered Jews along with Muslims. Robert S. Wistrich, professor of Jewish Studies at the University of London, describes the scene:

> The leader of the First Crusade, Godfrey Bouillon, who had sworn to avenge the blood of Christ on Israel and "leave no single member of the Jewish race alive," burnt the synagogue of Jerusalem to the ground, with all the Jews inside. . . . The Second Crusade (1146), like its successors, led to renewed anti-Jewish excesses with fatalities, though less severe than the first, still running into the hundreds.[81]

Such was the environment out of which there arose yet another prophet of doom: Joachim of Fiore. This Italian abbot has been called the "most influential European until Karl Marx."[82] According to University of Chicago Divinity School professor Bernard McGinn, he was "without doubt, the greatest medieval apocalyptic thinker."[83]

Visions at Fiore

Joachim (c. 1135–1202) began his religious life as a Cistercian monk from Calabria, Italy. His fame as a prophet began to spread after he had two visions that "gave him the gift of spiritual intelligence enabling him to understand the inner meaning of history."[84] At the encouragement of Pope Lucius III, he explained his beliefs in three major works: *Exposition of the*

Apocalypse, Concordance of the Old and New Testaments, and *Psaltry of Ten Strings.* These volumes made Joachim something of a prophetic celebrity. By the end of his life he had met with four popes and consulted with kings, queens, and emperors at his mountain retreat.[85] According to Joachim, history was unfolding in three epochs corresponding to Christianity's trinitarian concept of God.

God the Father represented the first stage in time, wherein humanity lived under the law as recorded in the Old Testament. The second historical age, that of the Son, was a period of grace lasting forty-two generations of thirty years that would end with the appearance of the Antichrist in 1260. (During an 1191 interview with Richard the Lion-Hearted, Joachim said that the Antichrist had already been born.)[86] Finally, there would come the third era of the Holy Spirit, which would be marked by increased spiritual intelligence and a new religious order that would convert the world to Christianity. Joachim discovered most of this during his first vision on one particular Easter night when he was deep in meditation.[87]

After Joachim's death in 1202, several new religious orders claimed to be the group that he prophesied would convert the world.[88] Obviously, the Church could not continue to support Joachim's teachings. His view of God was condemned at the Lateran Council of 1215, and by 1259 all of his writings were labeled heretical.[89] Nevertheless, his prophetic system outlining three stages of historical progression survived in various forms to influence, if only indirectly, the thinking of several notable personalities including Adolf Hitler. His Third Reich, like Joachim's third epoch, was supposed to have lasted forever.[90]

The Flagellants

The flagellants were the first group of people to believe that they were the religious order of whom Joachim had spoken. This movement, which numbered well into the thousands, started unexpectedly when "bands of men and boys carrying candles and banners began roaming through Italy."[91] Followers were named after their practice of self-flagellation — i.e., flogging and scourging themselves in an effort to imitate Christ's sufferings. The self-torture was done either to purge themselves of sins or to secure forgiveness for others. These extremists first appeared in Italy around 1260, which coincidentally, was Joachim's prophesied beginning of history's final phase.

It was an exceptionally harsh time to be living in Italy. The year 1258 had brought severe famine to the region and 1259 saw a serious outbreak of the plague. Warfare between the Guelphs (supporters of the Pope) and Ghibellines (supporters of the Emperor) was also destroying that country's peace. According to one chronicler of the flagellant movement, participants "behaved as though they feared that as a punishment for their sins God was about to destroy them all by earthquake and by fire from on high."[92] In hopes of pacifying God's wrath, flagellants punished themselves as they called out: " 'Holy Virgin take pity on us! Beg Jesus Christ to spare us!' and: 'Mercy, mercy! Peace, peace!' "[93] It was often a bloody spectacle featuring iron-spiked whips.[94]

Flagellants made extraordinary claims regarding the spiritual rewards received from self-torture. They not only received forgiveness for their own sins, thus assuring themselves a place in heaven, but "were empowered to drive out devils, to heal the sick, even to raise the dead. There were flagellants who claimed to eat and drink with Christ and to converse with the Virgin; at least one claimed to have risen from the dead. All these claims were eagerly accepted by the populace."[95]

Many observers of the movement actually brought sick loved ones to be healed by the flagellants. Townsfolk would dip their cloths in the flowing blood of these men "and treasured them as sacred relics. . . . On one occasion a dead child was carried round the circle during the flagellation in the hope that he would be resurrected."[96]

The New International Dictionary of the Christian Church notes that "the most spectacular appearance of the Flagellants took place in Northern Europe in 1349 and was associated with the outbreak of the Black Death."[97] They believed that their self-mutilation would save humanity at a point in time that was the end of the world. They also "called for the killing of the Jews, whom they believed were the enemies of God and responsible for the plague."[98] Their propaganda led to several Jewish massacres.[99]

As the years passed, flagellants became even bolder, killing not only Jews, but also priests and the wealthy. Although the Roman Catholic Church officially banned the practice and executed many participants as heretics, the movement continued to reappear sporadically in France, Italy, and Germany for many centuries. In fact, there still exists a group of men in Spain who whip themselves during an annual religious ceremony now sanctioned by the Roman Catholic Church and attended by priests.

Only a few minor changes have been made to the medieval ritual. The original flagellants wore white robes embroidered with red crosses, while modern-day flagellants wear red robes emblazoned with white crosses. Today's flagellants are also hooded to preserve anonymity, whereas participants in the 1200s allowed their identities to be known. Modern flagellants, who call themselves "The Brotherhood of the True Cross," are undoubtedly the spiritual progeny of the originators of self-flagellation.[100]

Death Takes No Holiday

The Black Plague began in central Asia in 1338 and by 1349 had swept through most of Europe and into London. When it finally subsided two years later, one third of Europe's population (20-30 million) was dead. In some sectors, the fatal infection killed thirty to forty percent of the urban population. Then, as if things were not bad enough, the populace faced a second outbreak of the deadly disease (1357–1362). Again, millions of people perished. The speed and severity of the disease had never been seen before, nor has it been seen since.

The city of Venice lost 100,000 residents. In Marseilles, 57,000 died in a single month. Bologna lost two thirds of its population; Florence, three-fifths. In England, "one-half of the population, or 2,500,000 people, fell victim to the dread disease."[101] Bodies littered the streets of Stockholm, and on the high seas, cargo vessels were adrift with their crews lying dead above and below deck. This "medically apocalyptic" situation prompted multiple predictions concerning the date of the Antichrist's arrival: 1346, 1347, 1348, 1360, 1365, 1375, 1387, 1396, 1400, 1417, and 1418, to name but a few.[102]

At this same time, more and more people were beginning to suspect that the Antichrist, if not connected to either the Muslims or Jews, was linked to nothing other than the Roman Catholic Church. One of the most vocal preachers to promote this view was the Czech theologian Jan Hus (c.

1372–1415), dean of philosophy at the University of Prague and rector of that city's Bethlehem Chapel.

The rise of the anti-Catholic Hussites actually began in the 1360s with John Milic (d. 1374), the archdeacon of Prague. Milic briskly attacked the Church of Rome, going so far as to declare that the Antichrist's reign had already begun and that "corruption in the church was proof that the End was imminent."[103] After Milic's death, his views were carried on by several like-minded reformers such as Matthew of Janov (d. 1394). He pointed to Pope Clement VII "as an antichrist if not perhaps the final Antichrist."[104]

Following in the footsteps of Milic and Matthew was Hus, who stressed personal piety and purity of life, as well as the authoritative role of Scripture in the Christian's life. He also spent a good deal of time exposing the corruption of the Roman Church. His thoughts were clearly expressed in *On the Church*, wherein he stated that the true church of God was the body of Christ (all believers), with Jesus as its *only* head. He additionally declared that only God could forgive sins. These and other statements put Hus in direct conflict with the Church at Rome:

> Hus believed that neither popes nor cardinals could establish doctrine which was contrary to Scripture, nor should any Christian obey an order from them which was plainly wrong. He condemned the corruptness of the clergy and criticized his people for worshipping images, belief in false miracles, and undertaking "superstitious pilgrimages."[105]

Hus's views led Prague residents to hold demonstrations against the papacy in 1411. For his part in the uprising, Hus was excommunicated. The Church's response only served to further infuriate Prague citizens. Then, in 1412, three of Hus's followers were executed and Hus was forced to flee to Bohemia. He continued to preach against the papacy until 1414, when he was lured under false pretenses to attend a papal conference. He was subsequently apprehended and placed on trial for heresy, even though he had never taught anything heretical. After a series of appearances at several courts, he was found guilty of heresy and burned at the stake on July 5, 1415.

After hearing of his murder, large numbers of peasants and townspeople joined forces, calling themselves Hussites. A more radical wing of the movement known as the Taborites also arose. The latter group's desire was not simply reform, but a complete economic and social revolution.[106] One Taborite preacher announced in 1419 that in 1420 God's fiery wrath would consume all areas except Taborite strongholds. They held other beliefs that were even stranger:

> Taborites believed that as soon as the world became free of sinners, Christ would appear on their Mount Tabor and then take his rightful place as the emperor of Bohemia. The third of Joachim's ages would begin, there would be no need of a church, all men and women would be healthy, free and equal. As an added bonus, women would bear children without either intercourse or pain. When the world didn't end in 1420, they formed armies. The most radical were urged by their leaders to take upon themselves the responsibility of ridding the world of evildoers.[107]

The Hussites — who by now had branched into two more sects known as the Utraquists and the moderate/Catholic-friendly Calixtines — soon found themselves at odds with the Taborites. All of these groups were to some degree in conflict with Romanist forces. A multi-sided civil war ensued until the mid-1400s, when the Hussites declared victory. The end of the world, however, never transpired.

Müntzer the Madman

The transitional years between the 1400s and 1500s were calmer than prior eras. By the 1400s, the Italian Renaissance had moved northward, where it took on a religious flare. This sparked a fascination with Christian classics such as the New Testament and the writings of the early church fathers. The Reformation was ignited when the masses discovered that for centuries the Roman Catholic Church had not been following the faith espoused by early Christians.

Especially disturbing was the obvious corruption that thoroughly permeated the Church's hierarchy. The papacy "had a long history of occupants insensitive to the spiritual needs of the faithful and more interested in real estate than reform, more concerned with politics than piety."[108] The popes and other high-ranking clergy had also burned, beheaded, and tortured to death numerous Christians who had either disagreed with the legitimacy of the papacy or exposed Church corruption.[109]

Widespread dissatisfaction with Romanism finally came to a head in 1517 when Martin Luther (1483–1546) — a monk and doctoral graduate of the University of Wittenberg — nailed his Ninety-Five Theses to the door of a Wittenberg church. Luther wrote the document in response to the actions of Johann Tetzel (c. 1465–1519), a Dominican monk. His historical claim to fame is the selling of indulgences, which amounted to granting people forgiveness in exchange for financial contributions to the Church and/or monetary support for its projects (e.g., the Crusades).[110]

Like most of the historical ages marked by radical social change and tensions, the Reformation period produced a wealth of apocalyptic material. Understandably, this era's end-time visions had a decidedly anti-Roman Catholic edge to them. Most reformers, including Luther, believed that either the pope or the office of the papacy was the physical manifestation of the Antichrist.[111] One reformer who seized on the idea of reformation was Thomas Müntzer (c. 1489–1525), a priest who helped organize the German Peasants' Revolt of 1524-1526. He identified "the whole religious and social hierarchy of the late medieval world as part of the Antichrist."[112]

Müntzer fueled the peasant rebellion by teaching that an extermination of the rich and powerful classes would initiate the return of Christ and the establishment of God's millennial kingdom of righteousness. "Harvest-time is here, so God himself has hired me for his harvest," Müntzer announced. "I have sharpened my scythe, for my thoughts are most strongly fixed on the truth, and my lips, hands, skin, hair, soul, body, life curse the unbelievers."[113] It was by use of inspirational messages like these that he was able to secure for himself a position as parish priest in the town of Allstedt. Civil authorities quickly marked Müntzer as a possible troublemaker and began to observe his conduct "with a mixture of curiosity and alarm."[114]

In 1524, Duke John of Chelsea traveled to Allstedt and asked Müntzer to preach a sermon to him so that he could better understand the priest's views. The end-time prophet obliged the duke, choosing for his text the apocalyptic Book of Daniel. His message called for the death of priests, monks, and rulers who did not agree with his version of godliness:

"The battle of the Angels" from the Apocalyptic Series
by Albrecht Durer (1471-1528).

[A] godless man has no right to live if he hinders the godly. . . . The sword is
necessary to exterminate them. And so that it shall be done honestly and properly,
our dear fathers the princes must do it, who confess Christ with us. But if they
don't do it, the sword shall be taken from them. . . . If they resist, let them be
slaughtered without mercy. . . . At the harvest-time one must pluck the weeds out
of God's vineyard. . . . But the angels who are sharpening their sickles for that work
are no other than the earnest servants of God. . . . For the ungodly have no right
to live, save what the Elect choose to allow them.[115]

Müntzer grew more radical, even denouncing Luther as part of the wicked system that had to be destroyed. Not content with his own following in Allstedt, he went to the large city of Mühlhausen, which for over a year had been experiencing a great deal of friction between the ruling class and peasants. "Obsessed as always by impending destruction of the ungodly, he had a red crucifix and a naked sword carried in front of him, when at the head of an armed band, he patrolled the streets of town."[116]

When open revolt ensued, Müntzer fled to Nuremberg, where he caused more trouble. From there, he wandered to the borders of Switzerland and then back again to Mühlhausen. This time he stayed, and in April 1525, set up a church over which hung a banner declaring that he would soon be marching out to meet the forces of evil with an army of 2,000 followers. An army of princes eventually marched to Frankenhausen (near Mühlhausen), where the rebellious peasants had organized themselves into a formidable army numbering 8,000 under Müntzer's leadership.

The princes, who held superior forces and military positioning, offered the peasants clear terms of surrender: their lives in return for Müntzer and his closest followers. Müntzer responded by making a passionate speech to his troops, telling them that "God had spoken to him and had promised victory; that he himself would catch the enemy cannon-balls in the sleeves of his cloak; and that in the end God would transform heaven and earth rather than allow his people to perish."[117]

When no reply was sent to the princes, they began firing their artillery. The ensuing battle ended with the capture of Frankenhausen by the army of princes. Only six of their men were lost. As for the peasants, 5,000 of them were slaughtered in one day. Müntzer, although he escaped from the battlefield, was found hiding in a cellar. He was tortured and finally beheaded on May 27, 1525.

MASSACRE AT MÜNSTER

A decade later, another "prophet" — Melchoir Hoffmann (c. 1495–1543) — announced that Jesus' return would take place in 1533. Unlike Müntzer, Hoffmann was a peaceful activist. He, in fact, had stood with Luther against

Title page from one of many pamphlets that announced the end of the world
via a flood that was supposed to have struck in 1524.

the teachings of Müntzer and the revolt. Nevertheless, for condemning the
papacy, Hoffmann spent the last years of his life in a prison at Strasbourg,
the city where he thought the New Jerusalem would descend. Historical
records reveal that he saw himself as another Elijah and believed he was
"writing in the midst of the final seven years of history."[118]

As Hoffmann wasted away in Strasbourg, a significant number of
followers "flocked to the north German city of Münster in 1533 and
1534."[119] It was in this religiously unstable region that Jan Matthys, a
Dutch supporter of Hoffmann, gained control of Münster's government and
expelled all Lutherans and Catholics who disagreed with his views. He
proceeded to preach violence to cleanse the ungodly from the earth in
preparation for Jesus' return and the world's destruction by Easter of 1534.

But Easter came and went, as did Matthys, who met a bloody end when
the city that he had conquered was besieged by an army of vengeful
Protestants and Catholics. But this did not end the conflict at Münster. A
close associate of Matthys named John Beukels took leadership of the group

and continued the fight. He "declared himself ruler of the world and added polygamy to the community of goods and other radical practices that had been instituted in the new messianic city."[120]

These Münsterites, as they came to be known, were defeated in June 1535 when an army of Protestants and Catholics took the city. Beukels and other leaders "were tortured to death in January 1536, and their bodies were hung in iron cages from the cathedral spire."[121]

OUT OF THE SHADOWS

The 1400s and 1500s saw a lengthy list of end-time prognosticators, some of whom would go on to be rather famous. For example, there was Christopher Columbus, who in 1501 claimed that he was the messiah to whom Joachim had pointed! Columbus believed that the next climax in history "would be a successful last crusade. His calling was to lead the Christian armies."[122] He went so far as to predict that the world would end in one hundred fifty-five more years: 1656.[123]

In the midst of the sixteenth century's momentous changes, there appeared a man who would become the most famous "prophet" of all. His prognostications would not only be accepted during his life, but well after his death. In fact, his popularity would increase over the years, since many of his predictions seemingly pointed to our century. He is today celebrated by occultists, New Agers, some Roman Catholics, and even a few evangelicals. He has a remarkably large following, even though he has been dead for nearly 500 years. His name was Michel de Nostredame, more commonly known as Nostradamus.

SIX

Nostradamus

In the year 1999, and seven months, from the sky will come the great King of Terror.

Nostradamus

(1503–1566)[1]

ON MAY 10, 1988, the Los Angeles Griffith Observatory received hundreds of phone calls from terrified California residents who wanted information about the massive earthquake scheduled to occur that day. Their fears were based on *The Man Who Saw Tomorrow*, a documentary-style movie that had recently aired on cable TV. This film, narrated by actor Orson Welles, convincingly presented the sixteenth century occult seer, Nostradamus, as a man with supernatural powers who could see into the future.[2] The program presented several predictions by Nostradamus, one of which included a seismic disturbance that would destroy an unnamed "new city" when various planets moved into a certain astrological positioning in May of an unspecified year. It was suggested that either San Francisco or Los Angeles might be the doomed city. When television viewers subsequently discovered that a planetary alignment was due on May 10, they reached a frightening conclusion that prompted them to call the observatory for details on what might transpire, and how they could prepare for the worst.[3]

Astronomers were not the only ones approached during this minor bout of mass hysteria. A May 3 article in the Santa Monica *Evening Outlook* quoted Red Cross spokesperson Peggy Brutsche: "We've had a number of calls from people clearly inquiring because of the Nostradamus thing. Some of the public seem to be genuinely frightened from what they've heard."[4] Prominent California weatherman Fritz Coleman told the *Los Angeles Times* that his TV station's phones were "ringing off the hook."[5] Even the crisis hotlines at Long Beach Charter Hospital were flooded, according to Nurse Betty Searcy: "They're really panicking. Some of them are shaky and crying. I've had a lot of parents call and say their children can't sleep at night because of the predictions."[6] When journalists asked California geologist Jim Berkland for his observations, he commented: "This has gone beyond fun speculation. People are close to panic."[7]

Other social responses traceable to the movie were equally impressive. For example, companies specializing in earthquake preparedness supplies posted a dramatic rise in sales for the week of May 10. One company, Extend-A-Life, experienced a tenfold increase in demand for purified water, survival cookie-bars, first aid kits, thermal blankets, and hand-cranked AM-FM radios. Psychologist Robert Butterworth revealed to the Los Angeles *Herald Examiner* that he knew of some people taking amphetamines to stay awake so that when the quake hit they would "be at their best."[8]

But May 10 came and went like any other day in California. Nonetheless, since *The Man Who Saw Tomorrow*, an endless stream of bestselling books and made-for-TV specials have elevated Nostradamus and his predictions to an unrivaled level of popularity among prophecy buffs and doomsday aficionados. Some of the most sensationalistic claims about him have been made by Hollywood productions bent on exploiting society's current obsession with doomsday. The 1997 Fox Television network special *Prophecies of the Millennium*, for instance, wrongly declared that Nostradamus accurately predicted the death of King Henry II, the Great Fire of London (1666), Napoleon's reign, World Wars I and II, and Hitler's rise to power.[9]

In truth, Nostradamus may actually be history's *worst* prognosticator. According to well-known illusionist/magician James Randi (famed debunker of fraudulent faith healers and psychics), an investigation of one hundred three prophecies by Nostradamus that specifically mention a date, place, or

Nostradamus

person yielded an amazing discovery: none of them came true![10] Yet somehow the famed seer continues to be celebrated as an end-time visionary able to "look into the future and actually be there and experience what was going on even though it was hundreds of years ahead of him."[11] How could a prophet so inaccurate gain such widespread notoriety? Read on.

THE MAN BEHIND THE MYTH

Nostradamus — whose given name was Michel de Nostredame — was born in St. Rémy, France in 1503 to Jewish parents who converted to Christianity. His father, Jacques, and paternal grandfather, Pierre, were grain dealers (not prominent physicians, as today's followers of Nostradamus claim). Michel's mother, Renée, was the daughter of a failed doctor who had become a tax collector.[12] By the time Michel was born, Jacques was a successful notary, "well able to support a family."[13] Consequently, Michel was privileged to receive an education in nearby Avignon, one that included classes in the art of astrology.

After finishing his primary studies, Michel enrolled in the prestigious University of Montpellier in Provence, where he pursued a medical degree. He was probably an excellent student since he graduated at the early age of twenty-two. His ensuing internship took him on a prolonged tour through rural France as a plague doctor who successfully treated a number of patients. He eventually returned to Montpellier and obtained his full license to practice medicine when he was still only twenty-six. By this time, Michel de Nostredame had changed his name to simply Nostradamus, a Latin form of the French name. This "was a common custom of most physicians and other scholars of the day. . . . [It] set them above the uneducated and declared their status clearly."[14]

In 1526, forty-one-year-old Nostradamus settled down in the small town of Agen. There, he met his first wife, with whom he had two children. Unfortunately, tragedy struck Nostradamus about twenty-five years later, when the plague killed his wife and children. He alone was spared an agonizing death because he happened to be away on a tour of Provence when the dreaded disease crept through the streets of Agen.

In an effort to soothe his conscience and comfort his soul, Nostradamus set off on a pilgrimage throughout France and Italy, treating plague victims as he wandered the countryside. He finally found himself back in Salon de Provence, not far from his boyhood home of St. Rémy. He again put down roots after meeting his second wife, Anna Ponce Gemelle, "a rich widow by whom he was to have three sons and three daughters."[15]

At the age of about fifty, Nostradamus began writing vague, four-line verses of poetry (quatrains) arranged in groups of one hundred, each of which he labeled a "century." These were supposed to be prophecies, "couched in an eccentric and already archaic form of Latinized French peppered with what appear to be various foreign words and expressions."[16] Ten "centuries" were eventually written and published in a book entitled *The Centuries*. The first edition, printed in 1555, was incomplete. It consisted only of Century One through Century Three, and just fifty-three quatrains of Century Four. A supplemental 1557 edition added the missing quatrains of Century Four, as well as Centuries Five through Six, plus forty verses of Century Seven.

Centuries Eight through Ten appeared in a separate 1558 volume, leaving Century Seven incomplete. Consequently, modern editions do not have 1,000 quatrains divided evenly among Ten Centuries, which seems to have been Nostradamus's intention. We, instead, have 940 quatrains that can legitimately be attributed to Nostradamus. To these, eight more verses of doubtful authenticity are often added. They mysteriously appeared in the first English edition of *The Centuries* (1672), titled *The True Prophecies or Prognostications of Michael Nostradamus, Physician to Henry II, Francis II, and Charles IX, Kings of France, And one of the best Astronomers that ever were.*

According to Nostradamus devotees (i.e., Nostradamites), the 940 to 948 cryptic verses found in the centuries have accurately predicted a host of world events ranging from historic human tragedies and triumphs (e.g., Chernobyl, the Challenger disaster, Gorbachev's *glasnost*, and Germany's reunification) to trivialities reminiscent of tabloid newspapers (e.g., the marriage of Prince Charles and Diana, actor Richard Gere's association with the Dalai Lama, and the activities of Jane Fonda and Ted Turner).[17]

In reality, writings of his which appear to point to events that, in his day, would have been in the future, have been cleverly manipulated by zealous Nostradamites to read like fulfilled prophecies. This has been accomplished through use of a wide assortment of propaganda tools: bad scholarship, historical inaccuracies, forged documents, half-truths, and outright lies. The public's willingness to see Nostradamus as someone with "a rare gift of prophetic vision"[18] is a remarkable example of just how gullible people can be.

CENTURY BY CENTURY

Nostradamus's reputation as a seer *extraordinaire* began almost immediately after the 1555 edition of *The Centuries* was released. In fact, within four months of its publication, the Queen of France (Catherine de' Medici) summoned Nostradamus to Paris. This royal invitation was a distinct honor, "since at that time Paris supported an estimated 30,000 sorcerers, alchemists, astrologers and a variety of sayers of sooth. . . . [Her] request for Nostradamus indicated her exceptional regard for his work."[19]

It is not surprising that Catherine — wife of France's King Henry II — would want to meet Nostradamus who, by this time, had become a renowned astrologer. Catherine was an extremely superstitious sovereign who consulted countless occultists for spiritual insight. In fact, "many books on the occult sciences written in her time were dedicated to her."[20] Interestingly, the "prophecy" most often repeated by Nostradamites seeking to prove the powers of their favorite seer relates to King Henry, not Catherine. It is found in Century 1, Quatrain 35 (C1:Q35), first published in 1555:

ORIGINAL FRENCH	ENGLISH TRANSLATION[21]
Le lyon jeune le vieux surmontera,	The young lion will overcome the old one,
En champ bellique par singulier duelle:	On the field of battle in single combat:
Dans caige d'or les yeux luy creuera,	He will burst his eyes in a cage of gold,
Deux classes vne, puis mourir, mort cruelle.	Two fleets one, then to die, a cruel death.

This is, "by all standards, the single most famous of the Nostradamus quatrains, one that in his day officially put him at the forefront of all the seers, and continues to do so today."[22] What event does it predict? Nostradamites claim that these verses provide the details surrounding King Henry's untimely demise, which resulted from a freak jousting accident. The historical tragedy took place in July 1559 during a celebration honoring the double marriage of Henry's daughter Elizabeth to King Philip II of Spain, and Henry's sister Marguerite to the Duke of Savoy. The wine flowed, the guests laughed, and the music played to everyone's delight, until the last day of the festivities.

A jousting tournament had been staged, and now Henry II — himself a distinguished jouster — would sportingly face a Scottish captain of the guard, Gabriel de Lorges, Comte de Montgomery. When the two men collided during their final run at each other, a slight miscalculation caused Montgomery's lance to shatter. A wooden splinter entered Henry's helmet and pierced his skull just above the right eye, penetrating his brain. It was a fatal wound that took the King's life ten days later.

Nostradamites are quick to point out the exactness of C1:Q35. Henry Roberts, for instance, in his book *The Complete Prophecies of Nostradamus*, writes: "The Young Lion [Montgomery] . . . in a tournament with King Henry II, the Old Lion, accidentally pierced his golden helmet with a splinter of his wooden lance, putting out his eye . . . causing the King to die 'a cruel death.' "[23] Another Nostradamite, Erika Cheetham, makes an added observation: "The reference to *lyon* [lion] is interesting in that both the king and Montgomery had a lion in their coat of arms."[24]

These assertions have been repeated as absolute fact *ad nauseam ad infinitum*. *Mysteries of the Unexplained*, printed by the Reader's Digest Association, says: "Henry II of France, who sometimes used the lion as his emblem, engaged in a jousting contest. The lance of his young opponent pierced the king's gilt helmet and wounded him."[25] Another relevant passage in *Nostradamus: The End of the Millennium*, published by Simon & Schuster, reads: "Henry's opponent, Montgomery, was younger than the King. The Lion was an emblem used by Henry. . . . Next comes the amazing description 'Eyes in a Golden Cage' — a reference to Henry himself, since he was wearing a gilt helmet with a barred visor."[26] Yet a third volume, *Eve of Destruction* by Eva Shaw, declares: "[Montgomery's] lance pierced the king's visor — a visor made of gold."[27]

The historical facts, however, do not fit the quatrain as well as Nostradamites would have us believe. Montgomery was indeed younger than the King, but only by three years. Henry himself was a mere forty-one years old. Their meeting was hardly a case of a *young* man battling an *old* king. Furthermore, neither Henry nor Montgomery had a lion in their coat of arms. French royalty used a fleur-di-lis and a fighting cock. "The French, as a matter of record, have never used a lion as a symbol of the monarchy."[28]

It must also be noted that the men did not meet on a "field of battle." Jousting was a light-hearted sport in which no blood was to be drawn. Injuring an opponent was considered a major *faux pas*.[29] Henry also did not wear a golden helmet, nor did his eyes (or even one eye) "burst"! The wound was in his forehead, *above* the right eye.

A final observation about C1:Q35 involves its last line: "Two fleets one, then to die, a cruel death." The reader may notice the rather out-of-place word "fleets" (i.e., army). Nostradamites, too, have noticed this awkward term. Cheetham writes: "The Latin *classus*, fleets, makes no sense here, since there was no union of fleets anywhere in the world at this time."[30] But such a problem is easily dealt with by Nostradamus' fans. They simply discard "fleets" and replace it with "wounds," a word much more relevant, even though it appears nowhere in the text.[31]

What exactly is Nostradamus talking about in C1:Q35? No one can know for sure. But one prediction he made can *definitely* be linked to the royal court. This particular prophecy does not appear in any of his centuries, but instead, is mentioned by none other than the Queen herself. In a letter dated 1564, Catherine informs her godfather of an answer she received from Nostradamus after asking him to make a prophecy about her son, Charles IX. The original document, located in the Bibliothèque Nationale in France, is the only letter in existence in which Catherine mentions Nostradamus by name:

> To my godfather, the Milord Conétable . . . [W]e have seen Nostradamus, who has promised to my son, the King [Charles IX], everything good, and also that he shall live as long as you yourself, who he says shall see your ninetieth year ere passing this life.[32]

In other words, Nostradamus prophesied that Catherine's godfather and her son would both live to be ninety years old. Things, however, turned out differently. Conétable passed away at the age of seventy-seven and Charles died from intestinal tuberculosis when only twenty-four. Despite such instances of failed prognostications, a significant number of people continue to maintain that some of Nostradamus' prophesies "are so remarkably clear that they seem beyond coincidence or wishful thinking."[33] This claim, as we shall now see, is also patently unjustifiable.

DIGGING DEEPER

There are many quatrains regularly touted by Nostradamus followers as proof of their prophet's powers. Like C1:Q35, however, these other passages are so nonsensical that they can be made to fit any number of historical events. All it takes is a little creativity. As we have already seen, Nostradamites will not hesitate to add words to their translations that appear nowhere in the French text and delete words that do not fit the particular event supposedly being prophesied.

In an effort to promote the misconception that Nostradamus was a gifted prophet, devotees of the seer have even resorted to combining a line (or two) from one century with a verse (or verses) from another century, thus creating an entirely new quatrain that Nostradamus never wrote![34] Consider the following quatrains that Nostradamites say are some of *the most impressive* "prophecies" penned by their prophet.

The Great Fire of London
(C2:Q51)

ORIGINAL FRENCH	ENGLISH TRANSLATION[35]
Le sang du iuste á Londres fera faulte,	The blood of the just shall be wanting in London,
Bruslés par fouldres de vint trois les six:	Burnt by thunderbolts of twenty three the Six(es),
La dame antique cherra de place haute,	The ancient dame shall fall from [her] high place,
De mesme secte plusieurs seront occis.	Of the same sect many shall be killed.

This quatrain is said to predict the Great Fire of London (1666) that destroyed four-fifths of the city. As with C1:Q35, a considerable amount of fantasy must be coupled with word juggling in order to arrive at the interpretation that impresses so many Nostradamites. First, *fouldres* ("thunderbolts") in line two must be changed to *feu* ("fire"). This alteration to the text suddenly appeared in the first English translation of 1672, which coincidentally, was just six years *after* the London blaze.

Second, the phrase *de vint trois les six* ("twenty three the Six[es]") is a linguistically tortured, desperate attempt to get a reading that sounds significantly more like 1666. It is invariably mistranslated as either "the year '66" or "three times twenty plus six."[36] Both renderings contain words that are not in the text (i.e., year, plus, times.).

Third, *La dame antique* ("The ancient dame") in line three is applied
to St. Paul's Cathedral, which was destroyed. Why is the phrase equated
with a cathedral? According to Cheetham, the not-so-flattering "ancient
dame" remark points to the church's large statue of the Virgin Mary that
"fell on people seeking refuge from the fire." A similar interpretation
from *The Book of Predictions* reads: "The Virgin's statue on St. Paul's
toppled."[37] Shaw, on the other hand, says the ancient *dame* is the church's
dome ceiling.[38] (It should here be noted that there was no statue of the
Virgin Mary on the cathedral. Moreover, it had a severe Gothic style
squared roof.)[39]

As imaginative as these interpretations may be, a more plausible
explanation exists, based on observations by historians, that most of the
quatrains are "clearly contemporary political lampoons."[40] It is likely that
C2:Q51, published in 1555, refers to England's Roman Catholic Queen
Mary I ("Bloody Mary") and her mass execution of Protestants *in London*
(line one). Line two seems to refer to how Mary's victims were killed. They
were burned at the stake with bags of gunpowder tied between their legs or
around their necks. When the fire reached them, an enormous explosion
occurred (i.e., *Bruslés par fouldres*, "Burnt by thunderbolts"). The condemned were executed in groups of six, beginning on January 22, 1555 (i.e.,
de vint trois les six, "of twenty three the Six[es]").

The "ancient dame" remark of line three might easily refer to Mary
herself, who was quite insane by the final years of her reign. Suffering from
congenital heart failure and a host of other medical disorders, she would
wander half-naked throughout her palace, babbling incoherently about
religion, lost love, and an imaginary pregnancy by her absent Spanish
husband Philip, who by 1555 had left both Mary and England.

Finally, line four's comment about many being killed of the same sect
probably refers to the 300 Protestants who ended up being executed.
(Interestingly, the first edition of *The Centuries*, in which this quatrain
originally appeared, is dated May 4, 1555 — barely three months *after*
Mary's bloody executions began.)[41]

"King" Napoleon and Two Popes
(C8:Q1)

ORIGINAL FRENCH	ENGLISH TRANSLATION[42]
PAU, NAY, LORON plus feu qu'à sang sera. *Laude nager, fuir grand aux surrez.* *Les agassas entrée refusera.* *Pampon, Durance les tiendra enserrez*	PAU, NAY, LORON will be more in fire than in blood. Swim in praise, the great one to flee the confluence (of rivers). He will refuse entry to the magpies. Pampon and the Durance will keep them confined.

The manner in which Napoleon is extracted from this quatrain is rather ingenious. Nostradamites nonchalantly pluck out the letter "y" from *NAY* and combine it with the letters "ro" from the middle of *LORON* to get the *roy* (French, "king") to be used later, even though the word is not actually in the text. This letter manipulation leaves "PAU, NA, LON." Next, the commas are dropped, the order of words switched, and all three pseudo-words are thrown together to create NAPAULON. Finally, the left over *roy* is inserted to discern an encrypted message: "Napoleon, the king." (Nostradamites seem unfazed by the fact that Napoleon was never a king.)

Another argument for the convoluted interpretation focuses on the archaic word *agassas* ("magpies") in line three. The modern French word for magpie (i.e., a noisy bird of the crow family, or a chattery person) is *pie*, pronounced "pee." This is also the French word for "pious," which supposedly confirms the connection to Napoleon because he imprisoned two popes: *Pious* VI and VII.

Such linguistic acrobatics only serve to obscure the more likely explanation that Nostradamus was simply commenting on some regional event. Three small towns — Pau, Nay, and Oloron (also Loron) — happen to be near Nostradamus' boyhood home. Equally noteworthy is the word *Laude* in line two. In several editions of *The Centuries*, this appears as *L'Aude*. Coincidentally, there is an Aude River located just north of Pau, Nay, and Oloron. *Pampon* is probably the city of Pamplona (located in northern Spain, south of Oloron). The *Durance* is undoubtedly the Durance River, a prominent tributary just north of Nostradamus's birthplace. C8:Q1 is obviously talking about events that had already taken place, or that would take place, in the area where Nostradamus lived. It has nothing to do with Napoleon.

But John Hogue, author of *Nostradamus and the Millennium*, adamantly states that this quatrain clearly refers to Napoleon Bonaparte and his imprisonment of the two popes. Hogue, who is perhaps the best known of all contemporary Nostradamites, has appeared on numerous TV specials (often wearing a long flowing black cloak) to proclaim the powers of his favorite soothsayer. He has even put an added spin on C8:Q1 that directly relates to end-time visions:

> Napoleon was the first of three Antichrists foreseen by Nostradamus. Each Antichrist will take us a step closer to the final Battle of Armageddon. Nostradamus named all three of these Antichrists. He called Napoleon, "Nay-pau-lon-roy." It's an anagram; a word play on the name Apollyon, the angel of the abyss in the book of Revelations [sic].[43]

Exactly how Hogue gets the Greek term *Apollyon* (Rev. 9:11) from Nay-pau-lon-roy remains a mystery since an anagram is formed when a word/phrase is rearranged into another word/phrase *using the same letters*. The term *Apollyon*, however, fails to use five letters from Nay-pau-lon-roy and adds an extra "l." But Nostradamites are habitually unconcerned with trivial details like the etymology of a word or the proper use of a literary device. Their thinking is rooted in the notion that if various words sound alike, then they must mean the same thing (cf. next two sections).

It is also somewhat revealing that Hogue does not even know the correct name for the last book of the Bible. He calls it Revelation*s* (plural), rather than Revelation (singular). Although a relatively minor error, it is indicative of a tendency toward overlooking details. This is a common trait among Nostradamites that opens up a world of possibilities for them when interpreting their prophet's quatrains.

Hitler's Verses
(C2:Q24 and C4:Q68)

ORIGINAL FRENCH	ENGLISH TRANSLATION[44]
Bestes farouches de Faim fleuues tranner,	Beasts wild with hunger will cross the rivers,
Plus part du champ encontre Ister sera.	The greater part of the battlefield will be against Hitler.
En caige de fer le grand fera treisner,	He will drag the great one in a cage of iron,
Quand rien enfant de Germain obseruera.	When the child of Germany observes no law.

ORIGINAL FRENCH	ENGLISH TRANSLATION[45]
En l'an bien proche non esloigne' de Venus,	At a nearby place not far from Venus,
Les deux plus grans de l'Asie & d'Affrique	The greater ones of Asia and Africa;
De Ryn & Ister qu'on dira sont venus,	From the Rhine and Hitler they will be said to have come.
Crys, pleurs à Malte & costé ligustique.	Cries and tears at Malta and Ligurian coast.

The first quatrain (C2:Q24) supposedly points to nations coming against Hitler (lines one and two), until he finally commits suicide (line three) in his bunker ("a cage of iron"), after gaining for himself a reputation as a German who observed no laws (line four). Cheetham claims "[t]here can be little doubt that Hitler is referred to."[46] The second quatrain (C4:Q68) is allegedly filled with all sorts of World War II events:

Venus, standing for Venice, is the clue . . . as it links Italy, costé ligustique [i.e., Ligurian coast of western Italy], with Hitler. The two dictators, Hitler and Mussolini, met at the Brenner Pass when they sealed the Tripartite Pact with Asia, that is to say the Japanese. The last line refers to the blockade of Malta by the Italians and the trouble in the Ligurian coast, to the Allied bombing of Genoa and the bombardments by British battleships operating out of Gibraltar.[47]

Even the most casual reader will notice that the name Hitler is in neither quatrain. The word *Ister*, however, does appear in both of them. This term, according to Nostradamites, is a veiled reference to Hitler for two reasons: 1) it sounds and looks like Hitler (but only if you add and "H" to make it "Hister"); and 2) Ister is an old name for the Danube River, on the banks of which Hitler grew up (i.e., in Austria). Furthermore, there is the reference to Germany ("Germain") in line four of C2:Q24.

There are so many problems with these interpretations it is difficult to know where to begin analyzing them. The best place to start may be with the word "Germain." Admittedly, "de Germain" can indeed be translated as "of Germany." It is even in *modern* French dictionaries. But that is precisely the problem, as James Randi explains:

> [F]rom the 12th to the 16th century, "de germain" meant "brother" or "near relative" and nothing else. The word "German" came to be used in France only after World War II, to mean an inhabitant of Germany.[48]

Claiming that "Hister" is an anagram for Hitler is as contrary to linguistic possibilities as Hogue's Apollyon/Nay-pau-lon-roy theory. "Ister" has long been used (since the era of the Roman Empire) to describe the lower part of the Danube River. There is no reason to assume that Nostradamus was using it as a projected reference to a future leader who would grow up in Austria. Besides, an anagram out of the name Hitler could not contain an "s." A real anagram for Hitler would look more like "Lethir."

Attempts to link the phrases "At a nearby place not far from Venus [Venice]" and "The greater ones of Asia and Africa" (C4:Q68) to the 1941 Tripartite Pact are built on nothing but conjectures. Nostradamite James Laver remarks: "If Mussolini might be called the greatest one in Africa and Japan the greatest one in Asia, then the second line refers to the Tripartite Pact."[49] Mussolini, of course, was from Italy, not Africa.

Furthermore, Laver arbitrarily switches how he interprets the poem by identifying "the greater" one from Africa as a person, while interpreting "the greater" one from Asia as a nation. To be consistent, "the greater ones" from Africa and Asia should be either two people or two nations. Using consistency, however, would totally ruin the desired interpretation.

Finally, there is no reason even given for why the "cage of iron" in C2:Q24 should be interpreted as the bunker where Hitler committed suicide. The assertion is simply made for gullible persons to believe, even though the bunker was actually concrete.[50]

Exactly who came up with the idea that these and other quatrains refer to Hitler? No one is certain. Until 1936, commentators on *The Centuries* interpreted *Hister* to mean only the Danube. But by the mid-1930s, everyone was seeing Hitler in the quatrain. *Der Führer*, too, was convinced that the words referred to him. In fact, Nostradamus' writings were used by Joseph Goebbels, Hitler's Minister of Propaganda. He manipulated them to prophesy Nazi victory and printed them on leaflets. These were distributed throughout occupied countries. British and American propagandists responded with their own Nostradamus tracts. They, of course, prophesied Allied victory.[51]

ANYTIME OR ANYWHERE

There is literally no end to the list of events allegedly prophesied in Nostradamus' verses: the hot air balloon (C5:Q57), radio (C3:Q44) (wherein the word *l'animal* [animal] is said to actually mean radio-waves), nuclear bombs (C2:Q3), Nagasaki and Hiroshima (C2:Q6), the Ayatollah Khomeini (C6:Q80), the Gulf War/Operation Desert Storm (C8:Q70), and Mikhail Gorbachev (C9:Q36).

We are additionally told that Nostradamus predicted President John Kennedy's assassination: "The ancient work will be accomplished, And from the roof evil ruin will fall on the great man. Being dead they accuse an innocent of the deed: the guilty one is hidden in the misty woods" (C6:Q37). The "roof" is interpreted as the book depository window from which Oswald shot Kennedy ("the great man"). And for conspiracy buffs, Eva Shaw points out that "the phrase, 'Being dead they accuse an innocent of the deed,' seems to concur with reports that there were two shots fired and that Oswald may not have been in the right position to kill the president."[52] No one, however, seems to know why Kennedy's assassination would be referred to as an "ancient work."

Also consider C3:Q75: "Pau, Verona, Vicenza, Saragossa, swords drip-
ping [or damp] with blood from distant lands. A very great plague will
come in the great shell [i.e., scab], relief near, but the remedies far away."
Both Cheetham and Shaw suggest that this quatrain is talking about AIDS.
Why? According to Shaw, 'swords damp with blood from distant lands' is a
direct reference to AIDS, with 'swords' referring to the disease's transmission through sexual penetration, and the 'blood from distant lands' reflecting the fact that the plague had started abroad."[53]

This bizarre interpretation is reminiscent of the prophetic ravings of David
Koresh, who claimed that the word "horn" in the Bible was actually a veiled
reference to the male sex organ, as in "horny."[54] And what does line three mean
about the plague coming "in the great shell [or scab]"? Scabs are not symptoms
of AIDS. Again, these trivial details are simply ignored by Nostradamites.

Also labeled as prophetic is C1:Q25, which is said to actually mention
Louis Pasteur. Eva Shaw excitedly notes, "Nostradamus comments specifically
on the scientist's discoveries, using the doctor's name, *333 years before his time*."
Shaw adds to this remark a stinging indictment against unbelievers: "Critics
can provide no explanation for this incredible coincidence; most refuse to
comment on it."[55] But critics have made a number of comments about C1:Q25.
The fact is that this quatrain does *not* mention "Louis Pasteur" by name. It
only speaks of an individual referred to as the *pastor* being "celebrated as a
god." The French word for a pastor happens to be *pasteur*, which is close
enough for Nostradamites to add Louis and apply it to the scientist.

Significantly, the centuries are always applied to an event only after
that event has taken place. For example, there are no books on Nostradamus
written prior to 1963 that interpret C6:Q37 as being a prophecy about a
president destined to be assassinated. The quatrain's pre-1963 interpretation was King Louis XVI's failed attempt to escape from the rebels, and his
capture "in a forest hiding-place."[56]

Other quatrains have had a similarly flexible history. The now famous
AIDS-related C3:Q75 used to be applied to the Spanish influenza epidemic
of 1918.[57] Before that, the quatrain was seen as a reference to some
unknown plague that would hit Italian cities and spread "due to lack of
organization" by city officials.[58] C6:Q74 has had even more interpretations
over the years; five in all, as of 1990.[59]

It is true that there have been *some* occasions on which Nostradamites have gone out on a prophetic limb to predict a future event. *The Man Who Saw Tomorrow*, for instance, made several prognostications based on Nostradamus' quatrains: a global famine in the 1980s, Ted Kennedy becoming president in 1984, the previously mentioned 1988 earthquake, and World War III in 1994. Obviously, none of these predictions came true.

In *Nostradamus: The End of the Millennium* (1991) by V. J. Hewitt and Peter Lorie, we also find a number of false predictions: an evacuation of California from 1992–1993, the sinking of San Diego into the ocean via a massive earthquake in May 1993, the utter destruction of Switzerland's financial system by 1995, an Arab invasion of Israel in 1995, a spacecraft crashes on American soil in 1997.[60]

LEGENDS AND LIES

In addition to *The Centuries*, there are a number of legends about Nostradamus that his followers regularly present to the credulous public. Predictably, these amazing stories are about as reliable as his quatrains. The following narratives are but three examples of the many yarns Nostradamites so dearly relish.

Tales from the Crypt

Nostradamus died in his sleep of congestive heart failure on July 2, 1566 and was buried in the chapel of St. Martha in Salon. The marble tablet erected over his grave can still be viewed by persons visiting the site:

> Here lie the bones of the illustrious Michael Nostradamus, whose almost divine pen alone, in the judgment of all mortals, was worthy to record, under the influence of stars, the future events of the whole world. . . . Posterity, disturb not his sweet rest!

According to our first tale, posterity — in the form of several French soldiers — did indeed disturb Nostradamus' rest. This macabre story takes place in May 1791, at the height of the French Revolution (1789–1799). An unspecified number of drunken soldiers (possibly three) were aware of a rumor that had long been circulating throughout Europe: anyone who exhumes the body of Nostradamus and drinks from his skull will instantly inherit all of the prophet's powers. But a curse was also present: he who drinks from the skull will die.

Despite the ominous warning, these foolish men waited until dark (possibly around midnight) and proceeded to the accursed tomb. After hours of digging, the intoxicated soldiers finally pulled Nostradamus' coffin from its resting place. They opened it and were met by a ghastly sight. The prophet was lying down with a plaque across his chest that read: "May 1791." The message, held in place by bony fingers, was Nostradamus' final prophecy. He somehow knew exactly when his body would be exhumed.

Undaunted, the soldiers removed the plaque and lifted the prophet's skull. The bravest soldier, or perhaps the most foolish one, filled it with wine and began to drink. Just then, a shot rang out from a nearby riot and a stray bullet hit the man in the head, killing him instantly. So ends the tale.

Of course, most of the above story is false. The only true aspect to it is that the prophet's grave, like many burial plots during the French Revolution, was looted. The rest of the embellishments seem to have been added by a devout monk trying to discourage others from desecrating tombs in the future. And like most tall tales, this story can be told in various ways. Details mean little. In *The Book of Predictions* (1981), we find the story recounted in the following way:

> Secretly, Nostradamus had arranged to have a metal plaque buried with him. In 1700, when his coffin was opened in order to move his remains to a newly built tomb, the metal plaque was discovered resting on his skeleton. On it was inscribed the date 1700.[61]

Why the changes? Perhaps the authors of this book preferred a simpler approach to storytelling and liked round numbers. In 1987, the 1700 version of the story was repeated by none other than the black-robed John Hogue in *Nostradamus and the Millennium*.[62] Hogue, however, changed the metal plaque to a beribboned medallion.

A Queen's Séance

The following episode is related as fact in *La vie de Nostradamus* (1930) and numerous other publications including the 1961 volume *Science, Prophecy, and Prediction*:

> Having correctly predicted the death of Henri II of France during a tournament . . . Henri's widow, Catherine de Medici . . . summoned Nostradamus [to her castle at Chaumont], and for 45 nights the two of them conducted spiritualist seances. Nostradamus managed to conjure up the angel Anael who showed Catherine the future of her children in a mirror. Her three sons, later to become kings of France, appeared first and paraded across the mirror, once for every year of their reign. Since none of them was destined to reign for long, the parade took up little time, but when Catherine's son-in-law, the King of Navarre, who later succeeded to the French throne as Henri IV of France, appeared in the mirror, he took 23 turns in it. Catherine was so frightened at this revelation that she desisted from pressing Nostradamus for any further glimpses of the future. Both Nostradamus and the angel Anael obliged and the mirror reverted to its former, more prosaic, role of ordinary looking glass.[63]

After much investigation, James Randi discovered an interesting and unexpected bit of information. The historian Nicolas Pasquier chronicles this exact same séance including the magic mirror, Catherine's presence, the moving visions of her three sons, and the location of the event as Chaumont. In the Pasquier account, however, the astrologer assisting Catherine is *not* Nostradamus. Another medium named Cosimo Ruggieri, a resident of Chaumont, is named as the assistant to Catherine. It seems that Nostradamus devotees, feeling somewhat possessive of the Queen's affections for their prophet, borrowed the Ruggieri episode and made it their own. Interestingly, Pasquier is the *only* historian to record the séance. No other history book even hints at any such event, which casts a significant shadow of doubt on even Pasquier's story.[64]

Black Pig/White Pig

The Black Pig/White Pig legend appears in countless books and is often re-
told on sensationalistic TV specials eager to continue the Nostradamus-was-
a-psychic misconception. The following version is taken from *They Foresaw
the Future* by Justine Glass. The book is dedicated to celebrated witch
Doreen Valiente, who helped Glass with a significant amount of research:

> [Nostradamus] could not help making predictions. And as these were fulfilled,
> more and more people believed him to have the gift of foretelling the future. They
> did not include the Seigneur de Florinville, at whose castle of Fains Nostradamus
> stayed when passing through Lorraine. To prove the foolishness of such belief, the
> seigneur pointed out to Nostradamus in the farmyard a black and a white sucking
> pig. "Foretell their future," he said. "You will eat the black one; a wolf will eat
> the white one," Nostradamus answered. To make sure the prophecy was not
> fulfilled, the seigneur presently told his cook to kill and serve the white pig for
> supper that night. The piglet having been killed, it was cooked and left on the
> table ready for dressing. While the cook was out of the kitchen, a wolf cub which
> some of the seigneur's servants were trying to tame got in and ate the pig.... [T]he
> cook [then] killed the black one and served it at supper that night. The seigneur
> no doubt took some pleasure in telling his guest that they were eating the white
> pig. When Nostradamus insisted that it was the black pig, the cook was sent for,
> to prove Nostradamus wrong. He confessed that the white pig had made, as the
> seer had predicted, the wolf cub's meal; the pork they had been eating had been
> the black pig, which was substituted for its white brother.[65]

This story, as it turns out, is also not original. Another version exalts a
nineteenth century Sicilian prophet named Gregorio Nuncio Adolfo Pal-
lantrini. A few of the details have been changed by modern Nostradamites,
but it is essentially the same fable:

> [Pallantrini] is said to have startled his father by warning him that he would be
> injured by a black cock that they observed running about the estate. Already aware
> of his son's prophetic abilities, so the story goes, the father ordered the bird killed
> and prepared for consumption by the servants. He also ordered a white cock to be
> prepared for his own table. Again, before dinner, Gregorio warned his father, who
> shrugged off his words, confident that the black cock was unable to harm him.

During the evening meal, however, the father began to choke violently and had to be relieved of a bone which had become lodged in his throat. Recovering, he was told by his son that he had been eating the black, not the white, cock. The cook, immediately questioned, admitted that a cat had stolen the white bird and that to conceal that fact, she had served the black one at the master's table.[66]

In *The Mask of Nostradamus*, James Randi humorously remarks: "The similarity of the two stories makes one wonder whether this is a standard tale told about all prophets, as soon as they attain enough fame."[67]

THE NEVERENDING STORY

1999, 2000, 2002, 3420, 3797, and 7000 have all been seen by Nostradamites as catastrophic dates for humanity. Each year, it has been theorized, may bring an end to the world as we know it. Given the flexibility of Nostradamus' quatrains, there will no doubt be more years added to this list. And should the planet keep revolving into the eighth millennium, events more mundane than planetary disasters will assuredly be paired with that seer of seers, Nostradamus.

Recently, in fact, a widely-read publication released a Nostradamus-related news article that shocked the world. Its headline read: "Nostradamus Predicts O. J. Trial — And the verdict!" The quatrain cited does indeed seem frighteningly accurate:

The hero's name is tarnished by a bloody glove,

The masses cry for vengeance, but truth prevails,

Nineteen hundred and ninety-five finds him free,

The monster confesses and loses his soul in eighteen months.

Is this final proof that Nostradamus really is a prophet? Hardly. The above quatrain is a total fabrication that appeared for the first time in the 1990s. A tabloid newspaper reporter created it. Perhaps in a few hundred years, however, it will have found its way into a newly printed edition of Nostradamus' quatrains entitled *The Lost Prophecies of Nostradamus*. If so, it will no doubt be a best-seller.

SEVEN

Miller's Millennial Madness

I am fully convinced that somewhere between March 21st, 1843 and March 21st, 1844, according to the Jewish mode of computation of time, Christ will come.

William Miller
(1782–1849)[1]

IT DID NOT TAKE LONG FOR EUROPEAN OBSESSION with the world's end to make its way to American shores. In fact, New England Puritans who had come to America to escape religious persecution in England were quite confident that doomsday was near. Cleric Michael Wigglesworth, for instance, penned a 224-stanza poem titled "The Day of Doom" (1662) that became immediately popular. Deacon William Aspinwall, of the state's General Court, predicted the world's demise "no later than 1673."[2] There was also influential Puritan Cotton Mather (1663–1728), who was convinced that all the prophecies that needed fulfillment before Jesus' second coming had occurred. He further reasoned that the world would end in 1697, but later changed this prediction to 1716. After that date passed, 1736 became his new deadline for Christ's return.

Perhaps the most famous group of end-timers to find their way to America from England were the Shakers, led by Ann Lee (1736–1784). The sect was founded in Manchester, England by Quakers Jane and James Wardley. Lee got involved with the Shakers after going through several tragic experiences including an "unenthusiastic marriage" to blacksmith Abraham Standerin and the death of four infants.[3] For some reason, she became convinced that the loss of her children was divine punishment for indulging sexual desires. Lee responded by withdrawing from her husband in 1766 and announcing that she had experienced a "complete conversion."[4]

The Shakers did not begin enjoying popularity until 1774, when Lee guided a band of eight believers to Watervliet, New York (near Albany). Lee's belief system, which rested on the doctrinal foundation of absolute celibacy for all followers, included: 1) communal living; 2) pacifism; 3) spiritual manifestations such as violent shaking, uncontrolled barking, and frenzied dance; and 4) a belief in the impending destruction of the world. Unlike most end-time movements, Shakers believed that Christ had already come, "embodied in an embryonic way in the Shaker community."[5]

These communities were adamantly against sexual intercourse, so much so that men and women were segregated into male/female dormitories and not allowed to even eat together unless chaperoned. (An added restriction was rather odd: it was considered sinful to watch animals copulate.) Married converts were actually "de-married" to further drive a wedge between the genders. This would eventually be the downfall of the Shakers. No procreation meant no new generation of believers. The Shakers, however, felt that there was no need to reproduce, since the world was going to end by 1792.

Although Ann Lee died well before doomsday's predicted date of arrival, her flock continued to flourish for several years under other leaders, each of which kept Lee's memory alive. The *Dictionary of Christianity in America* notes that through a prolonged reflection on Lee's role, Shakers gradually began to believe that "she was the second coming of Christ in female form. This belief was held most strongly during the Shaker spiritual revival, known as 'Mother Ann's Work' " from 1837–1847.[6] Coincidentally, these years also saw the rise and fall of the most notable doomsday movement of the nineteenth century: the Millerites.

A MAN NAMED MILLER

William Miller — born on February 15, 1782 in Pittsfield, Massachusetts — was raised on the rugged frontier of Low Hampton, New York. As the oldest of sixteen children in a poverty-stricken household, he received little more than a rudimentary education, but made up for his lack of formal schooling by reading numerous books borrowed from neighbors.

Although books greatly contributed to Miller's worldview, his most deeply ingrained lessons about life came from his mother, a devout Baptist whose father and two brothers served as ministers. She instructed her son to believe the Bible and to love Jesus Christ with all his heart, soul, mind and strength. Mrs. Miller may have even hoped that young William would someday become a preacher.

Christianity suited Miller well until 1803, when he married Lucy Smith and moved to Poultney, Vermont. His faith was critically damaged in this New England town by the hypocrisy he saw among professing Christians. The crisis of faith was intensified by his newly acquired circle of friends and acquaintances, who were educated, articulate, and refined. Their role models, rather than heroes of Scripture, were notable skeptics: David Hume, Voltaire, and Thomas Paine, all of whom Miller read with fascination. When Miller's new associates finally won him over to their "rational" way of thinking, he abandoned his faith in both the church and the God of the Bible.[7]

Like many of his skeptical friends, Miller turned to deism, a religious belief system that accepted the existence of a divine Creator, but denied that the Almighty personally interacted with his creation. God, according to deists, simply started the universe in motion like a clockmaker who "wound up the clock of the world once and for all at the beginning, so that it now proceeds as world history without the need for his further involvement."[8] Deism saw reality as being governed solely by natural law, leaving no room for the miraculous or supernatural. Consequently, Miller also found himself rejecting the Bible's divine inspiration, the deity of Christ, and the benefit of prayer.

Although Miller experienced a change of faith, his moral outlook remained much the same. He was a respected figure and recognized leader, who at various times served the community as a constable, justice of the peace, and deputy sheriff. When America found itself engaged in the war of 1812, Miller joined the militia as a captain in the infantry. He was a capable leader who immediately won praise and admiration from fellow soldiers. In fact, when he signed up for military service, forty-seven other men volunteered with him "on the condition that they serve directly under his command."[9]

By this time, however, Miller was struggling with his deism. Morality and reason, the cornerstones of deism, simply did not fill the spiritual void created by his abandonment of Christianity. A fatal blow to Miller's deistic outlook was delivered at the battle of Plattsburgh, where he and only about 5,000 other Americans squared off against a reported 15,000 British troops. Miller believed that they would experience a devastating defeat unless God intervened.

After several grueling skirmishes on both land and sea, the American forces scored a decisive victory over the British fleet on September 11, 1814. It was a battle in which Miller had played a "courageous part."[10] Plattsburgh ultimately spelled disaster not only for the king's invading units, but also for Miller's flagging deism. God, it seemed to Miller, had actually stepped into time and space to perform a miracle.

When the war ended in 1815, Miller moved with his family back to Low Hampton, and settled on a 200-acre farm near his boyhood home. There, he was regarded "with much esteem, as a benevolent, intelligent man, and a kind neighbor."[11] But as well as his life was going, he could not forget the events at Plattsburgh, which prompted more questions in his mind about various issues: heaven, hell, the reason for evil in the world, the problem of sin, the nature of humanity, and his own state of impiety:

> Eternity — what was it? And death — why was it? . . . The more I thought,
> the more scattered were my conclusions. I tried to stop thinking, but my
> thoughts would not be controlled. I was truly wretched, but did not understand
> the cause. I murmured and complained, but knew not of whom. I knew that
> there was a wrong, but knew not how or where to find the right. I mourned,
> but without hope.[12]

Miller sought to resolve the conflict in his soul by attending the local Baptist church pastored by his uncle. Though not an official member of the congregation, Miller was asked on several occasions to perform sermon readings. The reading on one occasion focused on Isaiah 53, a prophecy describing the coming Messiah's suffering and death for the sins of the

William Miller

world. Miller was so moved by the words of the passage that he had to sit down to regain his composure:

> I saw that the Bible did bring to view just such a Saviour as I needed. . . . I was constrained to admit that the Scriptures must be a revelation from God. They became my delight; and in Jesus I found a friend. . . . [T]he Scriptures, which before were dark and contradictory, now became the lamp to my feet and light to my path. My mind became settled and satisfied.[13]

Miller's spiritual search culminated in 1816 with a re-dedication of his life to Christianity. But he then had to face the criticisms of deist associates. As expected, they did not hesitate to level the same objections Miller himself had previously expressed against the Christian faith. This time, however, Miller resolved to find his own answers. Beginning with Genesis, he embarked on an intensive two-year study of Scripture. He tried so hard to avoid preconceived biases that he chose to use only a Bible concordance (a book grouping verses by key words) to guide him.

Miller pursued his studies with great diligence and sincerity, taking a keen interest in prophecy like so many of his countrymen. Along the way, however, he encountered many portions of Scripture that were particularly difficult to interpret. His difficulties were compounded by his refusal to use scholarly resources (such as Bible commentaries), lack of formal training, and limited linguistic skills. Unable to fully uncover the historical and grammatical context of various prophetic passages, Miller arrived at a staggering and erroneous deduction:

> I was thus brought, in 1818 . . . to the solemn conclusion, that in about twenty-five years from that time all the affairs of our present state would be wound up.[14]

In other words, Miller determined that the world was going to end around 1843 with Jesus' return and the establishment of God's millennial kingdom on Earth.

SETTING A DATE

The eschatology held by the majority of Christians during Miller's day was postmillennialism; namely, that the church would bring about a millennium (a 1,000-year period of peace and prosperity) that would culminate with Christ's return. Miller, on the other hand, believed that only *after* Christ's return would peace be established on Earth for 1,000 years (a view known as premillennialism). According to Miller, God had revealed the timing of the last days in Scripture, and it could be unraveled using the right calculation method. There were a few rules governing the time calculating process, but these were well within the grasp of untrained lay persons willing to take the time and effort required to learn them. He insisted that anyone of reasonable intelligence could decipher the prophecies and see, as he did, that in the Bible "the end of all things was clearly and emphatically predicted, both as to time and manner."[15]

Miller's foundational interpretive principle was that one prophetic day equals one literal year (Ezek. 4:6). Using this bedrock rule, he turned to two crucial biblical passages: 1) Daniel 9:24-27, which speaks of seventy weeks until the messiah comes to save Israel; and 2) Daniel 8:14, which mentions 2,300 days until God's sanctuary is cleansed. The seventy prophetic weeks (or 490 days) represented a 490-year period that began in 457 B.C. with King Artaxerxes' decree to rebuild Jerusalem (Ezra 7:11-26). Going 490 years forward from that date brought Miller to A.D. 33/34, the year that, according to some Christians, Jesus was crucified. Christ's first coming, then, was perfectly fulfilled at the end of Daniel's weeks. This discovery legitimized, at least in Miller's mind, his method of date calculation. He then applied his time computation to Daniel 8:14. He saw this passage as a reference to Christ's return, when the earth (i.e., "sanctuary") would be cleansed. Using the same principle as before, he added 2,300 *years* to the starting date of 457 B.C., which brought him to a target date A.D. 1843.[16]

The calculations clearly indicated to Miller that the apocalypse and the millennium were close at hand. As additional confirmation, he determined that 1843 would mark 6,000 years from the creation of Adam, which conveniently corresponded to the six days of creation in Genesis. On the seventh day, says Genesis 2:2, God rested. To Miller, this meant that the seventh day — or the beginning in the 7,000th year, prophetically speaking — would mark the completion of God's plan of redemption for humanity. It would be the beginning of Jesus' millennial kingdom of peace on earth.[17]

SPREADING THE WORD

Although Miller shared his insights privately with friends and relatives, it did not take long for him to realize that he needed to express his views on a much wider scale. Consequently, he wrote a series of sixteen articles in 1832 that were published in the *Vermont Telegraph*, a local Baptist periodical. A year later, he set forth a synopsis of his beliefs in a sixty-four-page pamphlet that enjoyed wide circulation.[18] In 1833 he also began to publicly preach, but only in reluctant response to what seemed to have been yet another sign from God:

> One Saturday, after breakfast, in the summer of 1833, I sat down at my desk to examine some point, and as I arose to go out to work, it came home to me with more force than ever, "Go and tell it to the world." The impression was so sudden, and came with such force, that I settled down into my chair, saying, "I can't go, Lord." "Why not ?" seemed to be the response; and then all my excuses came up, my want of ability, etc.; but my distress became so great, I entered into a solemn covenant with God, that, if he would open the way, I would go and perform my duty to the world. "What do you mean by opening the way ?" seemed to come to me. "Why," said I, "if I should have an invitation to speak publicly in any place, I will go and tell them what I find in the Bible about the Lord's coming." Instantly all my burden was gone, and I rejoiced that I should not probably be thus called upon, for I had never had such an invitation. . . . . In about half an hour from this time . . . a son of Mr. Guilford, of Dresden, about sixteen miles from my residence, came in and said that his father had sent for me, and wished me to go home with him. Supposing that he wished to see me on some business, I asked him what he wanted. He replied, that there was to be no preaching in their church the next day, and his father wished to have me come and talk to the people on the subject of the Lord's coming. . . . I left the boy, without giving him any answer, and retired in great distress to a grove near by. There I struggled with the Lord for about an hour, endeavoring to release myself from the covenant I had made with him, but could get no relief. . . . I finally submitted; . . . I returned to the house, and found the boy still waiting; . . . I returned with him to Dresden.[19]

Miller's sermon on prophecy was received with great enthusiasm and resulted in a deluge of invitations from other churches in New York and the northeastern United States. Within a year, he could accept no more than half of the speaking engagement requests he received from Baptist, Methodist, and Congregational churches.[20] Miller, once a simple country preacher, quickly developed into a powerful and engaging orator who attracted sizable crowds. On more than one occasion spiritual revivals broke out in churches and towns following his dramatic presentation of apocalyptic truths.[21]

Then, on November 13, 1833, the world witnessed what Miller and his followers interpreted as a sure sign of the end: a meteor shower that would later be described by astronomer W. J. Fisher as "the most magnificent meteor shower on record."[22] One eyewitness described the shower as "an incessant play of dazzling brilliant luminosities. . . . Some of these were of great magnitude and most peculiar form. . . . [T]he first appearance was that of fireworks of the most imposing grandeur, covering the entire vault of heaven with myriads of fireballs resembling skyrockets."[23]

Coincidentally, May 19, 1780 had brought another unusual phenomenon that affected the northeastern United States from New Jersey to Maine: several hours of complete darkness that began at high noon. Scientists have since discovered that this episode resulted from "vast forest fires raging unchecked in the unpopulated western territories."[24] The west-to-east flow of wind and weather made New England particularly susceptible to such a phenomenon. But the farmers and city dwellers who experienced the event only knew that the sun had disappeared. To them, it seemed like the end of the world had finally come. The House of Representatives in Hartford, Connecticut actually adjourned. The governor's council, however, continued their meeting at the urging of Colonel Abraham Davenport. "Either the day of judgment is at hand or it is not," Davenport thundered. "If it is not, there is no cause for adjournment. If it is, I wish to be found in the line of my duty."[25]

Miller and others could not help but see in all of these heavenly displays a fulfillment of Jesus' words: "Immediately after the tribulation in those days shall the sun be darkened and the moon shall not give her light, and the stars shall fall from heaven and the powers of heaven shall be shaken" (Matt. 24:29). The darkening of the sun in 1780, combined with the stars falling in 1833, convinced many devout believers that the second advent of Jesus was indeed near.[26]

Finally, in 1836, Miller penned his first book: *Evidence From Scripture and History of the Second Coming of Christ About the Year A.D. 1843*. The text would later be accentuated by various prophecy time charts that included a bevy of winged lions, leopards, bears, and dragons. These apocalyptic images gleaned from Daniel and Revelation tantalized Ameri-

A nineteenth century sketch of the celestial event that greatly agitated Millerite expectations:
the 1833 meteor shower. This drawing appeared in the 1883 volume *American Progress; or The
Great Events of the Greatest Century.*

cans interested in prophecy, a study which was fast becoming an obsession among people of all classes.

Miller proceeded to criss-cross the east coast and parts of Canada, preaching about "the time of the end" and the imminent second coming of Jesus Christ. (He would later claim to have delivered in excess of 4,500 lectures over a twelve-year span to more than a half million people.) At first, fellow clergymen viewed Miller with a skeptical eye. Soon, however, several leading ministers — e.g., Josiah Litch, Joshua V. Himes, Joseph Bates, and Charles Fitch — began spreading his message.

Especially important to Miller was Himes, a gifted organizer and promoter who converted to Miller's cause in 1839. He was instrumental in getting Miller in front of huge audiences in large cities. Himes was also responsible for introducing Miller's views via several national newspapers. He additionally established two significant periodicals to further spread Miller's teachings: *Signs of the Times* (later called *The Advent Herald*) and the *Midnight Cry*. Millennial madness quickly swept the country under the banner of the Millerite movement.

DOOMSDAY APPROACHES

Miller's prediction that Jesus would return around 1843 spread like wildfire across all denominational lines in the church, and within a few short years a bonifide religious movement was in full swing. It pulled followers from the Methodists, Baptists, Presbyterians, and Congregationalists. While determining the exact number of Millerites has proved elusive, conservative estimates range from fifty thousand to well over one hundred thousand. Soon, these so-called "Millerites" had inadvertently formed a new sect that religion watchers of the day labeled "Adventists."

Miller never intended to form a new sect, but such an outcome was unavoidable given the highly sensationalistic nature of his teachings. As the terminal date of history drew closer, Adventists became increasingly divisive and antagonistic toward fellow Christians who would not join the movement. They soon began to publicly denounce all churches that rejected Miller's message of the apocalypse, branding them "Babylon," the false religious system spoken of in Revelation 14:8, 17:5.

These drawings, which illustrate various prophetic symbols mentioned
in the Bible, appeared in a Millerite publication.

These churches, in turn, scorned the doomsday messengers, expelling and excommunicating from their ranks any ministers and lay persons supporting Miller. The Methodists went so far as to adopt an official resolution in 1843 that reflected the alarm of most mainstream clergyman and many churches:

> *Resolved:* That the peculiarities of that theory relative to the second coming
> of Christ and the end of the world, denominated Millerism, together with all
> its modifications, are contrary to the standards of the church, and we are
> constrained to regard them as among the erroneous and strange doctrines
> which we are pledged to banish and drive away.[27]

But America's new prophet remained resolute. "What have we believed that we have not been commanded to believe by the word of God, which you yourselves allow is the rule, and only rule, of our faith and practice?," asked Miller. "Our conclusions have been formed deliberately and prayerfully, as we have seen the evidence in the Scriptures."[28]

Millerites supplied the media with more than enough bizarre news stories on which to report. Tent meetings, for example, were sometimes marked by wild behavior that included frenzied dance, fainting, and screaming. A number of followers also threw away their possessions and fled from cities. Miller himself added even more fuel to the apocalyptic fire on January 1, 1843 by declaring a definitive time-frame:

> I am fully convinced that sometime between March 21st, 1843 and March 21st, 1844, according to the Jewish mode of computation of time, Christ will come, and Bring all His Saints with Him; and that then He will reward every man as his work shall be.[29]

Miller had previously been somewhat vague about the exact date of Christ's second advent, simply saying that it would occur "about 1843." But all of that had changed with this new proclamation. Miller's message became crystal clear: "The hour of God's judgment is at hand — prepare to meet thy God."[30]

As 1843 progressed, expectations reached an almost feverish pitch. Millerites were so numerous in some cities that it was impossible for them to find buildings large enough to accommodate their meetings. Another sure sign that the end was imminent appeared in the heavens in the form of a brilliant comet that blazed across the sky in February 1843. It was called the "Great Comet."[31] The celestial wonder was so bright that it could be seen during the day with the naked eye. The 1883 historical volume *American Progress: or The Great Events of the Greatest Century* devoted an entire chapter to describing the appearance of this spectacular event:

> The comet of 1843 is regarded as, perhaps, the most marvelous of the present age, having been observed in the daytime even before it was visible at night, — passing very near the sun, — exhibiting an enormous length of tail, — and arousing an interest in the public mind as universal and deep as it was unprecedented. It startled the world by its sudden apparition in the spring, in the western heavens, like a streak of aurora, streaming from the region of the sun, below the constellation of Orion. It was at first mistaken, by multitudes, for the zodiacal light; but its aspects and movements soon proved it to be a comet of the very

largest class. There were, too, some persons who, without regarding it, like many of the then numerous sect called Millerites, as foretokening the speedy destruction of the world, still could not gaze at it untroubled by a certain nameless feeling of doubt and fear. . . . The appearance, at first, was that of a luminous globular body with a short train. . . . The head of the comet, as observed by the naked eye, appeared circular; its light, at that time, equal to that of the moon at midnight in a clear sky; and its apparent size about one-eighth the area of the full moon. Some observers compared it to a small cloud strongly illuminated by the sun. The train was of a paler light, gradually diverging from the nucleus, and melting away into the brilliant sky. An observer at Woodstock, Vt., viewed the comet through a common three-feet telescope, and found that it presented a distinct and most beautiful appearance, exhibiting a very white and bright nucleus, and showing a tail which divided near the nucleus into two separate branches. . . . It was occasionally brilliant enough to throw a strong light upon the sea. . . . In regard to the extraordinary brilliance . . . this was due to the comet's proximity to the sun. . . . [I]t had almost grazed the sun's disk. . . . The comet on the twenty-eighth of February was red hot. . . . In the equatorial regions, the tail is described as resembling a stream of fire from a furnace. Such are some of the principal facts concerning this most wonderful comet of modern times.[32]

A nineteenth century sketch of the great comet of 1843. This drawing appeated in the 1883 volume *American Progress: or The Great Events of the Greatest Century.*

This same year also saw the building of a huge Millerite tabernacle in Boston. It was dedicated "with great pomp and circumstance in front of a group of more than three thousand followers."[33] Not everyone, however, was pleased. A Philadelphia newspaper story read as follows:

The Millerites have very properly been shut out of the buildings in which they have for some time been holding their orgies in Philadelphia, and we are happy to learn that the grand jury of the Boston municipal court has represented the great temple itself as a dangerous structure. After some half-dozen more deaths occur and a few more men and women are sent to madhouses by this miserable fanaticism perhaps some grand jury may think it worthwhile to indict the vagabonds who are the cause of so much mischief.[34]

Although the general public began to deride the Millerites, especially after March 21, 1843 had passed uneventfully, most Millerites remained unfazed. After all, Miller's prediction left a whole year for the second advent of Christ. Even at the end of 1843, the Millerites remained confident of their beliefs. In a New Year's address to his congregation, Miller declared the following:

> Brethren, the Roman [year] 1843 is past and our hopes are not realized. Shall we give up the ship? No, no. . . We do not believe our reckoning has run out. It takes all of 457 [years] and 1843 to make 2,300 [days], and must of course run as far into '44 as it began in the year 457 before Christ. [The Jewish sacred year would end in the spring of 1844.][35]

According to historian Clara Endicott Sears, the uneventful close of 1843 did cause a few Millerites to start harboring doubts, but these were soon dispelled after they spoke with persons who had been with the movement since its beginning:

> [I]t was recalled that as far back as 1839 Prophet Miller had stated on some occasion, which had been forgotten in the general excitement, that he was not positive that the event would take place during the Christian year from 1843 to 1844, and that he would claim the whole Jewish year which would carry the prophecy over to the 21st of March, 1844. An announcement to this effect was made, and by this time the delusion had taken such a firm hold upon the imaginations of his followers that any simple explanation, however crude, seemed sufficient to quiet all doubts and questions.[36]

Interestingly, this would be the same excuse used in 1994 by twentieth century prognosticator Harold Camping (see Chapter 3). Like Camping's followers, Miller's devotees accepted the time extension and renewed their work with vigor. Sears noted that Millerites seemed bent on terrifying unbelievers into belief by enumerating the horrors that awaited them. The approach also served to further strengthen the faith of those already in Miller's ranks. The tactic worked and the Millerites grew in number.

But as Miller's doomsday deadline drew nearer, he seemed to sense that the end would not come as he had predicted. On February 15, 1844, he said: "If we are mistaken in the time [of the March 21 return of Christ], we feel the fullest confidence that the event we have anticipated is the next great event in world history."[37] March 6, 1844 found Miller making this statement: "If Christ comes, as we expect, we will sing the song of victory soon; if not, we will watch, and pray, and preach until He comes, for soon our time, and all prophetic days, will have been filled."[38]

Sadly, the subtle message contained in these comments was utterly missed by Miller's flock. The *Midnight Cry* reported many people leaving their jobs and homes to warn the public about doomsday: "In Philadelphia, thirteen volunteered at one meeting (after hearing Brother Storrs) to go out and sound the alarm . . . in other cities, stores are being closed."[39] The growing fanaticism was widely condemned. Even the famous lexicographer Noah Webster voiced his disapproval to Miller:

> Your preaching can be of no use to society but it is a great annoyance. If you
> expect to frighten men and women into religion, you are probably mistaken.
> . . . If your preaching drives people into despair or insanity, you are responsible
> for the consequences. I advise you to abandon your preaching; you are doing
> no good, but you may do a great deal of harm.[40]

On March 21, 1844, some of the more fanatical Millerites completely lost control. A Boston journalist who had been following the story, reported to the *New York Herald* that many Millerites had actually jumped from roofs and treetops in hopes of timing their leaps with Christ's return. But Jesus did not return and those who jumped "were critically hurt, and some fell to their deaths."[41]

When March 21, 1844 came and went, the public had a field day. Miller's followers were subjected to merciless ridicule. The headline of one Boston newspaper read: "What! — not gone up yet? — We thought you'd gone up! Aren't you going up soon? — Wife didn't go up and leave you behind to burn, did she?"[42] Miller, confused, grief-stricken, and embarrassed, admitted his mistake in a May 2, 1844 letter, stating: "I *confess my error*, and acknowledge *my disappointment*." At the same time, however, Miller declared: "I still believe that the day of the Lord is near, even at the door."[43]

Despondent and disillusioned, some individuals abandoned the movement. A large number of believers, however, continued to anticipate the end of all things. These faithful devotees were finally given a much needed boost in August 1844, when Samuel S. Snow — a committed Millerite — claimed to have found the explanation for Miller's miscalculation. According to Snow, Jewish chronology indicated that Christ would return in the fall of 1844, rather than in the spring as Miller had indicated. He announced his discovery at a major five-day Millerite camp meeting near Exeter, New Hampshire. Snow even came out with a new day for the end: October 22, 1844.[44]

THE GREAT DISAPPOINTMENT

Millerite expectations were raised once again as people prepared for the revised date, which Snow had dubbed the "seven month message" (the seventh month in the Jewish calendar) and the "new midnight cry!" Although initially reluctant, Miller finally accepted the October date and aligned himself with the renewed movement. On October 6, he wrote to his good friend, Joshua Himes: "Now, blessed be the name of the Lord, I see a beauty, a harmony, and an agreement in the Scriptures, for which I have long prayed, but did not see until today. Thank the Lord . . . . I am almost home. Glory! Glory!! Glory!!!"[45] In this same letter, Miller also wrote: "If Christ does not come within twenty or twenty-five days, I shall feel twice the disappointment I did in the spring."[46]

Tremendous excitement surrounded the arrival of the final day. One man "put on turkey wings, got up in a tree and prayed that the Lord would take him up. He tried to fly, fell, and broke his arm."[47] Several land owners, who at one time had been wealthy, had been reduced to poverty after selling all of their property and donating the money toward the construction of Miller's tabernacle building in Boston. In one area of New Hampshire, several Millerite farmers refused to reap their harvest of corn and potatoes, nor let others take in their crop, "saying it was tempting Providence to store up grain for a season that could never arrive, the great catastrophe being so near at hand."[48] On October 11, Miller wrote to his friend Himes:

> I have never seen among our brethren such *faith* as is manifested in the seventh month. "He will come," is the common expression. "He will not tarry the second time," is their general reply. There is a forsaking of the world, an unconcern for the wants of life, a general searching of heart, confession of sin, and a deep feeling in prayer for Christ to come. A preparation of heart to meet Him seems to be the labor of their agonizing spirits. There is something in this present waking up different from anything I have ever before seen. . . . No arguments are used or needed: all seem convinced that they have the truth. There is no clashing of sentiments: all are of one heart and of one mind. Our meetings are all occupied with prayer, and exhortation to love and obedience. The general expression is, "Behold the Bridegroom cometh; go ye out to meet Him."[49]

But joy and enthusiasm turned to overwhelming disappointment because, as one witness put it, "[T]he day came. And Christ did not." October 22, 1844 went down in history as the "Great Disappointment." The emotional pain was overwhelming for thousands of faithful believers. Joseph Bates, a close associate of Miller's, wrote a friend on the following day: "You can have no idea of the feeling that seized me. I had been a respected citizen, and had with much confidence exhorted the people to be ready for the expected change. . . . If the earth could have opened and swallowed me up, it would have been sweetness compared to the distress I felt."[50] Millerite Hiram Edson, while reflecting on October 22, wrote: "Our fondest hopes and expectations were blasted, and such a spirit of weeping came over us as I never experienced before. It seemed that the loss of all earthly friends could have been no comparison. We wept, and wept, till the day dawn."[51] Millerite lecturer Luther Boutelle would also write an account of the event:

[T]he 22nd of October passed, making unspeakably sad the faithful and longing ones . . . . All was still. No *Advent Herald*; no meetings as formerly. Everyone felt lonely, with hardly a desire to speak to anyone. Still in the cold world! No deliverance — the Lord [had] not come! No words can express the feelings of disappointment of a true Adventist then. . . . It was a humiliating thing, and we all felt it alike. All were silent, save to inquire, "Where are we?" and "What next?" All were housed and searching their Bibles to learn what to do.[52]

As for Miller, he removed himself from active ministry and died in obscurity in 1849 — still looking for the apocalypse of Jesus that he had so longed to see. Like the comets and meteors that marked his years in the annals of Armageddon, Miller's end-time ministry appeared suddenly and burned bright. As one nineteenth century historian remarked: "Few men have attained a wider name or more rapid and remarkable note, in the American religious world, than Rev. William Miller, 'the prophet' — as he was familiarly called."[53]

The Millerite movement was irrevocably shattered on October 22, 1844, but many of its beliefs and methods of Bible interpretation found their way into the modern era. Furthermore, numerous individuals emerged from Miller's disappointed flock to start their own denominations such as the Seventh-day Adventists, under the leadership of Ellen G. White. This group was well on its way to becoming a stable denomination within two months of The Great Disappointment.

Several persons attempted to explain away what had happened by coming up with novel interpretations of Miller's miscalculations. White's Adventists, for example, claimed that the "cleansing of the sanctuary" about which Miller had spoken did indeed take place, but everyone had been mistaken about the nature of the *sanctuary*. It was not Earth, which the Millerites had erroneously thought would be cleansed at the second coming. The sanctuary was actually an invisible realm in the heavens.

A lessor-known faction retained the name Second Adventists. Unlike the Seventh-day Adventists, who wisely eschewed date-setting, Second Adventists continued to speculate about the timing of Christ's return. They actually set yet another date for Jesus' second coming: 1873/1874. As unbelievable as it sounds, a second doomsday movement was born. It, too, drew hundreds of followers, including one young man by the name of Charles Taze Russell.

Like Miller, Russell (1852–1916) was extremely articulate and preached with fire and zeal. By 1870, he had formed his own home Bible study group in Allegheny, Pennsylvania that focused primarily on biblical passages dealing with Christ's second coming. His small group of loyal followers would gradually emerge as one of the largest end-time cults of the twentieth century: the Jehovah's Witnesses.

EIGHT

Jehovah's Witnesses: Armageddon, Inc.

[People] have at hand the Bible, but it is little read or understood. So, does Jehovah have a prophet to help them, to warn them of dangers and to declare things to come? These questions can be answered in the affirmative. . . . This "prophet" was not one man, but was a body of men and women . . . . [known] as International Bible Students. Today they are known as Jehovah's Christian witnesses.

The Watchtower[1]
April 1, 1972

THE WATCH TOWER BIBLE AND TRACT SOCIETY (WTBTS) — commonly known as the Jehovah's Witnesses (hereafter referred to as JWs) — is one of the most deceptive and dangerous of today's apocalyptic cults. Like many other groups of this type, the JWs present a list of dos and don'ts that members must obey if they hope to earn salvation. Distinct to the Watch Tower, however, is its ban on activities not normally associated with religious activity. The organization does not allow members to observe holidays (e.g., Christmas, Thanksgiving, or Easter), nor can they celebrate birthdays, Mother's Day, Father's Day, or Valentine's Day. Members cannot vote in elections, salute their country's flag, or sing any national anthem. More devastating is the group's ban on blood transfusions, which has led to countless Witness deaths, including many children.[2]

Since its inception in the late 1800s, the group's hierarchy has kept rank-and-file members in line with a series of false prophecies, doctrinal flip-flops, scholastic dishonesty, and psychological manipulation via peer pressure, verbal intimidation, and threats of excommunication. Despite countless warnings about the WTBTS that have been issued by numerous counter-cult organizations, the Witnesses continue to thrive worldwide. Much of this cult's success can be attributed to the zealous proselytizing efforts of its members. In 1997, for instance, Jehovah's Witnesses spent a total of 1,179,735,841 hours preaching their message in two hundred thirty-two countries.[3]

The group's evangelistic strategy rests on door-to-door witnessing coupled with distribution of two semi-monthly magazines: *Awake!* and *The Watchtower.* The former publication targets non-members and focuses on current events, while the latter periodical is the group's "chief means of instructing members in doctrine and practice."[4] As of January 1998 circulation for *Awake!* was 18,350,000 in eighty languages and circulation for *The Watchtower* was 22,103,000 in one hundred twenty-eight languages.[5] The WTBTS has also produced a significant number of books throughout its history, and continues to do so at a rate of about one or two per year. These books promote basic doctrines, serve as instructional guides for living, and contain Bible studies.

JWs have even published their own translation of the Bible: *The New World Translation of the Holy Scriptures* (NWT). Most scholars have labeled it an obvious propaganda tool filled with deliberate mis-translations of the biblical Hebrew and Greek texts in order to promote the Witness doctrines.[6] Nevertheless, by 1998 more than 82,513,571 copies of the NWT had been published in thirty languages.[7] This impressive number of Bibles produced by the WTBTS does not mean that JWs are avid Bible students. Although many JWs may read their Bibles, they are allowed to do so only in conjunction with other WTBTS publications, which serve to interpret Scripture for them.

According to JWs, the Bible is actually an "organizational book" that is beyond the understanding of all persons except the Governing Body of the WTBTS (i.e., the ruling spiritual hierarchy of the organization). Scripture does not belong "to individuals, regardless of how sincerely they may believe that they can interpret the Bible."[8] JWs assert: "Only this organization functions for Jehovah's purpose and to his praise. To it [i.e., the

27-year-old Charles Taze Russell in 1879. His International Bible Students Association
would later evolve into the cult known as Jehovah's Witnesses.

organization] alone God's Sacred Word, the Bible, is not a sealed book."[9]
This method of keeping members obedient to a set of beliefs promoted by
WTBTS leaders can be traced to the organization's founder, Charles Taze
Russell, who stated that only through his writings could a proper under-
standing of Scripture be gained.[10]

RISE OF THE RUSSELLITES

As mentioned previously in Chapter 7, the roots of the Jehovah's Witnesses
go back several years before Charles Taze Russell was even born, to a time
in early nineteenth century American when apocalyptic expectations were
running high due to the Millerite movement. Although Millerism *per se*
died out, plenty of Second Adventists — i.e., individuals formerly of the
Millerite camp — continued to look for Jesus' imminent return, setting yet

another date for the end: 1873/74.

It was to this group of end-timers that young Charles Taze Russell found himself drawn. He was clearly another Miller: charismatic, bold, self-assured, striking in appearance, and imbued with an air of authority. Not surprisingly, he quickly succeeded in becoming a leader among the Second Adventists. His followers were dubbed Russellites. It was the Millerite movement all over again, except on a much smaller scale.

The Russellites (some of whom had lived through the "Great Disappointment") were understandably saddened when their 1873/74 date for Jesus' return went by uneventfully, just like Miller's date had passed thirty years earlier. Nevertheless, the Russellites continued to pursue their millennial dreams under Russell because he put forth a new way to explain the failed prophecy. Rather than admitting that there had been a time miscalculation, as Miller had done, Russell adopted a cleverly devised Second Adventist excuse. It was proposed that everyone had indeed been right about the *1874* date of Jesus' return, but were wrong about the *manner* in which he had appeared. Christ had returned invisibly and could only be seen with the eyes of faith! Russell explained it this way in *Zion's Watch Tower* and *Herald of Christ's Presence*, a periodical to be later renamed *The Watchtower*:

> Looking back to 1871, we see that many of our company were what are known as Second Adventists, and the light they held briefly stated, was that there would be a second advent of Jesus . . . . This they claimed would occur in 1873. . . . Well, 1873 came . . . and yet no burning of the world . . . . But prophecies were found which pointed positively to 1874 as the time when Jesus was due to be present . . . . The autumn of 1874, anxiously expected, finally came, but the earth rolled on as ever. . . . Then the prophetic arguments were carefully re-examined. Was an error found? No, they stood the test of all investigation . . . . Dark indeed seemed the outlook; all were discouraged. . . . Just at this time Bro. Keith, (one of our contributors) was used of the Lord to throw another beam of *light* on the subject which brought order out of confusion, and caused all of the former "light" to shine with tenfold brightness. . . . [A] new idea of *a presence* unseen, except by the eye of faith . . . . [W]e realized that when Jesus should come, it would be as unobserved by human eyes as

though an angel had come . . . . Here was a new thought: Could it be that the *time prophecies* . . . were really meant to indicate when the Lord would be *invisibly present* to set up his kingdom? . . . [T]he evidences satisfied me.[11]

Russell and his followers were thus able to cling to their end-time scenario and preach their message to the masses. To better disseminate his teachings, Russell founded and installed himself as president of Zion's Watch Tower Tract Society in 1884. This organization evolved into the Watch Tower Bible and Tract Society, which continues to serve as the legal corporation for Russell's spiritual progeny: the Jehovah's Witnesses.

ARMAGEDDON IS COMING!

Under Russell, The WTBS experienced tremendous growth. Members, then known collectively as the International Bible Students Association, looked exclusively to Russell for spiritual nourishment. Especially popular was his six-book series called Studies in the Scriptures.[12] Through these books, Russell not only taught that Jesus had turned invisibly in 1874, but claimed that his arrival in the heavenly realms marked the beginning of humanity's "Time of Trouble," which would culminate with the Battle of Armageddon in 1914 and the end of the world:

[W]e present the Bible evidence proving that the full end of the times of the Gentiles, i.e., the full end of their lease of dominion, will be reached in A.D. 1914; and that that date will be the farthest limit of the rule of imperfect men. . . . [A]t that date the Kingdom of God, for which our Lord taught us to pray, saying "Thy Kingdom come," will have obtained full, universal control, and that it will then be "set up," or firmly established, in the earth.[13]

[T]he "battle of the great day of God Almighty" (Rev. 16:14), which will end in A.D. 1914 with the complete overthrow of earth's present rulership, is already commenced.[14]

[A]ll present governments will be overthrown and dissolved. . . . [T]he full establishment of the Kingdom of God, will be accomplished by the end of A.D. 1914.[15]

This same prediction was printed in *Zion's Watch Tower & Herald of Christ's Presence.*[16] With the commencement of World War I in 1914, Russell proclaimed his message with even more zeal, declaring: "The present great war in Europe is the beginning of the Armageddon of the scriptures."[17] Russell, however, never lived to see Christ's return. He died on October 31, 1916, still believing that "the end" was near. He was wrong. But faithful followers continued to promote the prophetic chronology that their beloved pastor had so painstakingly formulated.

Many of the newer converts to Russell's flock held on to their expectations due in part to a concerted effort made by WTBTS leaders to cover up the various mistakes and false prophecies that had been published by group leaders. Russell himself had initiated this practice as his doomsday date drew nearer. For example, later editions of *Studies in the Scriptures* contained subtle changes in the text where Russell had made explicit declarations regarding the timing of the end. He deliberately altered them in an effort to give his predicted "end" more time to unfold. These alterations were made with no explanatory notes about the textual changes.

Compare the following photostatic reproductions of various passages found in volumes two, three, and four of different editions of *Studies in the Scriptures.* (The deceptive alterations have been underlined to assist the reader in locating them.):

Volume 2

(p. 99)

In view of this strong Bible evidence concerning the Times of the Gentiles, we consider it an established truth that the final end of the kingdoms of this world, and the full establishment of the Kingdom of God, will be accomplished by the end of A. D. 1914. Then the prayer of the Church, ever since her Lord took his departure—"Thy Kingdom come"—will be answered ; and under that wise and	In view of this strong Bible evidence concerning the Times of the Gentiles, we consider it an established truth that the final end of the kingdoms of this world, and the full establishment of the Kingdom of God, will be accomplished near the end of A.D. 1915. Then the prayer of the Church, ever since her Lord took his departure—"Thy Kingdom come"—will be answered ; and under that wise and
1906 edition	1913 edition

Volume 3

(p. 228)

power of Jehovah's Anointed. Just how long before 1914 the last living members of the body of Christ will be glorified, we are not directly informed ; but it certainly will not be until their work in the flesh is done ; nor can we reason-	power of Jehovah's Anointed. Just how long after 1914 the last living members of the body of Christ will be glorified, we are not directly informed ; but it certainly will not be until their work in the flesh is done ; nor can we reason-
1908 edition	1916 edition

Volume 4

(p. 604)

date;—the "harvest" or gathering time beginning October 1874; the organization of the Kingdom and the taking by our Lord of his great power as the King in April 1878, and the time of trouble or "day of wrath" which began October 1874 and will end October 1914; and the sprouting of the fig tree. Those who choose might with-	date;—the "harvest" or gathering time beginning October 1874; the organization of the Kingdom and the taking by our Lord of his great power as the King in April 1878, and the time of trouble or "day of wrath" which began October 1874, and will cease about 1915; and the sprouting of the fig tree. Those who choose might with-
1897 edition	1916 edition

The most fascinating change made to *Studies in the Scriptures* appears in volume three, where Russell sought to prove his Armageddon time-table through pyramidology (see Chapter 2). Russell taught that the pyramid was "God's Stone Witness" corroborating biblical prophecy. To Russell, the pyramid's "Descending Passage," which starts inside the structure's entrance and leads toward its "Subterranean Chamber" (or "Pit"), was a prophetic marker of world events.[18] He believed that the "Pit" designated the "Time of Trouble" — i.e., a period of catastrophe that he predicted would occur just prior to the 1914 Battle of Armageddon.

Russell further declared that each inch in the passage represented one year, and that by taking measurements of the "Descending Passage" and numerous intersecting passages, one could predict exactly when the world's Time of Trouble would begin. Predictably, Russell discovered that the measurements pointed to the very year that he himself had already arrived at through computations based on Bible chronology: 1874. It was yet another confirmation to Russell that 1874 marked the beginning of the end, which would culminate in 1914 with the Battle of Armageddon.

But as 1914 drew near, Russell began to worry that perhaps God's end-time battle would not take place after all. Consequently, he came up with an ingenious way to buy himself more time. He had volume three reprinted, and simply stretched the Great Pyramid's passage by forty-one inches. Each extra inch translated into an extra year. Suddenly, the WTBTS was teaching that the *beginning* of the end had *not* started in 1874. Instead, the year *1915* was the landmark date for the beginning of trouble to start:

Volume 3

(p. 342)

1902 edition	1916 edition
as the date at that point. Then measuring *down* the "Entrance Passage" from that point, to find the distance to the entrance of the "Pit," representing the great trouble and destruction with which this age is to close, when evil will be overthrown from power, we find it to be 3416 inches, symbolizing 3416 years from the above date, B. C. 1542. This calculation shows A. D. 1874 as marking the beginning of the period of trouble; for 1542 years B. C. plus 1874 years A. D. equals 3416 years. Thus the Pyramid witnesses that the close of 1874 was the *chronological* beginning of the time of trouble such as was not since there was a nation—no, nor ever shall be afterward. And thus it will be noted that this	Then measuring *down* the "Entrance Passage" from that point, to find the distance to the entrance of the "Pit," representing the great trouble and destruction with which this age is to close, when evil will be overthrown from power, we find it to be 3457 inches, symbolizing 3457 years from the above date, B. C. 1542. This calculation shows A. D. 1915 as marking the beginning of the period of trouble; for 1542 years B. C. plus 1915 years A. D. equals 3457 years. Thus the Pyramid witnesses that the close of 1914 will be the beginning of the time of trouble such as was not since there was a nation—no, nor ever shall be afterward. And thus it will be noted

By the early 1920s, most WTBTS leaders felt that the numerous changes to Russell's writings would garner their organization more than enough extra time for the world's end to occur. So confident were they that the planet's demise was near, that Russell's successor — J. F. Rutherford (1869–1942) — started making his own predictions. The year 1914 had easily replaced 1874 as the *beginning* of troubles. But what year would replace 1914 as the date of the end? Rutherford picked 1925.

1925 — DEFINITELY

Joseph Franklin Rutherford became president of the Watch Tower in 1917. He was an aggressive leader who rabidly attacked "Christendom" through radio programs, public speeches, convention lectures, books, pamphlets, and assorted publications. Under his control, the size of the Russell's organization grew exponentially. In fact, it was Rutherford who instituted the door-to-door preaching for which Witnesses have become so well-known. It was also Rutherford who introduced several new doctrines into the group, while at the same time contradicting a number of Russell's teachings.

His administration additionally saw the name "Jehovah's Witnesses" adopted in 1931 as a descriptive term that would forever identify the doctrinally shifting cult of "Bible Students" founded by Russell. The new name was adopted for two reasons: 1) to separate followers of the Watch Tower from traditional Christian groups; and 2) to delineate Rutherford's followers from those individuals who remained true to Russell's teachings and who had formed their own Russellite groups after his death.

A 1922 Watch Tower Bible & Tract Society flyer that advertizes an end of the world lecture by Fred Franz, who would eventually become president of the organization.

Perhaps the most infamous period of Rutherford's presidency was from 1918 to 1925. During this era of JW history, the Watch Tower Society declared with full assurance that 1925 would bring the complete overthrow of all worldly governments, the resurrection of Old Testament saints (e. g., Abraham and Jacob), and the establishment of God's earthly kingdom. In other words, 1925 would mark the end of the world.[19] Rutherford first announced this prophecy during a 1918 lecture that was eventually turned into a 1920 booklet entitled *Milllions Now Living Will Never Die*.

Throughout the early 1920s, this prediction was consistently reinforced by a nationwide campaign that included speaking engagements, posters, flyers, large billboards, and newspaper advertisements. Books published by the WTBTS during these years also supported the prediction.[20] The most authoritative pronouncements on the subject, however, appeared in *The Watchtower* magazine:

Abraham should enter upon the actual possession of his promised inheritance in the year 1925 A.D. [prophecy printed in 1917].[21]

If any one who has studied the Bible can travel through Europe and not be convinced that the world has ended, that the day of God's vengeance is here, and that the Messianic kingdom is at the door, then he has read his Bible in vain. . . . The date 1925 is even more distinctly indicated by the Scriptures because it is fixed by the law God gave Israel. . . . [E]ven before 1925 the great crisis will be reached and probably passed [prophecy printed in 1922].[22]

[T]he present crisis in the world is caused by the long-looked-for King of Glory, the Lord Jesus, taking unto himself his great power and . . . . making way for the era of peace and happiness in the joyous time just over the horizon of 1925, when God's will shall be done on earth as it is in heaven [prophecy printed in 1923].[23]

Rutherford claimed that his prediction was based on nothing less than "the promises set forth in the divine Word."[24] The certainty with which *The Watchtower* preached the world's demise brought many converts into the organization. But as God's day of judgment approached, the Watch Tower began once again to back away from the dogmatic assertions it had made. For example, the July 15, 1924 issue of *The Watchtower* stated: "The year 1925 is a date definitely and clearly marked in the Scriptures, even more clearly than that of 1914; but it would be presumptuous on the part of any faithful follower of the Lord to assume just what the Lord is going to do during that year."[25] The most obvious attempt at downplaying prior declarations about doomsday appeared in the January 1, 1925 issue of *The Watchtower*:

The year 1925 is here. With great expectation Christians have looked forward to this year. Many have confidently expected that all members of the body of Christ will be changed to heavenly glory during the year. This may be accomplished. It may not be.[26]

As more of 1925 slipped by, WTBTS leaders seemed to have completely forgotten about their previous statements regarding the year's significance. In one book they published that year, Rutherford declared that faithful followers should expect to see only one thing in 1925: "[E]xpect the people to begin to receive some knowledge concerning God's great plan of restoration."[27] In another 1925 booklet, he actually wrote: "Much has heretofore been said about 1925. . . . Many people are looking for something phenomenal to happen. . . . A careful consideration of prophecy will enable you to be fortified against whatsoever comes."[28]

The Watchtower of September 1, 1925 issued what was perhaps the most unbelievable warning: "It is to be expected that Satan will try to inject into the minds of the consecrated the thought that 1925 should see an end of the work."[29] What about all of the previous statements in The Watchtower concerning 1925? According to WTBTS leaders, rank-and-file members had misunderstood what was printed and erroneously "anticipated that the work would end in 1925, but the Lord did not so state."[30] This assertion, however, completely contradicted what WTBTS leaders had declared in the August 15, 1922 edition of The Watchtower: "This chronology is not of man but of God . . . of divine origin . . . absolutely and unqualifiedly correct."[31]

To date, the organization's Governing Body is still trying to convince Jehovah's Witnesses that the fiasco of 1925 was the fault of various members who had read too much into what appeared in official Watch Tower publications. The 1980 Yearbook of Jehovah's Witnesses, for instance, explains:

> The book Millions Now Living Will Never Die had been widely used . . . and on the basis of its contents, much was expected of 1925. . . . It was stated in the 'Millions' book that we might reasonably expect them [Abraham, Isaac, and Jacob] to return shortly after 1925, but this was merely an expressed opinion [emphasis added].[32]

But the Millions book clearly expresses more than just an opinion. Pages 89–90 read: "[T]he great jubilee cycle is due to begin in 1925. At that time the earthly phase of the kingdom shall be recognized. . . . Therefore we may confidently expect that 1925 will mark the return of Abraham, Isaac, Jacob and the faithful prophets of old [emphasis added]"[33] Rutherford's statements on page 97 are even more definitive:

> [T]he old order of things, the old world, is ending . . . and that the new order is coming in, and that 1925 shall mark the resurrection of the faithful worthies of

old. . . . [M]illions of people now on the earth will be still on the earth in 1925. Then, based upon the premises set forth in the divine Word, we must reach the positive and indisputable conclusion that millions now living will never die.[34]

Rutherford and other WTBTS officials obviously misled members into believing that God's Word pointed to 1925 as the end of the world. In fact, 1929 found them still promising that Armageddon was near: "It is a special pleasure to announce that the next few years [c. 1930s] will witness the full establishment of that kingdom which is to be the desire of all nations."[35] As we have already seen, this prediction was not the first false prophecy to be made by the Watch Tower, nor would it be the last. The next two presidents of the Jehovah's Witnesses — Nathan Knorr and Frederick Franz — would make their own false prophecies.

DOOMSDAY'S ALMOST HERE

When Nathan Knorr (1905–1977) took over for Rutherford in 1942, one of his first acts as president was to release a new book titled *The New World*. This volume continued promoting what had become a standard line of the WTBTS — i.e., that the Old Testament saints would soon be resurrected in order to assume their roles as earthly rulers in Jehovah's Kingdom. *The New World* proclaimed, "[T]hose faithful men of old may be expected back from the dead any day now."[36] A 1942 issue of *Consolation* additionally promised: "[T]hat these princes will *shortly* take office upon earth as perfect men is found in the prophecy of Daniel . . . . Proof is now submitted that we are now living at 'the end of the days,' and we may expect to see Daniel and the other mentioned princes any day now!"[37]

Such predictions came as a surprise to no one. The WTBTS had been suggesting for several years that Armageddon would occur in the 1940s as a result of World War II. An earlier *Consolation* article (October 1941) had stated: "[T]he German people are awakening to their horrible predicament. . . . [T]heir faces are . . . filled with forebodings of what the near future will bring and is already hastening to bring to them — Armageddon, the battle of that great day of God Almighty."[38] As far back as May 1940, the *Informant* — a members only publication — had declared: "The year 1940 is certain to be the most important year yet, because Armageddon is very near."[39]

In September 1940, WTBTS leaders reiterated: "The Kingdom is here, the King is enthroned. Armageddon is just ahead."[40] The September 15, 1941 issue of *The Watchtower* told readers that a recently released book entitled *Children* would be "the Lord's provided instrument for most effective work in the remaining months before Armageddon."[41] Tragically, these false prophecies were coupled with a series of directives that advised JWs to forsake marriage and child-rearing:

> There are now on earth Jonadabs [i.e., Jehovah's Witnesses] devoted to the Lord . . . . Would it be Scripturally proper for them to now marry and begin to rear children? No, is the answer, which is supported by the Scriptures.[42]
>
> Scriptures appear to clearly show that the survivors of Armageddon will be those Jonadabs who henceforth 'seek righteousness' . . . . SHOULD THEY MARRY NOW? . . . [S]hould the Jonadabs now be encouraged to marry and rear children? No, is the answer supported by the Scriptures.[43]
>
> [T]he great multitude who survive the battle of Armageddon will be the only ones of the human race to abide on the earth . . . . [S]hould those begin now to marry and bring forth children in fulfillment of the divine mandate? No, is the answer; which the Scriptures fully support.[44]

Countless JWs throughout the world made decisions about their future based on this advice that had appeared in official Watch Tower publications. But Armageddon never came, and many witnesses lived to regret not having followed through with their original plans to marry and/or bear children. Knorr responded by simply ignoring the misleading statements that the WTBTS had published. Then after more twenty years of continuing to preach the imminent arrival of Armageddon, Knorr chose yet another date for the end of human history: 1975.

JUST ONE MORE TRY

Pushing Armageddon all the way up to 1975 took quite a bit of work on the part of WTBTS leaders. They had to completely re-write Russell's outdated mode of end-time calculating. The 1943 book *The Truth Shall Make You Free* was Knorr's first step to formally erase what Witnesses had been believing since 1879. The volume completely did away with Russell's dating system, replacing it with the one currently being used by the Jehovah's Witnesses. According to the new system, Jesus did not return invisibly in 1874, but returned in 1914.[45]

It was further taught that many persons comprising "the generation" that was alive during 1914 would live to see Armageddon and God's kingdom established. This "1914 generation" time-table continued to be reinforced until 1966, when the book *Life Everlasting in Freedom of the Sons of God* set 1975 as the target date for Armageddon, the alleged end of 6,000 years of history since the creation of Adam.[46] In JW eschatology, this meant that the end of the world would occur within eight years. More importantly, plenty of people from the "1914 generation" would still be alive in 1975:

> [I]t was to our generation that Jesus referred when he added the key thought: "This generation will by no means pass away until all these things occur." (Matt. 24:34) The generation that saw the beginning of woes in 1914 would also see the end of Satan and his entire wicked system of things. Some who were alive then would still be alive when "the end" comes. It is to be carefully noted that the youngest of those who saw with understanding the developing sign of the end of this system of things from its start in 1914 are now well over sixty years of age![47]

By 1968 the WTBTS was boldly pushing 1975 as the completion date of human history.[48] A 1966 issue of *Awake!*, promised: "[W]ithin relatively few years we will witness the fulfillment of the remaining prophecies that have to do with the 'time of the end.'"[49] One especially influential article appearing in a 1968 issue of *The Watchtower* was entitled "WHY ARE YOU LOOKING FORWARD TO 1975?" The story continued: "Are we to assume from this study that the battle of Armageddon will be all over by the autumn of 1975, and the long-looked-for thousand-year reign of Christ will begin by then? . . . It may involve only a difference of weeks or months, not years."[50]

As in the 1940s, Witnesses were once more counseled to not get married or have children, and young adults were advised to forego higher education and professional careers in order to devote themselves to the organization in the months remaining before Armageddon:

[T]he end of this system is so very near! . . . Reports are heard of brothers selling their homes and property and planning to finish out the rest of their days in this old system in the pioneer service. . . . [T]his is a fine way to spend the short time remaining before the wicked world's end.[51]

Today there is a great crowd of people who are confident that a destruction of even greater magnitude is now imminent. The evidence is that Jesus' prophecy will shortly have a major fulfillment, upon this entire system of things. This has been a major factor in influencing many couples to decide not to have children at this time. They have chosen to remain childless so that they would be less encumbered to carry out the instructions of Jesus Christ to preach the good news of God's kingdom earth wide before the end of this system comes.[52]

Will you be finishing school soon? If so, what have you decided to do after you graduate? . . . Of course, there may be a tempting offer of higher education or of going into some field of work that promises material rewards. . . . In view of the short time left, a decision to pursue a career in this system of things is not only unwise but extremely dangerous. . . . Many young brothers and sisters were offered scholarships or employment that promised fine pay. However, they turned them down and put spiritual interests first.[53]

Although such statements were reminiscent of what had been said in the 1940s, WTBTS leaders had already taken steps to psychologically prepare JWs to tolerate more talk about "the end." By 1968, the Governing Body — under Knorr's leadership — was actually claiming that JW's during World War "didn't succomb" to any expectations about that war leading to Armageddon.[54] This was to make the new prophecy about 1975 seem even more reliable and trustworthy.

Adding considerable credence to the 1975 prediction wa s Watch Tower vice-president Frederick Franz (1893-1992) who would succeed Knorr as president in 1977. In fact, Franz was the Governing Body member who wrote *Life Everlasting in Freedom of the Sons of God.*[55] He would also be instrumental in explaining why 1975 did not bring the end as predicted. As in the past, the average Jehovah's Witness was blamed for having "missed the point" of all the WTBTS's statements, and erroneously "thinking that Bible chronology reveals the specific date."[56]

The most notable aspect of Franz's term as president was his steadfast adherence to the teaching that persons alive during 1914 (that "generation") would definitely see Armageddon. But when Franz died in 1992 at the age of ninety-nine, it became apparent that there were not many individuals left who had witnessed the events of 1914. This realization placed the Governing Body in a very precarious situation since much of the Watch Tower's doctrine has been based on the belief that the generation of 1914 would see Jehovah's Kingdom established. The problem, however, would be cleverly dealt with by Franz's successor: 72-year-old Milton G. Henschel.

LET'S CALL THE WHOLE THING OFF

Henschel's primary concern after taking office was figuring out how to rescue the WTBTS from total collapse. The death of Fred Franz, who was part of the 1914 generation, made it uncomfortably clear that few persons from that era were still alive. The long-held prophecy that the 1914 generation would see Jehovah's Kingdom established was set to crumble, and with it, the entire eschatology of "God's organization."

The prophecy originally held that persons old enough to see "with understanding" the events of 1914 would also live to see the world's end. Such individuals, according to WTBTS leaders, probably would have been no younger than fifteen years old in 1914.[57] It was taught that this 1914 generation "logically would not apply to babies born during World War I."[58] Then in the 1980s, the Watch Tower contradicted itself by revealing that the term "generation" applied to people who were only *babies* in 1914.[59] By extending "the generation" to babies, WTBTS leaders were able to continue maintaining that the end would come before that generation passed away.

But this left Henschel with no more ways to redefine the 1914 "generation." Consequently, he boldly discarded the entire generation prophecy in the November 1, 1995 issue of *The Watchtower*. This "new light"[60] of truth explained that the "generation" mentioned by Jesus in Matthew 24 has nothing to do with individuals — adults or babies — living in 1914. Now, the term simply applied to wicked mankind in general; more specifically, any and all people of the earth in any generation who "see the sign of Christ's appearance but fail to mend their ways."[61]

The all-important "generation of 1914" had been relegated to *everyone* living in today's wicked system; or perhaps in the wicked system of one hundred years from now, or one thousand years from now. All time elements had been completely removed. Although this major step contradicted the position that had been held by JWs for eighty years, it was a change that *had* to be made. One can only wonder how members of the Watch Tower psychologically justify God's prophecies changing so arbitrarily:

PRE-1995	POST-1995
"[T]he generation alive in 1914, some will see the major fulfillment of Christ Jesus' prophecy and destruction"[62] "What, then, is the 'generation that 'will by no means pass away until all these things occur'? . . . It is the generation of people who saw the catastrophic events that broke forth in connection with World War I. . . . We can be happy, therefore, for Jesus' assurance that there will be survivors of 'the generation of 1914' . . . when the 'great tribulation' rings down the curtain on this wicked system of things"[63] "[B]efore the 1914 generation completely dies out, God's judgment must be executed."[64]	"Jehovah's people have at times speculated about the time when the 'great tribulation' would break out, even tying this to calculations of what is the lifetime of a generation since 1914. . . .[But] rather than provide a rule for measuring time, the term "generation" as used by Jesus refers principally to contemporary people of a certain historical period, with their identifying characteristics."[65] "God's servants in modern times have tried to derive from what Jesus said about "generation" some clear time element calculated from 1914 . . . [T]he recent information in *The Watchtower* about 'this generation' . . . . did give us a clearer grasp of Jesus' use of the term "generation," helping us see that his usage was no basis for calculating — counting from 1914 — how close to the end we are."[66]

EXCUSES, EXCUSES, EXCUSES

Despite the many false prophecies that have been made by God's prophet-like organization, JWs continue to maintain that they are not false prophets, that they have never made *any* false prophecies, and that they do not fall under the Bible's condemnation of a false prophet: " 'How can we know when a message has not been spoken by the LORD?' If what a prophet proclaims in the name of the LORD does not take place or come true, that is a message the LORD has not spoken. That prophet has spoken presumptuously. Do not be afraid of him" (Deut. 18:20–22).

The all-important question that must be asked is quite simple: Has the WTBTS ever claimed to be a "collective prophet" that has made predictions in the name of God? Put another way, have the Jehovah's Witnesses ever attributed their predictions directly to God? The answer is easily documentable. *The Watchtower* of May 1, 1938 dogmatically asserted that God uses angels to supernaturally impart his divine messages to the writers of WTBTS literature. As a result, everything published by the WTBTS, including prophecies, must be received as God's words:

> The resolutions adopted by conventions of God's anointed people, booklets, magazines, and books published by them, contain the message of God's truth and are from the Almighty God, Jehovah, and provided by him through Christ Jesus and his underofficers [i.e., angels]. . . . The interpretation of prophecy, therefore, is not from man, but is from Jehovah . . . . It is his truth, and not man's.[67]

As if this statement were not clear enough, a 1943 issue of *The Watchtower* took great pains to explain that representatives of Jehovah's organization are *not* "an earthly tribunal of interpretation, delegated to interpret the Scriptures and its prophecies." According to this issue's article, it is God the Father who interprets prophecies and Jesus Christ who proclaims those prophecies to WTBTS leaders. The organization is merely used by God "to publish the interpretation after the [spiritual] Supreme Court by Jesus Christ reveals it."[68] Consider, too, the following excerpts from *The Watchtower* that clearly attribute the words of WTBTS publications directly to God:

Whom has God actually used as his prophet? . . . Jehovah's Witnesses are deeply grateful today that the plain facts show that God has been pleased to use them.[69]

Those who are convinced that The *Watchtower* is publishing the opinion or expression of a man should not waste time in looking it at it all. . . . Those who believe that God uses *The Watchtower* as a means of communicating to his people, or of calling attention to his prophecies, should study *The Watchtower*.[70]

All this information came not from or by man, but by the Lord God, being given to his people gathered under Christ at the temple, and these things learned by them in the secret place.[71]

The WTBTS has even published statements that specifically label the "1914 generation" prophecy as having come directly from God:

Jehovah's prophetic word through Jesus Christ is: 'This generation [of 1914] will by no means pass away until all things occur.' (Luke 21:32) And Jehovah, who is the source of inspired and unfailing prophecy, will bring about the fulfillment . . . . [P]rophecies regarding 'the time of the end' will be fulfilled *within the life span of the generation of 1914*" [emphasis added].[72]

[T]his magazine builds confidence in *the Creator's promise* of a peaceful and secure new order *before the generation that saw the events of 1914 C.E. passes away*" [emphasis added].[73]

[T]his magazine builds confidence in the *Creator's promise* of a peaceful and secure new world *before the generation that saw the events of 1914 passes away* [emphasis added].[74]

Ironically, an October 8, 1968 edition of *Awake!* reads: "True, there have been those in times past who predicted an 'end to the world,' even announcing a specific date. . . . The 'end' did not come. They were guilty of false prophesying. Why? What was missing? . . . Missing from such people were God's truths and the evidences that he was guiding and using them."[75]

In vacillating on their prophecies, JWs present nothing new to the field of religion. For thousands of years, false prophets have tried to salvage their false prognostications by changing dates and rearranging time-tables. The

JWs are somewhat different, however, in that they have regularly contradicted themselves on doctrines that have nothing to do with prophecy: e.g.,
the significance of the Great Pyramid, the pursuit of higher education by
members, and the legitimacy of organ transplants.[76] On some topics, the
WTBTS has repudiated itself more than once, and in doing so, has ended
up reverting back to the position it held more than one hundred years
earlier.[77]

An even more disturbing aspect of the Watch Tower Society is its
tendency to resort to lying in order to cover-up embarrassing doctrinal
mistakes and prophetic blunders. The attempts by WTBTS officials to re-
write their organization's history is reflective of the actions taken by "Big
Brother" in George Orwell's futuristic sci-fi thriller *1984*. The following
segment documents only a few of the many times JW leaders have blatantly
deceived their trusting followers.

WHAT'S MY LINE?

Watch Tower leaders readily admit that "[a] religion that teaches lies
cannot be true."[78] Yet this is precisely what the Watch Tower itself has done
on numerous occasions. For example, the WTBTS used to ban vaccinations
as being in "direct violation of the everlasting covenant that God made with
Noah after the flood."[79] The Society also warned: "Oh, yes, serums,
vaccines, toxins, inoculations, are all 'harmless,' because the man who is
selling them says so. You, my friends, believe this LIE, and continue to
submit your body to these violations, then all I can say is, 'God have mercy
on your soul.' . . . All vaccination is unphysiological — a crime against
nature."[80] Another condemnation of vaccinations appeared in the April 24,
1935 issue of *Golden Age* (now known as *Awake!*), wherein the court
testimony of a faithful JW (Maria Braught) was quoted: "[V]accination is a
direct violation of the holy law of Jehovah God. . . . I have no alternative. I
must obey Jehovah God's law" (p. 471).

Currently, however, WTBTS leaders not only allow vaccinations, but
claim that they *never* said vaccinations were sinful. A 1993 issue of *Awake!*
reads as follows: "Previous articles in this journal and its companion, *The*

Watchtower, have presented a *consistent position*: It would be up to the Bible-trained conscience of the individual Christian as to whether he would accept this treatment for himself and his family" (emphasis added).[81]

The Watch Tower has also attempted to cover up its history of date-setting errors. The following charts present recently made statements by Watch Tower Society leaders with declarations previously made by them:

"TIME OF THE END"

TRUTH	1993 COVER-UP
"The overthrow of that dominion in 1798 by the French Revolution marked the beginning of the 'time of the end' . . . ."[82] "The year 1799 marked the beginning of the 'time of the end,' when various events were to occur."[83] "Twelve hundred and sixty years from A.D. 539 brings us to 1799, which is another proof that 1799 definitely marks the beginning of 'the time of the end.' "[84]	"Jehovah's Witnesses have consistently shown from the Scriptures that the year 1914 marked the beginning of the world's time of the end."[85]

JESUS' INVISIBLE RETURN

TRUTH	1993 COVER-UP
"[T]he Bridegroom came in the Autumn of 1874, and he appeared to the eyes of faith."[86] "Our Lord, the appointed King, is now present, since October 1874, A.D."[87] "The Scriptural proof is that the second presence of the Lord Jesus Christ began in 1874 A.D."[88]	"The Watchtower has consistently presented evidence to honesthearted students of Bible prophecy that Jesus' presence in heavenly Kingdom power began in 1914. Events since that year testify to Jesus' *invisible* presence."[89]

One of the clearest examples of the Watch Tower's willingness to lie to members, especially new converts unaware of the Society's history, appeared in a 1988 issue of *The Watchtower*. In this magazine, an elderly JW named Matsue Ishii gives her testimony, claiming that in 1928/29 she learned that Christ's invisible presence began in 1914, discovering this doctrine from *The Harp of God* (1921) by J. F. Rutherford.[90] But such a claim cannot be true. In 1928 the WTBTS was still teaching that Jesus' invisible presence began in 1874, not 1914! In fact, pages 235–236 of the 1928 edition of *The Harp of God* reads: "This date, therefore, when understood, would certainly fix the time when the Lord is due at his second appearing . . . . [it] brings us to 1874 A.D., at which time, according to Biblical chronology, the Lord's second presence is due. . . . The time of the Lord's second presence dates from 1874, as above stated."[91]

A similar statement was made in the September 1, 1990 issue of *The Watchtower* where faithful JW, Jack Nathan, claims that shortly after 1920 he learned from a follower of Russell's that Jesus had returned invisibly in 1914.[92] Nathan maintains that this was confirmed to him through the *Studies in the Scriptures*. But in 1920, *The Watchtower* was still printing articles declaring that Jesus had returned invisibly in 1874. All the way up through 1929, in fact, *The Watchtower*, as well as all of Rutherford's books, presented the 1874 date.[93] Consequently, it would have been impossible for someone involved with the Society in 1920 to have told Nathan that Jesus had been present since 1914. It would have been equally impossible for Nathan to have gotten his information from Russell's books. The *Studies in the Scriptures* always taught that Jesus' invisible presence began in 1874.[94] Even later editions of the books never placed Jesus' return in 1914. Consider the following excerpts from 1923 editions:

> The date of our Lord's second advent, and the dawn of the Times of Restitution, we have already shown to be A.D. 1874.[95]
>
> Our Lord, the appointed King, is now present, since October 1874, A.D., according to the testimony of the prophets, to those who have ears to hear it.[96]

Another untruth regarding the WTBTS's teaching on Jesus' invisible presence in 1914 was repeated in the September 15, 1990 issue of *The*

Watchtower. It misleads readers into thinking that Rutherford taught Jesus' invisible return in 1914 rather than in 1874. The JW magazine does this by partially quoting Rutherford's speech during a 1922 convention. According to *The Watchtower* of 1990, Rutherford stated: "Since 1914 the King of Glory has taken his power."[97]

Such a quote does indeed appear to indicate that Rutherford believed Jesus had returned in 1914. But what 1990 issue fails to mention is that the Watch Tower president was *not* speaking about Jesus' return. He was talking about the beginning of Jesus' invisible *reign* in 1914 after Jesus' invisible *return* in 1874. A November 1, 1922 issue of *The Watchtower*, which fully quotes Rutherford, unquestionably shows the Society's teaching that Jesus had returned in 1874, *not* 1914: "Since 1874 the King of glory has been present. . . . Since 1914 the King of Glory has taken his power and reigns. . . . Do you believe it? Do you believe that the King of glory is present, and has been since 1874?"

Obviously WTBTS leaders are quite willing to rewrite history in an effort to present their organization as having consistently taught various doctrines throughout the years. JWs would do well to heed what the WTBTS itself stated in the 1974 book *Is This Life All There Is?*: "It is obvious that the true God, who is himself 'the God of truth' and who hates lies, will not look with favor on persons who cling to organizations that teach falsehood. . . . And, really, would you want to be even associated with a religion that had not been honest with you?"[98]

PART THREE

A Return to Sanity

This protester — marching outside the headquarters of the Jehovah's Witnesses in Brooklyn, New York — is demonstrating against the apocalyptic cult because of its many predictions regarding the end of the world.

NINE

Signs of the Times Revisited

For the first time ever, everything is in place for the battle of Armageddon and the Second Coming of Christ. . . . It can't be too long now. [The Bible's book of] Ezekiel says that fire and brimstone will be rained upon the enemies of God's people. That must mean that they will be destroyed by nuclear weapons.

Ronald Reagan
United States President[1]

No generation has ever had solid biblical reason for believing that it was living in the last of the last days preceding the second coming of Christ — no generation until ours. . . . [T]he present generation — unlike any generation before it — has more than sufficient reason for believing that the second coming is very near.

Dave Hunt
evangelical prophecy teacher[2]

DESPITE CENTURIES OF FAILED PREDICTIONS about doomsday coming in a particular year or on a specific occasion, innumerable individuals continue to assert that the end of the world is undeniably at hand. The assumption that seems to appear most frequently in the thinking of apocalyptic cultists, false prophets, and date-suggesters is that Armageddon's immediacy is reflected in current events. In *Countdown to the Second Coming*, for example, evangelical Dave Hunt declares that the Antichrist is "almost certainly alive. . . . based upon sober evaluation of current events." He continues: "[T]he present generation — *unlike any generation before it* — has more than sufficient reason for believing than the second coming is very near."[3]

Today's torchbearers of Armageddon further substantiate their assertions by pointing to nightly news reports. Network film footage, they claim, is cataloguing the most obvious signs of the planet's imminent end: devastating floods, massive earthquakes, monstrous hurricanes, deadly tornadoes, volcanic eruptions, freezing rain in the spring, and blistering heat in the fall. The atmosphere is going haywire! There are also various diseases (e.g., Ebola and AIDS), famines, and pestilence popping up all around the globe. These too are viewed as signs indicating that we are reaching the end of human history. The Bible foretold it all, says prophecy pundit Jack Van Impe:

> EARTHQUAKES, PLAGUES, AND FAMINE. . . . [A]ll this is only the tip of the apocalyptic iceberg. . . . [T]o the list of doom-and-gloom we can add increasingly strange, new weather patterns which are playing havoc with our world. . . . [W]e are poised at the very threshold of cataclysmic change. We're told to continue to watch for certain signs of the times — the advent of false prophets, widespread religious deception, international upheaval, an increase in great earthquakes, an even greater onslaught of devastating plagues, famines, and strange phenomena in the heavens, along with changing global weather patterns. . . . World events declare that Jesus Christ is coming soon. . . . Be ready for the world-shattering events of the year 2001 and beyond as we find ourselves teetering on the edge of eternity.[4]

Van Impe, of course, is not the first prognosticator to claim that the signs of the times point to an imminent Armageddon. Cyprian (third century A.D.) and Pope Gregory (sixth century A.D.) felt very much the same way:

> *Cyprian:* "That wars continue to prevail, that death and famine accumulate anxiety, that health is shuttered by raging diseases, that the human race is wasted by the desolation of pestilence, know that this was foretold; that evils should be multiplied in the last times, and that misfortunes should be varied; and that the day of judgment is now drawing nigh.[5]

> *Pope Gregory:* "Of all the signs described by our Lord as presaging the end of the world some we see already accomplished. . . . For we now see that nation

arises against nation and that they press and weigh upon the land in our own times as never before in the annals of the past. Earthquakes overwhelm countless cities, as we often hear from other parts of the world. Pestilence we endure without interruption."[6]

Twentieth century prophets can usually see prophetic significance in just about anything. Consider the words of David Allen Lewis, founder of the Missouri-based Springfield Regional Eschatology Club and publisher of the *Prophecy Watch International* newsletter. He lists even taxes and the Internet among the signs that indicate Jesus is coming soon to destroy ungodliness and usher in God's millennial kingdom on Earth:

> Signs! Distress! Confusion! Commotion! Another great sign is the obvious decay of society and the inevitable collapse of the world system. Never has chaos and confusion ruled as today. A few decades ago we did not have the massive problems of drug usage, abortion, pornography, rampant taxation, inflation, family breakup, children rebelling, assaulting, killing and raping other children, weapons of mass destruction, cults and false prophets, false Christs, occult invasion of the New Age Movement, Satanism, Wicca, violence in the streets, terrorism, UFO deception, euthanasia, suicide increase, human slavery again (Sudan), Mars rocks and government sponsored Search for Extra Terrestrial Intelligence (SETI), increase of knowledge, the World Wide Web, "virtual" reality and a growing inability to discern reality from fantasy, Hollywood and TV's moral corruption, Gulf War disease (now thought to be contagious), AIDS, pestilence, weird weather, increased earthquake activity, and on and on the list could go.... The signs all point to the glorious day of a new beginning.... There will be a complete disassembly of the physical universe, for complete cleansing, then the restoration of a perfect world, spoken of as the new earth in prophecy. ... The end is the beginning! Yes, the end of this age and this doomed anti God world system signals the beginning of the Millennial Kingdom and then the dawn of eternity which features a new heaven and a new earth![7]

End-time visionaries are thoroughly convinced that our era is experiencing natural disasters, man-made catastrophes, social/political unrest, and devastating diseases in record numbers and severity. Their contention is usually based on two Bible passages wherein Jesus enumerates those conditions that will mark the end of the age:

> [Y]ou will be hearing of wars and rumors of wars. . . . [N]ation will rise against nation, and kingdom against kingdom, and in various places there will be famines and earthquakes. (Matt. 24:6–7)
>
> Nation will rise against nation, and kingdom against kingdom, and there will be great earthquakes, and in various places plagues and famines; and there will be terrors and great signs in the heavens. . . . [T]here will be signs in sun and moon and stars, and upon the earth dismay among nations, in perplexity at the roaring of the sea and waves. (Luke. 21:10–11, 25)

According Van Impe, "[o]ne hardly needs to be a Bible scholar or student of prophecy to see these signs in the world today. Just pick up your daily newspaper or turn on the television news! The evidence is all around us."[8] But a little scholarship and historical study might help modern-day prophets see that they are quite mistaken in believing that our generation is uniquely qualified to be the final generation.

NATURAL DISASTERS

Natural disasters (often referred to as "earth changes" by individuals obsessed with doomsday) are easily the most popular "signs of the times."[9] Countless persons from widely divergent belief systems — e.g., occultists, Christians, New Agers, American Indians, near death experiencers (NDErs), numerologists, pyramidologists, and militiamen/patriots — although they may disagree on a number of spiritual beliefs, are united in thinking that there has been a marked increase in the frequency and intensity of earth changes over recent years. The facts, however, tell a different story.

Earthquakes

According to the article "No Such Thing as Doomsday?," which appeared in a 1997 issue of the patriot/militia movement's *Preparedness Journal*, earthquakes have become an increasingly "more frequent part of life during the last two decades."[10] This sentiment has been echoed incessantly by doomsayers such as Hal Lindsey who, in the early 1980s, claimed that the 1970s "experienced the largest increase in the number of quakes known to history."[11] Similarly, evangelical Bible teacher Peter LaLonde tells us that the number of quakes per decade "has roughly doubled since the 1950's."[12] David Allen Lewis, in *Signs of His Coming*, informs his followers that "there have been more earthquakes in the last 50 years than in the previous 1,500 years."[13] In 1994, prophecy preacher Michael D. Evans declared: "[T]he magnitude and frequency of earthquakes sets this decade apart from any other time in spiritual history."[14]

Not surprisingly, the devotees of prophecy pundits unquestionably believe their favorite end-time prognosticator and repeat their claims without hesitation. Consider the following statement posted in 1997 to the Internet newsgroup alt.talk.calvary.chapel. Its author, a Christian named Dave Brodie, called his posting "End Times Armageddon Scenario: An Overview of Events to Come." Brodie's statement is taken almost verbatim from an Internet "Intelligence Briefing" authored by none other than Jack Van Impe:

BRODIE	VAN IMPE
"History shows that the number of killer earthquakes worldwide remained constant until the 1950s, averaging between two to four per decade. In the 1950s there were nine. In the 1960s there were 13. In the 1970s there were 51. In the 1980s there were 86. From 1990 through 1996 there have been more than 150!"[15]	"History shows that the number of killer quakes remained fairly constant until the 1950s — averaging between two to four per decade. In the 1950s, there were nine. In the 1960s, there were 13. In the 1970s, there were 51. In the 1980s, there were 86. From 1990 through 1996, there have been more than 150."[16]

But seismologists unanimously disagree with the end-time interpretation of these statistics.[17] The *apparent* rise in earthquakes over the last several years is due to nothing more than the use of technologically advanced seismographs. In a 1969 issue of *Natural History*, Charles F. Richter — inventor of the Richter Scale, which measures earthquake intensity — explained that modern seismographs can record minor quakes that previously would have gone unnoticed.[18] In other words, because scientists are able to detect more earth tremors, it *seems* as if more quakes are actually taking place.

What about earthquake severity? Near death experiencer Susan Hickman, in a 1997 letter to fellow NDErs, stated that she has noticed a clear increase in "greater magnitude earthquakes."[19] Native American Indian prophets Sun Bear and Wabun Wind declare: "[I]ncreased seismic activity is taking place. And the earthquakes are getting larger. From 1950 to 1990, the number of large earthquakes — 6.0 or greater on the Richter scale — almost doubled compared to the first fifty years of this century."[20] A similar observation was made in a 1986 issue of *The Good News of the World Tomorrow*, published by the Worldwide Church of God:

> Did you know that from 1901 to 1944, during more than four decades, only three earthquakes measured magnitude 7 or over? . . . Then, in just 10 years from 1945 to 1954, the number leaped to 21 quakes measuring 7 or over. From then on, large earthquakes have increased dramatically. From 1955 to 1964 — in just one decade — 87 earthquakes measured 7 or over; from 1965 to 1974, 136; from 1975 to 1984, 133.[21]

But again, seismological data contradicts these watchers of end-time signs. According to geophysics professor Seweryn J. Duda — a renowned seismologist at the University of Hamburg, Germany — there has been no increase in "large earthquakes." Duda stated his position after being asked in 1986 to respond to *The Good News of the World Tomorrow* article. In a letter written to authors Carl Jonsson and Wolfgang Herbst, Duda revealed that the Worldwide Church of God was in error about there being only three quakes with a magnitude of 7 or higher between 1901 and 1944. Those years actually saw 1,000 quakes of that magnitude. He also made the following remarks:

It is not justified to claim that large earthquakes have increased dramatically from the mid-fifties to the present. There are indications that worldwide seismic activity — if expressed in terms of earthquakes with magnitude 7 or over — has decreased steadily in the time from the beginning of the 20th century until now.... There are no indications that the twentieth century is radically different from earlier centuries, as far as global seismic activity is concerned.[22]

A number of other respected seismologists have also tried to explain to the general populace that the number and severity of earthquakes has remained relatively constant throughout history:[23]

Wilbur Rinehart: "[T]here has been no significant increase in the numbers of earthquakes during this or any other century" (World Data Center of Boulder, Colorado).

Keiiti Aki: "I feel very strongly that the seismicity has been stationary for thousands of years. . . . Excellent geological evidence for the stationarity has been obtained by Prof. Kerry Sieh of Caltech, for the San Andreas fault" (Department of Geological Sciences at the University of Southern California)

Waverly Person: "Our records do not show any significant increase in great earthquakes" (United States Department of Interior, Denver, Colorado).

Clearly, earthquakes are not taking place with more frequency or intensity now than in centuries past. Tremors of varying strength have been occurring for centuries. The oldest quake recorded took place in China in 1831 B.C. The first recorded large quake occurred in A.D. 7 and destroyed the entire city of Hsien, China. Moreover, historical records indicate that citizens of the first century probably saw just as many quakes as we are seeing today. Consider the words of Roman philosopher Seneca (A.D. 65):

How often have cities in Asia, how often in Achaia, been laid low by a single shock of earthquake! How many towns in Syria, how many in Macedonia, have been swallowed up! How often has this kind of devastation laid Cyprus in ruins! How often has Paphos collapsed! Not infrequently are tidings brought to us of the utter destruction of entire cities.[24]

The fifth century also brought terrible disasters associated with earthquakes, as this excerpt from E. A. Thompson's *A History of Attila and the
Huns* (1948) notes:

> The series of earthquakes which shattered the Eastern Empire for four months
> beginning on 26 January 447 were, in the belief of Evagrius, the worst in its
> history. Entire villages were swallowed up and countless disasters occurred
> both on land and sea. Thrace, the Hellespont, and the Cyclades all suffered.
> For three or four days after the earthquakes began, the rain poured from the
> sky, we are told, in rivers of water. Hillocks were levelled with the ground.
> Countless buildings were thrown down in Constantinople, and, worst of all, a
> stretch of the massive ways of Anthemius, including no less than fifty-seven
> towers, fell to the ground.[25]

To date, historians have catalogued thousands of quakes that have been
taken place over the years. In 1971, seismologist N. N. Ambraseys at
London's Imperial College of Science and Technology identified 3,000
quakes (including 2,200 "larger shocks") that had hit the Eastern Mediterranean region between A.D. 10 and 1699. Robert Mallet, known as "the
first true seismologist," declared in the *Reports of the British Association* for
the years 1852–54 that his research into ancient documents uncovered
references to nearly 7,000 quakes between the years 1606 B.C. and A.D.
1850. In 1911, John Milne listed 4,151 destructive earthquakes that hit the
world between A.D. 7 and 1899.

The most extensive listing of tremors was compiled by Count F.
Montessus de Ballore. From 1885 to 1922 he researched historical
documents located in numerous countries and catalogued 171,434 quakes
in all parts of the world. His manuscript, which is now stored in the
library of the Geographical Society in Paris, occupies over eighty-four feet
of bookshelf space.[26] Even this incredible document, however, fails to
provide an accurate tally since it represents only widespread disasters
resulting from *large* quakes. Smaller quakes, according to seismologists
John Milne and A. W. Lee, are not mentioned in ancient documents for
two reasons: 1) they did not cause a great deal of damage; and 2) many
were not strong enough to be felt.[27]

To illustrate, it is estimated that each year "there are some 500,000 detectable seismic or microseismic disturbances." Of these, only 100,000 can be felt.[28] If, as seismologists say, the number of quakes worldwide has remained constant, then historical records prior to the 1800s only give us references to one-fifth the number of quakes that have taken place since the earliest times.

Contrary to these facts, many people continue to assert with certainty that *this* generation is seeing a unique display of tectonic disasters.[29] Documentation, of course, is either not provided, or taken out of context and presented in a deceptive way. For example, the Jehovah's Witness publication *You Can Live Forever In Paradise On Earth* (1982) makes the following declaration: "From 1914 until now, there have been many more major earthquakes than in other like periods in recorded history. For over 1,000 years, from the year 856 C.E. [i.e., A.D.] to 1914, there were only 24 major earthquakes causing some 1,973,000 deaths. But in the 63 years from 1915 to 1978, a total of some 1,600,000 persons died in 43 earthquakes."[30]

These particular assertions were refuted in 1983 after religion researcher Douglas T. Harris of Reachout Ministries in England contacted several earthquake organizations. He provided them with the Watch Tower quote and four questions: 1) Do you agree with this quotation according to your records; 2) Is the reason that more earthquakes are reported in recent history due to better research units like yourself? 3) According to your figures has there been an increase in earthquake activity since 1914?; and 4) If more people are dying today from earthquakes, is this related to the increase in world population? Harris received two responses. The first came from the Earthquake Research Unit, Tokyo University, Japan. He received a second reply from the International Seismological Centre, Newbury, Berks, England (see Table 9.1).[31]

Interestingly, earthquake-related casualties in exceptionally strong tremors have actually *decreased* over the years. More people died "between 1715 and 1783 from earthquakes (1,373,845) than between 1915 and 1983 (1,210,597)."[32] History is filled with deadly quakes, the worst of which killed nearly one million people in Shenshu, China back in 1556.[33] A brief listing of quakes from the past reveals that even the largest of modern tremors are rarely as destructive as those that occurred long ago and that

EARTHQUAKE RESEARCH UNIT	INTERNATIONAL SEISMOLOGICAL CENTRE
1. No. It is almost impossible to reply with reliable data on world earth-quakes because there is no such data. 2. Yes. 3. No. Records of earthquakes have increased but we cannot say that earthquake activity has increased. 4. (no answer given).	1. In general, I would not agree with the quotation. . . The earthquake reputed to have killed most people was in China in 1556, with 850,000 fatalities. This makes the pre-1914 figure you quote seem very small. 2. [Yes.] Instrumental recording was just starting around the turn of the century. 3. [No.] There is certainly no seismo-logical evidence to believe that more seismic energy has been released since 1914 than in comparable peri-ods in the past. 4. [Yes.] This point, regarding world population is a very valid one. [W]orld population has grown by a factor of 100 since Biblical times, and also populations have become more condensed.

Table 9.1

the number of reported deaths between 856 and 1914 is grossly understated by the Jehovah's Witnesses.(see table 9.2).[34]

The Jehovah's Witnesses have additionally claimed that the frequency of *major* quakes "has increased about 20 times what it was on an average during the two thousand years before 1914."[35] Such a claim is impossible to prove since the definition of a *major* quake rests within the field of modern seismology, which can be traced no further back in history than the late 1700s–early 1800s.[36] The first modern seismograph was not even invented until 1880 and it was not until the 1950s-1960s that a global network of seismologists was established to observe quake activity throughout the world.[37] Consequently, no accurate numerical/intensity comparisons can be made between modern-day tremors and quakes from centuries past.

DATE	LOCATION	DEATHS
A.D. 532	Syria	130,000
678	Syria	170,000
856	Iran: Qumis Damghan	200,000
893	India: Daipul	180,000
893	Iran: Ardabil	150,000
1138	Egypt, Syria	230,000
1139	Iran: Gansana	100,000
1290	China: Chihli	100,000
1556	China	830,000
1641	Iran: Dehkwargan, Tabriz	300,000
1662	China	300,000
1669	Sicily (Etna eruption)	100,000
1693	Sicily: Catania and Naples	100,000
1703	Japan (tsunami)	100,000
1721	Iran: Tabriz	100,000
1730	China: Chihli	100,000
1730	Japan: Hokkaido	137,000
1731	China: Peking	100,000
1737	India: Calcutta	300,000
1780	Iran: Tabriz	100,000
1850	China	300—400,000
1876	Bay of Bengal (tsunami)	215,000
1908	Italy: Messina/Reggio	110,000

Table 9.2

Recent data concerning just the last one hundred years actually shows that between 1897 and 1987 the number of "major" tremors (7.0 magnitude or greater) *decreased* worldwide, as did the number of "great" tremors (8.0 magnitude and greater). A chart illustrating this fact appeared in Steven A. Austin's 1989 article "Earthquakes in These Last Days." It is currently available from the Institute for Creation Research (see Figure 9.1)

One of the most interesting attempts to get around these statistics comes from Armageddon sign-watcher John Hagee, author of the *New York Times* bestseller *Beginning of the End*. In his book, he repeats the popular assertion that the increase in tremors is a sign of the end, stating: "[T]he number of earthquakes recorded has risen from 2,588 in 1983 to 4,084 in 1992."[38] According to Hagee's endnotes, he retrieved his information from "Fre-

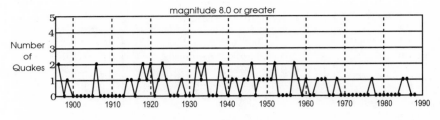

Fig 9.1

quency of Occurrence of Earthquakes" printed by the U.S. Geological Survey National Earthquake Information Center. Interestingly, Hagee's main text does not include the geological center's accompanying statement:

> As more and more seismographs are installed in the world, more earthquakes can be and have been located. However, the number of large earthquakes (magnitude 6.0 or greater) have stayed relatively constant. . . . [I]n fact, the last decade has produced substantially fewer large earthquakes than show in the long-term averages.[39]

How does Hagee reconcile his view with the indisputable fact that the *apparent* rise in earthquakes is only due to more and better seismographs? He claims that since the Bible predicts an increase in earthquakes, and the number of earthquakes *measured* between 1983 and 1992 has risen, then prophecy is indeed being fulfilled because higher earthquake numbers are being posted. In other words, the *real* number of earthquakes no longer has to rise in order to prove it is the last days. Only the *measured* number of earthquakes has to rise![40]

Fundamentalist J. R. Church, takes a different approach to explaining seismic data that contradicts his opinion. Rather than reinterpret prophecies, he just dismisses all contrary statements by geologists as unreliable because they are "schooled with the uniformitarian secular viewpoint."[41] To Church, only a select group of dedicated Christians can see through the deceptive statistics to discern an "emerging pattern" of increased earthquake activity.[42] Church is basically telling his followers to reject what the facts clearly indicate in favor of his interpretation of various Bible passages.

Church, like many people, does not seem to realize that seismology is an intricate field of study that includes many variables. Analyzing earthquakes is such a complex assignment that scientists sometimes disagree among themselves and ascribe "*different* intensities to the *same* earthquake."[43] There are even several scales that measure the various aspects of a quake: *qualitative intensity* per the Modified Mercalli Scale, *magnitude* per the Richter Scale, *moment magnitude* per the Moment Magnitude Scale (M_w), and additional measurements obtained by the Body-Wave Scale (m_b) and Surface-Wave Scale (M_s).[44]

The many exterior variables that contribute to a quake's effects must also be considered when analyzing seismic data. For example, the destruction caused by a high-magnitude quake centered on the ocean floor or in a sparsely populated region will be minor. A low-magnitude quake, however, that hits a densely populated area with poorly constructed dwellings will cause severe property damage and many casualties.

Obviously, end-time prophets are hardly qualified to draw conclusions based on seismological data. Nevertheless, their groundless assertions about earthquakes continue to go unchallenged by trusting followers, as do their pronouncements on other earth changes.

Hurricanes and Tornadoes

Hurricanes and tornadoes seem to be the most frequently mentioned disasters after earthquakes. In 1996, for instance, Jack Van Impe ominously revealed to his fans that in 1995 eleven Caribbean hurricanes had formed — "the most since 1933."[45] According to the 1996/97 four-part TV series *Ancient Prophecies* (The Learning Channel), we are living in "a unique period in the history of the world" because devastating floods, droughts, tidal waves, hurricanes and tornadoes are now occurring "with greater frequency and more devastating impact."[46] Doomsday lecturer Hal Lindsey has even made a video (*Apocalypse Planet Earth*) on the apocalyptic significance of weather signs, especially hurricanes. During an interview for Peter and Paul LaLonde's *This Week in Bible Prophecy* television program, Lindsey made the following remark:

> [T]he oceans of the equatorial part of the earth are really warming up and
> this is the place where this Super Storm Phenomena is being generated. So I
> think that when you look back just last year [1992] we had Hurricane Andrew
> which was the most powerful hurricane that ever hit this coast.[47]

But these statement are just as misleading as the many declarations
that have been made about seismic disturbances. Lindsey, for instance, was
incorrect on two points. First, there is no "super storm phenomenon"
occurring. Second, Andrew (a Category 4 hurricane) was *not* the most
powerful storm to hit the U.S. Coast. According to the U.S. National
Hurricane Center's 1997 statistical table of "The Most Intense Hurricanes
In The United States: 1900-1996," Andrew ranks third. The most powerful
cyclone to hit U.S. shores was the great 1935 hurricane (category 5) that
landed in the Florida Keys. The second most intense hurricane was Camille
(category 5), which devastated Mississippi, Louisiana, and Virginia in 1969.
Of the fourth through tenth most powerful storms, *none* took place later
than 1961 (see Table 9.3).

THE MOST INTENSE HURRICANES IN THE UNITED STATES: 1900-1996[48]

RANK/NAME	YEAR	CATEGORY STRENGTH
1. Unnamed	1935	5
2. Camille	1969	5
3. Andrew	1992	4
4. Unnamed	1919	4
5. Unnamed	1928	4
6. Donna	1960	4
7. Unnamed	1900	4
8. Unnamed	1909	4
9. Unnamed	1915	4
10. Carla	1961	4

Table 9.3

Doomsayers cannot even argue that the *deadliest* hurricanes have occurred in more recent years. As of late 1997, information from the U.S. National Hurricane Center showed that of the twenty-five deadliest tropical cyclones, only one struck in the 1960s, two hit in the 1970s, and *none* took place in either the 1980s or 1990s. The deadliest hurricane to hit U. S. shores swept across Galveston, Texas all the way back in 1900 (see table 9.4).

Moreover, a special 1997 project by the National Climatic Data Center[49] — "Evaluation and Extension of the Historical North Atlantic Ocean Tropical Cyclone Track Data Set" — discovered that data supposedly showing a rise in the *number* of hurricanes is due to the less than adequate means of gathering storm information "prior to the establishment of a modern tropical cyclone monitoring and detection system."[50] When researchers re-examined historical documents from 1851-1880 in an effort to "add to our understanding about the longer-term natural variability of tropical cyclone occurrence, physical characteristics, and threat," they found an additional ninety-three hurricanes that had previously gone unnoticed, bringing the total number of recorded storms from that period up from one hundred twenty-three to two hundred sixteen.

This latter figure is much closer to the total number of storms recorded for 1951–80 (292 hurricanes) and 1961–90 (290 hurricanes).[51] According to researchers, the job required "meticulous inspection of historical materials, such as newspapers, old books and journal publications" to evaluate the relevant information therein. They still concluded, however, that their new total of two hundred sixteen storms between 1851-1880 was still "a significant underestimate of the actual storm totals for this time, due to the much poorer system of communication and sparser population of that time."[52]

Like hurricanes, devastating tornadoes have also been regularly cited as a sign of the end. But the *apparent* rise in their numbers are likewise due to the poor information gathering techniques employed during the late nineteenth and early twentieth century. *The Weather Almanac* of 1992 plainly states that better record-keeping since 1953 has resulted in a dramatic increase of the number of tornadoes reported:

From 1916 through 1952, fewer than 300 tornadoes were reported in any one year. In 1953, when the U. S. Department of Commerce initiated its tornado

THE DEADLIEST HURRICANES: 1492-PRESENT

Rank/Location/Hurricane (if named)	Year
1. Martinique and Barbados	1780
2. Galveston, Texas	1900
3. Honduras (Fifi)	1974
4. Dominican Republic	1930
5. Haiti and Cuba (Flora)	1963
6. Pointe-a-Pitre Bay	1776
7. Newfoundland Banks	1775
8. Puerto Rico, Carolinas	1899
9. Florida, Puerto Rico	1922
10. Cuba, Jamaica	1932
11. Central Atlantic	1782
12. Martinique	1813
13. El Salvador	1934
14. Western Cuba	1791
15. Barbados	1831
16. Belize	1931
17. Haiti, Honduras, Jamaica	1935
18. Dominica and U. S. (David)	1979
19. Offshore Florida	1781
20. South Carolina	1893
21. Eastern Gulf of Mexico	1780
22. Cuba	1870
23. Louisiana	1893
24. Guadeloupe and Martinique	1666
25. Martinique	1767

Table 9.4

forecasting effort, more than 437 tornadoes were observed and reported, beginning the first period of reliable statistical history. Since 1953, partly through improved equipment and techniques, partly through increasing public participation, essentially complete tornado records have been available.[53]

Many of today's heralders of Armageddon are either unwilling or unable to accurately interpret statistics. This holds true not only with regard to tornadoes, hurricanes, and earthquakes, but also floods, droughts, and volcanic eruptions. The same can be said for their remarks about pestilence and famine, both of which have been around for thousands of years. But modern-day prophets say the worst examples of these tragedies are yet to come, and in fact, may already be here.

A PLAGUE UPON YOUR HOUSE

Although pestilence has been a persistent problem for thousands of years, many end-time prophets maintain that humanity is only now experiencing its full effects. Hence, we *must* be living in the last of the "last days." Elizabeth Clare Prophet, leader of a doomsday cult called the Church Universal and Triumphant, believes that our era is a "period of intensification" of "the last plagues."[54] Hal Lindsey feels the same way: "Jesus said plagues would sweep the world prior to his return. . . . . [I]n just the past few years great epidemics have killed millions."[55]

Acquired Immunodeficiency Disease (AIDS) seems to be the malady of choice among prophecy purveyors looking for an end-time epidemic. Bible teacher J. R. Church, for example, predicted that by 1991 everyone would personally know someone with AIDS.[56] Hal Lindsey, always willing to inspire fear in his audience, has often commented on AIDS, stating on one occasion that it is "clearly one of the worst plagues that mankind has ever seen, if not worse, because it is 100% fatal. It is so complex that no cure is in sight."[57] Another fundamentalist Christian — Noah Hutchings of the Southwest Radio Church — has dogmatically labeled AIDS "the worst plague in history."[58] According to Van Impe, the year 2020 may see the last human being "expiring on this earth, killed by AIDS."[59] He further maintains that there are already "30 new strains of the AIDS virus threatening to ravage the world's population."[60]

Although the spread of AIDS is certainly a major concern, such sensationalistic statements go far beyond what is known about the disease. For instance, Van Impe's assertion that there exists "30 new strains" of AIDS is untrue. According to the U.S. Center for Disease Control (CDC), AIDS can be caused by two separate viruses: HIV 1 and HIV 2. HIV 1 is the more widespread virus, while HIV 2 is confined to small area of Africa. To date, there are no officially named strains (or sub-type mutations) of HIV 2. With HIV 1, however, it is a different story. It has indeed mutated into various categorized strains. The CDC has divided HIV 1 into two large groups: "M" and "O," each of which contains several "sub-types of the groups." HIV 1 (M) has been divided into eight different strains (labeled A–H). As of 1998, HIV 1 (O) — which contains the rarest sub-types — has not been divided into named strains.[61] Thus, Van Impe's figure of "30 new strains" is unfounded.

What about the future of AIDS? In a 1996 *Intelligence Briefing* titled "The Age of Plagues," Van Impe declared that experts fear "110 million adults and some 10 million children would be infected by the year 2000."[62] But again, his fact-finding leaves much to be desired. At the 1994 conference on AIDS sponsored by the World Health Organization, experts estimated "a total of at least 40 million AIDS cases by the year 2000."[63] An even smaller estimation of 26.6 million AIDS-infected persons by 2000 was given in 1996 by the World Health Organization.[64]

It must also be acknowledged that AIDS is by no means the worst infectious disease to strike society. That distinction belongs to the Black Death (1347–1350), which killed one third to one half of all the people in Europe. A third of Egypt's population died, along with half of Italy's residents, two-thirds of Norway's populace, and three-quarters of Poland's inhabitants.[65] Every country affected by the plague posted similar statistics. Historians have labeled it the "most lethal disaster of recorded history."[66] Isaac Asimov, renowned scientist and cosmologist, called it the "greatest of all crises faced by the human species."[67] Other scientists and historians agree:

- "The Black Death was an unprecedented catastrophe for which the only parallels are the Biblical story of the Flood and the 20th-century predictions of the effects of an all-out nuclear war."[68]
- "Undoubtedly the worst disaster that has ever befallen mankind."[69]
- "The only possible comparison would be with the hypothetical results of a modern nuclear or bacteriological war."[70]

- "[T]he Black Death should be ranked as the greatest biological-environmental event in history, and one of the major turning points of Western Civilization."[71]

Another significant issue related to AIDS and end-time prognostications involves those remarks from doomsday prophets wherein AIDS is categorized as an *epidemic.* Such a description of the disease and its virulence among the populace is entirely inaccurate. An epidemic is defined as a contagious illness that breaks out suddenly and spreads rapidly in a particular area.[72] The Black Death, for example, struck without warning and spread to persons who had hardly any contact with those unfortunate enough to be infected. AIDS, on the other hand, is much more difficult to contract. In fact, more people die every year from malaria (up to four million) than from AIDS.[73]

HIV (the virus that many believe causes AIDS) is so fragile that it tends to die very quickly once it is outside of a person's body. The virus must be transmitted body to body. Consequently, a contaminated body fluid (e.g., blood, sweat, saliva, tears, urine, semen) only poses an HIV risk if it is introduced directly into another person's bloodstream (e.g., via an open cut, a blood transfusion, invasive sexual activity, etc.). Professor Sten Iwarson — a leading authority on AIDS who heads the infection clinic in Gothenburg, Sweden — comments:

> AIDS is the most dangerous disease today, but as a pestilence it is limited to certain risk groups. AIDS cannot be compared to the Black Death or the Spanish Flu in which people died by the millions. The way of transmission is different, and the society is different. . . . AIDS is transmitted through intercourse and via blood transfusions and is limited to certain risk groups. Although a lesser number outside the risk groups may also be stricken, there is actually nothing to indicate that it will develop into a general pestilence.[74]

Clearly, the virulence and world effects of AIDS pale in comparison to the ravaging power of the Black Death. The past has seen numerous outbreaks of pestilence that were far more devastating than anything we are seeing today:

- A.D. 165–180: For fifteen years the Roman Empire endured a smallpox epidemic that killed one-quarter to one-third of the population in affected areas throughout the land.

- 310–312: Approximately 98% to 99% of the entire population of the northwestern provinces of China was wiped out by pestilence.

- 542–565: Technically, the worst case of bubonic plague — the Plague of Justinian — occurred during this time throughout the Middle East, Europe, and Asia. Although it took the lives of an estimated 100 million people, it is not considered more devastating than the Black Death because it was actually a *series* of bubonic plague outbreaks, rather than a single outbreak of plague that continued to spread, which is what occurred during the days of the Black Death.

- 1500–1800: Called the era of syphilis and smallpox by some historians, these years saw the deaths of millions of people in Europe and the New World, especially Mexico. Spaniards, under the command of Cortez, imported these diseases to North America. Smallpox, in fact, is what eventually conquered the Aztec and Inca civilizations. By 1568, only fifty years after Cortez's conquest, disease had reduced the Mexican population from 25-30 million to just three million. Thanks to European invaders, malaria and yellow fever also struck the New World with deadly consequences. Eventually, disease-related deaths decreased the American Indian populations of North, Central and South America from more than 100 million to as low as 4-5 million.

- 1817–1896: Five outbreaks of cholera killed an estimated 100 million people worldwide.

- 1918–1919: An unparalleled pandemic of Spanish influenza resulted in 20 million deaths.[75]

It is true that society continues to be challenged by new diseases and the resurgence of old diseases, but thanks to modern medicine, today's populace has a fighting chance against infectious illnesses.[76]

STARVING TO DEATH

Although it is true that recent years have brought terrible famines to various parts of the world, this human tragedy has occurred time and again throughout history.[77]

MAJOR FAMINES

Egypt (c. 3500 B.C.)	The earliest written reference to a famine.
Rome (436 B.C.)	Thousands of starving people threw themselves into the Tiber River.
British Isles (A.D. 310)	Famine killed 40,000 people.
Wales (836)	This famine killed so many people that the ground was "covered with dead bodies of men and beasts."
Kashmir, India (917)	Historical documents say that the Jhelum River was filled with bodies. "The land became densely covered with bones in all directions, until it was like one great burial-ground, causing terror to all beings."
England (1004–1016)	This extended famine, according to some historical reports, killed one half the population of England.
Ireland (1116)	A famine so great that people resorted to cannibalism.
England (1235–1239)	Famine caused 20,000 deaths in London. People resorted to eating the bark of trees and grass in order to survive. People also "ate their children."
China (1333-37)	Four million were reported dead in one region alone. This famine may have been the source of Europe's Black Death.
Russia (1600)	500,000 died from both famine and plague.
India (1630)	This famine began when floods followed a severe drought. Parents apparently sold their children in exchange for food. In the city of Surat, 30,000 inhabitants died.
France (1769)	This second famine in France took place within seventy-five years of the country's first great famine (1693), which killed perhaps five percent of the population.
Ireland (1846)	The great potato famine killed at least 1 million people.

India (1899-1900)	Despite relief efforts, at least 250,000 starved. The estimated death toll from famine and subsequent disease was 3.25 million.
U. S. S. R. (1921-22)	250,000 to 5 million died.
Ethiopia (1973)	This drought-induced famine killed 100,000.
Somalia (1991-92)	Hundreds of thousands die, including one-fourth of all Somali children under age five. People ate their own clothes in an effort to survive.

Despite the clear facts of history, famines provide one of the most heart-wrenching signs of the end that doomsday cults and prophecy "experts" cannot resist citing. The Watch Tower Society (i.e., the Jehovah's Witnesses) has for many years been preaching that the "worst food shortages in human history followed on the heels of World War I"[78] and that "in the wake of World War I came the greatest famine of all history."[79] In reference to more recent times, Jack Van Impe has confidently announced that we are currently seeing "[t]he worst famines the world has ever known."[80]

But the Watch Tower, Van Impe, and similar doomsayers are mistaken. History's worst famines took place in the 1800s. The greatest series of famines hit China from 1810–1811, as well as in 1846 and 1849. The 1849 famine took fourteen million lives. The second deadliest famine struck India from 1876–1878 and killed over five million people. There was also the great Irish potato famine of 1846, which claimed the lives of more than one million people.[81]

Obviously, humankind has been the victim of natural disasters, disease, and famine since the beginning of time. These, however, are not the only alleged signs of the end that today's prophets use to captivate their listeners. Another great indicator of the world's imminent destruction is entirely man-made: war.

WAR: THE OLDEST "SIGN"

There have been very few years in recorded history when a war was not taking place somewhere on the planet. Many individuals, however, believe that World War I and World War II were especially significant. "So many lives were lost and so many countries were involved," they argue. "Surely these two conflicts signal the beginning of the end." The military conflicts after these two episodes have also sparked comments, such as this one made by Hal Lindsey in *The Late Great Planet Earth*: "War has greatly increased in frequency and intensity in this century."[82]

But once more, history reveals that proponents of the "we're-in-the-last-of-the-last-days" mentality are mistaken. World War I was not even really the *first* world war. That, according to historians, was actually the War of Spanish Succession (1702–1713). This conflict involved France, Britain, Holland and Austria. Historians R. R. Palmer and Joel Colton note that this was the true first world war because "it involved the overseas world together with the leading powers of Europe."[83] The legitimate second world war was the Seven Years' War (1756–1763). It involved all four continents and all of the major oceans.[84]

Well before these two "world wars," earlier conflicts led to widespread death and destruction. The Thirty Years War (1618–1648) involved ten nations and claimed the lives of two to three million soldiers. Thirty to forty percent of the civilian German population (i.e., seven to eight million people) died. Germany did not suffer such loses during World War II. Then there was the Manchu-Chinese War of 1644. It left twenty-five million dead. The Napoleonic Wars (1792–1815) took five to six million lives, and the Taiping Rebellion (1850–1864) — "the most destructive war of the entire 19th century" — resulted in the deaths of approximately thirty million![85] To get a perspective on these numbers, World War I claimed a total of ten to twelve million lives, including approximately eight and a half million soldiers.[86]

Popular evangelical author Tim LaHaye claims that the twentieth century has seen 180 million killed in wars, "more than all the wars of history put together."[87] This, says LaHaye, is a sure sign that warfare has increased and Armageddon looms on the horizon. But LaHaye's information, for which there is no source cited, is contradicted by a 1974 study of warfare. It found that approximately three billion people have been killed in more than 14,000 wars since 3600 B.C.[88] Contrary to what LaHaye and other end-time prophets may declare, the last one hundred years of warfare represent nothing more than the tail end of humanity's long and bloody history.

J. David Singer and Melvin Small, in their 1972 book *The Wages of War 1816–1965*, stated: "Is war on the increase, as many scholars as well as laymen of our generation have been inclined to believe? The answer would seem to be a very unambiguous negative. Whether we look at the number of wars, or their severity or magnitude, there is no significant trend upward or down over the past 150 years."[89]

Wars, famine, pestilence, earthquakes, hurricanes, and tornadoes have always been part of that perennial struggle called human survival. Even if for the sake of discussion, one were to agree that an increase in such tragedies was indeed supernaturally destined to be a signal of an approaching doomsday, the twentieth century would not qualify as the terminal generation. Ironically, the most vocal proponents of these signs — i.e., Christian prophecy teachers — virtually ignore what the Bible itself declares about predicting when the end of the world will occur: "But of that day or hour no one knows, not even the angels in heaven" (Mark 13:32).

TEN

The Bible Tells Me So?

Whenever history takes one of its unexpected turns, the doomsayers end up with prophetic egg on their faces. But when their schemes don't fit [current events] any more, you never see these folks owning up to it. They merely reshuffle and come out with another edition.

Tim Weber
church historian[1]

UNTOLD NUMBERS OF PEOPLE seek comfort and guidance from the Holy Bible, history's best-selling and most widely distributed book. Unfortunately, Scripture can be abused as well as used. It has often been cited in an effort to support all sorts of bizarre behaviors and beliefs. Some of our era's most infamous religious groups (e.g., Branch Davidians, Aum Shinrikyo, Order of the Solar Temple, and Heaven's Gate) have appealed to Scripture in an effort to legitimize their twisted ideas and deadly agendas. Although most end-time visionaries are not as morally and socially offensive as members of these groups, many are equally as guilty of perverting Holy Writ as was David Koresh, Shoko Asahara, Luc Jouret, or Marshall Applewhite, often in an attempt to make it say what it does not say; specifically, that we can know when doomsday will occur. Ironically, the actual message that Scripture imparts concerning this issue is in direct opposition to the pronouncements made by individuals obsessed with Armageddon.

VERSE AFTER VERSE

Previous chapters have already demonstrated that Christian prophecy pundits (both date-setters and date-suggesters), New Age gurus, apocalyptic cult leaders, and psychic prognosticators have all been preaching the same basic message — i.e., that the end of the world is set to occur very soon, probably somewhere around A.D. 2000. As pyramidologist Richard Kieninger says: "After Armageddon and Doom's Day [sic] less than a tenth of the world's population will be alive to see the year 2001 A.D."[2]

Christians are understandably the most influential and widespread purveyors of Bible-based "end of the world" predictions. Ever since the late 1800s, and especially since World War II, notable doomsayers within the Christian community have been declaring that Scripture *clearly* identifies "now" as the final moment before global destruction. Their pronouncements throughout every decade have been surprisingly similar. Consider, for instance, the text from *When Will It End?*, a pamphlet produced in 1931 by the Los Angeles Free Tract Society. It contains the transcript of an April 14, 1931 sermon delivered by Nathan Cohen Beskin, a Chicago preacher:

> EARTHQUAKES, in divers places. FAMINES in different parts of the world, WARS AND RUMORS OF WARS.... We are living in the day of mergers when all the governments are uniting into a United States of Europe.... Then will come the final culmination and the final war which will be known as The Battle of Armageddon when the great armies will encamp around the little group of faithful ones ready to devour them. But then the Lord will come with ten thousand of His saints. He will conquer the armies of the world, establish a reign of righteousness and peace upon the earth and for a thousand years there will be no more wars. This will be the last world war. When will it take place? I know not when it will end but I believe I have an idea as to when it will begin — in 1934.[3]

In *Time Cycles in the Bible*, another Free Tract Society publication from the same era, author Gus McKey wrote the following:

> We have discovered in the Scriptures various time measurements that locate the end time in a marvelous way. The measurements all terminate between 1931 and 1938 in such an orderly array of harmony, we are delighted with such revelation. It all comes through the Word in such a plain simple way, concealed for ages by its utter simplicity, to be revealed in the last time.[4]

One of the most popular "time measurements" is gleaned from the first two chapters of Genesis, which is the first book of the Bible's Old Testament. It revolves around the theory that the world was created in 4004 B.C.

Ussher's Miscalculation

According to numerous end-time prophets, doomsday is slated for around the year 2000 because that chronological milestone will mark the end of approximately six thousand years since the creation of the world. This theory is built on four notions: 1) God created the world in six literal days (Gen. 1–2), resting on the seventh day; 2) each Genesis "day" represents not only a literal day, but prophetically symbolizes a 1,000-year epoch because both the Old and New Testaments (Ps. 90:4; 2 Peter 3:9) declare that to God "one day is as a thousand years"; 3) the creation account in Genesis is a veiled reference to how long the universe will exist (i.e., six 1,000-year periods of activity after which comes a 1,000-year era of rest [Christ's millennial kingdom]); and 4) earth's creation dates to 4004 B.C., hence 6,000 of history have expired, which means that God's seventh "day" (or last 1,000-year period) of rest will begin shortly.

This "six-day theory," as it is called in Christian prophecy circles, stems from two sources. First, a number of Jewish rabbis and early Christian leaders (c. 1st-6th century A.D.) promoted the concept that God would allow humanity to toil for 6,000 years, then establish an earthly kingdom of righteousness. Second, the genealogies in the book of Genesis, when counted backward through time, seem to indicate that Adam and Eve were created in 4004 B.C. This latter idea is traceable to Irish archbishop James Ussher (1581–1656), who first published the Genesis genealogical calculations in his *Annales Veteris et Novi Testamenti* (1650-54).[5]

Recently, the "six-day theory" has been embraced by several prominent Christian preachers including Charles Capps, Ray Brubaker, Rod Parsley, Gordon Lindsay, and Rex Humbard.[6] Christ for the Nations Ministry founder Gordon Lindsay, who is billed in the book *He's Coming Soon* as "an outstanding Pentecostal/charismatic theologian," made the following comment in his 1968 volume *The World: 2000 A.D.*:

According to Bible chronology, there was from Adam's creation until Christ some 4,000 years. This means including the present dispensation approximately 5,968 years have elapsed since the fall of Adam — or nearly six of God's days. . . . All signs indicate that this time of trouble [the tribulation just before Jesus' return] will occur before the year 2000.[7]

One of the most forceful proponents of the six-day theory is Jack Van Impe (see Chapters 3 and 4). In numerous videotapes, television programs, publications, and Internet postings he has incessantly propagated the idea that 6,000 years since creation will culminate around the year 2000, at which time Christ will return to initiate God's seventh "day." During a July 2, 1997 television broadcast of *Jack Van Impe Presents*, Jack's wife Rexella related the view of second century church leader Irenaeus (c. 175–195), who believed that "after 6,000 years from the time Adam was created, the Lord's going to come again." Jack responded: "That's anywhere from 2001 to 2012, you've just heard it."[8] Consider a few other remarks Van Impe has made since the mid-1990s:

Well, it's 1995, friends and we're still here! . . . The world of A.D. 2000 and beyond holds a future that's intriguing, fascinating and challenging. Before us lies the most important decade in the history of the world. . . . [T]he Millennium will be God's "Heaven on Earth" for 1,000 years, somewhere after A.D. 2000-2007.[9]

Never before has the stage been so well set for the Second Coming. . . . From the time of Adam, we've got genealogical tables and charts [in the Bible] to show that 4,000 years passed from Adam's creation to Christ's birth. From Jesus' birth until the present age another 2,000 years has almost transpired, for a total of 6,000 years or six days. . . . [T]he entire prophetic scenario is being fulfilled before our eyes.[10]

Since God created the world in 6 days . . . and rested on the 7th (Genesis 2:2) then because 1,000 years is as one day (Ps. 90:4) . . . (2 Peter 3:8) — therefore, the world will go on for six days, for 6,000 years, and the Jews said Messiah would come, and the Christians say our Savior would return, and that comes out right at 2001 and onward. . . . So we're right on schedule. . . . What's coming? We believe the coming of Messiah. The coming of Messiah is near.[11]

Interestingly, numerous prognosticators throughout history have used the six-day theory to "prove" a variety of *different* dates for doomsday. Hippolytus (d. c. 236 A.D.), who coincidentally influenced the theology of Irenaeus, believed that Christ would indeed return 6,000 years after Adam's creation. This fact is often cited by modern-day doomsayers in an effort to lend credibility to their beliefs. But one piece of information that today's prophets consistently gloss over is the fact that Hippolytus, along with his contemporaries such as Irenaeus and Lactantius (c. 240–320), thought that God's 6,000 years would come to a close in 500 A.D., not the year 2000.

Twentieth century prophets also fail to mention how, as the year 500 approached, medieval church clerics "revised" their calculations and pushed ahead the end of the 6,000 years to 800 A.D. in an effort to forestall apocalyptic terrors.[12] After this date passed, the six-day theory was all but forgotten. Then Bishop Ussher came up with his 4004 B.C. tabulation, which in turn gave rise to new generations of six-day theory adherents such as John Cumming of the Scottish National Church. In 1855, he published two volumes, the latter of which declared that God's pre-ordained 6,000 years of history would come to an end in 1862.[13] Cumming was mistaken, but that only seemed to motivate others to try to pinpoint the conclusion of Earth's allotted 6,000 years.

Gus McKey, in an early twentieth century pamphlet titled *Time Cycles in the Bible*, authoritatively declared that the 6,000 years would end between 1931 and 1938.[14] Prophecy teacher Salem Kirban, in his 1968 book *Guide to Survival*, used Ussher's chronology to arrive at a 1989 date for the Rapture.[15] The widely circulated end-time tract titled *The Midnight Hour Approaches! Your Time Is Almost Over* by Ron Reese pointed to 1992-93, stating; "IN 6000 YEARS, THE LORD WILL BRING ALL THINGS TO AN END. . . . The 6,000 years are almost over."[16]

Currently we see the year 2000 and shortly thereafter being touted as "the end" based on Ussher's miscalculation. But these devout calendar watchers seem oblivious to several points that render their 4004 B.C. creation date an absurdity. First, ample historical and archeological data indicates that human civilizations existed prior to 4004 B.C. The most ancient ruins include Qalat Jarmo in Iraq (7000 B.C.), Catal Hüyük in

Turkey (6700–5650 B.C.), and the Hassuna and Tall Al-'Ubayd excavations in Mesopotamia (5750–3500 B.C.).[17]

Second, neither Psalm 90:4 nor 2 Peter 3:8 are intended to prove that one day equals 1,000 years in God's prophetic timetable. In fact, 2 Peter not only says that "one day is as a thousand years," but also states that one thousand years are as a day. The teaching here is simple: God is not limited by our concept of time. *The Tyndale New Testament Commentaries*, a conservative series on biblical interpretation, notes: "[Peter] emphasizes first the relativity of time. . . . What man regards as a long time is like a mere day in God's reckoning of time."[18] Protestant Reformer John Calvin (1509–1564) explained that Peter's message was actually intended to *prevent* Christians from speculating about the timing of "the end." According to Calvin, Peter was saying that when Christ's return is discussed, believers should recognize that God's timing is not theirs and in doing so, "will not subject the time appointed by God to their own ridiculous wishes."[19]

Third, the Genesis genealogies are incomplete and not intended to provide a chronology of human history dating back to Adam and Eve. They are simply a literary device used to highlight the individuals important to the unfolding biblical narrative. Several biblical genealogies are written in this way. For example, the genealogy in Luke chapter 3 lists Cainan (v. 36), but this same name is omitted in Genesis 11:12-13 (also compare 1 Chron. 23:15–16; 26:24 to Matt. 1; and Ezra 7:1–5 to 1 Chron 6:3–15).

Fourth, the Hebrew term for *father* in Old Testament genealogies does not necessarily mean direct fatherhood. It can also mean ancestor (cf. 2 Kings 16:1–2 with Matt. 3:9). Likewise, the Hebrew word translated in the Bible as *son* can actually mean descendant (cf. Matt. 1:1, where Jesus is called the Son of King David even though David lived centuries earlier). This means that there are a number of places where time gaps, perhaps as long as thousands of years, can fall into the Genesis genealogies. In other words, adding together the life spans of everyone mentioned in the Genesis reveals nothing about when the world was created.

Fifth, Ussher's chronology was not even based on the calendar we now use (Gregorian), which was instituted in 1582. The 4004 B.C. date is based on the old Julian Calendar, which is ten days out of synch with our current calendar. Moreover, Ussher's tabulations actually put the end of 6,000 years since creation on November 1, 1996![20]

Sixth, countless persons have come up with widely varying dates for the end of the 6,000 years since creation: 2017 by Jesuit thinker Petavius (1583–1652); 2040 by Martin Luther (1482–1546); 2048 by the eleventh century Anglo-Norman historian Orderic Vitalis; 2050 by the great classicist Joseph Justus Scalinger (1540–1609); and 2239, according to Jewish tradition.[21]

Seventh, the "1 day = 1,000 years" idea is of dubious origin. It first appeared in the *Secret Book of Enoch*, an ancient text of unknown Jewish origin that was written in the period between the composition of the Old and New Testament (mid-5th century B.C. – c. 65 A.D.).[22] The end-time theory eventually found its way into the *Epistle of Barnabas*, a spurious text allegedly written by the traveling companion of Paul the apostle (Acts 4:36, 11:22–26).[23] Both of these texts were rejected by the Christian church hundreds of years ago as being spurious and filled with unbiblical teachings. But this has not stopped Christian prophecy teachers from regularly appealing to them as if they were historically accepted texts within the Christian tradition.

Popular end-time preacher Ray Brubaker, for example, has offered copies of the *Epistle of Barnabas* on his radio program.[24] Jack Van Impe has endorsed this ancient manuscript as well, agreeing that it was written by "Barnabas who travelled with the apostle Paul."[25] What is never mentioned by the likes of Van Impe and Brubaker, however, is that the *Epistle of Barnabas* also teaches that hyenas change their sex every year, (Barn. 10:22–25), that God hates the weasel because it conceives with its mouth (Barn. 10:26–28), and that first century Jews who rejected Christianity did so due to the diabolical influence of an "evil angel" (Barn. 9:20).[26]

Interestingly, the apostle Paul wrote a lengthy command about 2,000 years ago that seems to marvelously address with succinct accuracy the 4004 B.C. "six-day theory" and those who promote it:

[C]ommand certain men not to teach false doctrines any longer nor to devote themselves to myths and endless genealogies. These promote controversies rather than God's work — which is by faith. The goal of this command is love, which comes from a pure heart and a good conscience and a sincere faith. Some have wandered away from these and turned to meaningless talk. They want to be teachers of the law, but they do not know what they are talking about or what they so confidently affirm. (1 Tim. 1:3–7)

Gog and Magog

Another biblical passage that is consistently interpreted in such a way as to place Armageddon in our century is Ezekiel 38–39 (written c. 597–570 B.C.), which mentions the mysterious Gog and Magog, as well as the words *Rosh*, *Meshech* and *Tubal*. (Concerning these latter terms, see Chapter 3.) To a majority of Christians, Gog and Magog refer to Russia. As Bible teacher Tim LaHaye says, "Russia is unquestionably the nation identified in the prophecies of Ezekiel 38 and 39."[27]

The biblical passage also supposedly predicts a Russian invasion of Israel in the near future. Hal Lindsey believes this invasion will occur by or before the year 2000.[28] In fact, during a September 25, 1997 broadcast of his *International Intelligence Briefing* television program, he predicted that Russia would probably attack Israel within eighteen months (i.e., sometime in 1998/1999).[29] Lindsey, of course, is not the only doomsayer who sees Russia in Ezekiel's writings. Note the following declarations from other influential prophecy teachers:

John Walvoord: "The prophetic chapters of Ezekiel 38 and 39 . . . clearly describe a horde of armed might invading Israel from the north. The names given to the leader, the country [i.e., Gog and Magog], and the cities, as well as the clear description of armies out of 'your place in the far north' (Ezek. 38:15), could only refer to what we know today as Russia."[30]

Dave Breese: "Ezekiel takes two chapters, starting with Ezekiel 38, to describe a fearsome battle. . . . [T]his passage tells us that the invading army will consist of Gog and Magog. . . . Here we have Russia moving with powerful forces in a program of conquest of the South."[31]

David Allen Lewis: "Friends, Magog is still Magog and Russia is still Russia and they are still the same thing. . . . Just look at a map of the world! Look at your globe! The only land mass that fits the description in relation to Israel [a place 'out of the north'] is Russia, the new C.I.S. [Commonwealth of Independent States of the former Soviet Union]."[32]

Prophecy teachers such as these are notorious for spreading erroneous information in a zealous attempt to "prove" their beliefs. Dave Breese, for instance, asserts that "Bible scholars, with virtual universality, have long believed that here [Ezekiel 38–39] we have a picture of Russia attacking the state of Israel and the Middle East."[33] This is simply untrue. A large number of conservative Christian scholars reject the "Gog/Magog=Russia" interpretation of Ezekiel 38 and 39.

It is true, however, that since the early twentieth century many end-time prophets have used the book of Ezekiel as the basis of their predictions about an imminent Armageddon preceded by a Russian invasion of Israel. For example, an Associated Press story of August 16, 1931 reported that one particular end-time prognosticator — Wilbur Glen Voliva — had reached a frightening conclusion based on his notion that Ezekiel did indeed describe Russia as a great northern colossus poised to attack Israel: "The World is going to go 'puff' and disappear in September, 1935."[34]

An equally erroneous statement about Gog was made in 1985 by prophecy teacher Charles Taylor. He presented the term as a prophetic acronym for Russian president Andrei **G**romyko, Warsaw Pact leader Marshall **O**garkov, and Soviet General Secretary Mikhail **G**orbachev.[35] When Gromyko was ousted and replaced by Gorbachev, Taylor then claimed that GOG actually represented the first three letters in the *real* Russian spelling of the name Gorbachev (i.e., GOGrbachev).[36] During an interview with journalist William Alnor, Alexander Bobilev — a University of Pennsylvania faculty lecturer in Slavic studies — could not help but laugh, bluntly stating: "He's making that up." According to Bobilev, Gorbachev's name is spelled in English the same as it is in Russian, except "the 'ch' in English is one letter in the Soviet language."[37]

The terms Gog and Magog have been identified in various ways throughout history. It has been applied to King Gyges (7th century B.C.) of Lydia, an ancient kingdom in Asia Minor, which some people saw as the land of Magog.[38] Throughout the closing years of the Roman Empire, the Patriarch of Constantinople, Proclus (434–47), interpreted *Rosh* and *Meshech* — often associated with Gog and Magog — as the invading Huns.[39] During the Dark Ages, the Goths and Visigoths were said to be Gog and Magog.[40] Then, the Turkish Ottoman Empire was identified as Gog and Magog. By the eighteenth century, Puritan writer Cotton Mather (1663–1728) was teaching that Gog and Magog were the American Indians![41]

More recently, contemporary prophets have had to drastically alter their own views of Gog and Magog because of the disintegration of the Soviet Union, which until the early 1990s was heralded as the infamous northern foe of Israel. Christian prophecy teacher Peter LaLonde, in his 1991 book *One World Under Anti-Christ*, issued several warnings based on what he termed unquestionably clear Bible prophecies:

> [T]he prophets told us, Israel will be regathered into her homeland.... [T]hey
> also saw that in this same time period another power would arise in the North
> and eventually invade the land of Israel. There is no question that the Soviet
> Union is the fulfillment of that prophecy.... **The Soviets Will Invade Israel**
> - The next thing of which we are certain is that at some point before the second
> coming of Jesus at the end of the tribulation period, the Soviet Union will
> invade the land of Israel.... [W]hen the Soviet Union does invade Israel no
> one will be expecting it.[42]

Hal Lindsey confidently presented a similar prediction in his 1980 book *The 1980s: Countdown to Armageddon*:

> For several centuries, both Rabbis and Christian theologians have identified the
> great northern power named in Ezekiel as being the Soviet Union. . . . Before
> Russia attacks Israel, however, it will first invade Iran, or Persia, as it is called
> in Ezekiel chapter 38, verse five. When we apply this prophecy to modern times,
> it becomes obvious that the Soviets will use their recent conquest of Afghanistan
> as a springboard to overthrow Iran and gain control of the Persian Gulf area.[43]

Note the specifics of Lindsey's "Bible-based" prognostication: 1) Ezekiel is speaking about the Soviet Union; 2) Russia, as the leader of the U.S.S.R., will invade Iran before attacking Israel; and 3) the Soviets will attack Iran from a Soviet-occupied Afghanistan. Unfortunately for Lindsey (and many other Christian prophecy buffs), the U.S.S.R. collapsed in 1989, which meant that there would be no Soviets, nor a Soviet Union, to launch an attack. The Russians also pulled out of Afghanistan and fostered good relations with Iran. Lindsey has responded by simply revising his interpretation of Ezekiel. He now claims that Ezekiel has always pointed only to "modern ethnic Russians" and that when *Russia* invades Israel it will be fighting "alongside the Muslims."[44]

Influential Christian leader Pat Robertson has had to make an equally significant about-face regarding the Soviet Union. In 1984 he stated: "The immediate event of greatest significance in the Middle East is the obvious growing influence of the Soviet Union, which one day will lead the invasion of Israel . . . according to Ezekiel 38."[45] In 1992, he adopted an entirely different view, saying in reference to Ezekiel 38 and 39: "I have begun to believe it is more likely the Muslim republics — such as Kazakhstan, Tadzikhstan, Uzbekstan, and Azerbaijan."[46]

An especially interesting series of reversals was made in the 1996 "revised" version of the 1980 bestseller *Apocalypse Next* by William R. Goetz. The updated text, which took into consideration the downfall of the U.S.S.R., epitomizes the ease with which end-time speculators adapt their views to newspaper headlines. He simply re-worded most of the 1980 text to fit the current world situation.

Occasionally, however, his statements were so erroneous that he had to completely excise them from the updated edition. Because the text makes no mention of these edits, unsuspecting readers are led to believe that Goetz has always viewed Gog and Magog as applying only to Russia, rather than to Russia *and* the Soviet Union, including the now non-existent East Germany (see Table 10.1).

Since the 1920s Christians have been announcing an imminent attack on Israel by satanically-inspired hordes from Russia/Gog-Magog.[47] But Ezekiel 38 and 39 have nothing to do with the U.S.S.R., Iran, Russia, Afghanistan, Turkey, or even a hostile Arab/Muslim confederation that will invade Israel under Russian leadership. In the first place, the soldiers mentioned in Ezekiel 38 are "wielding swords" (v. 4) and "riding on horses" (v. 15). Ezekiel 39 lists the weapons used by Israel's enemies as wooden "bows and arrows, war clubs and spears" (vv. 9–10). It is doubtful that a Russian-led army of Muslims would attack Israel using such primitive weapons.

Second, Genesis 10:2 reveals that Magog is not a country, but a person; specifically, one of the sons of Japheth. His descendants — i.e., the people of Magog — were the militarily powerful Scythians (7th–6th century B.C.),

APOCALYPSE NEXT (1980 1ST EDITION)	APOCALYPSE NEXT (1996 REVISED EDITION)
"Russia is going to invade Israel. . . . However, the big Red Bear's pounce upon tiny Israel will result, not in the annihilation of the Jews, but rather the crushing defeat of *the awesome Soviet war machine*" (emphasis added).[48]	"Russia is going to invade Israel. . . . However, the big Red Bear's pounce upon tiny Israel will result, not in the annihilation of the Jews, but rather the crushing defeat of *the northern power's awesome war machine*" (emphasis added).[51]
"Who are her [Russia's] allies? . . . GOMER. *Gomer* and his hordes is evidently Germany. . . . Obviously, then, Gomer and his hordes are that part of eastern Europe found behind the Iron curtain. . . . The first to be taken into the ranks [of the U.S.S.R.] was *East Germany* (*Gomer*) — at the close of World War II."[49]	"[W]hat is prophesied about the nations which are predicted to join Russia? . . . GOMER. Gomer was the first grandson of Noah . . . . [M]any of Gomer's people also settled . . . in the Southern Russian steppes . . . Later they were pushed . . . into part of modern Turkey . . . . TURKEY (*Gomer*)."[52]
"Apparently unusual disasters like earthquakes and upheaval, pestilence, torrential rain and hailstones combined with supernatural fire . . . will result in the destruction of five-sixths of the entire Soviet military force."[50]	"Apparently unusual disasters like earthquakes and upheaval, pestilence, torrential rain and hailstones combined with supernatural fire . . . . will result in the destruction of five-sixths of the entire northern military force."[53]

Table 10.1

who lived to the far north of Israel where Russia is now located.[54] This nomadic tribe was actually identified as the Magogites by the first century Jewish historian Josephus.[55]

Third, most of the nations that appear in connection with Magog in Ezekiel 38–39 are also listed in Genesis 10:2 (i.e., Gomer, Tubal, Meshech, Cush, and Put). *Gomer* describes the race of people whom the Assyrians called Gimirrai. (The Greeks called them the Cimmarians.) *Tubal* is listed in Genesis as the fifth son of Japheth. His descendants — variously identified by historians as the Scythians, Iberians, and Hittites — were known for having traded with the city of Tyre (Ezek. 27:13). The progeny of *Meshech* (another son of Japheth) inhabited the mountains north of Assyria from 1115–705 B.C. Finally, *Cush* and *Put* were ancient names for Ethiopians and Libyans. Obviously, all of these terms apply to nations that existed long before modern Russia.

Fourth, although Ezekiel says that Israel will be invaded from the north, this has nothing to do with Russia, which just happens to be located north of Israel. Why not? According to archeologist Barry Beitzel, an approach from the north was usually the way an enemy would attack ancient Israel, regardless of where that enemy resided. In *The Moody Atlas of Bible Lands*, Beitzel explains that "the Bible's use of the expression 'north' denotes the direction from which a foe would normally approach and not the location of its homeland."[56] In fact, the Bible actually labels several of Israel's enemies as being from the north, although they were all located in the east: Assyrians (Zeph. 2:13), Babylonians (Jer. 1:13-15; 6:22; Zech. 2:6–7), and Persians (Is. 41:25; Jer. 50:3).[57]

End-time prophets committed to making Ezekiel's words fit into today's world have responded to these facts by coming up with some clever ways of getting around the obvious problems inherent to their interpretations. The description of "horses," for instance, is said to be God's way of prophetically speaking about the "horse power" of modern war machines.[58] What about Ezekiel's references to soldiers using bows and arrows? These verses are explained away via a thought progression that goes something like this: a) arrows fly through the air; b) bullets and missiles fly through the air; c) an arrow can even be called a "missile," or projectile. Conclusion: Ezekiel *must* be talking about modern-day bullets and missiles, and his reference to "bows" (which launch arrows) *must* actually be referring to guns and missile launchers.[59]

This method of biblical interpretation cannot be supported grammatically, historically, culturally, theologically, or contextually. It does, however, give doomsday visionaries great freedom to produce literature that places Armageddon just around the corner. Best-selling author Hal Lindsey, for example, promotes such a view of Ezekiel's bows and arrows. Of course, this is not the only argument Lindsey presents for a Russian invasion of Israel. His most compelling reason to believe that modern-day Russia is Gog/Magog relates to the genealogy of Russians: "They're the ones that are the enemy from the north, because Magog is the forefather of the Scythians, who are modern Russians."[60] In other words, because today's Russians are direct descendants of the Magogites (i.e., the ancient Scythians), Ezekiel's prophecies apply to Russia.

In taking this approach, Lindsey runs into yet another historical snag. Modern Russians are *not* related to the Scythians/Magogites! The Scythians were all but completely wiped out as a people between the first century B.C. and second century A.D. through a series of confrontations with the Sarmatians (a related people), the Ostrogoths, and finally the Huns in 372 A.D., under the leadership of Attila.[61]

Where, then, did twentieth century Russians originate? They emerged from Slavic tribes that migrated into Russian territory after the Huns had removed the Scythians and Sarmatians from that area. Only after the Hun empire collapsed in 454 did the Slavs began to rise as a dominant group. The Russians, as a distinct nationality, did not branch off from the Slavic tribes until Prince Oleg unified the Varangian principality of the Rus in 880.[62] Put another way, today's Russians are a totally distinct people from the Scythians, and therefore, cannot be Magog.

To understand the book of Ezekiel, one must first recognize that the apocalyptic imagery used therein is not meant to be taken literally. For example, Ezekiel 39 describes the alleged "Russia vs. Israel" post-battle scene as being littered with so many slain enemies of Israel that it takes seven months to bury them! This same chapter has God instructing the victorious Israelites to eat the flesh and drink the blood of "the princes of the earth" (vv. 17–20), even though such cannibalistic acts would clearly violate God's commands elsewhere in the Old Testament (cf. Deut. 12:23).

The Wycliffe Bible Commentary on the Bible notes that illustrations in Ezekiel's writings "frequently have details that cannot be literally pressed (e.g., 16:46–51, 53-56, 61), but are part of the drapery of the story."[63] Therefore, rather that being a veiled reference to a future Russian/Arab invasion of Israel, Ezekiel 38–39 is probably a "prophetic parable illustrating a great truth," as the Wycliffe commentary explains:

> Here the elaborate and weird imagery [of Ezekiel] expresses a great truth. To
> Israel in Babylon [in captivity] this prophecy gave assurance that, once she was

restored to her land, the power of God would protect her from the worst foes imaginable. To the Church suffering at the hands of its most relentless persecutors, this is a promise of God's deliverance. The final triumph of the Messiah at the end time is also implicit in this parable. This view makes the passage pertinent to every period of history. The purpose of apocalyptic writing such as this is the unveiling of the future, showing God's Lordship over it. Thus it guides and strengthens the people of God in times of darkness.[64]

Bluntly stated, Ezekiel 38–39 was never meant to be read like tomorrow's newspaper. The passages were written to bring hope and comfort to Bible readers who, due to life's circumstances, feel like a nation with no hope of escaping from hostile enemies that are surrounding them. To such individuals, Ezekiel declares that God will rescue them and eventually give them peace of mind.

The "Fig Tree" Nation

Fitting Israel-related world events into various Bible verses is crucial to Christians bent on predicting when Armageddon will take place. Israel's statehood is seen as an "irrefutable sign" that we are living in the last of the last days.[65] One especially significant Bible passage that Christian prophecy teachers use in connection to this thought is Matthew 24:32–34, which contains Jesus' parable of the fig tree:

> Now learn the parable from the fig tree; when its branch has already become tender, and puts forth its leaves, you know that summer is near; even so you too, when you see all these things, recognize that He [i.e., the Messiah] is near, right at the door. Truly I say to you, this generation will not pass away until all these things take place.

According to eminent Bible scholar D. A. Carson — Professor of New Testament Studies at Trinity Evangelical Divinity School in Deerfield, Illinois — few chapters of the Bible "have called forth more disagreement among interpreters than Matthew 24 and its parallels."[66] The most popular interpretation of this passage is as follows: 1) the fig tree represents Israel;

2) the budding of the tree's leaves describes the re-establishment of Israel's statehood in 1948; and 3) the generation to see this event will see Jesus' return. The importance of this teaching cannot be overstated. It is high-lighted in virtually every end-time volume produced by the Christian publishing industry. *Storming Toward Armageddon: Essays in Apocalypse*, a 1992 volume co-written by several prophecy teachers, contains an entire chapter titled "Israel: The Clear Sign." Its author, William T. James, makes the following statement:

> Apocalypse and Armageddon loom just ahead. But, can we know if those long talked about, worried-over events will even come to pass, much less within our own lifetime? . . . [W]e will concern ourselves with the one sign Jesus gives that seems most directly to signal the beginning of the end. We have been living a part of that most dramatic sign since 1948, when the nation of Israel was born in a single day — May 14. . . . Jesus clearly used the fig tree parable to tell the last generation of believers that the re-establishment of the nation of Israel would be a key sign of His nearing second advent as well as a sign of the end of the world system.[67]

Christian writer Tim LaHaye says Israel's current status as an indepen-dent nation is the "Super Sign" of Christ's soon return. According to LaHaye, the generation to see this sign will surely see the end of the world.[68] But this was not always LaHaye's position. At one time he held a view similar to that of the Jehovah's Witnesses, declaring that World War I and the year 1914 was the beginning of the "generation" that would see the world's destruction and Jesus' second advent. He had to abandon this view, however, because most of the 1914 generation had died out by the 1990s.

Fortunately, the establishment of Israel's statehood in 1948 provided a new starting point at which LaHaye could position the beginning of the last generation. He expressed his updated view in the revised edition of *The Beginning of the End*. Interestingly, the first edition of this book (published in 1972) not only presented LaHaye's original view, but included a date-suggestion that put "the end" somewhere in the 1990s. Of course, the 1991 edition replaced this obviously false view with a different date-suggestion, which placed "the end" near 2028–2038. Readers of LaHaye's 1991 book were given no clue as to what he had taught twenty years earlier. A comparison of text from La Haye's original edition with the same text section from his updated edition clearly shows the textual deletions and additions he made to various paragraphs (see tables 10.2 and 10.3)

THE BEGINNING OF THE END (1972 1ST EDITION)	THE BEGINNING OF THE END (1991 REVISED EDITION)
"*The Key Generation* Now we are ready to examine the key to this whole passage as it relates to the time of Jesus' coming. . . . Carefully putting all this together, we now recognize this strategic generation. It is the generation that 'sees' the four-part sign of verse 7 [Matt. 24], or the people who saw the First World War [1914]. We must be careful here not to be dogmatic, but it would seem that these people are witnesses to the events, not necessarily participants in them."[69]	"**THE KEY GENERATION** Now we are ready to examine the key to this whole passage as it relates to the time of Jesus' coming. . . . Carefully putting all this together, we now recognize this strategic generation. It is the generation that 'sees' the events of 1948. We must be careful here not to become dogmatic, but it would seem that these people are witnesses to the events, not necessarily participants in them."[71]
"That would suggest they were at least old enough to understand the events if 1914–1918, not necessarily old enough to go to war. How old does one have to be to understand that the world is in a great war? . . . [P]erhaps somewhere between five years and fourteen years of age in 1914 [i.e., born 1900–1909]."[70]	"That would suggest they were at least old enough to understand the events of 1948 [REMAINING SENTENCES DELETED BY LA-HAYE]."[72]

Table 10.2

Historically speaking, the popularization of this notion that Israel's rebirth as a state holds prophetic significance is traceable to John Cumming, the mid-nineteenth century preacher. He saw the migration of Jews to Jerusalem as prophetic fulfillment of the fig tree parable. Furthermore, Cumming — who felt that he would see Jesus return by 1865 — was also an early promoter of the "Russia=Gog/Magog" view. He believed Russians were descended from *Rosh*, *Meshech*, and *Tubal*.[73] Cumming's ideas, including his identification of *Gomer* as Germany, have been repeated almost verbatim by "a multitude of later writers on the subject."[74]

THE BEGINNING OF THE END (1972 1ST EDITION)	THE BEGINNING OF THE END (1991 REVISED EDITION)
"I believe it is that generation which our Lord said 'will not pass away till all those things be fulfilled.' . . . How many people make up a generation? No particular number; just one person who comprehended the four parts of the 1914–1918 sign could represent the 'generation.' . . . We are acquainted with 90-year-old people, so this 'generation' is not limited to eighty years. However, neither should we expect the entire generation to pass away before Jesus returns!"[75]	"I believe it is that generation which our Lord said 'will not pass away till all those things be fulfilled.' . . . How many people make up a generation? No particular number; just one person who comprehended the significant events of 1948 could represent the 'generation.' . . . We are acquainted with ninety-year-old people, so 'this generation' is not limited to eighty years. However, neither should we expect the entire generation to pass away before Jesus returns!"[77]
"How Much Longer Do We Have?" All of us know gray-haired members of the generation that experienced the events of World War I. I know several who have already gone to be with the Lord [i.e., died], so the people of that generation do not have much more time on this earth. . . . We are in the twilight of that generation — that I firmly believe. . . . [I]f you think the above teachings indicate that time is short, you are right."[76]	**"HOW MUCH LONGER DO WE HAVE?** All of us know gray-haired members of the generation that witnessed the events of 1948. If indeed this is the generation our Lord had in view, and that does seem probable, we do not have much more time on earth. . . . We are in the twilight of that generation — that I firmly believe. . . . [I]f you think the above teachings indicate that time is short, you are right."[78]

Table 10.3

In the years following the publication of his works, many predictions were based on the "Israel=the fig tree" concept. Then, with the outbreak of World War I and the seemingly unavoidable re-establishment of Israel as a state, predicted dates for "the end" increased exponentially. In the May 13, 1916 issue of *The Alliance Weekly* there appeared an article authored by influential fundamentalist W. E. Blackstone, who calculated that the end of the world would come in 1915/16, 1926/27, or 1934/35.[79]

Into this apocalyptically expectant environment came the Balfour Declaration (1917). It pledged British support for a Jewish national home in Palestine, which at that time was still part of the Ottoman Empire. This declaration brought euphoria to countless Christians, as one article in the *Evangel* noted: "Do not we, who are looking for the coming of our Lord, and the 'New Jerusalem,' feel a thrill go through us as we read . . . the words of Christ when He said, 'Now learn a parable of the fig tree?' . . . Hallelujah, our summer is nigh!"[80] Another publication from the 1920s contained this editorial:

> Palestine for the Jews. The most striking sign of the times is the proposal to give Palestine to the Jews once more. . . . Prophecy revolves around the despised Jew: and if Jewish restoration is imminent (as it appears to be), how near must we be to the fulfillment of every vision!"[81]

But once again, Christian prophecy teachers have misunderstood the texts to which they so devoutly adhere. The fig tree in Matthew 24:32–34 probably does not represent Israel. In his book *99 Reasons Why No One Knows When Christ Will Return*, evangelical cult specialist B. J. Oropeza admirably attempts to bring some balance to the views of his fellow Christians by pointing out several relevant points:

> [W]e cannot discover the nation of Israel hidden among the leaves of every fig tree mentioned in Scripture. Sometimes a fig tree represents peace and prosperity (1 Kings 4:25; Mic. 4:4); sometimes it's just a plain old fig tree! In fact, there is no indication that Jesus intended his apostles to discern a secret reference to any particular nation in Matthew 24:32-34. In the parallel passage in Luke, Jesus says, "Look at the fig tree and *all the trees* [emphasis added]. When *they* sprout leaves, you can see for yourselves and know that the summer [the time] is near" (Luke 21:29–30). Since at the time he was sitting on the Mount of Olives (see Matt. 24:2–3) — famous for its fig trees — he was simply selecting the fig tree as an end-time illustration because it was the most immediate object lesson available. In one reference where scholars suggest the fig tree does represent Israel (Mark 11:12–14, 20–21; cf. Matt. 21:18–20), Jesus curses the tree so that it can never again bear fruit. He was saying that

Israel was spiritually dead. It is difficult to imagine that Israel, as a nation, is once again represented by the fig tree in Matthew 24:32–34 when Jesus has just cursed the nation forever in Matthew 21:18–20.[82]

Oropeza's most significant observation about Matthew 24 involves its parallel passage, Luke 21:29–30, which includes Jesus' statement about seeing *all* the trees sprouting leaves, not just the fig tree. If Christian prophecy teachers were to be consistent, then they would have to find numerous countries to correspond to *all* of the trees mentioned in Luke.[83] It must be further recognized that nowhere in Matthew 24 does Jesus declare that he is speaking to some future generation. In fact, he reiterates time and again that *his listeners* are the ones who will see the signs of the end. Note how the fig tree parable fits in the context of Matthew 24:4–34:

See that no one misleads *you*. . . . And *you* will be hearing of wars and rumors of wars; see that *you* are not frightened, for those things must take place, but that is not yet the end. . . . Then they will deliver *you* to tribulation, and will kill *you*, and *you* will be hated by all nations on account of My name. . . . Therefore when *you* see the abomination of desolation which was spoken of through Daniel the prophet, standing in the holy place [i.e., the Jerusalem Temple] . . . then let those who are in Judea flee to the mountains. . . . Now learn the parable of the fig tree; when its branch has already become tender, and puts forth its leaves, *you* know that summer is near; even so *you* too, when *you* see all of these things, recognize that He is near, right at the door. Truly I say to *you*, this generation [i.e., the generation hearing Jesus speak] will not pass away until all these things take place [emphasis added].

One question, however, must be answered: If Jesus was telling the Jews present with him in the first century that *they* were the generation who would see "the end," then is he guilty of making a false prophecy? No. The "end" about which he spoke may have been the end of Israel/Jerusalem (70 A.D.), not the end of the world. All of the "signs" enumerated by Jesus took place in the first century just before the destruction of Jerusalem under the Roman emperor Titus. Again, Oropeza provides us with insight:

The phrase "this generation" in Matthew 24:34 does not refer to our generation, which has seen Israel return to Palestine in 1948. It refers to the Jews
living in the first century. . . . Those living in the first century experienced
the wars, famines, earthquakes, pestilences, false Christs, persecutions and
tribulations mentioned in these passages. Other parts of the New Testament
tell us of false prophets and messiahs such as Theudas, Judas the Galilean and
Elymas in the first century (Acts 5:34-37; 13:4-12). Many false teachers
infiltrated the church (2 Cor. 11; Gal. 1:6-10; 2 Peter 2; Jude 4). Earthquakes
were abundant (Acts 16:26; Josephus *Wars* 4.4.5), as were famines, persecutions and other signs (Acts 8:1–4; 11:27–29; 12:1–23; Rom. 15:25–28; 1 Cor.
16:1–5). Such calamities are confirmed by writings of non-Christian historians
of the day such as Suetonius, Tacitus and Josephus. . . . The parable of the fig
tree in Matthew 24:32–34 was told for those living in the first century
regarding the destruction of the [Jerusalem] temple.[84]

Oropeza's interpretation, which is shared by many conservative Christians, shows that not every born-again believer who reads their Bible is
obsessed with doomsday. According to Dr. Ron Rhodes — a well-respected
conservative scholar, prolific book author, and graduate of Dallas Theological Seminary — dogmatic eschatological views (including date-setting and
date-suggesting) are opposed to Scripture. He feels that responsible Bible
teachers focus "on what the Scriptures say, not so much on what the
newspapers have to say."[85] Although Rhodes personally believes that we are
indeed living in the last days, he does not subscribe to sensationalism:

I plan my life like I'm going to be here my entire life. . . . Who knows how
long God's clock is going to tick? For that reason, I always advise people to
plan like they're going to be here their whole life. Don't make an irresponsible
decision to put off education, or put off saving for your retirement or anything
like that because you don't know what's going to happen. My feeling is that
that is the responsible thing to do. And I think that that's exactly what Jesus
taught, because Jesus said, "You don't know what's going to happen." Nobody
knows when it's [i.e., the end] going to happen. For that reason you need to
live your life in such a way so that when it does happen, you will be ready. . . .
You don't set dates. What you want to do is to live your life in such a way that

you're ready whenever Christ shows up. But between now and the time Christ comes our goal is not to set dates and be sensational, but to be sober-minded as we await the second coming. Christ himself indicated that we are to be sober-minded. . . . It is an unwise thing to imply or state that within "X-number" of months such and so is going to happen, because we don't know those things. Only God knows those things.[86]

There is certainly nothing wrong with Christians looking forward to the return of their Lord and Savior. The apostles John and Paul both prayed for Jesus to come back (1 Cor. 16:22; Rev. 22:20). Such a sincere desire imparts comfort and hope to individuals living in a decidedly difficult world full of complex problems. But no one has ever benefited from the disappointment and embarrassment inseparably linked to failed prophecies, predictions, and suggestions about "the end."

IN THE END

Scripture plainly teaches that we will never know when, or even *about* when, the apocalypse will occur:

- "Be on the alert, for you do not know which day your Lord is coming. . . . The Son of Man is coming at an hour when you do not think He will" (Matt. 24:42, 44; cf. Mark 13:35–37).
- "But of that day or hour no one knows, not even the angels in heaven" (Mark 13:32).
- "It is not for you to know times or epochs which the Father [i.e., God] has fixed by His own authority" (Acts 1:7).
- "Now as to the times and epochs, brethren, you have no need of anything to be written to you. For you yourselves know full well that the day of the Lord will come just like a thief in the night [i.e., when not expected]" (1 Thess. 5:1–2; cf. 2 Peter 3:10).
- "I will come like a thief, and you will not know at what hour I will come upon you" (Rev. 3:3).

Moreover, the Bible teaches that the "last days" actually began with the birth of Jesus in the first century (Heb. 1:2; 1 Peter 1:20). The apostle John went so far as to describe his own era as "the last hour" (1 John 2:18). Yet first century Christians were not exhorted to discover the date of the world's end, but were instead instructed to keep their eyes on Jesus, the author and perfecter of their faith (Heb. 12:2). All of the biblical passages admonishing Christians to expectantly look for their savior's return were written to help believers fix their hearts on God rather than on the attachments of earthly life, which according to the Christian worldview, pale in comparison to the heavenly awards that await them at Jesus' second advent (cf. 2 Peter 3:11–13; Heb. 11:13).[87]

Renowned Christian scholar F. F. Bruce pointedly notes in his foreword to *A Guide to Biblical Prophecy* that "Holy Writ does not provide us with the means of plotting the course of future events."[88] D. Brent Sandy — New Testament Professor at Liberty University in Lynchburg, Virginia — agrees, stating that prophetic passages of Scripture were written "both to warn and comfort, not assuage our curiosity about what next year will hold."[89] Consequently, today's Christians might do well to spend fewer hours studying prophecy books filled with pointless conjectures, and more hours plumbing the depths of biblical passages relating to love, kindness, self-control, patience, and thoughtfulness. According to the Bible, the timing of Jesus' second advent is not nearly as important as the events that took place during his first advent.

ELEVEN

Millennial Mindsets

The prophecies say it's all about to end. It seems without hope. The only thing we can have is faith and commitment to grab some meaning for our lives now, even though we know [that] in the end, it's all going to be destroyed.

Charles Strozier, Ph.D.[1]

John Jay College, Center on Violence and Human Survival

COUNTLESS AMERICANS took a terrifying walk on the road to Armageddon during the night of October 30, 1938, after tuning their radios to WABC. The station was broadcasting live orchestra music from New York's Hotel Park Plaza and all seemed normal, until the following news flash aired:

> Ladies and gentlemen, we interrupt our program of dance music to bring you a special bulletin from the Intercontinental Radio News. At twenty minutes before eight, Central Time, Professor Farrell of the Mt. Jennings Observatory — Chicago, Illinois — reports observing several explosions of incandescent gas occurring at regular intervals on the planet Mars. . . . Professor Pearson, of the observatory at Princeton, confirms Farrell's observation and describes the phenomenon as "like a jet of blue flame shot from a gun."

WABC's musical program resumed. Within the span of a few minutes, however, it was interrupted two more times for updates on the Mars story. The second bulletin included an interview at Princeton University with the aforementioned Professor Pearson, a "world famous astronomer." Interviewing him was reporter Carl Phillips:

Phillips: [H]ow do you account for these gas eruptions occurring on the surface of the planet [Mars] at regular intervals?

Pearson: Well, I, cannot account for them.

Phillips: By the way professor, for the benefit of our listeners, how far is Mars from the Earth?

Pearson: Approximately forty million miles.

Phillips: Well, that seems a safe enough distance. . . . Just a moment ladies and gentlemen. Someone has just handed Professor Pearson a message. While he reads it, let me remind you that we are speaking to you from the observatory at Princeton, New Jersey . . . . One moment, please. Professor Pearson has passed me a message which he has just received. Professor, may I read the message to the listening audience?

Pearson: Certainly.

Phillips: Ladies and gentlemen I shall read you a wire addressed to professor Pearson from Dr. Gray of the Natural History Museum, "New York: 9:15 p.m. Eastern Standard Time, seismograph registered shock of almost earthquake intensity occurring within a radius of twenty miles of Princeton. Please investigate. Signed Lloyd Gray, Chief of Astronomical Division." Professor Pearson, could this occurrence possibly have something to do with the disturbances observed on the planet Mars?

Pearson: Well, hardly, Mr. Phillips. This is probably a meteorite of unusual size and its arrival at this particular time is merely a coincidence.

The station once again continued its music broadcast. But as before, the program was periodically interrupted by news reports, each one more disturbing than the last. Listeners eventually learned that it was not a meteorite after all that had plummeted to Earth. According to Phillips and Pearson — who had driven eleven miles to reach the crash site near Grover's Mill, New Jersey — the "meteorite" was actually a smooth cylindrical object measuring thirty yards in diameter. While on the scene, Phillips informed his radio audience that a large contingency of police and firemen, along with dozens of curious onlookers, were already present. He then proceeded to describe the place in detail and conduct on-the-spot interviews.

Suddenly, everything went chaotic. Shouts could be heard in the background as Phillips nervously related an unbelievable series of events that left listeners stunned:

Something's happening. Ladies and gentlemen this is terrific. This end of the thing is beginning to flake off. The top is beginning to rotate like a screw . . . . [T]he thing must be hollow. Ladies and gentlemen, this is the most terrifying thing I've, I've ever witnessed. Wait a minute! Someone's crawling — someone, or something — I can see coming out of that black hole. Two luminous disks. . . . It might be a face. . . . [There's] something wiggling out of the shadow like a gray snake. Now it's another one, and another one, and another one. They look like tentacles to me. I, I can see the thing's body now. It's large; large as a bear. . . . Ladies and gentlemen it's indescribable. I can hardly force myself to keep looking at it, it's so awful. The eyes are black and they gleam like a serpent. The mouth is, is kind of V-shaped . . . . The thing's rising up now and the crowd falls back. . . . Ladies and gentlemen. Am I on? Ladies and gentlemen, ladies and gentlemen . . . . I'll give you every detail as long as I can talk; as long as I can stay here. More state police have arrived and they're drawing up a quadrant in front of the pit. . . . [A] captain and two policemen advance with something in their hands. I can see it now. It's a white handkerchief tied to a pole — a flag of truce, if those creatures know what that means; what anything means. Wait a minute. Something's happening. Some shape is rising out of the pit and it's letting out a small beam of light against a mirror. What's that? It's a jet of flames springing from that mirror . . . right at the advancing men! It's strikes them head-on!! . . . It's spreading everywhere!! It's coming this way now, about twenty yards to my left . . . .

Phillips was cut-off in mid-sentence. During the several seconds of deafening silence that followed, listeners could only imagine what caused his transmission to end so abruptly. WABC then made an announcement that was far from comforting: "Ladies and gentlemen, due to circumstances beyond our control we are unable to continue the broadcast from Grover's Mill. Evidently, there is some difficulty with our field transmission. However, we will return to that point at the earliest opportunity."

Persons listening to the broadcast began calling neighbors and word quickly spread throughout America that something horrific was happening in New Jersey. The end of the world, it seemed, had finally come in the form of monsters from Mars. Panic-stricken farmers living near Grover's Mill — although they themselves had neither heard nor seen anything out of the ordinary — grabbed their guns and headed out the door to defend both home and country. Police stations, army headquarters, newspapers, and radio stations were flooded with so many phone calls that switchboards were jammed. As the night wore on, more and more citizens turned to WABC in hopes of finding out what was occurring on America's east coast.

The news they heard was not good, and it was rapidly getting worse. According to the continuing coverage, central New Jersey had been placed under martial law and CBS's broadcasting facilities were being used exclusively by the state militia. As for Phillips, his charred body was identified among the obliterated remains of forty people, including six state troopers. Their bodies had been "burned and distorted beyond all possible recognition" by some kind of heat ray.

To make matters worse, Martian flying machines were reportedly heading for New York and destroying everything in their path! WABC additionally informed its anxious audience that several battles between the aliens and U.S. soldiers had left battalions of dead men scattered across the countryside. Not even a squadron of army bombers could stop the Martian's advance. Within one hour of WABC's initial news break-in, another journalist from the station was relaying a nightmarish message to a cowering nation: "I'm speaking from the roof of the Broadcasting Building, New York City. The bells you hear are ringing to warn people to evacuate the city as the Martians approach." WABC subsequently reported that millions of people lay dead. The alien menace had apparently sprayed New York with poison gas. It did indeed seem like the end of the world.

In reality, however, no invasion had occurred. It was only actor Orson Welles's radio presentation of H. G. Wells's 1898 sci-fi thriller, *The War of the Worlds*.[2] Nevertheless, the general public was more than willing to believe that doomsday had arrived. The nationwide panic had ensued even though the broadcast began with an announcement that The Mercury Players were performing a dramatization of Wells's novel. Three similar announcements were made *during* the show as well. Despite these warnings, pandemonium broke out everywhere. Frightened crowds flocked to police stations and persons trying to flee various metropolitan areas brought traffic to a snarl.

According to the *Encyclopedia of Hoaxes*, people "packed up clothes, ran into the street in their nightclothes, piled furniture on top of their car, and held wet handkerchiefs over their faces for prevention from gas attacks."[3] Similar reactions took place a few years later when Welles's play was adapted to air in South America; first in Santiago, Chile in November 1944, and then in Quito, Ecuador in February 1949:

> In Santiago, there were panic, injuries, and heart seizures. In Quito, the situation was far worse. After the panic, word was spread that the whole thing was a hoax. As a result, a huge angry crowd surrounded the building that housed the radio station and the newspaper, and began throwing rocks. Soon the building was set on fire and nearly destroyed. At least twenty people were killed in the fire, many by jumping from upper story windows, where the radio station was located. The response of the Ecuadorean government was to arrest the director of the newspaper and the two writers of the modified radio script on charges of inciting riot. Some of the rioters were also arrested. In the case of the South American broadcasts, not much warning (if any) that this broadcast was only fiction was announced.[4]

Unfortunately, when it comes to end-time terrors and doomsday delusions, we have not advanced very far beyond where we were in 1938, *or even in A.D. 38*, for that matter. Armageddon paranoia has been, and will undoubtedly continue to be, stoked by doomsayers, especially now when society is crossing into a new millennium. Predictions regarding doomsday via any number of catastrophic events (e.g., a "pole shift," Armageddon, a comet collision, invading UFOs, Christ's return, etc.) span the religious spectrum from Nation of Islam leader Louis Farrakhan, who in 1991 declared that the Gulf War would "be that [war] which the scriptures refer to as the War of Armageddon which is the final war,"[5] to Native American spiritual leader Sun Bear, who in 1990 said that the year 2000 would bring global destruction unless humanity makes a change of "consciousness and perspective."[6]

Why are persons so ready, willing, and able to embrace end-of-the-world beliefs, dates of doom, and Armageddon scenarios? Some reasons may be deeply complex, while others are rather superficial (e.g., selling prophecy can be a lucrative career). The remainder of this chapter will discuss the six main reasons why this last century has seen a proliferation of end-time date-setters and date-suggesters.

PROPHETS OR PROFITS?

Prophecy sells. Of this fact there is no doubt. A December 1996 *Bookstore Journal* article on popularity trends in Christian book sales named end-times/prophecy as one of the "hottest" of all categories.[7] In May 1997, the number one best-selling Christian non-fiction book was *Day of Deception* by John Hagee, the Pentecostal preacher who wrote the *New York Times* best-seller *Beginning of the End*, another doomsday tome.[8]

In July 1997, two more books dealing with the world's end — *Left Behind* and *Tribulation Force*, both written by Tim LaHaye and Jerry Jenkins — held the number one and three slots on the best-selling Christian *fiction* list.[9] By December 1997, not only were these volumes still sitting comfortably in the number one and two slots on the best-selling Christian paperback lists, but a third apocalyptic novel — *Nicolae*, also by LaHaye and Jenkins — had hit the number one spot on the best-selling Christian hardcover book list.[10] In reference to this novel, one religious book catalogue noted: "This action-filled, post-rapture drama will have you perched on the edge of your seat!"[11]

Hal Lindsey, meanwhile, has released yet another doomsday work titled *Apocalypse Code*, in an apparent attempt to capitalize on the public's obsession with coded messages allegedly hidden in Scripture (per Michael Drosnin's bestseller *The Bible Code*).[12] Lindsey has even found spare time to write his own end-time novel: *Blood Moon*. It sets Armageddon in the near future and is based on prophetic scenarios he has been preaching for twenty-five years. One ad for it reads: "It's the 21st century, and the tribulation has begun. Fasten your seatbelts . . . you're in for the apocalyptic ride of your life!"[13]

Obviously, the amount of cash that can be generated by doomsday-related books is phenomenal. But written words are not the only provisions that doomsday peddlers offer to their information-starved followers. They also sell videotapes that tantalize the visual senses with images of nuclear explosions, volcanic eruptions, earthquakes, and the horrors of war. To these pictures are invariably added a script complete with Bible "proof-texts" and interviews with prophecy "experts," all of whom agree that the end is indeed coming soon. Audio cassette recordings of lectures given by prophecy teachers while on their speaking circuits are usually sold at "bargain prices" as well. Also offered are a number of other prophecy-related odds-and-ends: e.g., "earth changes" maps, posters of images gleaned from the Book of Revelation, and magazine subscriptions).

How much money is to be made in end-time related audio-visual products? Consider a joint project launched in late 1997 by Jack Van Impe Ministries and Peter and Paul LaLonde's *This Week in Bible Prophecy* television show. According to *CBA Marketplace*, the two prophecy-driven ministries plan a $1 million promotional campaign for the feature film *Apocalypse*, which is based on an original screenplay by the writers of *Left Behind*, a video already produced by the LaLonde brothers. Promotional plans include eight-week campaigns on *This Week in Bible Prophecy* and Van Impe's *Jack Van Impe Presents* television program, publication of the film's story in novel form by the Lalondes, and release of a soundtrack featuring contemporary Christian artists.[14]

The rise of the end-time related patriot/militia movement has brought even more consumer goods into the prophecy market. In fact, each year several "Preparedness Expos" are held in large cities across America for persons interested in getting ready for the one-world, totalitarian, Antichrist-led, New World Order (see Chapter 4). Every conference boasts more than one hundred exhibitors and a roster of guest speakers that reads like a Who's Who of the patriot/militia movement. Past Expos have featured Mark Koernke ("Mark from Michigan"), John Trochmann (Militia of Montana), David Thibodeau (Branch Davidian survivor), Larry Pratt (Gun Owners of America), and Christian financial planner Don McAlvany.[15]

The products made available at these gatherings represent the finest in doomsday survival paraphernalia. Of course, not all of the supplies sold (or those made available through the bi-monthly *Preparedness Journal*) are equally functional or effective; some amount to little more than the twentieth century version of snake oil (admittedly, the legitimate and not-so-legitimate items present a list of interesting choices):

> "BLOW GUNS . . . . The greatest tool ever invented."
>
> "SUPER BLUE GREEN [ALGAE] . . . . The uniquely superior nutrition for the 90s."
>
> "INTERNATIONAL POWER FOODS. . . . We are your source for cutting edge detoxification."
>
> "JUICE PLUS. . . . A Revolutionary New Product!!"
>
> "JUNGLE OUTFITTERS. . . . Jungle has the 'NO BULL' answers to what really works."
>
> "STEVE VAUS PRODUCTIONS. . . . *Patriot recording artist.*"
>
> "UNIVERSAL FORCE DYNAMICS. . . . The best in personal and family defense books."
>
> "YOUNG LIVING ESSENTIAL OILS. . . . Essential oils are nature's most powerful anti-oxidents. . . . Scientists & doctors are discovering the ability of Essential oils to fight diseases & protect us. Essential oils are history's missing link."[16]

The truly high-ticket goods come from the gold, silver, precious metals, and survival gear dealers. These power-players in the game of prophecy-for-dollars include such notable figures as Don McAlvany, president and owner of International Collectors Associates, which is his gold, silver, and rare coin brokerage "specializing in precious metals and other conservative investments."[17] As previously mentioned in chapter four of this book, McAlvany also sells year-long food storage systems for $2,513 per person, or $10,000 for a family of four.[18]

In addition to paying exorbitant rates for prophecy-related newsletters/magazines and buying survival products, persons obsessed with the end-times are regularly appealed to for those last few donations before "the end" hits. It seems that foretelling Armageddon is often a perfect segue into an appeal for donations. In a 1987 issue of *Bible Prophecy News*, for instance, end-time preacher Charles Taylor revealed that various unnamed "intelligence experts" had confirmed that the U.S.S.R. was mobilizing for a "major military confrontation with the United States sometime in 1988." Taylor then added a bold plug for funds: "In this year just before the rapture, INVEST IN HEAVEN AND REAP DIVIDENDS FOR ETERNITY. YOU CAN'T TAKE IT WITH YOU!"[19]

In 1995, just after Harold Camping's failed prophecy about doomsday in 1994, his Family Radio Network was functioning on a new annual budget of $12 million, thanks to Camping's continued request for donations through the time he was declaring Christ's imminent return. High expenditures are also posted by Texe Marrs, an ardent conspiracy advocate who teaches that the last days could very well "wrap up by the year 2000," which he claims just happens to also be "the year the Devil proposes to bring his plan to fruition."[20] Marrs markets his end-of-the-world conspiracy materials through a monthly newsletter called *Flashpoint* that has a yearly budget of $700,000.[21]

Given these fiscal facts, it is easy to see why say selling prophecy has become big business in the twentieth century. This is not to say that anyone I have mentioned thus far — be they Christian prophecy teacher, occult prognosticator, or anti-New World Order patriot — is actually guilty of proclaiming doomsday just to make a quick buck. I am only saying that a great deal of money can be made in the arena of prophecy teaching and that it is within the realm of possibility that some unscrupulous charlatans are taking advantage of persons fearful of the times in which we live, which brings us to the second reason why many individuals are preaching Earth's imminent destruction.

THE FEAR FACTOR

Renowned scholar Norman Cohn has noted that obsession with the end of the world tends to increase "not when times are merely bad, but when they are *unprecedentedly* bad, when people are being uprooted and their traditional ways of life — however unpleasant they may have been — are being destroyed."[22] In agreement with Cohn, John Hegeland — Professor of Religious Studies at North Dakota State University — makes the following observation:

As one can see from the history of it [i.e., apocalyptic fear], it nearly always arises in times of suppression, chaos, fear, or disadvantage. As such, its first appearances are a register of the degree of social and psychological pain people are suffering. We are dealing with frightened people caught in the jaws of history, not kooks.

Hegeland is clearly describing an emotional state at which many people in modern society have arrived. A 1996 *Time*/CNN poll found that half of all Americans believe that their country "is in deep and serious trouble."[23] Moreover, recent economic reports indicate that a "vast major-ity of Americans either tread water economically or grow poorer."[24] One study noted that "the working farmer or the average employee has seen his standard of living drift downward since the 1970s.[25] According to political analyst Chip Berlet, there now exists a whole generation of U.S. citizens for whom the "American Dream" will never come true:

They bought into the American Dream, fought in the war, sent their kids to college so they'd have a better life — that was the social contract. Now they realize their children will have a lower economic status than they do, they see their pension eroding into a meaningless amount of money, and a lot of them have been downsized or moved into the service economy.[26]

Yet another social problem that has contributed greatly to feelings that the end must be near is crime, especially juvenile crime. Youth offenses are not only rising, but growing more violent each year.[27] Moreover, Princeton professor John J. DiIulio Jr. has noted that our modern culture is actually breeding a new generation of criminals that sociologists have labeled "juvenile superpredators."[28] They have no sense of right or wrong and seem incapable of feeling remorse. They kill, beat, rob, and destroy property for the sheer thrill of it. A frightening number of heinous crimes that at one time only the most hardened and cold-blooded adult criminals would dare perpetrate are now being committed by children.

In reference to the many youth-related violations of the law, James Alan Fox — Dean of the College of Criminal Justice at Northeastern University — remarks: "The really bad news is that the worst is yet to come. I believe we are on the verge of a crime wave that will last out the century. Unless we act today, I truly believe we will have a blood bath when all these kids grow up."[29] Doomsayers and their followers ask a thought-provoking question: How much longer can humanity survive if each generation is more violent and decadent than the last?

In addition to crime and economic instability, several other alarming situations have compelled end-time visionaries to raise their voices in a united chorus of warning: global warming, depletion of the ozone layer, political unrest in the Middle East, and water/air pollution. One must also not forget about the possible impact on Earth by any one of a number of comets and asteroids that regularly zip through our solar system. All of these threats have contributed to our culture's perpetual state of crisis, which is precisely the kind of environment wherein apocalyptic fears flourish.

Frank Giordano, who believed end-time prophet Harold Camping's prediction that 1994 would bring the rapture, is typical of many persons longing to be rescued from their fears and frustrations. When the 1994 date passed uneventfully, Giordano's hopes for himself and others were dashed to pieces. "I'm disappointed for my children that they have to grow up in this cruel world," said Giordano. "I guess Mr. Camping was wrong."[30]

GIVING UP AND GETTING OUT

Religion scholar Mircea Eliade has noted that widespread fixation on apocalypticism has historically arisen when people are experiencing "feelings of relative deprivation in matters of status, wealth, security, or self-esteem. Millenarian movements appear in periods of crisis, when such feelings become most painful. . . . [T]he crisis engenders personal fantasies of invulnerability and escape."[31] In other words, when there seems to be no escape from the daily traumas of societal living, people psychologically comfort themselves by looking to an imminent escape via divine intervention on their behalf.

This aptly describes the attitudes of many end-time believers who have adopted a decidedly pessimistic attitude when it comes to the world's current situation. Consider the words of Carl Holland, a preacher at York County, Virginia's Assembly of God church. "Society is gonna get worse and worse," says Holland. "We can't do anything to make it better. People who tell you we can make things better are lying."[32]

Holland feels that nothing short of Christ's return will be able to alleviate the problematic facets of modern life. His view, which reflects the mindset of vast numbers of persons obsessed with discerning the signs of the times, has been commented upon by numerous religious researchers. In his 1992 article "Lure of the Apocalypse," cult specialist and former Jehovah's Witness Randall Watters made this observation:

> Apocalyptic religions appeal primarily to those who have lost faith in the world and its political and reform systems. Lacking faith that the world could ever be a better place to live under man's influence, they look to God to destroy the world and start over.[33]

Watters's assertion has been confirmed again and again in the writings of prophecy teachers. In a 1997 issue of *Prophecy Watch International*, for instance, David Allen Lewis wrote: "The end is the beginning! Yes, the end of this age and this doomed anti-God world system signals the beginning of the Millennial Kingdom and then the dawn of eternity which features a new heaven and a new earth!"[34] By adopting a worldview which proposes an imminent end of all things— e.g., within "one generation" of 1948, "very near," "possibly by 2001," etc. — individuals are in a sense also saying to themselves, "All I have to do is make it through one more year, one more decade, or until the year 2001, then all my problems will be over!"

For people in emotional/psychological stress who have lost all confidence in human problem-solving abilities, this tactic is somewhat akin to the pain-tolerance technique of counting to ten while undergoing an uncomfortable medical procedure. A person using such a technique would begin counting to ten when, for example, a needle is inserted into their body. This enables their mind to focus on a certain point in time when they *know* the pain will end. When it comes to apocalypticism, fixating on a certain year or on a limited span of time (i.e., "one generation") enables a person to psychologically convince themselves that their "pain" will only last a little while longer.

What happens when that date passes and the difficulties of life, as well as the world in general, continue? People simply pick a new date that will get them through the next year, or five years, or ten years. In other words, taking on life just a few years at a time is psychologically easier then thinking that one must face an indefinite duration of trials, toil, and trouble.

IN SEARCH OF SIGNIFICANCE

For thousands of years, extraordinary individuals have periodically emerged from relative obscurity to change the course of human events. Such personalities — whether military, religious or political — have affected the lifestyles and philosophies of countless millions. Consider Buddha, Alexander the Great, Julius Caesar, Confucius, Jesus of Nazareth, Joan of Arc, Thomas Jefferson, Abraham Lincoln, Harriet Tubman, Gandhi, Corrie Ten Boom, and Martin Luther King, Jr. Each has exerted tremendous influence over humanity, and will forever be remembered for his or her extraordinary accomplishments.

But the vast majority of individuals who have lived and died have done so in relative obscurity. They have never had their name in the newspaper, seen their image on television, altered another person's philosophy, or made a major contribution to society. For many people, their only claim to fame will be that they were alive when something of historical importance occurred: e.g., World War II, Kennedy's assassination, the first moon walk, Elvis's overdose, the death of Princess Di.

The ultimate event, of course, is doomsday. Consequently, many people in their personal search for significance cling to a belief that tells them they are special. In all of history, they are the ones who will be alive during humanity's final moment, whether it be due to a "pole shift" or Jesus' second advent. This millennial mindset is concisely explained in *The Sign of the Last Days* by Carl Jonsson and Wolfgang Herbst:

> Perhaps because we are to such an extent "strangers to the past," we easily read into the events and circumstances of our own day a distinctiveness and

uniqueness that may not actually be there. In the minds of many religious people there is a belief that the final war of Armageddon, the coming of Christ Jesus for the final judgment, is sure to occur in their day. It is hard for a person to accept that an event of such momentous importance should not happen in his or her lifetime. One inwardly resists the thought of missing out on it, of not experiencing a personal "rendezvous with history," particularly divine history. Doubtless this is why books that feed and stimulate such expectations often enjoy great popularity. As just one example, the book *The Late Great Planet Earth*, by Hal Lindsey, reached a circulation of over 18 million copies in a number of languages. People obviously want to believe that their day is unique, singled out in Bible prophecy as special.[35]

In his 1994 book *Prince of Darkness: Antichrist and the New World Order*, prophecy author Grant Jeffrey clearly gives special significance to "our generation." He intimates that out of all the persons who have ever lived, we are special: "The Scriptures teach that a single generation will witness the rebirth of Israel and the coming of the promised Messiah. . . . Our generation will witness the triumphant victory of Jesus."[36] Jack Van Impe preaches a similar message: "[T]he entire prophetic scenario is being fulfilled before our eyes. Jesus is coming back, and He's preparing for a thousand-year reign of peace on earth. . . . Isn't this exciting news?"[37] Finally, the closing words from an episode of Peter and Paul LaLonde's television show *This Week in Bible Prophecy* paints our generation as divinely chosen: "What exciting times we live in that we are able to witness the fulfillment of prophecies that so many have yearned to see over the generations. We're seeing it fulfilled right before our eyes. The Lord is coming back soon."[38]

The inescapable theme permeating the messages of these prophecy pundits could not be any clearer: we are a special generation. Hence, we as individuals must also be unique in God's eyes. Every person alive has the distinction of being picked to see history's culmination. Such a notion is much more appealing than the thought of having to work a boring job for the next twenty to thirty years, only to die in obscurity as billions of people have previously done. Many cannot resist believing that they stand at the very pinnacle of history.

TRUSTING SOULS

This facet of human behavior is summed up very well in a statement that is often, yet erroneously, attributed to P.T. Barnum, the renowned circus promoter: "There's a sucker born every minute." The observation is perfectly illustrated by individuals obsessed with doomsday. They will believe practically anything, as long as the person who is speaking has an air of authority.

Most people are simply too busy to verify all of the information they hear relating to increased earthquake activity, Bible prophecies, or secret legislation designed to enslave humanity to one world government. Moreover, few persons have the researching skills necessary to investigate the data they are given. They must accept what they hear by default. Their only alternative is to remain in a psychological state that offers them no answers for why the world is in such bad shape, and gives them no hope of imminent deliverance.

One must also remember that the success of any end-time prophet or preacher is directly related to how much trust he can engender in his followers. A charismatic doomsayer will usually never have his or her statements challenged or verified. This is perhaps most apparent within the Christian community, where the average believer implicitly trusts anyone who identifies himself or herself as a follower of Christ, especially when the one being trusted has gained a certain degree of notoriety. To many Christians, it is unthinkable that a radio Bible teacher, pastor, or televangelist would lie, since lying is clearly condemned in the Bible (Lev. 19:11; Col. 3:9).

Nevertheless, a number of end-time speakers, be they Christian or non-Christian, have resorted to spreading "facts" that seem less than 100% accurate. Consider, for example, three widely known lecturers who have been influential among both Christians and non-Christians in the patriot/militia movement: Mark Koernke, Linda Thompson, and Chuck Missler. Each has resorted to telling fanciful tales that portray them as authorities on world events, and how those events relate to the end-times.

Mark from Michigan

Mark Koernke is the undisputed father of the patriot movement's conspiracy theories (see Chapter 4). His 1993 videos, *America in Peril* and *A Call to Arms*, have a combined circulation of more than one million copies. According to the *Patriot Report*, he was the first person to come forward with information about the New World Order. He allegedly gathered his evidence "while serving in the U.S. Military Intelligence." His earliest lectures, which took place in the fall of 1992, contain information that is foundational to all patriot conspiracy theories:

- The use of foreign troops under U.N. control to police America with military power.
- The use of unmarked black helicopters to transport troops and/or dissident prisoners .
- The expansion of prison camps for large numbers of patriot resistors.[39]

How did Koernke acquire all of this secret information? He claims to have "handled a lot of classified documents" while in the U.S. Army as an intelligence analyst who held "a TSBI [top secret] clearance." He further maintains that he worked as "a counter-intelligence coordinator" and commanded the second and third brigades of "special warfare units that train U.S. military forces in foreign warfare and tactics."[40] (A brigade is usually composed of at least 5,000 soldiers.)

One of Koernke's supporters — fifty-six-year-old Morris Wilson of Topeka, Kansas — turned to Koernke's teachings in October 1995. Wilson could no longer make a living as a floor-covering installation contractor because of taxes and regulations. He wanted an answer to why life in America had become so difficult. Koernke's conspiratorial theories provided the answer. Wilson remembers: "With his [Koernke's] background in military intelligence, he has access to information that we don't have. . . . He explained about the black helicopters."[41] Like Wilson, many patriots believe Koernke's anti-government, end-time theories because of his military background. He is regularly billed as an "ex-military intelligence analyst . . . in a unique position to see first-hand how the conspirators for a one-world government have been planning to replace our Constitution and use foreign troops to police America."[42]

U.S. Army documents tell a different story.[43] Koernke's military records indicate that he served from December 22, 1977 to December 21, 1983 in the U.S. Army *Reserves*.[44] He "spent no time on active duty analyzing intelligence."[45] His only contact with analyzing intelligence data was as a student at the U.S. Army Intelligence Center and Schools.[46] Furthermore, Koernke could not have commanded two brigades since the highest rank he achieved was Specialist 5th Class.[47] According to Staff Sergeant Kenneth Klenk, Commander of the Mission Viejo, California Army Recruiting Station, the lowest rank allowed to command a brigade is a full Colonel (a high-ranking commissioned officer).[48]

Although Koernke's level of advancement, known as E-5, is no longer used by the Army or Army Reserves, it is comparable to the current rank of Sergeant. Such a rank is several steps below the highest non-commissioned officer grade, which is an E-9 (sergeant major). In response to Koernke's claims, Sergeant Klenk did not hesitate to speak in the bluntest terms: "I would think that he sold you a bill of goods . . . . A 1st Cook in the Mess Hall was a Spec. 5 in charge of KP [Kitchen Patrol] and the rank doesn't vary throughout the military that much."[49]

Koernke spins many fantastic yarns to keep up his public image. For instance, there is the dramatic account of a "face-to-face" confrontation between an unnamed patriot friend of his and NWO agents. Military Police allegedly escorted Koernke's friend to an interrogation room where he was left alone with a file on the desk. The patriot reportedly pulled the file toward him and opened it up to see a folded two and a half feet by one and a half foot "rap sheet" containing a "spider web of names of people to be arrested." Koernke's story ends predictably: "My name was at the top for the State of Michigan, so I can be proud. I'm number one and I don't have to try harder."[50]

For several years now, Koernke has been criss-crossing the country warning the masses about America's impending destruction, and exposing the evil New World Order regime now seeking to solidify their power. In reference to his outspoken tactics, Koernke notes with a flair of humor: "Big Brother is watching [and] Little Brother has a very big mouth."[51] Few would argue with this assertion. In fact, a 1995 *Time* article entitled "Mark

Koernke" stated that he is one of the most vocal of all the opinion leaders in the patriot movement.[52] As of 1998, he was still being revered at weekend militia conventions and nightly patriot meetings as Mark Koernke, former brigade commander and intelligence analyst for the U.S. Army.

"General" Thompson

If Mark Koernke is the patriot movement's father, then Indiana attorney Linda Thompson is its mother.[53] Her videotapes *Waco: The Big Lie* and *Waco II: The Lie Continues*, which are filled with deceptive anti-government propaganda, have succeeded in fostering a great deal of hatred for federal officials. Koernke and Thompson share an identically twisted view of the world. At one point during 1994, she and Koernke even worked together.[54]

Who is Linda D. Thompson? Her resumé states that she is a 40-year-old married mother of three who served in the U.S. Army until 1978, when she was honorably discharged at the rank of Sgt. 1st Class. She adopted the grandiose title of Acting Adjutant General of the Unorganized Militia of the United States of America in March 1993, when she attempted to rally Americans to meet in Waco for a protest against the government's handling of the Davidian standoff.[55]

She claims to be a "disabled Vietnam conflict veteran." However, her military file indicates that she did not join the Army until December 19, 1974[56] — almost two years *after* the January 23, 1973 Paris Peace Agreement was signed, which required United States troop withdrawal from Vietnam to begin within sixty days and prohibited the United States from sending any more troops into South Vietnam.

How then can Thompson claim to be a Vietnam veteran? Technically, a Vietnam veteran is anyone who served during that war's era, even though he or she may never have seen action. Thompson, then, is being *technically* truthful. But anyone reading "disabled Vietnam conflict veteran" will assume that Thompson was injured in Southeast Asia. She, of course, never served in Vietnam.[57] Thompson was injured during a training exercise in the U.S.[58]

The Indiana attorney also says she served in the Netherlands as an assistant to the U.S. Army Commanding General, NATO, Allied Forces Central Europe with a Cosmic Top Secret/Atomal security clearance.

Again, U.S. Army records shed light on Thompson's claims. She did indeed serve in Europe, and was even an assistant to the U.S. Army Commanding General of NATO — but only as a stenographer.[59] Her U.S. military file lists her principal duty for all years of service as: stenographer, secretary/steno, secretary/typist, and clerk typist.[60]

She additionally claims to have helped revise the NATO war plans manuals "while stationed at Allied forces Central Europe."[61] This also may be true, according to Staff Sergeant Kenneth Klenk, but only if one considers a secretary's task of typing up a document equivalent to making a revision. Klenk feels that Thompson may have "worked on" the NATO documents as a clerk typist, but could not have actually revised them because all revisions are done by Pentagon personnel and other high-ranking strategic command individuals.[62]

Concerning her domestic credentials, Thompson has stated that she is a member of the Indiana Bar Association.[63] But Thomas A. Pyrz — Executive Director of the Indiana State Bar Association — denies her claim. In a letter to John Reynolds of the *Free Spirit Press*, Pyrz writes: "Our records reflect that Ms. Thompson is not an Association member and apparently never has been a member."[64] After word spread regarding this particular oversight on Thompson's part, she began sending out a new resume with the Indiana State Bar Association credit deleted.

If Thompson is anything, she is dedicated and serious. In preparation for the New World Order's coming onslaught, she has organized a Ready Response Communications Network (RRCN) designed to relay news of importance to the patriot community. A 1994 American Justice Federation recorded telephone message states that persons wanting to join the RRCN must "pledge allegiance to the Constitution of the United States of America." Prospective members of the "ready response team" are also told another important point: "[T]he penalty for the knowing or intentional violation of your pledge is death."[65]

Idaho Chuck

Prophecy teacher Chuck Missler (see Chapter 4) gained popularity among Christians primarily through his close affiliation with the Calvary Chapel system of churches based in California. He graduated in 1956 from the U.S. Naval Academy "with distinction" (i.e., in the top ten percent of his class) and went on to eventually serve as the CEO for four public corporations. But some of the other information he has disseminated about himself appears to be rather exaggerated. Additionally, it has been discovered that Missler tends to "hide information that works against his claims."[66] A number of evangelicals have even accused him of propagating outright lies.[67]

Missler seems especially prone to telling tall tales when promoting Armageddon-related New World Order conspiracy theories, or when seeking to portray himself as a political insider and professional journalist who regularly moves in elite circles. For example, during a 1994 lecture at Calvary Chapel of Costa Mesa, California, Missler claimed that he had recently been "a keynote speaker" at the "governor's breakfast in Idaho."[68] As he continued his story, he painted himself as a sort of fearless Christian hero in a den of unbelieving politicians:

> When you have a group of politicians at something like the governors breakfast, it's a great opportunity to create problems [audience laughter]. I pointed out to the staff, and to the head table, I had to confess rather blatantly that I am neither a Republican nor Democrat — that got their attention. I said, "I'm a Monarchist." And they looked at me a little strangely. I said, "In fact, I'd like to close by telling you a little bit about *my* candidate [loud applause and cheers]. Yeah! I said, "My candidate is King of the Jews. . . . My candidate is also King of Israel. . . . He's the King of the Ages, the King of Heaven, the King of Glory, the King of Kings and Lord of Lords!

Sadly, none of Missler's admiring followers knew that the rousing story being told to them was completely false. I uncovered the truth about Missler's claims on November 1, 1997, after contacting five individuals who for many years have been intimately acquainted and involved with the Idaho Governor's Breakfast. My contacts included long-time attendee Harold Thomas (a retired businessman), Eloise Fisher (wife of Merold Fisher [co-founder of, and historian for, the Idaho Governor's Breakfast]), Orvil Stiles (co-founder of the Idaho Governor's Breakfast), Loren Ellis (former emcee for the event), and Dick Cooke (former General Chairman and current Program Chairman for the Idaho Governor's Breakfast). None of these persons had even heard of Chuck Missler. I also learned that "Governor's Breakfast" is the old name for the event that was replaced in the late 1980s with the label "State Leadership Prayer Breakfast."

Ellis remarked: "If you just want to dismiss this thing, you pretty well can. Chuck Missler definitely was not the keynote speaker at the State Leadership Prayer Breakfast — whoever he is."[69] Eloise Fisher's statement confirmed Ellis' claim: "For thirty-some years I've been to every one of them [Governor's Breakfasts] and I don't remember *ever* listening to a Chuck Missler."[70] Cooke agreed, stating: "Any person that was a speaker, I would recognize the name. And I have no recollection of this Missler."[71]

An even more dubious claim by Missler involves a private luncheon he allegedly had with Prince Nicholas of Liechtenstein. Missler discussed this impressive encounter during the same 1994 lecture in which he discussed the Idaho Governor's Breakfast. He intimated that he had received a great deal of important information from Prince Nicholas, including an admission from the Prince that he had dismissed "his parliament in order to get [the] Maastricht [Treaty] through."[72] (Because the Maastricht Treaty brings Europe one step closer to complete unification, it is often cited by end-time extremists as a sure sign of a coming one-world government under the Antichrist.)

But these claims are unlikely for two reasons. First, Liechtenstein has never voted on the Maastricht Treaty because it is not now, nor has it ever been, a member-state of the European Union. Second, the ratification process of the Maastricht Treaty required a vote by the general electorate, *not* the parliament of each member-state of the European Union. In other words, even if Liechtenstein had been allowed to vote, the balloting would have had nothing to do with its parliament.[73]

Unfortunately, Missler's fabrications are usually accepted as fact. Of course, not everything he says is a lie. Sometimes he simply fails to reveal all of the truth. For instance, he has greatly succeeded in adding a degree of credibility to his words by publicizing the fact that he is a "member of the International Press Association" (IPA).[74] This impressive-sounding affiliation naturally leads people to believe that he has acquired membership in a widely-recognized news organization limited to professional journalists. The true story, however, leaves Missler in a much less glamorous light.

His membership is in an organization that was started in 1991 by Steve Atkin, a born-again Christian who works for Calvary Chapel of Costa Mesa (a church where Missler is a frequent speaker). Just about any "Christian" can join this particular IPA for a mere $5 a month. They only need to be involved in news coverage "in some way" or at least have "a sincere desire to do writing, film, or radio work." They must also be willing to cover newsworthy events "from a Christian perspective."[75]

Atkin's organization holds its members to no legitimate journalistic qualifications whatsoever. Persons interested in obtaining membership do not even have to prove that they have been published in a trade periodical or newspaper. Most of the members, says Atkin, "just represent their own publications."[76] These range from homemade newsletters to small-scale Christian periodicals such as the monthly *Personal Update* pamphlet self-published by Missler.

Like Koernke and Thompson, Missler obviously understands that impressing others with important-sounding credentials and impressive accomplishments is an effective way to sell your views, even if those credentials and accomplishments, in reality, are non-existent.

MATTERS OF FAITH

Two more reasons why countless persons believe that the end of the world is near involve the very foundation of religion: faith. First, apparent fulfillment of prophecy serves to solidify one's confidence in related religious beliefs that they have chosen to embrace. As prophecy teacher David Allen Lewis says, "We live by faith, but we like proof as well."[77] Prophecy conveniently serves as the "proof" that many individuals need in order to validate their faith. Paul Boyer — history professor at the University of Wisconsin, Madison and author of *When Time Shall Be No More: Prophecy Belief in Modern American Culture* — states that this search for validation is one reason biblical prophecy has always appealed to some segment of the population.[78]

Second, doomsday pronouncements are an excellent means of gaining converts to one's particular belief system. Various religious groups, in an effort to gain new members, often exploit the fact this world is a very troubling place and that imminent destruction of our planet may be near. Publications produced by the Jehovah's Witness, for example, are packed with stories about the horrors of current society: crime, war, famines, natural disasters, government corruption, and diseases. These "common ground" issues on which most people can agree are used as a springboard to evangelism. Nearly every article appearing in Watch Tower tracts, pamphlets, and books include penetrating questions such as: Wouldn't you like to know when the horror will end? Is there a way to escape the destruction humanity now faces?

The answers found in the literature invariably involves coming to the Watch Tower Bible and Tract Organization — God's "one true organization." For some potential converts, just hearing Witnesses speak out forcefully against war, corrupt government, and crime are enough to get them involved in the organization. Once inside the cult, many persons then find it extremely satisfying to have every aspect of their life ordered by clear dos and don'ts. Especially vulnerable are young people with no practical living skills and adults who are simply tired of making decisions about life in an ever-increasingly complex world of alternatives.

Cults, of course, are not the only religious belief systems that utilize end-time predictions and threats of an imminent holocaust. Some segments of mainstream Christianity have used doomsday as an evangelistic tool as well. This is often done regardless of whether the facts presented are accurate. In *Raging into Apocalypse: Essays in Apocalypse IV* (1995), for instance, a chapter dealing with the alleged future invasion of Israel by Russia ends with this warning from Bible teacher Chuck Missler:

> If you are reading this and you don't know Jesus, I encourage you, in the privacy of your own will, to hand your life over to Him. he will take it from there. You will then be on the winning side, God's side, when Russia makes her fatal thrust to the south.[79]

In their book *The Mark of the Beast*, evangelicals Peter and Paul LaLonde warn that "Armageddon is coming. The day is fast approaching when the armies of the antichrist will stand as one to oppose the return of the Prince of Peace." The LaLondes go on to make a sincere plea: "Where will you stand in this battle to end all battles? . . . Who in their right mind would choose to fight with the antichrist against God? . . . Today each of us faces his or her own personal Armageddon. We must choose which side we will be on. . . . Choose this day whom you will serve!"[80]

Of course, using prophecy as a method of persuading people into a particular religion has its drawbacks. When the predicted date or suggested year of either Christ's return or Armageddon does not occur, individuals who came to "faith" or became "saved" due to end-time teachings run the risk of becoming disillusioned and forsaking the religious belief system they adopted. This can be psychologically traumatic for such persons and lead to any number of unhealthful emotions such as bitterness, resentment, and feelings of betrayal.

In the 1970–1980s, for instance, a significant number of individuals attending the widely respected Calvary Chapel system of churches experienced this kind of unfortunate disappointment. For many years the church's founder, Pastor Chuck Smith, had been suggesting that the year 1981 would bring the rapture.[81] In his 1978 booklet *Future Survival*, Smith declared: "Forty years after 1948 would bring us to 1988. . . . From my understanding of biblical prophecies, I'm convinced that the Lord is coming for His Church before the end of 1981."[82]

Smith based his belief primarily on Hal Lindsey's prophetic timetable as found in the original edition of *The Late Great Planet Earth*. When no rapture came at the expected time, numerous followers were stunned; some eventually left the church altogether. David Hocking, a former pastor at Smith's church, reminisced about the events of those years during a pastor's conference:

> I was in a conference in New York with Dave Hunt [another prophecy teacher] recently and he said something very provocative . . . . He went back a few years, especially in the early days when Calvary Chapel was beginning. How excited we were. Oh, some of the prophecy preachers got a little out of hand and those plagues like Revelation 9 were Vietnam helicopters and you know we sort of started dating things and we were even told that a generation is

forty years, and when Israel became a nation in 1948 it would be forty years
and the Lord would come. So we back it up seven. So the rapture's coming in
1981. I've met people all over this country who believed that, followed that,
and anticipated that. It did not come and as a result many of them bombed
out, dropped out, copped out — they're not around anymore.[83]

Although Hocking's comment addresses what happens to some individuals, the vast majority of persons obsessed with end-time speculation
simply re-adjust their thinking to allow for any errors. This may be possible
because the emotional/psychological benefits of clinging to one's eschatological views exceed the benefits of facing cold reality. For example, holding
on to one's belief that some fast approaching date will bring the "rapture"
of all Christians to heaven provides a measure of expectation that at any
moment all of one's *other* beliefs will be vindicated. Consider the following
remark about the rapture made by Assemblies of God preacher Carl
Holland: "People [i.e., Christians], in the twinkling of an eye, will disappear. Cars will go off the freeway. Airplanes will crash because the pilots are
gone. It will cause chaos on Earth. Some people are going to be real
surprised. Me? I'll be saying, 'I told you so.'"[84]

It is not difficult to detect a note of glee in Holland's voice over the
plight of those left behind because they were not "enlightened" enough to
see the truth in what he has been preaching for so many years. His end-time
beliefs not only provide emotional comfort to his followers, but serve to
deflect any and all criticisms of his broader Christian worldview; he is, in
effect, saying that one day he will be able to declare "I told you so" to the
entire unbelieving world.

A FINAL THOUGHT

Perhaps occult doomsayers, apocalyptic cult leaders, and Christian prophecy
teachers are not really all that different from everybody else. The truth is
that most people want to see into the future. There is nothing as disconcerting as facing the unknown, yet this is exactly what each of us does every
moment of every day. For some people, confronting an unending series of

tomorrows filled with uncertainty is unendurable. Hence, they invent a future scenario that is full of set expectations, even if those expectations are of an imminent doom via Armageddon. At least with this mindset, they know *exactly* what is coming . . . .**THE END**.

The NDE Mystery Solved

ALTHOUGH THE PHENOMENON of near death experiences (NDEs) was briefly discussed in Chapter 2, some questions were left unanswered: 1) What exactly are NDEs if they are not temporary excursions into the afterlife; and 2) Why were there so many NDE-related prophecies about the end of the world occurring in 1988/1989? The answer to the first question, which has been presented by several reputable investigators, is that NDEs are subjective, physiologically-based hallucinations that take place in the brain in response to physical/psychological trauma. The answer to the second question involves that function of the brain that we call our memory.

CONSISTENT INCONSISTENCIES

It has been clearly established that an NDE is built around a person's subjective life experiences, personal beliefs, and memories.[1] NDEs are highly individualized from person to person and from culture to culture, having no basis in objective reality. These individualizations, which can sometimes be quite humorous from an outsider's point of view, demonstrate that the experiences during a typical NDE are entirely subjective. One South Asian Hindu, for instance, "ventured to heaven on the back of a 'bespeckled cow' " to get to the light at the end of his tunnel. An American, however, "hailed a taxicab" to get to the light.[2]

In countries where Christianity thrives, people usually see a heaven that reflects "the pastoral meadows, formal gardens, seraphic choirs, life-giving trees and fountains, spacious courts, golden gates, and shining walled cities of biblical and early Christian revelation.[3] But people uninfluenced by Christianity picture a heaven that is quite different. Natives of Micronesia often see heaven as "a large, brightly lit American city with loud, noisy cars and tall buildings."[4] East Indians "sometimes see heaven as a giant bureaucracy, and frequently report being sent back because of clerical errors."[5]

One incident that shows the subjective nature of NDEs involves two people who were in an accident together. The woman lost consciousness, but her male companion did not. During the woman's NDE, "she perceived the two of them in an out-of-body state, yet her friend never blacked out" (emphasis added).[6] Obviously, the woman knew that she was in the car with her friend, and while unconscious, internally visualized the two of them traveling together in an out-of-body state.

Such examples of NDE subjectivity are rarely mentioned in popular literature. It is also uncommon for the general public to hear about NDErs encountering living persons during their NDEs. Psychiatrist Dr. William J. Serdahely — Professor of Health Sciences at Montana State University — conducted a study in which one subject saw a living female friend in "the tunnel" who told her to return to her body.[7]

The NDEs of children are most enlightening when it comes to this aspect of the phenomenon. NDE researcher and pediatrician Dr. Melvin Morse found that children often meet not only living persons, but also living pets during an NDE.[8] According to Morse, children even encounter their favorite fictional characters:

> [A] lot of kids see it as a living teacher; a living teacher! So, see what I mean? A living teacher. So, that says it all to me. I've had two or three cases like that. Or, a guy [kid] says it's a wizard dressed in white—and he's crazy about Nintendo. This ten-year-old boy says it's a wizard dressed in white who told him, "Struggle and you shall live."[9]

Morse obtained an especially interesting NDE account from a little five-year-old named Jane that perfectly illustrates the subjective nature of NDEs. During her experience, she met Jesus and subsequently drew a picture of him for Morse. After completing her portrait, she whispered: "I didn't think I was supposed to see Jesus. I didn't think He would look like that." Morse looked at her drawing and understood her comment. Jesus looked amazingly like Santa Claus or a clown, complete with a big red cap. Morse appropriately entitled the drawing "Jesus With the Red Hat."[10]

A final NDE story especially supportive of the subjectivist view comes from a 45-year-old Midwestern teacher who had a "light" encounter tailor-made for the supermarket tabloids:

> I entered into a dark tunnel and suddenly I was in a place filled up with love and a beautiful, bright light. The place seemed holy. My father, who had died two years earlier, was there, as were my grandparents. Everyone was happy to see me, but my father told me it was not my time and I would be going back. Just as I turned to go, I caught sight of Elvis! He was standing in this place of intense bright light. He just came over to me, took my hand and said: "Hi Bev, do you remember me?"[11]

Most people do not realize that NDEs have even occurred in persons nowhere near death, as psychiatrists Glen Gabbard and Stuart Twemlow explain:

> [D]o near-death experiences occur only near death?—we can state more emphatically today that no, of course, they don't . . . . Our experiences have led us to conclude that the state of *mind* of the near-death subject is far more important that the state of the *body*.[12]

It is also a little known fact that NDE-like experiences have been artificially created under laboratory settings in *conscious* test subjects. During the 1930s, well-known Canadian neurosurgeon Wilder Penfield made history by directly stimulating the brains of epileptic patients while investigating their psychical seizures. He tested possible seizure sites by "electrically stimulating different regions of the temporal and parietal lobes [non-motor portions] in partially exposed brains."[13] Because the brain itself is insensitive to pain, Penfield was able to open the skull using only a local anesthetic on the scalp. This left his patients conscious and capable of verbally responding throughout the procedure. By stimulating the sensory cortex, Penfield caused his subjects to experience sights, sounds, smells and other sensations.[14] Cardiologist Michael Sabom lists what Penfield's patients reported:[15]

- Sensory illusions, both visual (distortion of size and location of nearby objects) and auditory (intensity of sounds).
- Feelings of detachment from self and environment (illusions of remoteness).
- Emotions: fear, sadness, loneliness, happiness or other positive emotional states.
- Hallucinations including "perceptions of human-like figures of a "horrible and threatening nature;" strange music or voices; and "replays" of previous life experiences.
- Forced thinking, or "the crowding of random thoughts and ideas into the mind of the patient in an automatic and obtrusive way."

During these experiments, one patient exclaimed, " 'Oh God! I am leaving my body.' "[16] Patients also experienced life reviews or "flashbacks":

On the first occasion, when one of these "flashbacks" was reported to me by a conscious patient (1933), I was incredulous. On each subsequent occasion, I marveled. For example, when a mother told me she was suddenly aware, as my electrode touched the cortex, of being in her kitchen listening to the voice of her little boy who was playing outside in the yard. She was aware of the neighborhood noises, such as passing motor cars . . . . A young man stated he was sitting at a baseball game in a small town and watching a little boy crawl under the fence to join the audience. Another was in a concert hall listening to music.[17]

Recent experiments probing deeper into the temporal lobe have evoked additional effects such as "floating and rising sensations, out-of-body sensations, mystical and religious experiences and dream-like sequences."[18]

THE RIDDLE OF 1988/1989

Recognizing NDEs as subjective still does not solve the riddle of the widespread 1988/1989 date for doomsday (see Chapter 2). The solution to this curious phenomenon may be a psychological affliction known as False Memory Syndrome (FMS). It has been documented that the passage of time and its effects on the malleable mind can actually cause persons to "recall" experiences or visions that never really happened.

The NDE of Göran Grip is highly relevant as a case in point. He apparently "remembered" his entire NDE only after reading Raymond Moody's *Life After Life* and Dr. Michael Sabom's NDE-related book, *Recollections of Death* (1982). Grip also admits that he cannot tie his NDE to *any* event in his life such as an accident or illness. Nevertheless, he maintains that he *must* have had an NDE, especially after reading books about the subject:

> It was not until I read *Life After Life* . . . that I realized that I had had an NDE. . . . At first I thought I had read it before, but I soon realized that my recognition was on a far deeper level . . . . With the help of his books and, later *Recollections of Death* . . . I was able to revive more and more details of my own experience, and I understand that what had been half asleep in my memory for so long was no less than an NDE. However, no matter how much I scrutinize my memory I have to this day not been able to put a date and external circumstances to my experience . . . . I don't know of any instance where I have been close to death. But I have been through two operations as a child, and both times I was put to sleep with ether.[19]

According to research psychologist Elizabeth Loftus, about twenty-five percent of all individuals "can be easily induced to remember events that never happened to them—false memories that feel absolutely real."[20] A 1995 *Psychology Today* article examining Loftus' experiments relates what the researcher was able to accomplish:

> [S]he can prompt volunteers to "remember nonexistent broken glass and tape recorders; to think of a clean-shaven man as having a mustache, of straight hair as curly, of hammers as screwdrivers . . . . to believe in characters who never existed and events that never happened.[21]

This rather bizarre capability of the mind has, in recent years, led to countless tales involving persons who, through psychotherapy, have "recovered" memories of "satanic cults, butchered babies, and incest that have spawned church scandals, lawsuits, suicides, splintered families, murders, and endless fodder for talk shows."[22] Few of these "memories" have ever been validated. Many of them, in fact, have actually been proven false and a majority of those who originally recalled such "memories" have retracted their stories.

Members of the NDE community easily fit the profile of persons susceptible to the false memory phenomenon. Moreover, NDErs tend to be very close-knit and often hold conferences and informal gatherings at which they share their experiences. Consequently, enough talk about a 1988 date that may have shown up in *one* person's prophetic vision could have inspired a whole pack of NDErs to falsely remember that they, too, saw 1988 in their NDE just like Göran Grip remembered an entire episode.

Although this might adequately account for *some* NDE-related prophetic visions, the possibility still exists that many NDErs accurately remembered their experiences and that the date 1988 did indeed appear in all of them. How could this be accounted for? The answer to this question lies in the tendency NDErs have for tainting their testimony with bits and pieces of information they have subconsciously assimilated from other stories that they have heard. A person already interested in the subject of NDEs, the occult, psychics, pyramidology, or any other prophecy-related topic could have easily picked up on the 1988 date *before their NDE* and incorporated it into their experience. In Kenneth Ring's book, *Heading Toward Omega*, one NDEr admitted as much in reference to his NDE:

> I'm acutely aware of all the "visions" and predictions of late across the globe about war, but I recognize a sameness to them that occurred once before that I can remember — and that was in April of 1969. About six months before a certain date in April, psychics suddenly started declaring that on that date California would sink into the ocean and the West Coast would be destroyed. Everyone started picking up the same date in their dreams — everywhere — be they psychic or not. A hit song was written about it, warning everyone to boat up to Idaho. I picked it up, too, along with everyone else I knew. . . . That crazy date was popping up everywhere.[23]

Calendar Confusion

AS PREVIOUSLY DISCUSSED in this book, the year 2000 and the years soon thereafter seem to be the doomsday deadline of choice for numerous end-time prophets and their followers. Such individuals, however, appear to be unaware that this historical milestone is really nothing more than an arbitrary number affixed to our own particular method of time measurement. Moreover, attempting to use our calendar to accurately plot "time" is a futile project rife with problems.

Take, for example, everyone's notion that the new millennium starts on January 1, 2000. In reality, the new millennium begins on January 1, 2001 because the calendar we now use begins at the year 1, rather than 0. A zero was left out of the transition from B.C. to A.D. (In other words, the transitional sequence of years ran 3 B.C., 2 B.C., 1 B.C. — A.D. 1, A.D. 2, A.D. 3.)[1] Thus, every new century does not *begin* with a double-zero year (e.g., 100, 1600, 1900), but *concludes* with a double-zero year; the corollary to this fact being that each new century begins with a "01" year (e.g., 101, 1601, 1901).

But this relatively minor problem regarding time calculation is only the beginning of much more complex errors inherent to using our dating system. For instance, even January 1, 2001 is not *really* the new millennium. Why? Because in the Western world we measure time by the birth of Jesus Christ, who was actually born somewhere between four to six years *before* the year A.D. 1 (no one knows exactly when). This means that the *real* third millennium began somewhere around 1996!

Of course, not everyone measures time by the birth of Christ. Muslims hold to a calendar that began when their prophet Mohammed traveled from Mecca to Medina in A.D. 622. Furthermore, the Islamic year is only

354 days long, which means that 1997 was the year 1418 to Muslims. The Chinese were already celebrating the year 4695 in 1997. According to the Jewish calendar, 1997 was the year 5757![2]

The calendar we now use (the Gregorian) was not even introduced until 1582, after Pope Gregory XIII grew weary of everyone celebrating New Year's Day at a different time. Europeans had previously gone by the old Julian Calendar (instituted by Julius Caesar), which was a full ten days out of synch with today's calendar. Before that, Rome had a calendar that divided the year into only ten months. "The first month was March and the last month was December. At the end of December, everyone just stopped counting for sixty days until March came back."[3] Thanks to the Egyptians of that era, two extra months — dubbed January and February in 153 B.C. — were added to the ten-month cycle. The Greeks, of course, had their own calendar, as did the Babylonians, Egyptians, and Anglo-Saxons.

After the fall of Rome, nearly everyone followed a slightly different calendar. Britain declared New Year's Eve to be December 25. That lasted until William the Conqueror — crowned on January 1, 1066 — changed New Year's to fall on the anniversary of his coronation. Later, Britain changed its New Year's celebration to March 25. By that time, the French had placed New Year's Day on Easter Sunday, while Italy preferred Christmas Day, and Spain was holding fast to January 1.[4] For the Chinese, the New Year falls somewhere around the end of February. For observant Jews, New Year is the first day of *Tishri*, usually in September.

The various measurements of time are entirely arbitrary calculations that fluctuate from culture to culture. In fact, for about sixty-five percent of the world's population, the Christian year 2000 will, from a calendrical perspective, be absolutely meaningless.[5] As Christian author William David Spencer noted in a 1995 *Christianity Today* article: "[T]he next time somebody comes up to you and informs you that the world is ending in A.D. 2000 [or any other year] . . . . Pull yourself up to your full height, look into that person's eyes, and ask: 'Yeah? By whose calendar?' "[6]

Timeline of Doom

A.D. 60–100: Clement (c. 30–100), an early leader of the church at Rome, declares: "Soon and suddenly shall his will [i.e., the establishment of God's kingdom] be accomplished."

c. 100: Ignatius (d. 98/117), Bishop of Antioch, writes: "The last times are upon us."

c. 150–179: Montanus, Priscilla and Maximilla — leaders of the Montanism movement — prophesy that the end of the world would come within their lifetimes.

c. 250: Cyprian (c. 200–258), Bishop of Carthage, says: "The kingdom of God, beloved brethren, is beginning to be at hand."

c. 375–400: Saint Martin of Tours (c. 316–397), who served as Bishop of Gaul, teaches that the Antichrist exists in his day, writing: "There is no doubt that the Antichrist has already been born. Firmly established already in his early years, he will, after reaching maturity, achieve supreme power."

500: Hippolytus (d. 236) predicts that this year will see the consummation of the ages.

800: The Spanish monk Beatus (d. 798) feels that he will live to see the Antichrist and the end of the world by the year 800.

848: A prophetess named Thiota is able to gather a sizable following by announcing that the end of the world would take place by 848.

1000: Belief throughout Europe during the 900s is that the end of the world would occur in 1000 (see Chapter 5).

1033: This year is targeted as "the end" after the year 1000 passed uneventfully.

1184: The coming of the Antichrist in this year is predicted by various Christian prophets.

1186: The populace fears that a planetary alignment would bring the end of the world.

1260: Joachim of Fiore (c. 1135–1202) preaches that 1260 will see the appearance of the Antichrist, followed by the world's destruction. During an 1191 interview with King Richard the Lion-Hearted, Joachim says that the Antichrist had already been born.

1345–1385: The coming of the Antichrist is predicted for these years.

1420: The Taborites, an extremist Christian sect, held that in 1420 God's fiery wrath would consume the world.

February 20, 1524: A predicted flood is supposed to destroy the world.

1533: According to Melchoir Hoffmann (c. 1495–1543), Jesus' return takes place during this year.

1534: Jan Matthys, a Dutch supporter of Hoffmann, preaches violence to cleanse the ungodly from the earth in preparation for Jesus' return and the world's destruction by Easter 1534.

1656: The year that Christopher Columbus said would bring an end to the world.

1673: Deacon William Aspinwall, of the state's General Court, predicts the world's demise "no later than 1673."

1697, 1716, 1736: Influential Puritan Cotton Mather (1663–1728) preaches that 1697 would be the year of the world's end. He later changes his prediction to 1716. After that date passes, 1736 becomes his new deadline for Christ's return.

1792: The Shakers, believe that the world will end by this year.

1843–1844: William Miller and the Millerites expect Jesus' second advent. Their belief results in "The Great Disappointment" of October 22, 1844.

1868: The Rev. M. Baxter (Church of England) predicts that the Battle of Armageddon would occur during this year. His booklet predicting the dreadful conflict between good and evil had a rather interesting, and lengthy, title: *Louis Napolean, the Infidel Antichrist Predicted in Prophecy to Confirm A Seven Years Covenant With the Jews, About*

*the Year 1861, and Nearly to Succeed in Gaining A Universal Empire;
and Then to be Deified, and Idolatrously Worshipped, and Also to
Institute A 3 1/2 Years Sanguinary Persecution Against the Christian
Church, From 1864–1865 to 1868, During Which Time Wars, Famine,
Pestilences & Earthquakes, If Not Religious Persecution, Will Pre-
vail in England and America Until the Slaughter of the Witnesses,
Elias and Another Prophet; After Which Napolean, Their Destroyer,
Together with the Pope Are Foreshown to Be Cast Alive Into the Lake
of Fire At the Descent of Christ At Armageddon About the Year 1868.*

1874: Jesus' second advent is expected by former Millerites who had
banded together to form the Second Adventist movement.

1908: Lee T. Spangler — a grocery store owner in York, Pennsylvania —
announces that the world would end by fire in October 1908.

1910: Many people think that the arrival of Halley's comet will destroy
the earth.

1914: The Jehovah's Witnesses point to this year as the time when the Battle of Armageddon would take place.

1925: The Jehovah's Witnesses begin proclaiming in 1920 that 1925 would
bring the Battle of Armageddon, to be immediately followed by
the resurrection of Old Testament saints such as Abraham, Isaac,
Jacob, and King David.

1936: The June/July 1934 issue of *Plain Truth*, the magazine launched by
Worldwide Church of God founder Herbert W. Armstrong, predicts that the economic depression and fear of war marking the
early 1930's would continue until 1936. Then, said Armstrong,
"we may expect to see the heavenly signs of the sun and moon
becoming dark . . . which shall be followed by the 'Day of the
Lord' " (p. 5).

October 30, 1938: The Halloween broadcast of Orson Welles' "War of the
Worlds" radio play convinces thousands of Americans that the end
of the world has come via a Martian invasion.

1940s: The Jehovah's Witnesses declare that only a few months were left
before Armageddon.

1954: Forty-four-year-old Charles Laughead, a respected physician at
Michigan State College, shocks friends and relatives by proclaiming that doomsday would occur on December 20, 1954.

February 4, 1962: Many people throughout the world fear that the planetary alignment of this day would bring global destruction.

1975: This is the first "end of the world" year in a long string of years named by Christian prophecy extremist Charles Taylor. Other years that Taylor has predicted for doomsday include: 1975, 1976, 1980, 1981, 1982, 1983, 1985, 1986, 1987, 1988, 1989, 1992, 1994.

1975–1977: In the February 1967 issue of *Plain Truth*, Worldwide church of God founder Herbert W. Armstrong's predicts: "The 'Day of the Eternal' . . . is going to strike between five and ten years from now! . . . I am not writing foolishly, but very soberly, on the authority of the living Christ" (p. 47).

1975: The Jehovah's Witnesses announce that this year will bring the end of 6,000 years since Adam's creation and possible establishment of God's Kingdom on the earth. Many other groups and prophecy teachers not connected to either Armstrong or the Jehovah's Witnesses also point to 1979 as the possible end of the world.

1979: Herbert W. Armstrong, in the June 1968 issue of his *Plain Truth* magazine, declares that universal peace would be "coming in our time — and not later than the decade of the 1970's. . . . To save human life from annihilation Jesus Christ will come again, this time to set up the very kingdom of God on earth, and to establish the wonderful world of Utopia tomorrow" (p. 23).

1981: Based on the information in the first edition of Hal Lindsey's bestseller *The Late Great Planet Earth*, vast numbers of Christians believe that "the rapture" and the beginning of the tribulation will occur before December 31, 1981.

1982: Many persons from widely diverse religious belief systems fear that an alignment of the planets during 1982 (and its resulting "Jupiter Effect") will bring doomsday.

1985: Pentecostal preacher Lester Sumrall says the end of the world will occur this year. Sumrall later revises his prediction in a new book titled *I Predict 2000*.

September 11–September 13, 1988: Christian preacher Edgar Whisenant claims that these dates will bring the rapture — i.e., the miraculous transportation of all Christians from the earth to heaven.

1991: Nation of Islam leader Louis Farrakhan announces that the Gulf War will "be that [war] which the scriptures refer to as the War of Armageddon which is the final war."

October 28, 1992: The Korean *Hyoo-go* movement predicts that this day will bring the rapture.

September 7, 1994: According to Harold Camping, this date should have witnessed Jesus' second coming.

December 17, 1996: According to California psychic Sheldon Nidle, the end of the world was to occur on this day with the arrival of "millions of spaceships" and accompanying angels.

August 18, 1999: In 1968, the psychic Criswell gives this date for doomsday, saying: "The world as we know it will cease to exist . . . on August 18, 1999."

2000: It would be impossible to list the many persons declaring that the world may end in the year 2000. Such predictions are coming from widely divergent belief systems that are usually at odds with each other. For example, Christian prophecy teacher Grant Jeffrey has declared that the year 2000 will be the "probable termination point for the 'last days' " when Christ "may commence His Kingdom." In fact, Jeffrey has gone so far as to suggest that this event could fall on October 9, 2000. At the same time, the Process Church and the Foundation Church of the Millennium — two Satanism-related churches — also see the world coming to an imminent end. The latter organization believes that global destruction will occur around the year 2000. They have arrived at this belief by combining biblical prophecies with the writings of Nostradamus and the predictions of psychics Edgar Cayce and Jeane Dixon.

2001: The year that Edgar Cayce (1877-1945) prophesied would bring a globally devastating "pole shift."

2003–2012: *2001: On the Edge of Eternity,* a 1996 video produced by Christian prophecy teacher Jack Van Impe, puts Jesus' second coming "perhaps as far ahead as the year 2012." During a July 2, 1997 television broadcast, Van Impe declares: "The Bible teaches that an Antichrist comes to power (Rev. 13:1) — a world dictator. . . . This world dictator could appear anywhere from now to 2003. . . .

It means Jesus is about to return folks! Oh, the year 2000 is so important. *Are you ready.*"

2012: According to many apprehensive date-watchers, the world will end on December 21-23, 2012 when the ancient Mayan calendar runs out.

Inside Heaven's Gate

Although the circumstances surrounding the Heaven's Gate mass suicide have been widely publicized, little attention has been paid to the group's religious teachings. The following story is a synopsis of the history of the world according to Heaven's Gate leader Marshall Applewhite. The quotes appearing throughout the account are taken directly from videotaped teachings by Applewhite, as well as from the cult's self-published book *How and When Heaven's Gate May Be Entered*. This narrative may sound like a fable reminiscent of *Star Wars*, but it accurately represents the beliefs that ultimately led Heaven's Gate members to take their lives. (The synopsis is written in a matter-of-fact style that presents Heaven's Gate teachings as if a member of the group were explaining it to the reader. It is not my intention to endorse or support any of the following beliefs.)

Long ago, a highly advanced civilization of benevolent space beings from a far off galaxy called "The Evolutionary Level Above Human" (T.E.L.A.H.) — also known as the "Next Level," "Kingdom of God," or "Kingdom of Heaven" — decided to turn Earth into a garden. So they "planted it with a variety of life forms, including human." The "Human Kingdom," as well as those kingdom levels beneath human (e.g., the Animal Kingdom, Insect Kingdom, etc.), were created "according to a specific and carefully crafted design — and with a specific purpose in mind." This garden was to serve as "a transitional training ground — a proving ground for potential new members of the Kingdom of Heaven." Prospective members would be "birthed" from the Human Level into the Next Level (i.e., the level above human) through a "metamorphic process" that would occur in a select group of human plants, all of whom were created with a body and spirit.

The gardeners from T.E.L.A.H. planted their "crop" in a neutral condition so that each human would "have the chance to choose the direction of their growth." Every person placed here had three basic options: 1) go completely awry, separate from God, and ultimately be recycled (destroyed) like weeds that are "spaded under"; 2) overcome the human condition and leave it by becoming a member of God's Kingdom; or 3) join the opposition — i.e., groups of evil space alien races collectively known as Luciferians because they are under the direction of Lucifer, an extremely powerful "plant" from a prior Earth civilization who, after advancing to T.E.L.A.H., rebelled against God.

God, by the way, is not some spirit deity, as most religions teach. He is the most powerful member of the Next Level. As such, he not only functions as the top commander of T.E.L.A.H.'s whole star fleet, but has dictatorial charge of the entire Kingdom of Heaven, which is "a physical level of existence in deepest space (outside of man's concept of time) beyond this human level — advanced physically, technologically, behaviorally, ethically, genetically, and in the wisdom and knowledge of service in the Creator's world." Regarding Lucifer/Satan, he became evil when he "got to be too big for his britches, stopped looking to his Heavenly Father, and thought he knew so much he could 'run his own show.'" This arrogant Next Level member went so far as to start his own world in an attempt to create another heaven. He also took with him one-third of the creatures who were young members of T.E.L.A.H., "for they were still susceptible to his leadership." Those beings are the individuals who now circulate "in the Heavens as various 'Luciferian' space races (who also travel in their more primitive spacecrafts, or UFOs)."

Throughout Earth's long history numerous civilizations/gardens have been planted by Next Level botanists under God's direction. Our present civilization is only one of many that have been allowed to progress for thousands of years until that civilization's "Final Age" or "harvest" arrived. The harvest is a time of great joy for members of T.E.L.A.H., who are finally able to take to the Next Level all the human plants that have sufficiently matured. To stimulate growth of their plants toward this end, the gardeners have periodically related in a "hands on" way to each civilization "at its beginning stage, and subsequently (with few exceptions) at approximately 2,000-year intervals." The Bible — although it has been hopelessly marred by Luciferian-minded religionists throughout the ages — still provides a glimpse of the Next Level's dealings with this present civilization, which began about 6,000 years ago with Adam. He was the first plant from whom all other humans have descended.

After the planting-harvesting season runs its course (approximately 6,000 years), the rest of the garden, including all remaining plants, is annihilated ("spaded under"). The planet is then cleaned up and refurbished. A fresh crop is planted and the entire process starts all over again. Such radical action must be taken because each garden eventually becomes overrun by weeds, which are reprobate human plants with no possibility of renewal to the Next Level.

One might be tempted to think that Earth's extraterrestrial horticulturists have only themselves to blame for such a tragedy, since they are the ones who abandon the planet for 2,000 years at a stretch. In reality, however, Next Level gardeners are very attentive to their little plants. The epoch during which they are gone actually amounts to only about forty-eight hours from their perspective. The Bible even hints at this long-forgotten mode of time calculation: "[W]ith the Lord one day is as a thousand years, and a thousand years as one day" (2 Peter 3:8). In reality, then, the only ones responsible for the garden's ultimate state of irreparable damage are the weeds, and of course, the Luciferians who consistently use the weeds to keep propagating human behavior rather than T.E.L.A.H.-like thinking.

So how do Next Level gardeners help their plants mature into humans worthy of transition into the Kingdom of Heaven? This is perhaps the most fascinating part of the Heaven's Gate scenario. As previously mentioned, humans are composed of two separate parts: 1) the body, which is nothing more than a container; and 2) a spirit, which functions as "the informational mind or 'software' [in computer talk] of a human plant." But a human plant with only these two components will *never* advance to the Next Level. A third element is needed: a soul, which is comparable to a "seed" or "micro-chip" programmed with all the information necessary to begin and complete a plant's metamorphosis into a candidate for T.E.L.A.H. Moreover, this soul allegedly has its own "brain" that accumulates information from the Next Level, which is then made available to the plant.

Humans can only receive a soul from Next Level gardeners who, during their periodic visits to Earth, scan the human population for individuals "that seem to have potential." Such persons are then implanted with a "deposit," which is an actual storage bin of some kind, that houses a soul tuned into the wavelength of "the Next Level mind (mind that comes from the Creator, the Chief of Chiefs, or Most High God — the term you use is not important)."

Unfortunately, the primitive nature of human plants renders them unable to take advantage of the information contained in the soul. To remedy this minor problem, Next Level gardeners further program soul deposits to act as "tiny computer chips programmed with a sort of [two-way] 'homing device.' " Its primary signal functions as a beacon that can be locked on to by yet another group of visitors from T.E.L.A.H. — "Next Level Representatives." They periodically come to Earth in "Away Team" crews, complete with a captain, lieutenant, communication's officer, etc., and travel here via a spaceship, equipped with devices that can get a "readout" on where, and in whom, the deposit transmitters have been placed. The first responsibility of these special emissaries from the Kingdom of Heaven is to locate plants that have been "tagged" with soul deposits by Next Level gardeners. The mission continues as away team members shed their individual genderless bodies/vehicles ("similar to putting it in a closet, like a suit of clothes that doesn't need to be worn for awhile"), and attempt to take bodily possession of a "tagged" human who wants to begin the metamorphic process.

Here is where the soul deposit's secondary signal comes into play. It causes the human host to feel great inner turmoil and a need for the spiritual "nourishment" that can only come from a T.E.L.A.H. representative: "The first reaction to the deposit may be, 'What is happening? Goodness, none of this has any meaning for me anymore. Is there something, somewhere that has some meaning? I've got to find something, I don't even know what, but there must be something that can take me farther than where I am.' " In other words, the host's world "starts falling apart." This is the "awakening" process wherein an implanted human will think: "I don't fit here," "I hate this corrupt world," or "I just want to go home to God."

Such thoughts and anxieties, coupled with transmissions from the soul deposit itself, serve to direct the recipient toward a Kingdom of Heaven representative. "Without these 'deposits of recognition,' no choice of becoming a student is within the will of a human." The deposit also helps a plant recognize the representative assigned to it and assists the host human in mustering up the courage it takes to allow his or her body to be possessed. "When the deposit makes contact with the representative, it is an actual physical contact between the mind of the deposit and the mind or information brought by that member of the Next Level."

All "tagged" plants who choose to undergo the metamorphic process subsequently enter the "classroom" led by the away team's commanding officer who also has taken possession of a human body. It is during the classroom's course of rigorous study that the T.E.L.A.H representatives "nurture" each soul deposit with "Next Level thinking, behavior, and all the information required" for each participating plant to effectively "fluff off" all human/mammalian ways. As the human plant's "humanness" is gradually lost, the soul residing within it grows and the *mind* of the "soul" along with the mind of the representative begins to override the mind of the human plant. If all goes well, the representative inhabiting the human plant's body is able to utterly "take over" the functions of that body. At the same time, the human spirit within the vehicle/body is actually bonding (i.e., grafting) to the Next Level representative that is possessing the body. If the human plant is able to endure the entire transition classroom, then the human plant's spirit will be able to go with his or her representative when that representative departs for T.E.L.A.H. at the mission's conclusion.

Harvest comes at the end of a civilization's era. This joyous event is marked by the departure of the latest away team and those human plants to whom they have been grafted. A human plant can only arrive in T.E.L.A.H., attached to a T.E.L.A.H. representative. Therefore, it is crucial that each human spirit leave with their respective representatives when all of the representatives depart. Staying behind on Earth when one's representative leaves results in a severing of one's graft with their representative and effectively leaves the human host stranded on Earth to face the planet's recycling ("spading under"). Human plants in the classroom of T.E.L.A.H.

must be prepared to drop their physical bodies (containers/vehicles) at a moment's notice.

If it becomes necessary, a plant may actually have to force a shutdown of the body (i.e., commit suicide) in order to evacuate it. This final act of metamorphosis is the ultimate separation, or "disconnection," from the Human Kingdom and releases the human plant from the human environment. The next stop is the next world, or the physical environment of the Next Level, where each plant's transition to the Kingdom of heaven is supervised by senior members of the Next Level. All of the evacuees — the T.E.L.A.H. representatives and the human plants to which they have been grafted — rendezvous "in the clouds (a giant mothership)" for a briefing and final journey to the Kingdom of the Heaven.

This process has been going on for thousands of years. In fact, Jesus of Nazareth was a "tagged" plant that was possessed by the captain of an away team that came to Earth 2,000 years ago. He tried to bring the aforementioned "good news" to people of his time, but the Luciferians had him killed by wicked, human weeds. Jesus' disciples — who were themselves inhabited by the rest of the T.E.L.A.H. away team — tried in vain to continue preaching Jesus' message, but they, too, were murdered. For the last 2,000 years the world has become horribly overgrown with weeds. Furthermore, because of the Luciferians' extensive tampering with Earth's present civilization, "it has not been able to significantly serve as a stepping stone toward the Next Evolutionary Level." Earth's next "spading under" is due very soon (i.e., before A.D. 2000). The harvest is now.

Notes

INTRODUCTION

1. Billy Graham, quoted in Frank S. Mead, ed., *The Encyclopedia of Religious Quotations* (Westwood, NJ: Fleming H. Revell, 1965), 368.

2. Eugene Taylor, "Desperately Seeking Spirituality," *Psychology Today*, November/December 1994, 57.

3. Timothy Jones, "Great Awakenings," *Christianity Today*, November 8, 1993, 24.

4. Taylor, 56–58, 60, 62, 64, 66, 68; Bob McCullough, "The New Spin is Spirituality," *Publishers Weekly*, May 16, 1994, 40–43; Francine Prose, "The Power of Faith," *Redbook*, December 1994, 47–48, 50; Barbara Kantrowitz, "In Search of the Sacred," *Newsweek*, November 28, 1994, 52–55; and John Balzar, "Exploring Spiritual Approach to Business-World Challenges," *Los Angeles Times*, December 17, 1996, A5.

5. Kate Greer, "Are American Families Finding New Strength In Spirituality?," *Better Homes and Gardens*, January 1988, 19.

6. Kantrowitz, 54.

7. Kantrowitz, 54.

8. "What Does America Believe?," *George*, December 1996, 115; Kenneth L. Woodward, "Is God Listening?," *Newsweek*, March 31, 1997, 59; and David Van Biema, "Does Heaven Exist?," *Time*, March 24, 1997, 73.

9. Taylor, 64.

10. Taylor, 56.

11. Bob Ortega, "Research Institute Shows People a Way Out of Their Bodies," *Wall Street Journal*, September 20, 1994, A1.

12. Jeffery L. Sheler, "The Christmas Covenant," *U.S. News and World Report*, December 19, 1994, 64. As far back as 1991, a Gallup poll revealed that one out of six Americans thought the Gulf War would lead to the Battle of Armageddon. B. J. Oropeza, *99 Reasons Why No One Knows When Christ Will Return* (Downers Grove: InterVarsity Press, 1994), 13.

13. These persons, along with a number of individuals making similar claims, were featured in the four-part television series *Ancient Prophecies* (The Learning Channel, 1996–1997). Eleazer, Castro and Singer appeared in *Ancient Prophecies IV* (The Learning Channel, July 20, 1997).

14. "Mysteries of the Millennium" (CBS), May 1, 1996. In reference to the year 2000, Stuart Vyse of the psychology department at Connecticut College in New London observes: "[P]eople have this feeling of portent, that something is going to happen, and this is a momentous moment. More TV programs will come out that have to do with prophecy." Stuart Vyse, quoted in Julia Duin, "Wizards and Witches Go Mainstream," *Christian Research Journal*, vol. 19(2), Fall 1996, 44–45.

15. *Los Angeles/Cox Communication TV Guide*, February 7, 1997, 69.

16. *Boston Commons* (NBC), February 16, 1997.

17.   Joseph Gallagher, "Don't Count on Millennium to Be 'The End,' " *National Catholic Reporter*, August 11, 1995 (Orange County California Public Library Online System); also see "Poll Finds Americans Believe the End is Nigh," *Skeptic*, vol. 3(2), 1995, 10.

18.   This is a paraphrase of a 1990 statement made by Christian prophecy teacher Hal Lindsey, author of the *New York Times* bestseller *The Late Great Planet Earth*. His exact words were as follows: "All of this [i.e., earthquakes, famines, wars, AIDS, etc.] leads up to one thing. . . . Jesus said, 'This generation will not pass away unless all these thing are fulfilled.' What generation? . . . The generation that would see all these signs. *We are that generation!* I believe you cannot miss it. We're that generation, and I believe we're rapidly moving toward the coming of Christ." Hal Lindsey, *Apocalypse Planet Earth* videotape (Palos Verdes, CA: Hal Lindsey Ministries, 1990).

19.   Dinita Smith, "With the Apocalypse Almost Now, It Becomes a New Field of Study," *New York Times*, November 8, 1997, B11.

20.   Smith, B11.

21.   Stephen O'Leary, "Seeds of Apocalypse Are Among Us," *Los Angeles Times*, April 22, 1997, B7.

CHAPTER ONE

1.   Jim Jones, quoted in Simon Dwyer, "A Revolutionary Suicide: Jonestown, Guyana," *Rapid Eye 1*, 1995 ed. (London: Creation Books, 1989), 224–229. This excerpt is from a cassette recording of Jim Jones speaking to his followers as they were being forced to drink a lethal cocktail of cyanide, strawberry cola/Kool-Aid and tranquilizers. The recording, which was made by a person (or persons) unknown, was originally filed as "confidential" by the U.S. Government. It was eventually leaked to reporters in England who, with the help of the World Surrealist Network, produced a complete transcript of Jones' statements.

2.   According to religion researcher J. Gordon Melton (*Encyclopedic Handbook of Cults in America* [New York: Garland Publishing, 1992], 3), churches have historically been thought of as "large denominations [e.g., Roman Catholicism, Methodism, Lutheranism] characterized by their inclusive approach to life and their identification with the prevailing culture." Sects, on the other hand, have traditionally been seen as groups that have broken away from established churches. Although sects tend to retain most of the doctrines and practices of their parent church, they usually add to, or subtract from, the various teachings of the larger religious body from which they emerge. Many sects end up growing into established churches and/or religions. Christianity, for instance, began as a sect of Judaism. Protestantism started out as a sect of Roman Catholicism.

3.   Daniel G. Reid et al., *Dictionary of Christianity in America* (Downers Grove: InterVarsity Press, 1990), 331.

4.   Identifying a religious organization as cultic from a *sociological* perspective involves determining whether that group's religious practices and day-to-day behavior are normative for the surrounding culture. From a sociological perspective, the primary indicator of a group's cultic nature is complete withdrawal from society into a communal lifestyle that isolates members from the rest of the world. Secondary sociological marks of a cult — at least in America — that are *sometimes* present include polygamy, incest, adult-child sexual contact, use of illegal narcotics, physical abuse, murder, and the stockpiling of weapons, both legal and illegal. Obviously, sociological red flags tend to appear more frequently in groups that run afoul of the law. A *psychological* definition of a "cult" is often associated with thought reform

(popularly known as "brainwashing") and/or deceptive recruitment tactics. Psychologist Michael Langone, who has been aggressively studying the psychological dynamics of cults since 1978, offers what may be the most concise definition of a cult from a psychological perspective in his book *Recovery From Cults* (New York: W. W. Norton & Company, 1993): "A cult is a group or movement that, to a significant degree, (a) exhibits great or excessive devotion or dedication to some person, idea, or thing, (b) uses a thought-reform program to persuade, control, and socialize members (i.e., to integrate them into the group's unique pattern of relationships, beliefs, values, and practices), (c) systematically induces states of psychological dependency in members, (d) exploits members to advance the leadership's goals, and (e) causes psychological harm to members, their families, and the community" (p. 5). Through counseling hundreds of former cultists, Langone has discovered several psychological red flags common to cults. Each reveals the psychologically manipulative nature of cults: 1) information is withheld from new converts about the group's ultimate agenda; 2) the presence of a dictatorial leadership that tells with "excruciating specificity" exactly how members are to think, feel and act; and 3) an absence of leader accountability to persons outside the group's power structure (Langone, 5). Defining a cult from a *theological* perspective involves judging a group's doctrines against the beliefs of the major religion with which it claims association. This method of cult identification is used not only by Christians, but also by members of other major religions. For example, the Nation of Islam (Black Muslims) is a cult of Islam. Aum Shinrikyo is a cult of Buddhism. The International Society for Krishna Consciousness (ISKCON) — known as the Hare Krishnas — is a Hindu cult. Christianity, too, has its share of cults, which are appropriately termed pseudo-Christian. Several evangelicals have offered varying definitions for these groups. Cult expert Dr. Walter Martin offered the following definition in the 1985 edition of his landmark book *The Kingdom of the Cults* (Minneapolis: Bethany House Publishers, 1965): ["A] group of people gathered about a specific person or person's misinterpretation of the Bible. . . . [C]ults contain major deviations from historic Christianity. Yet, paradoxically, they continue to insist that they are entitled to be classified as Christians" (p. 11). Included among the many groups that would fall into this category would be the Mormons, Jehovah's Witnesses, and Oneness Pentecostals.

5.   Reuters, "Korean Sect Stunned As 'Rapture' Doesn't Come," *Orange County Register,* October 29, 1992, A21; Mark Potok and J. Michael Kennedy, "4 Federal Agents Killed In Shootout With Cult In Texas," *Los Angeles Times,* March 1, 1993, A1; Reuters, "Kiev Cult's Doomsday Prediction Draws Parents Searching For Children," *Orange County Register,* November 15, 1993, 15 (news section); Robert Davis and Juan J. Walte, "Swiss Cult's Bizarre Last Act Leaves 'Wax Museum' Of Death," *USA Today,* October 6, 1994, 6A; David Holley, "Secretive Japanese Cult Linked to Germ Weapons Plan," *Los Angeles Times,* March 28, 1995, A3; and *Newsweek* (cover), April 7, 1997.

6.   George Santayana, *Life of Reason,* vol. 1 of *Reason in Common Sense* (1905–1906), quoted in Robert Andrews, *The Columbia Dictionary of Quotations* (New York: Columbia University, 1993), 409.

7.   B. J. Oropeza, *99 Reasons Why No One Knows When Christ Will Return* (Downers Grove: InterVarsity Press, 1994), 168.

8.   *EP News Service,* October 9, 1992, quoted in Oropeza, 11.

9.   Taberah World Missions, *Rapture!* (Seoul: Taberah World Missions, 1992), 3–4.

10. *Rapture!,* 5–6.

11.   *The Last Plan of God*, 94, quoted in Oropeza, 37. The name Bang-Ik Ha sometimes
       appears as Ha Bang-Ik, because in the Korean language a person's last name is stated
       first. The former version of Bang-Ik's name usually appears in literature originally
       written in English, whereas the latter version is commonly used when a Korean
       publication is translated into English.

12.   *Rapture!*, 6.

13.   According to *The Last Plan of God*, "God showed his mother Hyun Jung Lee in her
       dream a child with a sword and a book in his hand who was taller than mountains in
       the midst of storms and peals of thunder and blood. Then a scroll came down from
       Heaven that said 'the Book of Revelation'" (pp. 94–96, quoted in Oropeza, 37). In
       other words, Bank Ik Ha would fulfill the prophecies of Revelation.

14.   Dang Ho Cha, *The True Holy Spirit Comes From A Single Root* (San Diego: Faithful
       Korean Church, 1992), 24.

15.   *Rapture!*, 2–3 reads: "Only a small number of Christians sanctified as brides of Jesus
       will be raptured while others are saved through martyrdom during the Great
       Tribulation."

16.   This information was obtained by author B. J. Oropeza, who interviewed Maranatha
       Mission Church member Na Huhn (Oropeza, 172).

17.   Oropeza, 173.

18.   *EP News Service*, November 6, 1992, 5; cf. Oropeza, 171.

19.   *EP News Service*, November 6.

20.   Reuters, "Korean Sect Stunned."

21.   *EP News Service*, November 6, 1995.

22.   "Seoul Sect Leader Gets Two Years For Fraud," *Los Angeles Times*, December 5,
       1992, A22; cf. Russell Chandler, *Doomsday* (Ann Arbor: Servant Publications, 1993),
       261.

23.   In a July 13, 1995 statement to the press, the U.S. Treasury Department's Director of
       Public Affairs, Chris Peacock, listed the number and types of weapons recovered from
       the ashes of the Branch Davidian compound. The Davidians possessed an extensive
       arsenal that included three hundred firearms and hundreds of thousands of rounds
       of ammunition. Among the weapons found were "semiautomatic firearms illegally
       modified to fire in full automatic mode, as well as grenades and silencers. All of these
       weapons were unlawfully possessed." The following excerpt from the Treasury
       Department's press release discusses the many illegal weapons found in the com-
       pound: "The FBI determined that 46 semiautomatic firearms had been modified to
       fire in full automatic mode: 22 M-16 Type Rifles, 20 AK-47 Type Rifles, 2 Heckler
       and Koch SP-89, 2 M-11/Nine. The FBI also determined that two AR-15 lower
       receivers had been modified to fire in full automatic mode. Silencers: 21 Sound
       suppressers or silencers. Hand Grenades: 4 Live M-21 Practice Hand Grenades. The
       possession of lawfully manufactured machine-guns, silencers, or grenades requires
       the owner to register the weapon with the Bureau of Alcohol, Tobacco & Firearms.
       None of the compound's residents were registered to own such a weapon, therefore it
       would have been illegal for them to possess these weapons." See also "Expert Says
       Cult Had Illegal Arms," *New York Times*, January 15, 1994, 10; Gordon Witkin,
       "Raking Up the Ashes," *U.S. News & World Report*, July 24, 1995, 30; Ken Carter,
       "Branch Davidian Firearms," *Machine Gun News*, March 1994, 5.

24.   Linda Thompson, *Waco: The Big Lie* videotape (Indianapolis: American Justice
       Federation, 1993).

25. Mike McNulty, "Waco: An Apparent Deviation" press release (California Organization of Public Safety Statement), December 28, 1993; cf. Mark England, "Think Tank Chief Adds Fuel to Cult-Fire," *Waco Tribune-Herald*, January 16, 1994, 1A.

26. Tom Morganthau, "Janet Reno Confronts Waco's Bitter Legacy," *Newsweek*, May 15, 1995, 26; "Cultists Spread Fuel Before Fire, Transcript Says," *Orange County Register*, February 15, 1994, 14 (news section); "In Tapes From Sect's Compound, Members Talk About Setting Fire," *New York Times*, February 15, 1994, A15.

27. I obtained Robyn's Bible through her brother, David Bunds, who is a personal friend of mine. Referenced pages from her Bible were copied and reside in my private files.

28. Stephen Braun, "Koresh Sends Doom-Laden Letter to FBI," *Los Angeles Times*, April 11, 1993, A9.

29. "Koresh Sends 2nd Threatening Letter," *Orange County Register*, April 13, 1993, 6 (news section).

30. Why did the fire not begin until between 11:55 A.M. and 12:07 P.M.? The mystery is possibly solved by Amos 8:9, which states: "And it shall come to pass in that day, saith the LORD God, that I will cause the sun to go down at noon and I will darken the earth in the clear day." (KJV) Next to the words "at noon," Robyn had transcribed Koresh's final prophecy: "DEATH OF CYRUS." Cyrus was a regal title Koresh applied to himself. Another piece of evidence that supports this theory is a January 10, 1987 taped teaching by Koresh. During the recorded study, the Davidian prophet tests his class with a penetrating question: "[T]hose who dwell in the land during this time shall be what?" A lone voice responds: "Consumed." Koresh verbally reacts to the unsatisfactory answer — "Burned!" He then continues: "[T]he whole land shall be devoured by the fire of his jealousy: for he shall make a speedy riddance of all them that dwell in the land." Wanting to make sure his flock got the message, Koresh again prods them again for an answer: "Going to be devoured by what?" The class replies with one voice: "The fire of his jealousy." David Koresh, *Study on the Assyrians* taped lecture, January 10, 1987.

31. Scott Mabb and Jake Mabb, quoted in Sara Rimer, "Cult's Surviving Children: New Lives, New Ordeals," *New York Times*, April 27, 1993, A1.

32. Dana Okimoto, author's May 30, 1993 recorded interview with Okimoto.

33. Poia Viega, author's May 11, 1993 recorded interview with Viega.

34. David Koresh, *The Foundation* taped lecture, 1989.

35. Although the Russian Orthodox Church continued to exist during the communist regime, its message was considerably watered down and priests were carefully screened by the state. Documents recently released from the Soviet archives confirm that many of the approved priests, as well as a significant number of high-ranking clergy, collaborated with various agencies of oppression such as the KGB. Persons attempting to practice a genuine faith suffered harsh punishment. A 1995 presidential commission concluded that during communist rule, Soviet authorities murdered 200,000 religious leaders and persecuted another 500,000. Serge Schmemann, "Religion Returns to Russia, With a Vengeance," *New York Times*, July 28, 1993, A6; Galina Dutkina, transl. from Russian by Catherine A. Fitzpatrick, *Moscow Days* (New York: Kodansha International, 1996), 193; Edith Coron, "Russia's Religious Revival," *Christian Science Monitor*, November 25, 1996, 9.

36. Tony Carnes, "Modern Moscow: Its Religions and Moral Values," *Urban Mission*, March 1996, 31.

37. Jo Biddle, "Russians Flock to Discover the Joy of Sects," *The European*, April 30 - May 6, 1993, n.p. In 1993, Father Francios Euvé — a French Jesuit — observed: "There is an identity crisis in Russia today. Old values have disappeared and there is no

structured ideology. People want religion to restructure their world — to give them values and point of reference."

38.   Richard Lacayo, "The Lure of the Cult," *Time*, April 7, 1997, 46. Internet edition at http://www.pathfinder.com/@@cVpTRwYAjTjNGAbQ/time/reports/cult/killer/killer3.html

39.   Richard Wurmbrand, "Faith and Credulity," *The Voice of the Martyrs*, May 1993, 2.

40.   Nickolai Porublev, "A Dangerous New Cult in CIS Called The Great White Brotherhood," *Take A Closer Look*, October 1993, 14.

41.   Porublev, 15.

42.   Vasily Zakrevsky, "Beware. Sects. Amnestied But Dangerous," *Izvestiia*, August 21,1997.

43.   Porublev, 15.

44.   Letter from Nina V, reprinted in *Current Digest of the Post-Soviet Press*, vol. XLV(30), 1993, 16.

45.   "As a few disciples became disenchanted, the stories crept out of the fortress. Inside, obedience was everything, they said. All worldly goods went to Krivonogov. Ceremonies for baptism involved- fasting for days, refusing sleep, and drinking a glass of what was supposed to be water from the River Jordan. Mothers were said to hand over their virgin daughters for Krivonogov's sex rituals — sacrificing their children for peace of mind. Understandably, the members had to make one crucial promise in order to stay inside the group — absolute secrecy" (Randolph, 324).

46.   Olga Iwaniak, "Ukraine's Far-Out Sects," *Zycie Warszawy*, February 7, 1996. Reprinted in *World Press Review*, June 1996, 46. Grieving mothers in Donetsk finally sent an appeal to the newspaper *Argumenty I Fakty*, which re-printed the text in condensed form: "Our underage children have been drawn into a pseudo religious cult called the 'White Brotherhood,' which they carefully hid from us that they were attending. . . . April 16 of this year, brother Sergei secretly took a group of teenagers to Moscow Province, and since then we haven't heard anything about most of them. . . . In most cases, the 'White brotherhood rents apartments in cities. . . . [I]f through your newspaper we could ask readers to be sure to report such apartments to the precinct police officer, then a document check on the people living there would immediately make it clear who is from the 'White Brotherhood,' who is a minor (and not local), and who should be returned to their parents." V. Vasilenko, A Batrakova, and others, "Give Us Back Our Children," *Argumenty I Fakty*, July 1993, 12, reprinted in *Current Digest of the Post-Soviet Press*, vol. XLV(30), 1993, 15.

47.   Nikolai Burbyag and Aleksei Grigoryev, "Heavenly Father and Heavenly Mother of the World," *Current Digest of the Post-Soviet Press*, vol. XLV(30), 1993, 17.

48.   Reuters, "Kiev Braces for Influx of Cult Members for Whom Mass Suicide is Central Tenet," *Orange County Register*, October 30, 1993, 25 (news section).

49.   Mary Mycio, "Cult's Suicide Threats Rattle Ukraine," *Los Angeles Times*, November 9, 1993, A7.

50.   Mycio, A7.

51.   The Great White Brotherhood, anonymously written flyer, quoted in Malcolm Gray, "Kiev's Cult of Doom," *Maclean's*, November 22, 1993, 32.

52.   Andrei Zamula, "Religious Wars Expected In Arkhangeisk," *Current Digest of the Post-Soviet Press*, vol. XLV(30), 1993, 16.

53.   Mary Mycio, "Ukrainians Seize 2 Fugitive Cult Leaders," *Los Angeles Times*, November 12, 1993, A16.

54.   Maria Devi Khristos, quoted in Gray, 33.

55.   Reuters, "Kiev Braces," 25.

56.   "Deadly Cult Active in Petersburg," *St. Petersburg Press*, May 28, 1997, Internet edition at http://www.spb.ru:8100/sppress/111/deadly.html.

57.   Richard Lacayo, "In the Reign of Fire," *Time*, October 17, 1994, 59.

58.   Tom Post, "Mystery of the Solar Temple," *Newsweek*, October 17, 1994, 42.

59.   "53 Cultists Found Dead in Switzerland and Canada," *Facts on File*, 748.

60.   Michael S. Serrill, "Remains of the Day," *Time*, October 24, 1994, 42.

61.   Lacayo, "In the Reign," 59.

62.   "53 Cultists Found," 748.

63.   "53 Cultists Found," 748.

64.   Post, 44.

65.   *Transit pour le Futur.* As reprinted in Ted Daniels, "Solar Temple Letters 3: Transit pour le Future," *Millennial Prophecy Report*, vol. 3(5), 1994, Internet edition at http://www.channel1.com/mpr/transit.htm.

66.   "53 Cultists Found," 748.

67.   Luc Jouret, taped message, quoted in Post, 43.

68.   David and Walte, 6A, see note 5 above.

69.   Scott Kraft, "Cult Ritual Suspected in Deaths," *Los Angeles Times*, December 24, 1995, A3.

70.   James Walsh, "The Sunburst Sacrifices," *Time*, January 8, 1996.

71.   Kraft, A3.

72.   Associated Press, "French Police End Cult Probe," November 11, 1996, America Online.

73.   Katherine Wilton, "Police Probe Rumor of Third Solar Temple Suicide," *The* (Montreal, Canada) *Gazette*, April 4, 1996, A3.

74.   Associated Press, "Teens Who Escape Cult Suicide Leave For France," May 6, 1997, America Online.

75.   Walsh, 45.

76.   Patrick Vuarnet, letter to Alain Vuarnet, quoted in Walsh, 45.

77.   Fred Guterl, "Nerve Gas in the Subway," *Discover*, January 1996, 73.

78.   David E. Kaplan and Andrew Marshall, *The Cult at the End of the World* (New York: Crown Publishers, 1996), 16.

79.   Kaplan and Marshall, 17.

80.   Teresa Watanabe, "Japanese Police Seek Sect Chief in Wider Probe," *Los Angeles Times*, March 24, 1995, A10.

81.   Anthony Spaeth, "Engineer of Doom," *Time*, June 12, 1995, 57.

82.   Shoko Asahara, *Declaring Myself The Christ*, quoted in Gwen Robinson, "Aum Shinrikyo: The Blind Leading the Blinded," *The Australian*, May 18, 1995, 9.

83.   Shoko Asahara, quoted in Edward W. Desmond, "Under Arrest — Finally," *Time*, May 9, 1995, 43.

84.   Peter Landers, "Cult Leader's Life Story Is Nothing If Not Bizarre," *San Francisco Chronicle*, March 24, 1995, A10. One of Asahara's fake drugs was nothing more than tangerine peel blended with alcohol (see Kaplan and Marshall, 9).

85.   Aum Shinrikyo advertisement, quoted in Kaplan and Marshall, 14.

86.   Shoko Asahara, quoted in *Twilight Zone*, cited in David Holley, "Japan Guru — Young Bully's Power Quest," *Los Angeles Times*, March 27, 1995, A6.

87.   John Burnham Schwartz, "Terror in Tokyo" *Newsday*, July 7, 1996, C35, Internet edition at http://www.elibrary.com:80/get-doc.cgi?id=54648250x0y370&Form=EN&Button=MEM

88.   Steven Strasser, "Tokyo Grabs the Doomsday Guru," *Newsweek*, May 29, 1995, 48.

89. Senator Sam Nunn, "The New Terror: Nutcakes With Nukes," *New Perspectives Quarterly*, January 1, 1996, 32. Internet edition at http://www.elibrary.com:80/getdoc.cgi?id=54648250x0y 370&OIDS=0Q004D018&Form=RL.

90. Murray Sayle, "Nerve Gas and the Four Noble Truths," *The New Yorker*, April 1, 1996, 64.

91. Strasser, 48.

92. Teresa Watanabe and Carol J. Williams, "Japan Sect Uses Pain to Impel Faith," *Los Angeles Times*, March 25, 1995, A13. This same device could be rented for approximately $8,000–$10,000 a month.

93. David Holley, "Cult Attracted Many Followers and Notoriety," *Los Angeles Times*, March 23, 1995, A19.

94. Teresa Watanabe, "Police Seize Toxic Chemicals in Raid On Japanese Sect," *Los Angeles Times*, March 23, 1995, A1, A18.

95. Watanabe and Williams, A12; cf. Kaplan and Marshall, 178–181.

96. David E. Kaplan and Andrew Marshall, "The Cult at the End of the World," *Wired*, July 1996, 178.

97. "Aum Shinrikyo's Cultic Style," *The Cult Observer*, vol. 12(4), 1995, 3. This counter-cult periodical is published by the American Family Federation (Box 2265, Bonita Springs, FL 34133).

98. Kaplan and Marshall, "The Cult," *Wired*, 177; cf. Kaplan and Marshall, *The Cult*, 182–183.

99. David Holley, "Police Search for Bodies At Sect's Compound," *Los Angeles Times*, March 29, 1995, A8.

100. Sayle, 56; cf. Kaplan and Marshall, *The Cult*, 172–173.

101. "A six-man Aum hit team . . . had entered the lawyer's apartment shortly before dawn, killed the sleeping family, wrapped their bodies in futons, and removed them under cover of darkness. . . . [T]he team strangled Sakamoto and his wife, and smothered their baby. Nakagawa said that Asahara personally ordered the lawyer killed." Sayle, 61. Kaplan and Marshall's *The Cult at the End of the World* contains a detailed and rather grisly account of these murders based on Nakagawa's confession to police (pp. 41–43).

102. "Asahara and O. J.," *The Economist*, May 4, 1996. Internet edition at http://www.enews.com/magazines/economist/archive/05/960504-001.html.

103. Associated Press, "Japan Guru Ordered From Court," November 8, 1996, America Online.

104. Associated Press, "Japan Guru Ordered."

105. Kyodo News Service, "Aum Leader Only One Who Could Have Ordered Murders," September 5, 1997.

106. Kevin Sullivan, "Japan Cult Survives While Guru is Jailed: Group Worships Leader on Trial in Gas Attack," *Washington Post*, September 28, 1997, A21.

107. UPI, "Japanese Warn of New Dangers from Cult," August 27, 1997, America Online.

108. Sullivan.

109. Sullivan.

110. Kaplan and Marshall, "The Cult," *Wired*, 136–137, 176.

111. Strasser, 48; cf. "The Cult's Broad Reach," *Newsweek*, May 8, 1995, 54.

112. "The Cult's Broad Reach," 54.

113. Kyodo News Service, "U.S. Designates Aum Shinrikyo As Terrorist Group," October 8, 1997. The entire list of foreign terrorist organizations released by the Office of the Coordinator for Counterterrorism, U.S. Department of State can be found on the Internet at http://www.state.gov/www/global/terrorism/terrorist_orgs_list.html.

114. Deputy Robert Brunk, author's recorded statement by Brunk at San Diego Medical Examiner's News Conference, March 21, 1997.

115. As told by deputies Robert Brunk and Laura Gacek at the March 21, 1997 San Diego Medical Examiner's news conference that was attended by this author.

116. Deputy Brunk.

117. In a 1976 interview, Nettles claimed the following: "[The monk] stands beside me when I interpret the charts," Nettles revealed during one interview. "There can be several meanings to them, and if I'm wrong, he will correct me." Bonnie Nettles, quoted in James Phelan, "Looking for The Next World," *New York Times Magazine*, February 29, 1976. Internet edition at *New York Times* online.

118. Marshall Applewhite, "Do's Intro: Purpose — Belief by The Present Representative Do," in *How and When Heaven's Gate May Be Entered*, posted on the Internet at www.heavensgate.com; cf. Marshall Applewhite, "Undercover 'Jesus' Surfaces Before Departure" in *How and When Heaven's Gate May Be Entered*, posted on the Internet at www.heavensgate.com.

119. Applewhite, " 'Undercover 'Jesus' Surfaces."

120. *Special Report: Mass Suicide Rancho Sante Fe* (CBS), Channel 2 News, March 27, 1997.

121. Joan Culpepper, *Extra* (NBC), April 1, 1997.

122. The Two attracted seven hundred people at a speaking engagement in San Francisco and completely filled a college lecture hall in San Diego (see Phelan).

123. Aaron Greenberg, *Extra* (NBC), March 31, 1997.

124. Joan Culpepper, quoted in Phelan.

125. Phelan, also see Marshall Applewhite, *Beyond Human — The Last Call* (videotaped teaching), Session 4 of 12.

126. Phelan.

127. Cited in Phelan.

128. Phelan.

129. Associated Press, "Heaven's Gate Member Profiles," *New York Times*, March 30, 1997, America Online.

130. Phelan.

131. Phelan.

132. The following statement was made by Heaven's Gate member Lvvody: "It was in late June/early July of 1976 that Ti and Do gathered all their surviving new students/ disciples together in Medicine Bow National Forest in Wyoming. Here is where the intensive 'classroom' for learning Next Level ways and behavior began. . . . Ti and Do really began taking us through the process of 'incarnating' — what Ti and Do must have told us a million times before we finally began to grasp it" (Lvvody, "Ingredients of a Deposit — Becoming a New Creature," in *How and When Heaven's Gate May Be Entered*, March 16, 1996, posted on the Internet at http://www.heavensgate.com.

133. Frank Brunni, "Cult's Two Decade Odyssey of Regimentation," *New York Times*, March 29, 1997, Internet edition at *New York Times* online.

134. Applewhite, *Beyond Human*, Session 3 of 12.

135. Applewhite, *Beyond Human*, Session 6 of 12.

136. Applewhite, *Beyond Human*, Session 6 of 12.

137. Stmody, "Evolutionary 'Rights' for 'Victims'," in *How and When Heaven's Gate May Be Entered*, April 18, 1996, posted on the Internet at http://www.heavensgate.com.

138. Glnody, *Earth Exit Statement*, March 19, 1997, posted on the Internet at http://www.levelabovehuman.com.

139.   Chkody, *Earth Exit Statement*, March 19, 1997, posted on the Internet at http://www.levelabovehuman.com.

140.   In a 1997 interview with MSNBC news, Heaven's Gate member Wayne Cooke — who missed the first round of suicides, but eventually killed himself within weeks of the initial deaths — stated the following with regard to independent thinking: "There's no room in the classroom as you grow towards being a member of the next level, which is what the classroom is about. There's less and less room for this kind of thinking and kind of action [i.e., independent thinking]. . . . It's teamwork, it's true mindedness, it's looking to your older member. Your teacher, and your teacher looks to his teacher — or his older member — and it's a chain of minds that goes all the way up to the creator, the top man. And that's how things can work without getting off track."

141.   Brnody, "Up The Chain," in *How and When Heaven's Gate May Be Entered*, April 16, 1996, posted on the Internet at http://www.heavensgate.com.

142.   Applewhite, "Undercover 'Jesus' Surfaces Before Departure"; cf. Applewhite, *Beyond Human*, Session 9 of 12.

143.   Dick Joslyn, *Impact* (CNN), March 27, 1997.

144.   Joslyn, *Impact*.

145.   Jwnody, "Overview of Present Mission," in *How and When Heaven's Gate May Be Entered*, April 1996, posted on the Internet at http://www.heavensgate.com.

146.   Jwnody. On October 11, 1995, Heaven's Gate released a similar, yet slightly reworded declaration called " '95 Statement by an E.T. Presently Incarnate."

147.   In "Overview of Present Mission," Jwnody explained: "The response was extremely animated and somewhat mixed. However, the loudest voices were those expressing ridicule, hostility, or both — so quick to judge that which they could not comprehend. This was the signal to us to begin our preparations to return 'home.' The weeds have taken over the garden and truly disturbed its usefulness beyond repair — it is time for the civilization to be recycled — 'spaded under.' "

148.   George Johnson, "Comets Spawn Fear, Fascination, and Web Sites," *New York Times*, March 28, 1997. Internet edition at *New York Times* online.

149.   Chuck Shramek, quoted in "What's the Harm in Believing in UFOs & Pseudo-science?: Heaven's Gate Cult Mass Suicide Answers the Question," *Skeptic*, vol. 5(1), 1997, 11.

150.   Alan Hale, "Hale-Bopp Comet Madness," *Skeptical Inquirer*, March 1997, Internet edition at http://www.halebopp.com/slo3.htm. Hale stated: "[O]nce I was able to examine the images in question, and could match the surrounding star field with a photograph of the same region of the sky taken during the course of the Palomar Sky Survey in the early 1950s, I found that the location of the "Saturn-like object" coincided perfectly with a bright 8th-magnitude star that the comet just happened to be located next to on the night in question. The "Saturn-like rings" extending from the "object" were apparently nothing more than a diffraction effect, a common occurrence with over-exposed stellar images on astronomical photographs."

151.   Hale.

152.   Chuck Shramek, Public Statement, Internet text at Chuck Shramek's Home Page, http://www.neosoft.com/~cshramek/.

153.   Jwnody, " 'Away Team' from Deep Space Surfaces Before Departure," in *How and When Heaven's Gate May Be Entered*, April 8, 1996, posted on the Internet at http://www.heavensgate.com.

154.   Marshall Applewhite, quoted in Phelan.

CHAPTER TWO

1. Criswell, *Criswell Predicts* (Anderson, South Carolina: Droke House Publishers, 1968), 141.

2. Neville Drury, *Dictionary of Mysticism and the Occult* (San Francisco: Harper & Row, 1985), 216. The term "psychic" was first used by French astronomer Camille Flammarion (1842–1925), whose main interest lay in the area of necromancy (communication with the dead) via mediums. In England, the term was first used by Edward Cox (1809–1879), a renowned investigator of the paranormal.

3. Lewis Spence, *The Encyclopedia of the Occult* (London: Bracken Books, 1994), 330.

4. David Wallechinsky, Amy Wallace, and Irving Wallace, *Book of Predictions* (New York: William Morrow, 1981), 446–447; Nidle's 1996 prophecy is discussed in James Randi, "The Official Pigasus Awards From the James Randi Educational Foundation," *Swift*, vol. 1(1), 1997, 2, reprinted in *Skeptic*, vol. 5(1), 1997.

5. David McCallum, *Ancient Prophecies II* (The Learning Channel), March 30, 1997 and *Ancient Prophecies III* (The Learning Channel), June 1, 1997.

6. Ken Hollings, "Criswell Predicts: Lost Voices From a Forgotten Future, 1956–59," January 11, 1996, *CTheory: Theory, Technology, and Culture*, Internet edition at http://www.ctheory.com/a35-criswell_predicts.html; cf. "Criswell the Propheseer," Internet site at http://members.wbs.net/homepages/s/p/y/spychick0007.html and "CRISWELL," Internet site at http://members.wbs.net/homepages/b/i/g/bigblueassbaby.html.

7. Hollings.

8. Criswell, 23.

9. A list of films by Wood can be found on the Internet at http://garnet.acns.fsu.edu/~lflynn/edwood.html.

10. In 1997, *Plan 9 From Outer Space* made the top ten list of cult films along with *Blood Feast* (1963), *Faster, Pussycat! Kill! Kill!* (1966), and *Bad Girls Go to Hell* (1965). Richard Corliss, "Sex! Violence! Trash!," *Time*, July 7, 1997, 103.

11. Criswell, 9, 16.

12. Criswell, 15.

13. Gordon-Michael Scallion, *Earth Changes Report*, "About Gordon-Michael Scallion," Internet edition at http://www.ecrnews.com/gmsbio.html.

14. Gordon-Michael Scallion, interview on *Coast to Coast* with Art Bell, December 8, 1995, Internet transcript at http://nen.sedona.net/nhne/bellinterview.html.

15. Scallion, Art Bell interview.

16. Gordon-Michael Scallion, *Ancient Prophecies I* (The Learning Channel), December 31, 1996.

17. Scallion, Art Bell interview.

18. David Sunfellow, "Gordon-Michael Scallion: A Summary of His Most Important Predictions," *New Heaven / New Earth*, November 11, 1994, Internet edition at http://www.newage.com.au/library/scallion.html. This same document can also be found at http://www.newciv.org/~albert/earth/scallion1.

19. Sunfellow.

20. Scallion, *Ancient Prophecies I*.

21. Elliot Miller, *A Crash Course on the New Age Movement* (Grand Rapids: Baker Books, 1989), 36.

22. Gordon-Michael Scallion, *Tribulation: The Coming Earth Changes* videotape (Chesterfield, NH: Matrix Institute), cited in Sunfellow. David Sunfellow, in "Gordon-Michael Scallion's Predictions For 1995 (& Beyond)," *New Heaven / New Earth*,

January 5, 1995 (Internet edition at http://nen.sedona.net/nhne/scallion95.html), quotes the January 1995 issue of *Earth Changes Report* wherein GMS explains how he has a vision: "Visions come to me in a random fashion. If a vision repeats itself, I attempt to gain greater insight through meditation. For me, meditation begins with a prayer followed by my mentally focusing on the flickering of a candle. As I drift into a heightened state of awareness, I reach a point where the light becomes bright and fills my inner screen. At this point I seem to split into two consciousness. One part of me is aware — the observer. The other part is a presenter of information and ideas — the teacher. The teacher directs visions and sometimes even comments with one or two short sentences. I have, at times, been able to have a dialogue with my intuitive counterpart... the observer and teacher are not separate personalities. They are part of the whole of me, perhaps best described as aspects."

23. Jon Klimo, *Channeling* (Los Angeles: J. P. Tarcher, 1987), 347.

24. Scallion, *Ancient Prophecies I.*

25. Larry van Leeuwen-Smith and Elvire van Leeuwen-Smith, "The Matrix Institute and Gordon-Michael Scallion — Futurist," *Karinya*, Internet edition at http://www.karinya.com/matrix.htm.

26. Matrix Institute, Introductory Statement, http://www.ecrnews.com/welcome.html.

27. Scallion, Art Bell interview.

28. Leeuwen-Smith.

29. David Sunfellow, "A Review of Gordon-Michael Scallion's Predictions for 1995," February 20, 1996, *New Heaven / New Earth*, Internet edition at http://nen.sedona.net/nhne/scallion95review.html.

30. Sunfellow, "A Review of Gordon-Michael . . ."

31. Sunfellow, "A Review of Gordon-Michael . . ."

32. Andy Lutts, "15.5 Million Spaceships," *Salem New Age Center Newsletter*, January 1997, Internet edition at http://www.newage.com.au/library/snac7.html.

33. Scallion made the following statement on his 1998–2002 future map of the United States: "A vision I've seen for the year 2002 is of a new Earth — reborn — with its people living in harmony with each other. Lush tropical settings cover many parts of the United States. Communities seem to be located more in rural areas than in cities. The air is clean, and there no longer is an ozone hole." This statement is available on the Internet at http://www.newage.com.au/library/scallion.html.

34. Leslie Shepard, ed., *Encyclopedia Occultism and Parapsychology*, vol. 1 (Detroit: Gale Research, 1991), 263.

35. Rudolf Steiner Publications, *The Steinerbooks Dictionary of the Psychic, Mystic, Occult* (Blauvelt, NY: Rudolf Steiner Publications, 1973), 39.

36. Reading #1 (Edgar Cayce Reading #3976-15, January 19, 1934), Reading #2 (Edgar Cayce Reading # 1152-11, August 13, 1941), Reading #3 (Edgar Cayce Reading #826-8, no date). All three of these readings are available from Cayce's Association for Research and Enlightenment. They may also be obtained from the Internet at http://www.newage.com.au/library/scallion.html.

37. John Van Auken., quoted in Ken Baker, "End of the World Is Rapidly Approaching," Knight-Ridder/Tribune News Service, January 11, 1995 (Orange County California Public Library Online System).

38. Edgar Cayce, A.R.E. Reading Index # 3976-15; cf. A. T. Mann, *Millennium Prophecies: Predictions for the Year 2000* (Rockport, MA: Element Books, 1992), 88.

39. Edgar Cayce, *Edgar Cayce On Atlantis* (New York: Hawthorne Books, 1968), 158–159.

40. James Randi, *Flim-Flam* (Buffalo: Prometheus, 1982), 191.

41. Randi, 192.

42. Gordon Stein, ed., *The Encyclopedia of the Paranormal* (Buffalo: Prometheus Books, 1996), 152.

43. Stein, 152.

44. Randi, 191.

45. Randi, 195.

46. Drury, 65.

47. There are two basic kinds of astrology: 1) *Judicial*, which foretells the future of individuals and nations; and 2) *Natural*, which predicts changes in the weather and the influence of stars on natural things (see Shepard, 102).

48. Kenneth Miller, "Star Struck," *Life*, July 1997, 40. A 1990 Gallup poll found similar results: seventy-five percent of Americans read their horoscopes at least occasionally and 25% believed the tenets of astrology (George H. Gallup and Frank Newport, "Belief in Paranormal Phenomena Among Adult Americans," *Skeptical Inquirer*, vol. 15(2), winter 1995, 137.

49. Doris Chase Doane, *Astrology: Thirty Years Research* (Tempe, AZ: American Federation of Astrologers, 1985), 154.

50. Quoted in Daniel Cohen, *Waiting for Apocalypse*, 1983 edition (Buffalo: Prometheus Books, 1973), 85.

51. Alan Hale, "Hale-Bopp Comet Madness," *Skeptical Inquirer*, March 1997, Internet edition at http://www.halebopp.com/slo3.htm; and Richard Lacayo, "The Lure of the Cult," *Time*, April 7, 1997, 46.

52. Berossus, cited by Seneca, as quoted in Charles Berlitz, *Doomsday 1999 A.D.* (New York: Doubleday, 1981), 18.

53. Cohen, 54.

54. Wallechinsky, Wallace, and Wallace, 441.

55. James Randi, "The Third Millennium — Or Bust," *Skeptic*, vol. 2(4), 1994, 30.

56. Wallechinsky, Wallace, and Wallace, 442.

57. Wallechinsky, Wallace, and Wallace, 446.

58. Wallechinsky, Wallace, and Wallace, 449–450: "In one marathon invoking Chandi Path, the goddess of power, one and a half tons of pure butter and thousands of marigolds were burned. The Hindu liturgy was intoned 4,800,000 times by a relay of 250 priests. U Nu, the prime minister of Burma, released 3 bullocks, 3 pigs, 9 goats, 60 hens, 60 ducks, 120 doves, 120 fish, and 218 crabs in the hope of averting the evil forces."

59. Robert S. Richardson, *Griffith Observer*, May 1962, quoted in John Mosley, "The Millennium Is Coming," *Skeptic*, vol. 4(4), 1996, 46.

60. Cohen, 54.

61. John Gribbin and Stephen Plagemann, *The Jupiter Effect* (London: Macmillan, 1974).

62. K. F. "The Jupiter Noneffect," *The Skeptical Inquirer*, vol. 5(1), 1980, 7.

63. Hal Lindsey, *The 1980s: Countdown to Armageddon* (New York: Bantam, 1981 paperback), 29–30.

64. K. F., 6.

65. John Gribbin, "Jupiter's Noneffect," *Omni*, June 1980.

66. Mosley, 49.

67. Richard Noone, *Enter Darkness / Enter Light* (New Millennium Productions, 1996). Transcribed quote available on the Internet at http://www.futurefate.com/graphic/predict/pspred.shtml.

68. Mosley, 49.

69.   Richard W. Noone, *5/5/2000* (New York: Harmony Books, 1994), 53.

70.   Mosley, 52.

71.   L. G. Thompson, "On the Trail of the Jupiter Effect," *Sky & Telescope*, September 1981, 220.

72.   Thompson, 53.

73.   Eklal Kueshana (a.k.a. Richard Kieninger), *The Ultimate Frontier* (Stelle, IL: The Stelle Group, 1963). quoted in *Future Fate* advertisement available on the Internet at http://www.futurefate.com/graphic/predict/mecpred.shtml.

74.   Donna Kossy, *Kooks: Guide to the Outer Limits of Human Belief* (Portland: Feral House, 1994), 133.

75.   Kossy, 136–137.

76.   Tim Wilhelm, quoted in Kossy, 136.

77.   Wallechinsky, Wallace, and Wallace, 340.

78.   Richard Cavendish editor-in-chief, *Man, Myth & Magic*, vol. 17 (New York: Marshall Cavendish Corporation, 1995), 2143.

79.   George Constable ed., *Mystic Places* of *Mysteries of the Unknown* (Alexandria, VA: Time-Life Books, 1987), 57.

80.   Peter Tompkins, *Secrets of the Great Pyramid* (New York: Harper & Row, 1971), 72.

81.   Constable, 58.

82.   Adam Rutherford, *Pyramidology: Book I* (Bedfordshire, Great Britain: The Institute of Pyramidology, 1961), 77–78.

83.   Geoffrey W. Bromiley, gen. ed., *The International Standard Bible Encyclopedia*, vol. 1, 1989 edition (Grand Rapids: William B. Eerdmans, 1979), 832; cf. Walter A. Elwell gen. ed., *Baker Encyclopedia of the Bible*, vol. 1, 1995 edition (Grand Rapids: Baker Books, 1988), 559. The Israelite cubit — approximately eighteen inches — follows the example of other Near East nations that used the average distance from a man's elbow to the end of his middle finger as a unit of measure (i.e., the forearm). Obviously, using such a loose standard led to various "cubit" measurements in different nations. In Mesopotamia, for instance, the cubit was about 19.5 inches. The average Egyptian cubit was approximately 20.5 inches. These cubits even varied within their own nations. In Egypt, archeologists have recovered cubit sticks from the twelfth dynasty (c. 1570–1310 B.C.) that vary as much as an inch in length. No ancient cubits, however, especially those used by the Israelites, would have been twenty-five inches.

84.   Charles Piazzi Smyth, *The Great Pyramid and the Royal Society* (London: 1874), 3–4.

85.   The popular occult book series *Man Myth and Magic* explains: "By taking detailed measurements of the perimeter, sides, outer courses of masonry, inner chambers, galleries and corridors, by dividing the result by certain numbers held to be significant in the construction of the pyramid, and by relating the results to biblical chronology and to the history of Christianity, exact correspondences were discovered. By the same token, an understanding of the cipher was supposed to permit the making of prophecies up to the Second Coming [of Jesus] which, following the pyramid-inch- per-year theory up the Grand Gallery, was clearly close at hand" (p. 2144).

86.   Basil Stewart, statement of February 16, 1928, quoted in Robert W. Smith, *The "Last Days"* (Salt Lake City: Pyramid Press, 1932), 36.

87.   John Edgar and Morton Edgar, *The Great Pyramid Passages and Chambers*, vol. 2 (London: The Marshall Press, 1924), 6-7.

88.   Thomas Foster, *Great Pyramid Power* (Blackburn, Victoria: Acacia Press, n.d.), 54–62.

89. Charles Piazzi Smyth, *Our Inheritance In the Great Pyramid*, 1880 edition (London: William Isbister, 1864), 546–547; Morton Edgar, *The Great Pyramid: Its Scientific Features* (Glasgow: Maclure, MacDonald & Co., 1924), 166–167; Francis M. Darter, "Our Bible In Stone," 144, reprinted in Benjamin S. Stringham, "Markings on the Highway of Life," in *L.D.S. Compendium*, 271 (no publishing information available), quoted in Robert W. Smith, *The "Last Days"* (Salt Lake City: Pyramid Press, 1932), 31; D. Davidson and H. Aldersmith, *The Great Pyramid: Its Divine Message* (London: Williams & Norgate, 1937), 390–391, 412; Rutherford, 145.

90. Martin Gardner, quoted in Randi, *Flim-Flam*, 116.

91. John Warwick Montgomery, *Principalities and Powers* (Minneapolis: Bethany House, 1973), 53.

92. Wallechinsky, Wallace, and Wallace, 342.

93. Matthew Scully, "The Light Brigade," *National Review*, September 12, 1994, 83.

94. Kenneth Ring, *Heading Toward Omega*, 1985 edition (New York: William Morrow, 1984), 195.

95. Ring, 200–201.

96. The following 1988 NDE prophecies are recorded in Ring's book, pages 204–205: "I think you can expect to see some of the most disastrous upheavals between now and 1988"; "It is to be 1988 or was to be. That [would] be the year everything would be wiped away if we didn't change"; "I think around 1984,1985, possibly even sooner [will see] the beginnings of droughts.... Anyway, by 1988, that will be when tensions finally grow to the point [of nuclear war]." More 1988/1989 NDE predictions were recorded in Margot Grey, *Return From Death* (London: Arkana, 1985), page 130–131: "Third World War. I would say 1988 is the most likely year for it all to happen"; "As time does not exist in the dimension where it is possible for this information to be given and received, it's very difficult to be accurate on this point. But the impression I gained was that the most difficult time was going to be around 1988"; "I think the most likely year for the events I can see arising to take place will be in 1988."

97. Raymond Moody, "Family Reunions: Visionary Encounters with the Departed in a Modern-Day Psychomanteum," *Journal of Near-Death Studies*, vol. 11(2), Winter 1992, p. 103.

98. Moody, 84–85, 103.

99. Moody, 85.

100. Darlene Brunson, *Ancient Prophecies II*.

101. *Ancient Prophecies II*.

102. *Ancient Prophecies IV* (The Learning Channel), July 20, 1997.

103. Linda Schele, quoted in "Armadas of Asteroids, and Other Heavenly Events," *Newsweek*, February 10, 1997, 14.

104. Philip Berg, *Ancient Prophecies II*.

105. Ariel Tzadok, *Ancient Prophecies II*.

106. Berg, *Ancient Prophecies II*.

CHAPTER THREE

1. David Allen Lewis, "Creation and the End Times," *Prophecy Watch International*, 1996 Special Edition, 3.

2. J. R. Church, "Chronology of the End Time," *Prophecy in the News*, November 1994, 4.

3. David Allen Lewis, *Signs of His Coming* (Green Forest, AR: New Leaf Press, 1997), 43.

4. Church, 6.

5. Terry Cook, *Satan's System: 666* videotape (San Bernardino, CA: Terry Cook Productions, 1994).

6. Richard Abanes, *American Militias: Rebellion, Racism and Religion* (Downers Grove: InterVarsity Press, 1996). Many of these survivalist groups are not Christian at all, but are offshoots of the virulently racist Christian Identity Movement discussed in Chapter 4.

7. Tim Weber, quoted in Steve Rabey, "Warning: The End Is Near, Again," *Gazette Telegraph*, December 28, 1991, D2.

8. Frank Flinn, "Government Shouldn't Fulfill Militia's Apocalyptic Prophecies," *Insight*, May 29, 1995, 38.

9. Russell Chandler, *Doomsday* (Ann Arbor, MI: Vine Books, 1993), 250.

10. Hal Lindsey, *The Late Great Planet Earth* (Grand Rapids: Zondervan, 1970), 54.

11. Lindsey 54.

12. Chandler, 250.

13. Hal Lindsey, *Countdown to Armageddon* long-playing record, 1980, quoted in William Alnor, *Soothsayers of the Second Advent* (Old Tappan, NJ: Fleming H. Revell, 1989), 67.

14. Lindsey, *The 1980s: Countdown to Armageddon* (New York: Bantam, 1981), back cover.

15. Michael E. Rench, "The End of the 'End Times,'" *Chalcedon Report*, November 1994, 37.

16. Hal Lindsey, *The Rapture* (New York: Bantam, 1983), 1, 23.

17. Hal Lindsey, *Planet Earth: 2000 A.D.*, (Palos Verdes: Western Front Ltd., 1994), 144, quoted in Tim Callahan, "The Fall of the Soviet Union & the Changing Game of Biblical Prophecy," *Skeptic*, vol. 3 no. 2 (1995), 94.

18. Hal Lindsey, "John Stewart Live," KBRT (Costa Mesa, CA), August 4, 1992; cf. Roy Rivenburg, "Is the End Still Near?," *Los Angeles Times*, July 30, 1992, E1–E2.

19. Callahan, 92.

20. Lindsey, *The Late Great*, 64–65.

21. Rivenburg, E4.

22. Ralph H. Alexander, "Ezekiel," in *The Expositors Bible Commentary*, Frank E. Gabelein gen. ed., 12 vols. (Grand Rapids: Zondervan, 1986), 6:930.

23. Lindsey, *The Late Great*, 66.

24. Lindsey, *The Late Great*, 69–70. Lindsey also made this claim in his 1981 book *The 1980s: Countdown to Armageddon*.

25. Hal Lindsey, quoted in Rivenburg, E4.

26. Rivenburg, E4; cf. Lindsey, *Planet Earth: 2000 A.D.*, 200.

27. C. Marvin Pate and Calvin B. Haines, *Doomsday Delusions* (Downers Grove: InterVarsity Press, 1995), 137.

28. Kathryn Lindskoog, *Fakes, Frauds & Other Malarkey* (Grand Rapids: Zondervan, 1993), 121. Yamauchi states that the Hebrew word *Rosh* has nothing to do with Russia: "This would be a gross anachronism, for the modern name is based upon the name *Rus*, which was brought into the region of Kiev, north of the Black Sea, by the Vikings only in the Middle Ages." Edwin Yamauchi, *Foes from the Northern Frontier* (Grand Rapids: Baker Books, 1982), 20; cf. David Wilson, *The Vikings and their Origins* (London: Thames and Hudson, 1970), 102–104 and Basil Dmytryshyn, *A History of Russia* (Englewood Cliffs, NJ: Prentice-Hall, 1977), 37–41. Yamauchi additionally explains that the names *Meshech* and *Tubal* are not related at all to Moscow or Tobolsk. Greek historian Herodotus identified *Meshech* and *Tubal* as the

Moschoi and Tibarenoi tribes who lived in central and eastern Anatolia between the eleventh and sixth centuries before Christ. Concerning Gog and Magog, these might refer to Spain, the Celts, Huns, Mongols, Arabians or Turks — but not Russia.

29. Rivenburg, E5.

30. Edwin Yamauchi, author's January 16, 1996 interview with Yamauchi; cf. letter from Baker Books to Edwin Yamauchi, November 16, 1992.

31. The following charts give a few examples of Missler's apparent plagiarism:

Foes from the Northern Frontier (1982) by Edwin Yamauchi	*The Magog Factor* (1995) by Chuck Missler
"Herodotus distinguishes three groups of Scyths in this area: "1. The agricultural Scythians (Herodotus 4.17–18) lived in the interior; northwest of the Crimea. 2. The nomadic Scythians (4.19) lived to the east of the agricultural Scythians. 3. The royal Scythians (4.20) lived in the Crimea and the area directly to the north" (p. 65).	"Herodotus distinguishes three groups of Scyths in this area: "1) The agricultural Scythians who lived in the interior, northwest of the Crimea; 2) The nomadic Scythians who lived to the east of the agricultural Sythians; 3) The royal Scythians who lived in the area directly to the north and to the east" (p. 52).
"A spectacular discovery of treasure at Ziwiye in this area now offers corroborative evidence of the Herodotus accounts. . . . The name Ziwiye may preserve the Akkadian name Zibie (Izibie), a site attacked by Sargon II in 716 and by Ashurbanipal in about 665" (p. 54).	"A spectacular discovery of treasure at Ziwiye in this area now offers corroborative evidence of the Scythian presence. . . . The name *Ziwiye* may preserve the Akkadian name *Zibie* (*Izibie*), a site attacked by Sargon II in 716 and by Ashurbanipal in about 665" (pp. 72–73).
"That the Scythian culture extended over 2,000 miles east from the Ukraine was demonstrated by the sensational discovery of tombs in the Chilikta Valley of East Kazakhstan. The results were published in Russian in 1965" (p. 112).	"The fact that the Scythian culture extended more than 2,000 miles east from the Ukraine was demonstrated by the sensational discovery of tombs in the Chilikta Valley of East Kazakhstan, published in Russian in 1965" (p. 52).

32. Chuck Missler, "Whoops! Our Slip is Showing," Internet posted statement at http://www.khouse.org/slip.html.

33. Hal Lindsey, quoted in "Special Correspondent's Report," *This Week in Bible Prophecy Magazine*, vol. 1(4), 1993, 9, quoted in B. J. Oropeza, *99 Reasons Why No One Knows When Christ Will Return* (Downers Grove: InterVarsity Press, 1994), 88.

34. Hal Lindsey, *Apocalypse Planet Earth* videotape (Palos Verdes, CA: Hal Lindsey Ministries, 1990).

35. *Bookstore Journal*, October 1995, 122.

36. Doug Clark, *When Planets Align . . . EARTHQUAKE 1982!!* (Garden Grove, CA: Lyfe Production Publication, 1976), 9, quoted in Alnor, 65.

37. Alnor, 65.

38. Clark, 28.

39. Clark, 39.

40. Doug Clark, *Final Shockwaves of Armageddon* (Garden Grove, CA: Doug Clark Ministries, 1982), introduction.

41. Doug Clark, interview with Alnor, April 11, 1989. Alnor, 69.

42. Doug Clark, interview on *Praise the Lord*, April 26, 1989, Trinity Broadcasting Network, quoted in Alnor, 92.

43. Author's June 26 interviews with U. S. Marshall's Service (Houston, TX) and the Federal Bureau of Prisons (Bastrop, TX). Clark's prisoner I.D. registration number was #682-32-079.

44. Edgar Whisenant, *On Borrowed Time* (Nashville: World Bible Society, 1988) and Edgar Whisenant, *88 Reasons Why the Rapture Could Be In 1988* (Nashville: World Bible Society, 1988).

45. Edgar Whisenant, quoted in *A Critique on the 1988 Rapture Theory* (Oklahoma City: Southwest Radio Church, 1988), 2.

46. Edgar Whisenant, interview with radio host "Greg" (no last name). Tape available at the Christian Research Institute, Rancho Santa Margarita, California.

47. Hart Armstrong, *Till There Is No Remedy*, tract #43222 (Wichita, KS: Christian Communications, 1988), 12, quoted in Alnor, 29.

48. Alnor, 28.

49. Chandler, 273.

50. David Aikman, "End-Times Fever," *Charisma & Christian Life*, February 1997, 72.

51. Edgar Whisenant, quoted in Joe Drape, "Ready or Not, the Rapture Didn't Come," *Atlanta Journal & Constitution*, September 14, 1988, 1A, quoted in Gary DeMar, *Last Days Madness* (Atlanta, GA: American Vision, Inc., 1994), 48.

52. Dean C. Halverson. "88 Reasons: What Went Wrong?," *Christian Research Journal*, vol. 11(2), Fall 1988, 14; cf. "Rapture Seer Hedges on Latest Guess," *Christianity Today*, October 21, 1988, 43.

53. Edgar Whisenant, *Tyler Morning Telegraph*, August 25, 1989, quoted in Dwight Wilson, *Armageddon Now* (Tyler, TX: Institute for Christian Economics, 1991), 6.

54. Chandler, 273

55. Harold Camping, *1994?* (New York: Vantage Press, 1992), 533.

56. Camping, xv.

57. Harold Camping, quoted in *New York Times*. Reprinted in *Buffalo News*, July 16, 1994, cited in Barry Karr, "It's the End of the World (And I Feel Fine)" *Skeptical Briefs*, Internet edition at http://www.csicop.org/sb/9409/endofworld.html.

58. Harold Camping, quoted in David Briggs, "Broadcaster Sees World's Sign-Off," *Orange County Register*, July 15, 1994, 6 (news section).

59. Harold Camping, quoted in Perrucci Ferraiuolo, "Could '1994' Be the End of Family Radio?," *Christian Research Journal*, vol. 16(1), Summer 1993, 6.

60. Harold Camping, quoted in Don Lattin, "The Man Who Prophesied the End of the World," *San Francisco Chronicle*, March 12, 1995, Z1.

61. Lattin, Z1.

62. Karr.

63. Michael D. Evans, *Seven Years of Shaking: A Vision* (Euless, TX: Mike Evans Ministry, 1994), 3, 6.

64. Evans, 10.

65. Evans, 37.

66. Evans, 39.

67. Evans, 27.

68. Evans, 39.

69. Evans, 10.

70. Evans, 3.

71. Evans states: "Why is this such a special time in spiritual history? Jesus said . . . . *This generation shall not pass, till all these things be fulfilled (Matthew 24:34)*. What generation was Jesus referring to here? The generation that sees the budding of the fig tree." Evans, 157.

72. Evans, 157.

73. Evans, 158.

74. Evans, 158.

75. Evans 159.

76. Evans, 23.

77. The Christian prophecy teachers discussed in this chapter and the facts surrounding their false predictions is a distillation of documents and information contained in numerous books, especially William Alnor's *Soothsayers of the Second Advent* and B. J. Oropeza's *99 Reasons Why No One Knows When Christ Will Return*. These volumes also discuss the following persons:

    Colin Deal: In 1979, this North Carolina prophecy teacher stated: "Christ will return bodily to the earth or in the air for the church by 1988." Colin Deal, *Christ Returns by 1988: 101 Reasons* (Rutherford College, NC: Colin Deal, 1979), 158.

    Mary Stewart Relfe: World War III, according to Relfe, was supposed to have started in 1989. The Great Tribulation, which Relfe said would begin in 1990, was to culminate with Jesus' return seven years later "just after Armageddon." Mary Stewart Relfe, *Economic Advisor,* February 1983, quoted in Alnor, 35. She even worked Halley's comet into her end-time scenario, stating that the comet's 1986 return could "be given the most distinguished honor yet, heralding the LORD OF LORDS AND KING OF KINGS!" Mary Stewart Relfe, *Relfe's Newsletter,* April 30, 1981, 8. When these years did not pan out as Relfe had expected, she updated her timetable by claiming that America would "burn" by 1993/1994, about three years before the Battle of Armageddon in 1997. Mary Stewart Relfe, Relfe's Review, February 1983, 5, quoted in Oropeza, 104. She additionally claimed that Christ's kingdom on Earth would be established by 1998. Mary Stewart Relfe, *Relfe's Review,* February 1983, 5, quoted in Oropeza, 115. Relfe said her information had come directly from God via divine revelation.

    Reginald Dunlop: This end-time prognosticator said that a 1986 worldwide famine would be so bad that "human body parts would be sold in stores." Reginald Dunlop, *The Coming Russian Invasion of America — Why? When? Where?* (Ontario, California: Reginald Dunlop, 1977), 327. The Antichrist was supposed to emerge "around the year 1989 or 1990, perhaps sooner" and the rapture was going to occur in 1991. Dunlop, 318. Of this scenario, he claimed to be "MORE than positive." Dunlop, 297. Dunlop believes that he can interpret the signs of the times because he has been specially chosen by God for that purpose. Dunlop, 304.

78. Peter LaLonde and Paul LaLonde, *The Mark of the Beast* (Eugene, OR: Harvest House, 1994), 186. Peter Lalonde, like other date suggesters, declares: "As citizens of the 1990s we have front row seats to those very events that will culminate with the return of Jesus Christ to this planet and the establishment of His kingdom!" Peter LaLonde, *One World Under Anti-Christ* (Eugene, OR: Harvest House, 1991), 11.

79. Lester Sumrall, *I Predict 2000 A.D.* (South Bend, IN: LeSEA Publishing Co., 1987), 74.

80. Lester Sumrall, *I Predict 1985* (South Bend, IN: LeSEA Publishing Co., 1984).

81. Alnor, 135–142; DeMar, 18; and Oropeza, 57.

82. Charles Taylor, *Bible Prophecy News*, vol. 15(1), January/February/March, 1986, 6.

83.   Alnor, 68, citing Emil Gaverluk, *Gospel Truths*, September 1979.

84.   Alnor, 108–109. Emil Gaverluk claimed in his 1986 book *The Rapture in the Old Testament* that NASA may actually have charted Heaven "using data obtained from high-flying" U-2 planes. According to Gaverluk, God's dwelling place might be in the direction of Virgo. Alnor, 110. Closely connected to this fanciful tale is the theory put forth by both Webber and Hutchings that "hell" may be either a white dwarf star somewhere or a black hole. David Webber and Noah Hutchings, *Apocalyptic Signs in the Heavens* (Oklahoma City, OK: Southwest Radio Church, 1979), 33–35. At the same time, Webber and Hutchings have suggested that hell may be housed on Venus: "[That planet] is a literal bottomless pit, a hell hole burning with fire and brimstone." Webber and Hutchings, *Apocalyptic Signs*, 54.

85.   David Webber, *Satan's Kingdom and the Second Coming* (Oklahoma City, OK: Southwest Radio Church, undated, c. 1973), 38, quoted in Alnor, 108.

86.   David Webber and Noah Hutchings, *Is This the Last Century?* (Nashville: Thomas Nelson, 1979), 49.

87.   David Webber and Noah Hutchings, *Gospel Truth*, June, 1987, 1.

88.   David Webber, William Alnor's April 19, 1989 interview with Webber, quoted in Alnor, 38.

89.   Alnor, 110.

90.   *Ancient Prophecies III* (The Learning Channel), June 1, 1997.

91.   *Ancient III*.

92.   *Ancient III*.

93.   J. R. Church, *Hidden Prophecies in the Psalms*, 1990 edition (Oklahoma City, OK: Prophecy Publications, 1986), 14.

94.   Church, *Hidden Prophecies* (1986 edition), 15, quoted in Alnor. 165.

95.   Alnor. 165; cf. Church, *Hidden Prophecies* (1986 edition), 246–260.

96.   Church, *Hidden Prophecies* (1990 edition), 252–253.

97.   Church, *Hidden Prophecies* (1990 edition), 61–62.

98.   Church, *Hidden Prophecies* (1990 edition), 67.

99.   Church, *Hidden Prophecies* (1990 edition), 88.

100. *Ancient Prophecies III*.

101. J. R. Church, "In the Beauties of Holiness," *Prophecy in the News*, May 1995, 25.

102. J. R. Church, "From the Womb of the Morning," *Prophecy in the News*, April 1995, 6–8.

103. J. R. Church, "Let There Be Light?," *Prophecy in the News*, January 1996, 4.

104. Church, *Hidden Prophecies* (1990 edition), 13–14.

105. Grant R. Jeffrey, *Armageddon: Appointment with Destiny* (Toronto: Frontier Research, 1988), 191–193.

106. Jeffrey, 192.

107. Oropeza, 58.

108. Geoffrey W. Bromiley gen. ed., *The International Standard Bible Encyclopedia*, vol. 2, 1990 ed. (Grand Rapids: William B. Eerdmans, 1982), 910; Walter A. Elwell gen. ed., *Baker Encyclopedia of the Bible*, vol. 1, 1995 ed. (Grand Rapids: Baker Books, 1988), 1056.

109. Donald Guthrie gen. ed., *The Eerdmans Bible Commentary*, 1989 ed. (Grand Rapids: William B. Eerdmans, 1970), 232.

110. Grant Jeffrey, *Final Warning* (Eugene, OR: Harvest House, 1996), 9.

111. Jeffrey, *Final Warning* 10–11.

112. Jeffrey, *Final Warning* 9.

113.   Jeffrey, *Final Warning*, "Notice to the reader about *Final Warning*," after acknowl-
       edgments, n.p.
114.   Salem Kirban, *I Predict* advertisement flyer (c. 1970).
115.   Kirban.
116.   Salem Kirban, *I Predict* (Iowa Falls, IA: Riverside Book & Bible House, 1970), 114–
       146; and Salem Kirban, *What in the World Will Happen Next?* (Huntingdon Valley,
       PA: Salem Kirban, 1974), 35, 43.
117.   Criswell, *Criswell Predicts* (Anderson, South Carolina: Droke House Publishers,
       1968), 14, 42, 77, 110, 112.
118.   Jeane Dixon, quoted in Ruth Montgomery, *A Gift of Prophecy* (New York: Bantam,
       1965), 181.
119.   Edgar Whisenant, *88 Reasons*, quoted in Alnor, 161.
120.   Jack Van Impe, *2001: On the Edge of Eternity* (Dallas: Word, 1996), 154; cf. Jack Van
       Impe, "Signs of the Times," *Van Impe Intelligence Briefing*, 1996 special edition,
       Internet edition at http://www.jvim.com/PerhapsToday/Special1996/signs.html
121.   Jack Van Impe, interview on *Praise the Lord* television program (Trinity Broadcast-
       ing network), April 21, 1994; Gregory S. Camp, *Selling Fear* (Grand Rapids: Baker
       Books, 1997), 186–187.
122.   Alnor, 168–172.
123.   Elliot Miller, "Cabala" (one page statement #DC-40), November 1992, published by
       the Christian Research Institute. This countercult institute may be reached by
       writing to: CRI, 30162 Tomas, Rncho. Snta. Mrgita, CA 92688.
124.   Leslie A. Shepard, *Encyclopedia of Occultism & Parapsychology*, vol. 2 (Detroit: Gale
       Research, 1991), 1191–1192.
125.   Deal, 124; cf. Alnor, 153–162.
126.   Colin Deal, *The Day and Hour Jesus Will Return* (Rutherford College, NC: Colin
       Deal, 1981), 96–97.
127.   Reginald Dunlop, *Flee to the Mountains — God's Message for Survival — No Time
       to Spare — Imminent End-Time Destruction* (Ontario, CA: Reginald Dunlop, c. 1975),
       125.
128.   David Webber and Noah Hutchings, *Prophecy in Stone* (Fort Worth, TX: Harvest
       press, 1974), 65; cf. David Webber, *Countdown for Antichrist* (Oklahoma City, OK:
       Southwest Radio Church, 1976), 22.
129.   David Webber and Noah Hutchings, *New Light on the Great Pyramid* (Fort Worth,
       TX: Harvest press, 1974), 65.

CHAPTER 4

1.   Don McAlvany, "The Waco Massacre: A Case Study on the Emerging American
     Police State," *McAlvany Intelligence Advisor*, July 1993, 1–2.
2.   John Trochmann, transcripts of ABC's *Primetime Live*, transcript #399, April 25,
     1995, 25.
3.   Daniel Junas, "Angry White Guys With Guns: The Rise of the Militias," *Covert
     Action Quarterly*, Spring 1995, 21; cf. Jill Smolowe, "Enemies of the State," *Time*,
     May 8, 1995, 61. This membership estimate was confirmed by James. L. Brown —
     Deputy Associate Director for Criminal Enforcement of BATF — during his
     testimony before the 1995 United States Senate Subcommittee on Terrorism,
     Technology, and Government Information of the Committee on the Judiciary. "The
     Militia Movement in the United States," June 15, 1995, 31. Dean Compton, leader of
     the California-based National Alliance of Christian Militia, stated that militia

membership alone could be as high as ten million. Author's November 17, 1995 interview with Compton.

4. Paul Henderson, "We're Not Saluting Hitler — We're Saluting God," *Seattle Times*, April 17, 1983, 7.

5. William Pierce (a. k. a. Andrew Macdonald), *The Turner Diaries* (Hillsboro, WV: National Vanguard Books, 1978; 1995 edition), 149–150, 158, 162–163. During his testimony before Congressman Charles Shumer's informal forum on "The Militia Movement and Hate Groups in America," July 11, 1995 (p. 3), Kenneth S. Stern noted that *The Turner Diaries* is a "key piece of fiction for white supremacists and neo-Nazis." The volume is nothing more than a 211-page cesspool of hate directed at Jews, blacks and other non-Anglo-Saxons, who are regularly knifed, shot, beaten and hung throughout the text. The fictional story — set between the years 1991 and 1993 — is the diary of Earl Turner, a rank-and-file member of The Order, an elite inner circle of militant revolutionaries who are part of a much larger terrorist group known as The Organization. The novel chronicles Turner's adventures during the two years prior to the conclusion of the "Great Revolution," a guerrilla war waged against the U.S. government by white patriots (p. iii). It paints Jews as the world's behind-the-scenes rulers and names "the Jewish-liberal-democratic-equalitarian plague" [sic] as the cause of society's moral decay (p. 42). There is, for instance, the Jewish man described as "Kappy the Kike . . . who makes his living in the White slave trade." This character sells young white girls to exclusive clubs in New York where wealthy Jews go "to satisfy strange and perverted appetites" (pp. 84–85). Blacks are portrayed in a similarly negative light, appearing sporadically throughout the book as brainless sub-humans who are either raping young white girls or beating up white patriots. An especially abhorrent portion of Pierce's book depicts blacks as natural-born cannibals who resort to eating defenseless whites when food grows scarce (pp. 24, 91, 92, 114, 147, 152, 179, 187, 205). For two years, Turner and his fellow freedom fighters crisscross the country, robbing, beating and murdering blacks and Jews along the way. Eventually, the organization successfully brings down the government as each state is systematically taken over by white revolutionary forces. Global victory, the murder of all nonwhites, and "the dream of a White world" is finally achieved by 1999 (p. 210). The book's climax is the "Day of the Rope." This gruesome event opens with white revolutionary forces sweeping through Los Angeles and surrounding neighborhoods to find race traitors — i.e., persons who had either engaged in, or encouraged, interracial relationships and racial equality programs. In ten hours, white patriots hang 55,000 to 60,000 victims, including government officials, lawyers, businessmen, TV newscasters, newspaper reporters and editors, judges, teachers, school officials, civic leaders, preachers, real estate brokers and prominent actors and actresses involved in "interracial 'love' epics" (pp. 162, 163).

6. James Johnson, transcripts of the United States Senate Subcommittee on Terrorism, Technology, and Government Information of the Committee on the Judiciary, "The Militia Movement in the United States," June 15, 1995, 113.

7. John Trochmann, transcripts of the United States Senate Subcommittee on Terrorism, Technology, and Government Information of the Committee on the Judiciary, "The Militia Movement in the United States," June 15, 1995, 128.

8. Ken Adams, transcripts of the United States Senate Subcommittee on Terrorism, Technology, and Government Information of the Committee on the Judiciary, "The Militia Movement in the United States," June 15, 1995, 84.

9.   The number of patriot/militia-related incidents of violence are far too numerous to
      mention. The following episodes, however, are indicative of what is happening
      throughout America:

      • In 1994, members of Virginia's Blue Ridge Hunt Club (BRHC) militia were charged
        with stockpiling machine guns and planning to raid a National Guard armory. A
        BRHC computer disk found by authorities contained information detailing a plan
        to destroy telephone relay centers, bridges, fuel storage tanks, radio stations, and
        airports. The militia was also planning to murder "human targets" such as police
        officers, political figures, and snitches. BRHC leader James Mullins was sen-
        tenced to a five- year prison term for violating federal firearms regulations.
        Senator Herb Kohl, transcripts of the United States Senate Subcommittee on
        Terrorism, Technology, and Government Information of the Committee on the
        Judiciary, "The Militia Movement in the United States," June 15, 1995, 5–6.

      • On February 28, 1995, four members of the Minnesota Patriots Council — LeRoy
        Wheeler, Duane Baker, Dennis Henderson, and Richard Oelrich — were con-
        victed under the U.S. Biological Weapons Anti-Terrorism Act of 1989 for planning
        to kill law enforcement agents with ricin, a deadly neurotoxin that they had
        manufactured. The men possessed enough ricin to kill 1,400 people. Richard A.
        Serrano, "7 Militiamen Held in Plot to Blow Up FBI Facility," *Los Angeles Times*,
        October 12, 1996, A27.

      • In 1996, self-proclaimed prophet Willie Ray Lampley, his wife, Cecilia, and associate
        John Baird were convicted for making bombs to blow up federal offices. All three
        were members of the Oklahoma Constitutional Militia. Serrano, A27.

      • In March 1997, ten members of the Arizona Viper Militia were convicted of
        explosives and weapons violations. All were sentenced to varying prison terms and
        fines. "Militia Member Gets 9-Year Prison Term," *Los Angeles Times*, March 21,
        1997, A21; cf. Associated Press, "Members of Viper Militia Sentenced," Los
        Angeles Times, March 20, 1997, A15.

      • In mid-1997, Ohio militia member Larry Martz was jailed after assaulting a state
        trooper and carrying a concealed weapon. Associated Press, "FBI: Militia Plotted
        'Holy War' On U.S., Death of Officials," *Los Angeles Times*, June 13, 1997, A8.

      • On August 8, 1997, Floyd Looker —leader of the Mountaineer Militia in West
        Virginia — was convicted of conspiring with two co-defendants to manufacture
        and deal explosives. Prior to the conviction, Looker's co-defendants had already
        pleaded guilty. The men were involved in a plot to blow up an FBI facility.
        Associated Press, "Militia Leader Guilty of Conspiracy to Manufacture Explo-
        sives," August 9, 1997, America Online.

10.   Josh Meyer, Paul Feldman and Eric Lichtblau, "Militia Members' Threats, Attack on
      Officials Escalate," *Los Angeles Times*, April 27, 1995, A1.

11.   *Militia of Montana Catalog* (November 1994), 9.

12.   "1996: Been There — Done That, 1997: Now What?," *Unraveling The New World
      Order*, January 1997, 1. Such ideas can be traced to the 1962 movie *The Manchurian
      Candidate*, which is about an American soldier transformed into a human time bomb
      after being subjected to an experimental drug and hypnosis. The concept crept into
      the patriot movement through patriot spokesperson Mark Koernke, who coined the
      term "bio bombs" to describe innocent citizens transformed into automatons via
      microchip implants. Koernke reveals: "Whenever the feds need an atrocity to advance
      their agenda. . . . they trigger one of these 'bio bombs.' " Mark Koernke, quoted in
      "Mark from Michigan," *Soldier of Fortune*, August 1995, 46.

13. Phil Agre, unpublished essay on the Oklahoma City bombing, Internet posting, April 23, 1995. Confirmed by author's January 19, 1995 telephone interview with Agre.

14. Susan Ladd and Stan Swofford, "Fearing for Our Country," *News & Record* (Greensboro, NC), June 25, 1995, Internet edition at http://www.infi.net/nr/extra/ militias/m-fearing.htm.

15. George Eaton, "America Is Lost Because the People are Lost," *Patriot Report*, October 1994, 2.

16. Michael Barkun, "Militias, Christian Identity and the Radical Right," *Christian Century*, August 2–9, 1995, 739.

17. George Bush, ABC's *Prime Time Live*, transcript #399, April 25, 1995, 22.

18. Caspar W. Weinberger, "Commentary on Events at Home and Abroad," *Forbes*, February 15, 1993, 35.

19. Jack McLamb, *Operation Vampire Killer 2000* (Phoenix: PATNWO, 1992), 3.

20. Linda Thompson, *Waco, Another Perspective* (Indianapolis: American Justice Federation, n.d.), 4.

21. McLamb, 32.

22. Thompson, 4.

23. "Another U.N. Outrage," *American's Bulletin* [sic], June 1995, 5.

24. *Militia of Montana Catalog*, November 1994, 14.

25. Jim Keith, *Black Helicopters Over America: Strikeforce for the New World Order* (Lilburn, GA: IllumiNet Press, 1994), 151.

26. According to Charles Strozier, Ph.D. of John Jay College's Center on Violence and Human Survival, "There is a huge overlap between militias and Christian fundamentalists." Peter Doskoch, "The Mind of the Militias," *Psychology Today*, July/August 1995, 12. This observation of the patriot militia movement was confirmed to me during my November 17, 1995 interview with Dean Compton, founder of the North American Alliance of Christian Militia. "[M]ost of the people of the patriot movement are born-again believers," said Compton. [And it is] "closely interwoven with mainstream Christianity."

27. Christian Civil Liberties Association, quoted in Bill Wallace, "Heated Rhetoric Set Stage for Oklahoma Blast," *San Francisco Chronicle*, May 1, 1995, Internet edition at http://www.sfgate.com/chronicle/index.shtml.

28. J. R. Church, "Tragedy Strikes Oklahoma City," *Prophecy in the News*, May 1995, 6.

29. Terry Cook, *Satan's System: 666* videotape (San Bernardino, CA: Terry Cook Productions, 1994).

30. Hal Lindsey, *Apocalypse Planet Earth* videotape (Palos Verdes, CA: Hal Lindsey Ministries, 1990).

31. Several fine books discuss the many attempts to identify the Antichrist: B. J. Oropeza, *99 Reasons Why No One Knows When Christ Will Return* (Downers Grove: InterVarsity Press, 1994); Russell Chandler, *Doomsday* (Ann Arbor: Servant, 1993); William Alnor, *Soothsayers of the Second Advent* (Grand Rapids: Fleming H. Revell, 1989); Robert C. Fuller, *Naming the Antichrist* (New York: Oxford University Press, 1995); and Bernard McGinn, *Antichrist* (San Francisco: Harper San Francisco, 1994). The first three books listed are written from a conservative Christian perspective. The latter two books are written from a secular point of view.

32. Pat Robertson, *700 Club Newsletter*, February-March 1980, quoted Fuller, 166.

33. Alnor, 23–25.

34. *Militia of Montana Catalog*, 5.

35. Hal Lindsey, *The 1980s: Countdown to Armageddon* (King of Prussia, PA: Westgate Press, 1980), 15.

36. John Hagee, *Beginning of the End* (Nashville: Thomas Nelson, 1996), 135.

37. Dave Hunt, *Global Peace and the Rise of the Antichrist* (Eugene, OR: Harvest House, 1990), 5.

38. Saint Martin of Tours, quoted in Otto Friedrich, *The End of the World: A History* (New York: Coward, McCann and Geoghegan, 1982), 27; cf. Gary DeMar, *Last Days Madness* (Atlanta: American Vision, 1994), 196–197.

39. Walter Laqueur, *Black Hundred* (New York: Harper Collins, 1993; paperback edition), 55.

40. DeMar, 199.

41. Benjamin Warfield, "Antichrist," in *Selected Shorter Writings of Benjamin B. Warfield*, vol. 1 (Nutley, NJ: Presbyterian and Reformed, 1970), John E. Meeter, ed., 356, quoted in DeMar, 200.

42. C. Marvin Pate and Calvin B. Haines, *Doomsday Delusions* (Downers Grove: InterVarsity Press, 1995), 41–42.

43. Oropeza, 155.

44. Colin Deal, *Christ Returns by 1988 — 101 Reasons Why* (Rutherford College, NC: Colin Deal, 1979), 86, quoted in Fuller, 181.

45. Ed Hindson, *Final Signs* (Eugene, OR: Harvest House, 1996), 157. Harvest House has published numerous end-time volumes by various prophetic speculators including Grant Jeffrey.

46. Joe Musser, quoted in G. R. Fischer, *The Quarterly Journal* (St. Louis: Personal Freedom Outreach), July-September 1989, 8, reprinted in Oropeza, 156.

47. Jennifer Ferranti, "Marine Worries ID Is Satanic," *Christianity Today*, November 13, 1995, 77; cf. Wendy Wallace, "The Four Horsemen of the Apocalypse," *Paranoia*, Spring 1995, 27.

48. Mary Stewart Relfe. Cited in Alnor, 83.

49. John Dart, "Religious Objections to DMV Upheld in L.A.," *Los Angeles Times*, October 25, 1997, A12. This article highlights the first court decision regarding persons who, for religious reasons, refuse to use their social security numbers to obtain a driver's license. The case involved five California men who would not use their Social Security numbers when seeking a license from the California Department of Motor Vehicles. In handing down the decision, Superior Court Judge Diane Wayne said that the state agency "could use another method of identification in light of the men's 'sincerely held religious convictions . . . that anyone who uses his or her Social Security number is in danger of not receiving eternal life." In an interview with the Los Angeles Times, one of the men — Paul Villandry — stated: "If I'm locked into that number, I'm going to hell. I chose to serve God and let God work it out for me."

50. David Webber and Noah Hutchings, *Computers and the Beast of Revelation* (Shreveport, LA: Huntington House, 1986), 129.

51. Texe Marrs, "New Money or Beast '666' Currency," *Flashpoint*, March 1995, 2.

52. Jean Paul Creusat and Anthony S. Halaris, "L.U.C.I.D.© & The Counter-Terrorism Act of 1995," *The Narc Officer*, September/October 1995, 56.

53. Creusat and Halaris, 55.

54. Texe Marrs, "Project L.U.C.I.D. is Here!," *Flashpoint*, September 1996, 1–2.

55. Marrs, "Project L.U.C.I.D.", 1–2.

56. Jack Van Impe, *11:59 . . . And Counting!* (Troy, MI: Jack Van Impe Ministries, 1983; 1987 edition), 105. Van Impe has since come up with another theory about the mark of the beast. As of 1997, Van Impe was teaching that the 666 mark may turn out to be a prefix number used in conjunction with "the international, national, and area computer codes presently in use (or being implemented), plus an individual number such as the person's Social Security number." Jack Van Impe, *2001: On the Edge of Eternity* (Nashville: Thomas Nelson, 1996), 125.

57. Van Impe, *11:59*, 106–107.

58. Oropeza, 160.

59. Cook, see note 32 above.

60. Gary Null, radio broadcast, WBAI-FM (99.5), reprinted as "Beyond AMERICA IN PERIL: Confirming Mark Koernke's Warnings," *THE PEOPLE'S SPELL-BREAKER*, John DiNardo, ed., Internet posting in the Patriot Archives, pathway starts at http://www.tezcat.com/, to Tezcat Archives, to Patriot folder, to New World Order folder, to Beyond_America_in_Peril.txt.

61. John Hanna, "Exodus," in *The Bible Knowledge Commentary: Old Testament*, John F, Walvoord and Roy B. Zuck eds., (Wheaton, IL: Victor Books, 1985), 130, quoted in Gary DeMar, "High-Tech Eschatology," *Biblical Worldview*, May 1994, 12.

62. Hanna, 130, quoted in DeMar, "High-Tech," 12.

63. Webber and Hutchings, 127; cf. Grant Jeffrey, *Prince of Darkness* (Toronto: Frontier Research Publications, 1994), 275–276.

64. For example, in an letter to the military-oriented magazine *Soldier of Fortune*, a Marine Corp sergeant observed the following: "[T]he United Nations is a nutless bureaucracy that carries no weight with its title and serves the sole purpose of wasting money and the lives of troopers from all nations." "Sickening Stats," *Soldier of Fortune*, November 1995, 28.

65. Reuters, "U.S. Spurns Idea of UN Taxes," January 19, 1996, America Online.

66. Klaus Larres, "Recycling Old Ideas," *History Today*, October 1993, 13.

67. *The Concise Columbia Encyclopedia* (New York: Columbia University Press, 1983; 1989 second edition), 872.

68. Larres, 14.

69. Jennifer Morrison Taw and Robert C. Leicht, *The New World Order and Army Doctrine* (Santa Monica, CA: RAND, 1992), 1.

70. Matthew Lyons and Chip Berlet , "Militia Nation," *The Progressive*, June 1995, 23.

71. Kenneth S. Stern, testimony before Congressman Charles Shumer's informal forum on "The Militia Movement and Hate Groups in America," July 11, 1995, 10–11.

72. Michael Barkun, "Reflections After Waco: Millennialists and the State," *Christian Century*, June 2–9, 1993, 599.

73. David Scoffins, "Choose You This Day Whom You Will Serve," *Calling Our Nation*, no. 29, 30; cf. Don Black, "The Ku Klux Klan Has A Plan" (flyer), early 1980s. Bob Miles served six years in prison for "conspiring to violate civil rights and possession of explosives for the bombings of ten empty school buses used for integration purposes in Pontiac, Michigan." John George and Laird Wilcox, *Nazis, Communists, Klansmen, and Others on the Fringe* (Buffalo: Prometheus Books, 1992), 370. Miles was also "convicted of an attack on a Willow Run, Michigan school principal, who was tarred and feathered." James Ridgeway, *Blood in the Face* (New York: Thunder's Mouth Press, 1990), 85.

74. Charles Lee Mange, *The Two Seeds of Genesis 3:15* (Nevada, MO: Wake Up America, n.d.), 5–9. There are some Christian Identity followers who do not hold to the serpent seed doctrine (e.g., Jack Mohr and Pete Peters). They define Jews as racially impure

converts to the satanically-inspired religion of Judaism. Most modern-day Jews, according to this position, are actually descendants of the Khazars (a nation of people living in Southeast Russia that converted to Judaism in the eighth century A.D.). Jack Mohr, *Seed of Satan: Literal or Figurative?* (Bay St. Louis, MS: Jack Mohr, n.d.), 16.

75. This belief contradicts the historic Christian position that Eve is the mother of *all* humanity (Gen. 3:20).

76. Bertrand Comparet, *The Cain-Satanic Seed Line* (Hayden Lake Idaho: Church of Jesus Christ Christian, n.d.), 5, 7. The publisher of this pamphlet — Church of Jesus Christ Christian — is not a Christian church. It is the church pastored by neo-Nazi Richard Butler, who founded the Aryan Nations. The church is located in Butler's Aryan Nations compound in Hayden Lake, Idaho.

77. Richard Butler, quoted in Brad Knickerbocker, "Followers See Validation for their Views in the Bible," *Christian Science Monitor,* April 20, 1995, 10.

78. "Why Oppose the Jews," *Calling Our Nation,* no. 15, 6.

79. Pete Peters, *Inter-Racial Marriage* (part1), audio-cassette #170 (La Porta, CO; Scriptures for America, n.d.). Quoted in Viola Larson, "Identity: A 'Christian' Religion for White Racists," *Christian Research Journal,* vol. 15(2), 1992, 25.

80. David Tate, "WHY?," *Aryan Nations,* no. 25, 12. Tate is currently serving a life sentence for machine-gunning to death in 1985 thirty-one-year-old Missouri State Trooper Jimmie Linegar.

81. Richard Butler, letter to an Aryan Kinsman, *Aryan Nations,* no. 25, 20.

82. David Lane, "Migration," *Calling Our Nation,* no. 59, 9. In 1985, Lane was convicted of racketeering and conspiracy to launch a race war against Blacks and Jews in order to establish a White nation. He was sentenced to forty years in prison. He was also convicted in 1987 for his role in the Alan Berg murder and sentenced to additional 150 years. He continues to contribute articles and letters to various white supremacist publications, especially those distributed by Richard Butler's Aryan Nations.

83. Michael. L. Hansen, "The Aryan Art of War," *Calling Our Nation,* no. 34, 6.

84. Ken Toole, quoted in Marc Cooper, "A Visit with MOM," *The Nation,* May 22, 1995, reprinted in Don Hazen, Larry Smith and Christine Triano, eds. *Militias in America 1995* (San Francisco: Institute for Alternative Journalism, 1995), 46.

85. Robin Wright and Josh Meyer, "Tradition-Rooted 'Patriot' Groups Strive to Curtail Modern 'Tyranny,'" *Los Angeles Times,* April 24, 1995, A12.

86. Loretta J. Ross, testimony before Congressman Charles Shumer's informal forum on "America Under the Gun: The Militia Movement and Hate Groups in America," July 11, 1995, 1.

87. Lyons habitually represents members of the Ku Klux Klan as well as the Klan as a collective entity. He has also worked as attorney for the Aryan Nations, founded be neo-Nazi Richard Butler.

88. Fred Mills, transcripts of the United States Senate Subcommittee on Terrorism, Technology, and Government Information of the Committee on the Judiciary, "The Militia Movement in the United States," June 15, 1995, 72. Mills stated: "We have had militias in Arizona . . . [as far back] as 1971 . . . . There has been sort of the white supremacist, the racist attitude in existence with many of the militia members for a long period of time . . . . What we have noticed recently is that they have changed their tune . . . . They have used examples of Ruby Ridge and Waco and the Brady Bill as examples of where Government is going beyond what it should be doing, and thus recruiting in perhaps more numbers."

89. Sons of Liberty, *1995 Sons of Liberty Book and Video Cassette List* (Arabi, LA: Sons of Liberty, 1995), 33. Among the hate literature sold through this catalogue is an

interesting booklet titled *This New World Order: Whose Concept Is It?* by Bertha
Glebe. The publication, which first began to be circulated in the late 1930s, allegedly
exposes "the plan for World Government with a proposed capital in Jerusalem under
Jewish control." This book, along with similar publications, is listed in the Sons of
Liberty catalogue under the subheading "THE NEW (JEW) WORLD ORDER" (p.
33).

90.   William Pierce, " 'Free' Trade, and the Deindustrialization of America, *National
      Vanguard Magazine*, Internet edition at National Alliance Home Page, http://
      www.natvan.com/NATVAN/NATVANDIR.HTML

91.   Barkun, "Militias, Christian Identity," 740.

92.   Barkun, "Militias, Christian Identity," 740.

93.   Pete Peters, quoted in Leslie Jorgensen, "Preaching the Patriot Gospel," *Freedom
      Writer*, August 1996, Internet edition at http://apocalypse.berkshire.net/~ifas/fw/
      9608/patriot.html.

94.   Nesta Webster, *Secret Societies and Subversive Movements* (Hollywood: Angriff Press,
      1972); cf. Jacob Heilbrunn, "On Pat Robertson: His Anti-Semitic Sources," *New York
      Review of Books*, April 20, 1995. The following excerpts are from *Secret Societies and
      Subversive Movements* by Webster:

      • In reference to the oft-mentioned Freemasonry/Illuminati conspiracy to which
        many Christians subscribe: "Either Freemasonry is the cover under which the
        Jews, like the Illuminati, prefer to work, so that where cover is not available they
        are obliged to come out more into the open, or that Grand Orient Masonry is the
        directing power which employs Jews as agents in those countries where it cannot
        work on its own account." (p. 383).

      • In reference to Karl Marx: "Can we not see him, like some veteran Jewish rag-and-
        bone merchant, going over the accumulated debris of past social schemes, passing
        through his fingers the dry bones of dead philosophies, the shreds and tatters of
        worn- out doctrines, the dust and ashes of exploded theories, and with the
        practical cunning of the German and Hebrew brain shrewdly recognizing the use
        that might be made of all this lumber by skillfully welding it into one subversive
        whole?"(p. 169).

      • In reference to global conspirators: "There is another power at work, a power far
        older, that seeks to destroy all national spirit, all ordered government in every
        country, Germany included. What is this power? A large body of opinion replies:
        the Jewish power" (p. 368).

      • In reference to communism: "The Jewish agitator is the tsetse fly carrying the poison
        germ of Bolshevism from the breeding-ground of Germany" (p. 309).

95.   Sons of Liberty, 7.

96.   Michael Howard, *The Occult Conspiracy* (Rochester, VT: Destiny Books, 1989), 161–
      162, quoted in Callahan.

97.   Sons of Liberty, 29.

98.   Eustace Mullins, *Murder by Injection*, as advertised in *1995 Sons of Liberty Book and
      Video Cassette List*, 15.

99.   Manfred Roeder, "Teutonic Unity," *Aryan Nations Newsletter*, no. 44 (July-August
      1982), 3.

100. Eustace Mullins, Radio Free America interview, October 28, 1994, hosted by Tom
      Valentine, transcripts posted on the Internet at http://lablinks.com/sumeria/poli-
      tics/eustace.html.

101. Eustace Mullins, epilogue in Bruce Brown, *The World's Trouble Makers* (Metairie,
      LA: Sons of Liberty, 1985), 145–146.

102. Jerome R. Chanes, *Antisemitism in America Today* (New York: Birch Lane Press, 1995) 299.

103. Pat Robertson, *Pat Robertson's Perspective*, February/March 1980, 3; cf. Chandler, 256.

104. Robertson, *Pat Robertson's Perspective*, 3. Robertson stated: "Ezekiel indicates enormous earthquake activity and severe hailstones in Israel at the time of the predicted Russian invasion.... According to these scientists [Gribbin and Plagemann], in 1982 there will be an alignment of planets on the same side of the sun which will exert a sufficiently strong additional gravitational pull on the earth to cause disruptions in the earth's upper atmosphere, radical changes in climatic conditions (hailstones?), and severe earthquakes."

105. Pat Robertson, *The New Millennium* (Dallas: Word Publishing, 1990), 312.

106. Chuck Missler, *Signs in the Heavens* cassette-tape series (Coeur d'Alene, ID: Koinonia House, n.d.). This form of astrology has been popularized primarily through two books: *The Witness of the Stars* (1893) by E. W. Bullinger and *The Gospel in the Stars* (1972) by Joseph Seiss. Missler, like many other Christians, see astrology as having originated with God. According to this view, God originally created the Zodiac to reveal his plan of salvation for humanity through Jesus Christ, but the correct interpretation of the Zodiac was lost as pagan occultists perverted the meaning of the stars. The majority of conservative Christian scholars and theologians, however, disagree with such a theory since it is without historical or biblical merit. Christianity and astrology have always been at odds with one another. On page 22 of *The Facts On Astrology* (Eugene, OR: Harvest House, 1988), conservative Christian cult specialists John Weldon and John Ankerberg comment: "Just as oil and water do not mix, the Bible and astrology are utterly irreconcilable." Moreover, there exists no record of a standard astrological system of zodiacal interpretation before ancient Babylon, let alone a zodiacal system that reflected the Christian gospel; Chuck Missler, *Personal Update*, February 1995, Internet edition at http://www.khouse.org/panin.html. Missler endorses the numerology outlined by Dr. Ivan Panin (1855–1942), whose work highlighted his discovery of hidden multiples of the number seven in various biblical passages. For example, Genesis 1:1 contains seven words totaling 28 letters (4 x 7). But Panin's discovery means nothing. Countless sentences contain seven words totaling 28 letters (e.g., "We had tea and toast for breakfast"; "Hurry, girls, or we'll miss the train"). This issue was dealt with in B. J. Oropeza's *99 Reasons . . .* (p. 47); During the fall of 1991, Missler conducted a series of lectures at Calvary Chapel (Costa Mesa, California) during which he gave an uncritical presentation of pyramidology, complete with an outline of the connection between the Great Pyramid, Stonehenge, and the alleged "face on Mars." As of 1997, the cassette recordings of these lectures — titled *Monuments: Sacred or Profane* — were still available through his ministry, Hal Lindsey Ministries, and Calvary Chapel. This fact has been referenced before in John Baskette, *Pyramidology?: Key to Biblical Prophecy* (Costa Mesa, CA: Answers In Action, 1992), 4. Baskette's difficult-to-find booklet is available through Answers In Action, PO Box 2067, Costa Mesa, CA 92628.

107. Chuck Missler, "Clear and Present Danger," *Personal Update*, July 1995, 8.

108. Missler, 6–9.

109. Chuck Missler, "The Genealogy of the Antichrist," *Personal Update*, September 1995, 9.

110. Missler, "The Genealogy," 9. Missler again used the patriot catch-phrase "District of Corruption in his July 1997 issue of *Personal Update*, Internet edition at http://www.khouse.org. This latter article, titled "None Dare Call It Fascism: Reflections on

Our Republic," is filled with classic patriot propaganda and anti-government rhetoric.

111. Jim Thomas, "From the Publisher," *Media Bypass*, August 1995, 4.

112. Chuck Missler, "Constitution a Crime?," *Personal Update*, November 1995, 3.

113. George and Wilcox, 372.

114. The number of articles found on relevant topics are as follows: New World Order — 75; Anti-Israel — 50; Anti-international Jewish bankers — 40; Anti-Black or pro-Apartheid — 28; Jewish holocaust denial — 13.

115. Chuck Missler, private recording of lecture, February 14, 1997, Calvary Chapel (Costa Mesa, California).

116. To understand the level of racism promoted by the Liberty Lobby, one need look only to the philosophy of its founder Willis Carto, who in 1955 boldly identified America's enemy: "History plainly tells us who our Enemy is. Our Enemy today is the same Enemy of 50 years ago and before — and that was before Communism . . . . The Jews came first and remain Public Enemy Number One. . . . Hitler's defeat was the defeat of Europe. And America. How could we have been so blind?" Willis Carto, letter to Earnest Sevier Cox, reprinted in C.H. Simonds, "The Strange Story of Willis Carto — His Fronts, His Friends, His Philosophy, His Lobby for 'Patriotism' " *National Review*, September 10, 1971, 979; cf. Scott McLemee, "Spotlight on the Liberty Lobby," *Covert Action Quarterly*, no. 50, Fall 1994, 24.

117. Chuck Missler, 1994 *Prophecy Update* lecture (tape #CC262), April 9, 1994.

118. "Foreign Police, Why?," *Free American*, September 1995, 15.

119. Peter Maas, "The Menace of China White," *Parade Magazine*, September 18, 1994, 4.

120. Maas, 6.

121. FBI Director Louis Freeh clarified this during a 1994 interview with *Parade Magazine*: "Our first need is to have people who have command of the language, and we don't have that yet." Freeh subsequently asked for changes in the law to allow for the use of personnel who "know the language and the culture." This is why Attorney General Janet Reno approved recruitment of Hong Kong and Taiwanese police into federal law enforcement agencies. (Maas, 6.)

122. Tim Callahan, "The End of the World & the New World Order, *Skeptic*, vol. 4(3), 1996, 45.

123. Chuck Missler, "Constitution a Crime?," 3.

124. Declassified version of PDD #25. This document clearly states that although U. S. forces may *temporarily* be under the "operational control" of a competent U. N. commander, U. S. commanders will continue to report separately to higher *U. S. military authorities* while taking part in U. N. operations. U. S. commanders are specifically authorized to do so if any U. N. commander issues orders that are "illegal under U. S. or international law, or are outside the mandate of the mission."

125. Missler, 1994 *Prophecy Update* lecture.

126. Doyle McManus, "Nuclear Dominoes: The Perils of Proliferation," *Los Angeles Times*, May 8, 1994, A1.

127. Doyle McManus, "Unwanted Russian Warheads a Prize Waiting to Fall Into Wrong Hands," *Los Angeles Times*, May 8, 1994, A14.

128. McManus, A14.

129. Chuck Missler, *Return of the Nephilim* cassette-tape series (Coeur d'Alene, ID: Koinonia House, 1997); cf. Chuck Missler, "The Return of the Nephilim?, *Personal Update*, September 1997, 6.

130. Missler, *Return of the Nephilim*; cf. Chuck Missler, interview with James Whalen (United Kingdom Radio), April 24, 1997, Internet real audio available at http://www.khouse.org.

131. Chuck Missler, *The Missler Report* radio talk show, July 2, 1997, Internet real audio at http://www.khouse.org.

132. Missler, *The Missler Report*.

133. C. F. Keil and F. Delitzsch, *Commentary on the Old Testament*, 10 vols. (Peabody, MA: Hendrickson, 1996), 1:81.

134. Geoffrey W. Bromiley gen. ed., *The International Standard Bible Encyclopedia*, vol. 3, 1989 edition (Grand Rapids: William B. Eerdmans, 1979), 519.

135. R. C. Sproul, for example, one of the most widely respected conservative theologians of recent times, rejects the "Sons of God = angels" view. The late Dr. Walter Martin, another conservative theologian who was best known for his landmark work in the area of cultic studies (*The Kingdom of the Cults* [Minneapolis: Bethany House, 1965; 1985 edition]), also rejected the "Sons of God = angels" interpretation of Genesis 6.

136. Chuck Missler, "Peace and Safety," *Personal Update*, October 1993, 6.

137. Chuck Missler, "Romanov Eagle Returns," *Personal Update*, January 1994, 4.

138. Missler, *Return of the Nephilim*. A real audio sound clip of Missler making this statement is available on the Internet at http://village.ios.com/~dougg/calvary/calvary.htm.

139. Don McAlvany, *Financial & Spiritual Preparation for the '90s* lecture, Christian Conference (Vail, Colorado), August 11, 1994.

140. Don McAlvany, "The Fourth Reich: Toward An American Police State," *McAlvany Intelligence Advisor*, January 1993, reprinted in NEXUS *New Times Magazine*, vol. 2 no. 13.

141. Don McAlvany, "The Waco Massacre: "A Case Study on the Emerging American Police State," *McAlvany Intelligence Advisor*, July 1993, 21.

142. Don McAlvany, "America At the Crossroads: Freedom or Slavery?," *McAlvany Intelligence Advisor*, August 1994, 7; "The Waco," 13, 16; and Don McAlvany, "Greater Self-Sufficiency for Troubled Times: Getting Out of Harms Way," *McAlvany Intelligence Advisor*, September, 1993, 10.

143. Don McAlvany, "Greater Self-Sufficiency," 10.

144. Don McAlvany, "POLICE STATE BRIEFS," *McAlvany Intelligence Advisor*, July 1995, 17.

145. Jennifer Chapman, author's December 27, 1995 interview with Chapman.

146. McAlvany, "The Waco," 21.

147. McAlvany, "The Waco," 19.

148. Bruce Perry, quoted in Gordon Witkin, "Raking Up the Ashes," *U.S. News & World Report*, July 24, 1995, 32.

149. Sophfronia Scott Gregory, "Children of a Lesser God," Time, May 17, 1993, 54; J. Michael Kennedy, "Doctors Get A Clearer Picture of How Cult Children Lived," Los Angeles Times, May 5, 1993, A24; Ginny Carol, "Children of the Cult," Newsweek, May 17, 1993, 48–50; "Texas Still Monitoring 12 Branch Davidian Kids," Orange County Register, September 28, 1993, 7; "Cult Children Tell of Abuse in Compound," Los Angeles Times, May 4, 1993, A16; Mark Potok, "Cult Kids' Story of Horror," The Sacramento Bee, May 5, 1993, A8. The following examples of abuse came directly from testimony given by children released from the Branch Davidian compound:

- The children described urinating and defecating in pots they were made to empty daily.
- Food was withheld from them for sometimes as long as a full day as punishment.

- Only Koresh could be called father. Children were made to call their biological parents dogs.
- From a very early age, girls were groomed for becoming Koresh's mate. Once a girl had been made "ready," she received a little plastic Star of David.
- For infractions as minor as spilling milk, children were beaten with "the helper," an instrument variously described as the broken paddle end of an oar or a rice stirrer. Several young girls had circular lesions on their buttocks, presumably from "the helper."
- Koresh's sermons, which children were allowed to hear, included graphic descriptions of sexual acts.

150. Lonnie Little, a Michigan man whose thirty-two-year-old son died in the Davidian fire, saw a child being beaten with a stick for fifteen minutes nonstop in 1990 (Carol, 49). In a signed affidavit, former Davidian Michelle Tom states that she watched Koresh beat her eight-month-old daughter "for forty minutes because she did not sit on his lap." Michelle Tom, signed affidavit, n.d., on file with this author. Debbie Bunds, another former Davidian who is now a conservative born-again Christian, witnessed this beating: "He [Koresh] took the baby . . . and pulled down her diaper and started beating her with a wooden spoon. He beat that baby for forty minutes. He kept saying, "I'm not going to stop 'till you stop cryin.' . . . I mean he put his hand way up in the air and he came down as hard as he could. . . . You try to imagine enduring that for forty minutes." Debbie Bunds, author's June 10, 1993 interview with Bunds.

151. "Welfare Worker Says She Was Warned Off Koresh Investigation," *Orange County Register*, October 11, 1993, 18.

152. Don McAlvany, "Terminating the U.S. Constitution: The Conference of States," *McAlvany Intelligence Advisor*, April 1995, 3, 23, 27; cf. McAlvany, "The Waco," 21, 28.

153. Don McAlvany, "Political Briefs," *McAlvany Intelligence Advisor*, February 1995, 19. The statement by Newt Gingrich to which McAlvany responded is as follows: "I'm for limited government, but a very strong limited government."

154. McAlvany, "Terminating," 3.

155. McAlvany, *Steeling the Mind of America Conference* lecture, Internet real audio edition at audio available at http://www.khouse.org.

156. Don McAlvany, "Reflections on America on a Quiet Summer Day," *McAlvany Intelligence Advisor*, July, 1995, 20; cf. Don McAlvany, "America At the Crossroads," 28.

157. Don McAlvany, "Conclusion and Recommendation," *McAlvany Intelligence Advisor*, August 1993, 19.

158. McAlvany, "Conclusion and Recommendation," 11.

159. McAlvany, "Conclusion and Recommendation," 12.

160. Persons interested in learning more about the coming horrors of the New World Order can get McAlvany's monthly newsletter for an annual subscription rate of $115.

161. Don McAlvany, "Toward A Soviet America: Strangling Americans' Freedom and Constitution," *McAlvany Intelligence Advisor*, March 1994, 26.

162. Don McAlvany, "Toward Medical Self-Sufficiency: Understanding Alternate Medicine," *McAlvany Intelligence Advisor*, August 1995, 28.

163. Don McAlvany, cited in Chuck Missler, "Vail Conference," *Personal Update*, October 1993, 8.

164. Missler, "Vail Conference," 7.

165. Don McAlvany, "Precious Metals in Uncertain Times: The Lull Before the Store," *McAlvany Intelligence Advisor*, September 1995, 13.

166. Rex Turner (ICA), author's February 14, 1995 interview with Turner.

167. Texe Marrs, flyer advertisement for *Circle of Intrigue*, n.d.

168. Texe Marrs, "Dark Majesty: Unmasking the Secret Brotherhood," *Flashpoint*, Special Edition, n.d., 1.

169. Texe Marrs, "Devil Companies, Devil Products, Devil Logos?," *Flashpoint*, December 1997, 1–2.

170. Marrs, "Devil Companies," 1–2.

171. Texe Marrs, "The Cult of Diana," *Flashpoint*, November 1997, 2.

172. Marrs, "The Cult," 3.

173. Texe Marrs, mass mailing appeal letter, n.d., 1.

174. Texe Marrs, "Campaign '92," *Flashpoint*, Special Edition, n.d., 3.

175. Texe Marrs, *Report from Iron Mountain* audiotape (Texe Marrs Ministries, 1995).

176. Texe Marrs, mass mailing appeal letter, c. 1995.

177. Marrs, "Dark Majesty," 1; Texe Marrs, "The Masonic Plan for America," *Flashpoint*, January 1995, 1–2; Texe Marrs, "The Treaty From Hell," *Flashpoint*, May 1995, 2; Texe Marrs, "The Pope Over Jerusalem," *Flashpoint*, May 1995, 5; Texe Marrs, "All Fall Down: The Plot to Crown the Pope the Prince of Peace," flyer advertisement for *All Fall Down*, n.d.; Texe Marrs, "The United Nations Plot," *Flashpoint*, September 1993, 4; Texe Marrs, "Foreign Occupation Troops in America," *Flashpoint*, December 1994, 3; Texe Marrs, "Are Christian Leaders Anti-Semitic, Neo-Nazi Bigots?," *Flashpoint*, September 1994, 1–2; Texe Marrs, "Pope Meets With ADL Henchmen," *Flashpoint*, April 1995, 1–2.

178. Texe Marrs, "What's Ahead for 1996–1999," *Flashpoint*, February 1996, 6.

179. Texe Marrs, "New Videos Document Power of Bible Prophecy," advertisement flyer, n.d. Marrs also promotes the standard stories about black helicopters (see Richard Abanes, *American Militias: Rebellion, Racism, and Religion* [InterVarsity Press, 1996]). He offers Jim Keith's book *Black Helicopters Over America*, and has had Keith as a guest on his World of Prophecy radio program (see *Flashpoint*, May 1995, 4, 5).

180. Texe Marrs, "Concentration Camps in America," *Flashpoint*, September 1994, 5.

181. Texe Marrs, "A Slime Pit of Sexual Depravity," *Flashpoint*, January 1994, 1.

182. Texe Marrs, "Who Slaughtered the Innocents in Oklahoma City," flyer advertisement for *Fascist Terror Stalking America*, n.d.

183. Texe Marrs, "Illuminata: The Secret New Age Occultism of Bill and Hillary Clinton," *Flashpoint*, April 1995, 5.

184. Texe Marrs, "A Slime Pit," 1.

185. Jack McLamb, *Operation Vampire Killer 2000* (Phoenix: PATNWO, 1992), 38.

186. Pete Peters, "Book Review: Big Sister is Watching You," *Scriptures for America Newsletter*, vol. 4, 1994, 8.

187. Peters, 8.

188. Texe Marrs, advertisement flyer for *ChequeMate: The Game of Princes*, n.d.

189. Jeffrey Baker, *ChequeMate: The Game of Princes* (Springdale, PA: Whitaker House, 1993), 47–53, 62, 69, 70, 79, 134, 141-142, 150–151, 154, 157–164, 243.

190. Abanes, 133–143.

191. Texe Marrs, "Night Cometh!" in *Storming Toward Armageddon: Essays in Apocalypse*, William T. James, ed. (Green Forest, AR: New Leaf Press, 1992), 130.

192. Jack Van Impe, *A. D. 2000 . . . The End?* videotape (Troy, MI: Jack Van Impe Ministries, 1990).

193. *The Mark of the Beast* videotape advertisement, *CBA Marketplace*, September 1997, 17; Jack Van Impe Ministries advertisement, *Charisma*, June 1997, 87.

194. Van Impe, *A.D. 2000 . . . The End?* videotape (Troy, MI: Jack Van Impe Ministries, 1990).

195. Jack Van Impe, "Messiah 1975? The Tribulation 1976?," *The Jack Van Impe Crusade Newsletter*, April 1975, 1, quoted in DeMar, *Last Days Madness*, 99.

196. Jack Van Impe, quoted in Chandler, 254.

197. Steve Rabey, "Warning: The End is Near, Again," *Gazette Telegraph*, December 28, 1991, D1; cf. Oropeza, 89.

198. Oropeza, 89.

199. Van Impe, *A.D. 2000*.

200. Jack Van Impe, quoted in Chandler, 254.

201. *2001: Countdown to Eternity* advertisement, *Bookstore Journal*, July 1995, 40; Van Impe, *2001: On the Edge of Eternity* (Dallas: Word, 1996), 16.

202. Jack Van Impe, *Jack Van Impe Presents* television program (Trinity Broadcasting Network), July 2, 1997.

203. Van Impe, *Jack Van Impe Presents*.

204. Dave Helms, "Massive Plot?: Some Truth, Wild Theories," *Mobile (Alabama) Press Register*, 1A.

205. "News Briefs & National Shorts," *Patriot Report*, October 1994, 7.

206. Helms, 4A.

207. Helms, 4A.

208. Jack Van Impe, quoted in Helms, 4A.

209. Craig B. Hulet, "All the News That's Fit to Invent," *Soldier of Fortune*, August 1995, 61; cf. Helms, 1A, 4A.

210. Hulet, 61.

211. Helms, 4A.

212. David and Michele, letter to the Christian Research Institute, December 7, 1992, quoted in Oropeza, 32–33.

213. Jack Van Impe, *Jack Van Impe Presents* television program (Trinity Broadcasting network), November 1, 1995.

214. In direct conflict with the biblical mandate for Christians to separate from strange and demonic doctrines (1 Tim. 1:3; 4:1), conservatives have allied themselves with racists and white supremacists. They have also disregarded biblical command for believers to be "subject to rulers, to authorities" (Titus 3:1) and to "honor the king" (1 Pet. 2:17). Moreover, Paul the apostle instructed Christians to not be bound together with unbelievers: "What partnership has righteousness with lawlessness? What fellowship has light with darkness? What harmony has Christ with Belial" (2 Cor. 6:14-15). Clearly, followers of Jesus must stand against anyone who promotes an unbiblical ideology, especially when that ideology advocates hatred and violence toward God's chosen people according to the flesh (i.e., the Jews, see Rom. 9:4-5), toward other races created in God's image (Gen. 1:26-27; Acts 17:26), and toward governmental authority, which God Himself has established and commanded us to obey (Rom. 13:1-7). Those who ignore these admonitions live under the threat of divine judgment. The prophet Samuel warned, "Rebellion is as the sin of witchcraft and insubordination is as iniquity and idolatry" (1 Sam. 15:23).

215. For an explanation of Trochmann's ties to the Aryan Nations, see Abanes, 178–180.

216. "CONFAB Draws National Coverage," *Spotlight*, September 18, 1995, 12.

217. *Demons: True Life Evil Forces* (His Majesty's Media, 1995).

218. Pete Peters, "Concerning our Television Debut," *Scriptures for America Newsletter*, vol. 4, 1993, 5.

219. Skipp Porteous, "Anti-Semitism: Its Prevalence Within the Christian Right," *Freedom Writer*, May 1994, Internet edition posted at http://www.berkshire.net/~ifas/fw/9405/antisemitism.html.

220. Prior to getting his own program on KIN, Peters was a guest on the network's very popular show *Keystone on the Line* (October 19, 1993). This broadcast reached the entire American continent, as well as Hawaii and the Virgin Islands. Host Jerry Jacobs used the program to praise and recommend Peters' book *America the Conquered*. According to Peters, this one show brought new responses from forty states. Peters, "Concerning our Television Debut," 5, see note 219 above.

221. Beverly LaHaye, quoted in endorsements flyer, received from Gary Kah Ministries, 1.

222. Gary Kah, *En Route to Global Occupation* (Lafayette, LA: Huntington House, 1991), 25, 26,61, 62,100,102,104,108,109,117.

223. Kah, 117.

224. Leonard Dinnerstein, *Antisemitism in America* (New York: Oxford University Press, 1994), 112.

225. John George and Laird Wilcox, *Nazis, Communists, Klansmen, and Others on the Fringe* (Buffalo: Prometheus Books, 1992), 206.

226. Anti-Defamation League, *Extremism on the Right* (New York: Anti-Defamation League, 1988), 175.

227. Chuck Smith, quoted in endorsements flyer, received from Gary Kah Ministries, 1.

228. Wendy Wallace, "The Four Horsemen of the Apocalypse," *Paranoia*, Spring 1995, 24.

229. Craig B. Hulet, "Patriots or Paranoids?," *Soldier of Fortune*, August, 1995, 85.

CHAPTER 5

1. Richard Cavendish, editor-in-chief, *Man, Myth & Magic*, vol. 6 (New York: Marshall Cavendish, 1995), 754.

2. Yuri Rubinsky and Ian Wiseman, *A History of the End of the World* (New York: Quill, 1982), 24–29.

3. Eva Shaw, *Eve of Destruction* (Chicago: Contemporary Books, 1995), xiii–xiv.

4. Felix Guirand gen. ed., *New Larousse Encyclopedia of Mythology*, 1973 edition (London: Hamlyn Publishing Group, 1959), 62–63, first published in France by Augé, Gillon, Hollier-Larousse, Moreau et Cie, the Librairie Larousse, Paris, transl., Richard Aldington and Delano Ames; cf. Shaw, 3. The main text from which the *Epic of Gilgamesh* is derived comes from the Library of Ashurbanipal of Ninevah and dates from the seventh century B.C.

5. Charles Berlitz, *Doomsday 1999 A.D.* (New York: Doubleday, 1981), 150–169.

6. Paul Edwards editor-in-chief, *The Encyclopedia of Philosophy*, vol. 8, four volume combined set edition (New York: MacMillan, 1967), 21.

7. Rubinsky and Wiseman, 25.

8. Cavendish, 756.

9. "From the very beginning the earth seemed close to its end. When Zeus made war on his father, Cronos, there was a great battle of rocks and thunderbolts. The earth shook and the oceans boiled; wild winds fanned fires that leveled the forests. When the dust and ash settled, Zeus had won and Cronos was banished to the underworld. As an aftereffect of this war, Atlas was doomed to carry the heavens on his shoulders so they would not fall and crush the earth. . . . In another myth, the gods came close to terminating the world by fire. . . . [Apollo] unwisely allowed his son to drive the chariot of the sun one day, and the horses, unaccustomed to the lighter load, spooked and bolted. First they swung too high, scorching the stars, and then too low, passing

between the earth and the moon, igniting the clouds and the mountains. The earth caught on fire. The desert of Libya dried to the condition in which it exists today, and the Ethiopians became black for the first time. Zeus, realizing all was lost unless he took swift action, hurled a thunderbolt and killed the boy, setting the chariot back on its usual path. Once again the world didn't end." Rubinsky and Wiseman, 24.

10.   Shaw, 4.

11.   The term *ragna rök*, often written as Ragnarok, is usually translated to mean "Twilight of the Gods" due to the alternate spelling *ragna rökkr*, which appears in some ancient Norse manuscripts. The main source of this end-time vision is the Teutonic poem *Völuspá*.

12.   The *ragna rök* myth is as follows: "The terror begins with the coming of the Great Winter, which lasts three years on end with no summer to break it, and with much wickedness among men, the breaking of oaths, murders among kindred, incest, and bitter warfare. Then come great earthquakes, when rocks are shattered and mountains crumble, as the monsters and hostile giants, imagined to dwell deep in the depths of the earth, begin to work their will . . . ." "The earth itself was beginning to lose its shape. Already the stars were coming adrift from the sky and falling into the gaping void. . . . The giant [named] Surt set the entire earth on fire; the universe was no longer more than an immense furnace. Flames spurted from fissures in the rocks; everywhere there was the hissing of steam. All living things, all plant life, were blotted out. Only the naked soil remained, but like the sky itself the earth was no more than cracks and crevasses. And now all the rivers, all the seas rose and overflowed. From every side waves lashed against waves. They swelled and boiled and slowly covered all things. The earth sank beneath the sea, and the vast field of battle where the lords of the universe had faced each other was no longer visible. All was finished." Cavendish, vol. 16, 2292; Guirand, 276.

13.   Guirand, 276–277.

14.   Rubinsky and Wiseman, 26.

15.   Rubinsky and Wiseman, 26.

16.   Rubinsky and Wiseman, 26.

17.   Rubinsky and Wiseman, 27.

18.   Mircea Eliade editor-in-chief, *The Encyclopedia of Religion*, vol. 5, 8 volume set edition(New York: MacMillan, 1987), 150–151.

19.   Tim Dowley organizing editor, *Eerdmans' Handbook to the History of Christianity* (Grand Rapids: Eerdmans, 1977), 65.

20.   The historian Tacitus, in reference to Nero's persecution, wrote the following: "[T]hose who confessed themselves Christians were arrested; next, on their disclosures, a vast multitude were convicted . . . . And their death was made a matter of sport: they were covered in wild beasts' skins and torn to pieces by dogs; or were fastened to crosses and set on fire in order to serve as torches by night when daylight failed. Nero had offered his gardens for the spectacle and gave an exhibition in his circus, mingling with the crowd in the guise of a charioteer or mounted on his chariot. Hence, in spite of a guilt which had earned the most exemplary punishment, there arose a feeling of pity, because it was felt that they were being sacrificed not for the common good but to gratify the savagery of one man." Dowley, 72.

21.   F. F. Bruce, *The Spreading Flame* (Grand Rapids: Eerdmans Publishing Co., 1958; 1995 edition), 178.

22.   Bruce, 218.

23.   Montanus, quoted in K. Aland, "Bemerkungen zum Montanismus und zur frühchristlichen Eschatologie," in *Kirchengeschichtliche Entwürfe* (Germany: Gütersloh,

1960), 105–148, cited in David E. Aune, *Prophecy in Early Christianity and the Ancient Mediterranean World* (Grand Rapids: Eerdmans Publishing Co., 1983), 314.

24.   An anonymous source quoted by Eusebius (d. 341/342), Bishop of Caesarea, describes the beginning of the movement: "[Montanus] in the unbounded lust of his soul for leadership gave access to himself to the adversary [Satan], became obsessed and suddenly fell into frenzy and convulsions. He began to be ecstatic and to speak and to talk strangely, prophesying contrary to the custom which belong to the tradition and succession of the church from the beginning. . . . [H]e raised up two more women and filled them with the bastard spirit so that they spoke madly and improperly and strangely, like Montanus. The [evil] spirit gave blessings to those who rejoiced and were proud in him, and puffed them up by the greatness of its promises." Eusebius, *Historia Ecclesiastica*, 16:6–9, quoted in Aune, 313.

25.   Priscilla, quoted in Aune, 315.

26.   Daniel Cohen, *Waiting for the Apocalypse* (Buffalo, NY: Prometheus Books, 1983), 49.

27.   Cohen, 49.

28.   Philip Schaff, *History of the Church*, vol. 2, "Nicene and Post-Nicene Christianity" (Grand Rapids: William B. Eerdmans, 1950 edition), 417.

29.   Schaff, 419, 424, 426.

30.   Rubinsky and Wiseman, 55.

31.   Maximilla, quoted in Aune, 315.

32.   Montanism's two female leaders received especially harsh condemnation. Consider this comment by Hippolytus, writing in A.D. 215: "[Montanists] have been deceived by two females, Priscilla and Maximilla by name, whom they hold to be prophetesses . . . . They magnify these females above the Apostles and every gift of grace, so that some of them go so far as to say that there is in them something more than Christ." Hippolytus, quoted in Rubinsky and Wiseman, 55.

33.   Montanus, quoted in Aune, 314.

34.   David Christie-Murray, *A History of Heresies* (New York: Oxford University Press, 1976), 35.

35.   Robert G. Clouse, "The Danger of Mistaken Hopes," in *A Guide to Biblical Prophecy*, Carl E. Armerding and W. Ward Gasque, eds., (Peabody, MA: Hendrickson, 1989), 29.

36.   Maximilla, quoted in Dowley, 74.

37.   Maximilla, quoted in J. D. Douglas general editor, 1978 revised edition, *The New International Dictionary of the Christian Church* (Grand Rapids: Zondervan, 1974), 644.

38.   Christie-Murray, 36.

39.   Will Durant, *The Story of Civilization*, vol. 3, "Ceasar and Christ" (New York: Simon & Schuster, 1944), 666.

40.   Durant, 668–669.

41.   Will Durant, *The Story of Civilization*, vol. 4, "The Age of Faith" (New York: Simon & Schuster, 1944), 36.

42.   Durant, vol. 4, 42.

43.   The term "Dark Ages," which many scholars avoid using in favor of the more accurate "Middle Ages," usually applies to the six centuries leading up to the year 1100. It represents the period when the Roman Empire was divided into four main nations: the Romanic/Latin (in Southern Europe, consisting of Italians, Spaniards, Portuguese, French), Celtic (consisting of the Gauls, Britons, Picts, Scots, Welsh, and Irish) Teutonic/Germanic (Germans, Swiss, Dutch, Scandinavian, Russian), and Slavs (includes the Bulgarians, Czechs, Moravians, Slovaks, Serbs, Croats, and Poles).

44. Gregory of Tours, *Historiae* 10:25, transl. by L. Thorpe, *History of the Franks*, 584–86; cf. Richard Landes, "On Owls, Roosters, and Apocalyptic Time: A Historical Method for Reading a Refractory Documentation," *Union Seminary Quarterly Review* (1996), 49:165–185, Internet edition at http://www.mille.org/landes-rob.htm.

45. Norman Cohn, *The Pursuit of the Millennium* (New York: Oxford University Press, 1961; 1980 edition), 41.

46. Cohn, 41.

47. Cohn, 41.

48. Cohn, 42.

49. *Passion of Leodeger* 1.15 in MGH. script. rer. Meroving. 5:296, quoted in Bernard McGinn, *Antichrist* (San Francisco: Harper San Francisco, 1994), 84.

50. McGinn, 85. Citing Beatus, *Commentary on the Apocalypse* 4; cf. Richard Landes, "Lest the Millennium Be Fulfilled: Apocalyptic Expectations and the Pattern of Western Chronography 100–800 C.E.," in Werner Verbeke, Daniel Verhelst, and Andries Welkenhuysen, eds., *Use and Abuse of Eschatology in the Middle Ages* (Leuven, Belgium: Leuven University Press, 1988), 193–194. Beatus began his three-part commentary in 776. He wrote part two in 784 and part three in 786.

51. Douglas, 114 and McGinn, 85; cf. John Williams, "Purpose and Imagery in the Apocalypse Commentary of Beatus of Liébana," in *The Apocalypse in the Middle Ages*, Richard K. Emmerson and Bernard McGinn, eds. (Ithaca, NY: Cornell University Press, 1992), 217–233.

52. *Letters of the Bishops of Spain to the Bishops of Gaul* 5 in *Corpus Scriptorum Muzarabicorum*, Ioannes Gil, ed. (Madrid: Instituto "Antonio de Nebrija," 1973), 92, quoted in McGinn, 85.

53. McGinn, 304 (see McGinn's endnote #25).

54. Rudolf of Fulda, *Annales Fuldenses*, ad. an. 847, MGH SS 1.365, transl. by Timothy Reuter, *The Annales of Fulda* (New York: Manchester University Press, 1992), 26–27; cf. Richard Landes, "While God Tarried: Disappointed Millennialism and the Making of the Modern West," *Deolog* (1997), 4:1, 6–9, 22–27, 41, 45, Internet edition at http://www.mille.org/wgt-prec.html.

55. McGinn, 85.

56. McGinn, 86.

57. Eulogius, *Memorial of the Saints* II.1.2 (PL 115:766), quoted in McGinn, 86.

58. McGinn, 87.

59. McGinn, 87.

60. Durant, vol. 4, 444.

61. Charles Mackay, *Extraordinary Popular Delusions and the Madness of Crowds* (London: Richard Bentley, 1841; 1980 reprint by Harmony Books of New York), 257–258.

62. Peter N. Stearns, *Millennium III, Century XXI* (New York: Westview Press, 1996), 25–26; cf. Cohen, 51–52.

63. Stearns, 29.

64. Stearns, 26.

65. Stearns, 26–27.

66. These examples of year 1000-related comments are listed in Richard Landes, "The Apocalyptic Dossier: 967–1033," Internet article at http://www.mille.org/1000-dos.htm. The text translation of Abbo's reference to the Antichrist can be found in McGinn, 310.

67. Landes, "On Owls."

68. Richard Landes, "While God Tarried."

69. Landes, "On Owls" and Johannes Fried, "Endzeiterwartung um die Jahrtausend-wende," *Deutsches Archiv für Erforschung des Mittelalters*, 45:2 (1989), 385–473; cf. Richard Landes, *Relics, Apocalypse and the Deceits of History: Ademar of Chabannes, 989–1034* (Cambridge, MA: Harvard University Press, 1995), especially chaps. 14–15.

70. Landes, "The Apocalyptic Dossier."

71. The 1033 pilgrimage was described in *Five Books of Histories* (completed in 1044), written by Radulphus Glaber, a Burgundian monk who witnessed the event :??[A]n innumerable multitude of people from the whole world, greater than any man before could have hoped to see, began to travel to the holy sepulcher of the Savior in Jerusalem. Many did not want to return at all, and prayed on the Mount of Olives for Christ to take them up. First the order of the inferior plebs then those of middling estate, and after these, the great men, that is kings, counts, marchlords and bishops, and eventually, and this was unheard of before, many women, noble and poor, undertook the journey. Many wished to die there before they returned to their own lands . . . [indeed] a certain Burgundian called Lethbaud went to the Mount of Olives whence the Savior ascended into heaven with the promise that he would return to judge both the quick and the dead. There [he prayed for Christ to take him up into heaven]" (Radulphus Glaber, quoted in Landes, "On Owls").

72. Landes, "While God Tarried."

73. Landes, "While God Tarried."

74. Landes, "While God Tarried."

75. Landes, "While God Tarried."

76. Pope Innocent III, quoted in Robert S. Wistrich, *Antisemitism: The Longest Hatred* (New York: Schocken Books, 1991), 25.

77. Wistrich, 25–26.

78. John George and Laird Wilcox, *Nazis, Communists, Klansmen, and Others on the Fringe* (Buffalo, NY: Prometheus Books, 1992), 442.

79. Leonard Dinnerstein, *Anti-Semitism in America* (New York: Oxford University Press, 1994), xxiii; Cf. Douglas, 50.

80. The most famous blood accusation occurred in England following the death in 1255 of a child, Hugh of Lincoln: "After a woman found the body of her eight-year-old child in a well a Jew who lived nearby was arrested and tortured into confessing his culpability. On the basis of this 'confession,' he and ninety-two other Jews were imprisoned and had their possessions confiscated. Eighteen of them were hanged. Throughout the village of Lincoln people first whispered that Hugh had been tortured and crucified but as the story passed from one lip to another it was further embellished. The boy had supposedly been stolen away, his body fattened on white bread and milk for ten days, and then slaughtered so that his blood could by used by Jews for ritual purposes. The alleged crime had occurred near Passover and Easter, and over the years rumor had it either that during Passover week the Jews crucified Christian children to reenact the execution of Jesus, or that the child was killed so that Jews might use his blood in the food for their Passover service." Dinnerstein, xxiii.

81. Wistrich, 24.

82. Rubinsky and Wiseman, 77.

83. McGinn, 115.

84. Douglas, 536.

85. Rubinsky and Wiseman, 77.

86. Rubinsky and Wiseman, 77.

87. One of Joachim's visions is described as follows: "[A] stream of brilliant light was all at once poured into his soul, and a divine revelation made all the mysteries of the Scriptures as clear to him as they had been to the Biblical prophets themselves. The contents of the Apocalypse were laid open to him, and the harmony of the Old Testament with the New, so difficult for theologians, became an open book to him." Henry James Forman, *The Story of Prophecy* (New York: Farrar & Rinehart, Inc., 1936), 109.

88. The Franciscan order — founded by St. Francis of Assisi — was perhaps the most famous religious group to lay claim to Joachim's prophecy. After the death of St. Francis, his monks fell into the Church's disfavor. They in turn began to see themselves as the persecuted order of whom Joachim had prophesied. Perhaps the most prominent of these Spiritual Franciscans, as they were called, was Peter John Olivi (1248–1298). He predicted that the end of Joachim' second epoch, and the beginning of the third era of peace, would occur in 1300. Amerding and Gasque, 30.

89. Christie-Murray, 111. A significant number of Joachim's followers ended up accusing Pope John XXII (1316-1334) of being the Antichrist, or at the very least, the forerunner of the Antichrist.

90. Cohn, 109.

91. Rubinsky and Wiseman, 82.

92. Cohn, 128.

93. Cohn 129.

94. For an in-depth treatment of the flagellants, see Cohn's *The Pursuit of the Millennium*, chapter seven. Consider the following excerpt: "The flagellants proceeded in bands varying in size from fifty to 500 or more. . . . [T]hey wore a uniform; in this case a white robe with a red cross before and behind and a hat or hood similarly marked. Each band of flagellants was commanded by a leader . . . . This 'Master' or 'Father,' as he was called, heard the confessions of the members and — as the clergy noted with horror — imposed penances and granted absolution, both during the public flagellations and in private. Each member had to swear absolute obedience to his Master for the duration of the procession [thirty-three and a half days]. . . . During that period the flagellants were subject to a rigorous discipline. They were not allowed to bathe or shave or change their clothes or sleep in soft beds. If they were offered hospitality they could wash their hands only when kneeling on the floor as a token of humility. They were not allowed to speak to one another without the Master's permission. Above all they were forbidden to have any dealings with women. They had to avoid their wives; in the houses where they lodged they could not be served at table by women. If a flagellant spoke a single word to a woman he had to kneel down before the Master, who would beat him, saying: 'Arise by the honour of pure martyrdom, and henceforth guard yourself against sin!' When they came to a town the flagellants would make their way to a church, form a circle in front of it, take off their clothes and shoes and put on a sort of skirt reaching from the waist to the feet. . . . . The penitents marched round in a circle and one by one threw themselves on their faces and lay motionless, with outstretched arms, in the form of a crucifix. Those behind stepped over the prostrate body, striking it gently with their scourges as they passed. . . . When the last man had lain down all rose to their feet and the flagellation began. The men beat themselves rhythmically with leather scourges armed with iron spikes, singing hymns . . . . At certain passages — three times in each hymn — all would fall down 'as though struck by lightning' and lie with outstretched arms, sobbing and praying. . . . The Master walked amongst them, bidding them pray to God to have mercy on all sinners. After a while the men stood up, lifted their arms

towards heaven and sang; then they recommenced their flagellation. If by any chance a woman or a priest entered the circle the whole flagellation became invalid and had to be repeated from the beginning. Each day two complete flagellations were performed in public; and each night a third was performed in the privacy of the bedroom. The flagellants did their work with such thoroughness that often the spikes of the scourge stuck in the flesh and had to be wrenched out. Their blood spurted on to the walls and their bodies turned to swollen masses of blue flesh." Cohn, 132–134.

95.   Cohn, 135.
96.   Cohn, 135.
97.   Douglas, 379.
98.   Douglas, 379.
99.   Cohn notes the following episode: "When in July 1349 flagellants entered Frankfurt, they rushed straight to the Jewish quarter, where the townsfolk joined them in exterminating the entire community. . . . A month later massacres took place simultaneously at Mainz and at Cologne. During a flagellant ceremony at Mainz the crowd of spectators suddenly ran amok and fell upon Jews, with the result that the largest community in Germany was annihilated. . . . At Brussels too it was the approach of the flagellants, coupled with the rumour of well-poisoning, that launched the massacre in which the whole community of 600 Jews was killed. . . . Through large areas of the Low Countries the flagellants, aided by the masses of the poor, burnt and drowned all the Jews they could find, 'because they thought to please God in that way.' " Cohn, 139.
100. *Rituals of the World: Rites of Pain*, The Learning Channel (TLC), August 8, 1997.
101. Schaff, vol. 6, 100–101.
102. McGinn, 173.
103. Rubinsky and Wiseman, 88.
104. McGinn, 183.
105. Dowley, 330.
106. Rubinsky and Wiseman, 88.
107. Rubinsky and Wiseman, 88.
108. Douglas, 836.
109. See Christie-Murray's *A History of Heresies*.
110. Selling indulgences was a common practice that started with the First Crusade, when Pope Urban II promised that those who joined the battle would immediately have all their sins forgiven. Later, the concept was extended to those who simply gave financial support to the crusades or the church. Tetzel's deeds were especially offensive to Luther because the Roman Catholic representative had sold forgiveness to citizens in Luther's home town. Luther responded with his set of theses, which in turn sparked the Protestant Reformation.
111. For examples, see McGinn, 187–218.
112. McGinn, 214.
113. Thomas Müntzer, quoted in Cohn, 237.
114. Cohn, 238.
115. Thomas Müntzer, quoted in Cohn, 239.
116. Cohn, 245.
117. Cohn, 250.
118. McGinn, 215.
119. McGinn, 215.
120. McGinn, 215.
121. McGinn, 216.

122. Rubinsky and Wiseman, 90.

123. B. J. Oropeza, *99 Reasons Why No One Knows When Christ Will Return* (Downers Grover: InterVarsity Press, 1994), 13.

CHAPTER 6

1. Nostradamus, Century 10, Quatrain 72, quoted in Erika Cheetham, *The Final Prophecies of Nostradamus* (New York: Perigree Books, 1989), 424.

2. John Mosley, "The Millennium Is Coming!," *Skeptic*, vol. 4(4), 1996, 47; cf. Bill Girdner, "Dispelling the Myths of Ignorance," *Boston Globe*, May 10, 1988, 2. The Warner Brothers film *The Man Who Saw Tomorrow* is still available on videotape from libraries and video rental stores.

3. Mosley, 47 and Girdner, 2.

4. Peggy Brutsche, quoted in Mosley, 48.

5. Fritz Coleman, quoted in Mosley, 48.

6. Betty Searcy, quoted in Mosley, 48.

7. Jim Berkland, quoted in Mosley, 48.

8. Mosley, 48.

9. *Prophecies of the Millennium* (Fox Television), July 30, 1997.

10. James Randi, interview on *Larry King Live*, September 21, 1990; cf. Russell Chandler, *Doomsday* (Ann Arbor, MI: Servant, 1993), 67.

11. *Future Sight: The Year 2000 and Beyond* videotape (Dan Dalton Production, 1996).

12. James Randi, *The Mask of Nostradamus* (New York: Charles Scribner's Sons, 1990), 10–11. These facts about Nostradamus and his family are verifiable through records in the archives of Avignon and St. Rémy.

13. Randi, *The Mask*, 12.

14. Randi, *The Mask*, 12.

15. Randi, *The Mask*, 16.

16. James Randi, "Nostradamus: The Prophet for All Seasons," *The Skeptical Inquirer*, vol. 7(1), Fall 1982, 30.

17. V. J. Hewitt and Peter Lorie, *Nostradamus: The End of the Millennium* (New York: Simon & Schuster, 1991).

18. Leslie A. Shepard, *Encyclopedia of Occultism & Parapsychology*, vol. 2 (Detroit: Gale Research, 1991), 1191.

19. Randi, *The Mask*, 21. Randi notes that as of 1990, New York City police estimated that the Big Apple "only" had 8,000 fortune tellers and astrologers.

20. Randi, *The Mask*, 42.

21. Translation taken from Gordon Stein ed., *The Encyclopedia of the Paranormal* (Amherst, NY: Prometheus, 1996), 461.

22. Randi, *The Mask*, 170.

23. Henry C. Roberts, *The Complete Prophecies of Nostradamus* (Oyster Bay, NY: Nostradamus Co., 1947; 1982 edition), 20.

24. Cheetham, 59.

25. Carroll C. Calkins, *Mysteries of the Unexplained* (Pleasantville, NY: Reader's Digest Association, 1982), 17.

26. Hewitt and Lorie, 189.

27. Eva Shaw, *Eve of Destruction* (Chicago: Contemporary Books, 1995), 50.

28. Randi, *The Mask*, 174.

29. Randi, *The Mask*, 175.

30. Cheetham, 58.

31. Cheetham, 58; cf. Roberts, 20.

32. Catherine de Medicis, letter to Conétable, quoted in Randi, *The Mask*, 43.

33. Shepard, 1191.

34. In the movie *The Man Who Saw Tomorrow*, a false quatrain was presented in order to make it seem as if Nostradamus had prophesied an earthquake for Los Angeles or San Francisco. The fabricated quatrain was created by joining the first two lines from C1:Q87 with the last two lines of C10:Q67.

35. Translation taken from Stein, 461.

36. Shaw, 51 and Cheetham, 113.

37. David Wallechinsky, Amy Wallace, and Irving Wallace, *The Book of Predictions* (New York: William Morrow, 1980), 354.

38. Cheetham, 113 and Shaw, 51.

39. Randi, *The Mask*, 91.

40. Randi, "Nostradamus," 31.

41. This insightful interpretation of C2:Q51 can be found in Randi, *The Mask*, 91–192.

42. This particular English translation is taken from Erika Cheetham, 316. Although inaccurate, it is one of the translations consistently used by Nostradamites to further their erroneous views. A more accurate translation appears in Randi's *The Mask of Nostradamus*: "PAU, NAY, LORON will be more in fire than in blood. Swimming the Aude, the great one fleeing to the mountains [Randi gets "mountains" from *surrez* because there is no word *surrez* in French, suggesting that it is a derivation from *serrez*, i.e., hills/mountains]. He refuses the magpies entrance. Pamplona, the Durance River will keep them confined." Randi, *The Mask*, 207.

43. John Hogue, interview in *Ancient Prophecies I* (The Learning Channel), December 31, 1996.

44. Translation as found in Cheetham, 101. Only modern translations of this verse have the word "Hister." In the original verse penned by Nostradamus, however, the word in place of "Hister" is "Ister." Consequently, I have removed "Hister" from this translation.

45. Translation as found in Cheetham, 205. See note above.

46. Cheetham, 101.

47. Cheetham, 205.

48. Randi, *The Mask*, 214.

49. James Laver, *Nostradamus, or The Future Foretold*, quoted in Randi, *The Mask*, 215.

50. As Henry Roberts says in *The Complete Prophecies of Nostradamus*: "[C2:Q24 is a] true prediction of the fate of Adolf Hitler. His demise in the bomb shelter bunker in Berlin . . . as his 'iron cage.' "

51. Randi, "Nostradamus," 31.

52. Shaw, 53.

53. Shaw, 54.

54. David Koresh, *The Foundation* taped lecture, 1989.

55. Shaw, 46.

56. Roberts, 191.

57. Shaw, 54.

58. Roberts, 102.

59. Randi, *The Mask*, 217–218. The six different interpretations of C6:Q74 are as follows: 1) Charles II will return to the English throne; 2) the advent of communism in France, which will last three years and seventy days; 3) Nazis returning to Germany after World War II; 4) communist rule in Russia for seventy-three years; and 5) the French Revolution.

60. Hewitt and Lorie, 58, 68, 82, 86.

61.   Wallechinsky, Wallace, and Wallace, 355.

62.   John Hogue, *Nostradamus and the Millennium* (Garden City, NY: 1987), 198.

63.   Richard Lewinsohn, *Science, Prophecy, and Prediction* (New York: Bell Publishing, 1961), 85–86. Originally published in Germany as *Die Enthüllung der Zukunft* and in England as *Prophets and Predictions*.

64.   Randi, *The Mask*, 28.

65.   Justine Glass, *They Foresaw the Future* (New York: Putnam's Sons, 1969), 116–117.

66.   Randi, *The Mask*, 27.

67.   Randi, *The Mask*, 28.

CHAPTER 7

1.   William Miller, quoted in J. Gordon Melton, *Encyclopedia of American Religions* (Detroit: Gale Research, 1996), 113.

2.   Russell Chandler, *Doomsday* (Ann Arbor: Servant, 1993), 71.

3.   Daniel G. Reed, coordinating editor, *Dictionary of Christianity in America* (Downers Grove: InterVarsity Press, 1990), 639.

4.   J. D. Douglas, *The New International Dictionary of the Christian Church*, 1978 edition (Grand Rapids: Zondervan, 1974), 588.

5.   Reed, 1079.

6.   Reed, 639.

7.   Anne Devereaux Jordan, *The Seventh-day Adventists: A History* (New York: Hippocrene Books, 1988), 26.

8.   Walter A. Elwell gen. ed., *Evangelical Dictionary of Theology*, 1996 edition (Grand Rapids: Baker Books, 1984), 304.

9.   Jordan, 26; cf. C. Mervyn Maxwell, *Tell it to the World* (Mountain View, CA: Pacific Press, 1977), 11.

10.   R. M. Devens, *American Progress: or The Great Events of the Greatest Century* (Chicago: Hugh Heron, 1883), 308.

11.   Devens, 308.

12.   William Miller, quoted in Ellen G. White, *The Great Controversy*, 1927 edition (Mountain View, CA: Pacific Press Publishing, 1888), 364–365.

13.   William Miller, quoted in Ken Samples, Erwin deCastro, Richard Abanes and Robert Lyle, *Prophets of the Apocalypse* (Grand Rapids: Baker Books, 1994), 100.

14.   William Miller, quoted in Leroy Edwin Froom, *The Prophetic Faith of Our Fathers*, 4 vols. (Washington D. C.: Review & Herald Publishing Assn., 1954), 4:463; cf. Anthony Hoekema, *Seventh-day Adventists*, 1990 edition (Grand Rapids: William B. Eerdmans, 1963), 9.

15.   William Miller, quoted in Wendy Murray Zorba, "Furture Tense," *Christianity Today*, October 2, 1995, 20–21.

16.   Melton, 113.

17.   Melton, 113.

18.   According to the 1883 volume *American Progress: or The Great Events of the Greatest Century* by R. M. Devens, Miller published a series of sixteen articles in the *Vermont Telegraph* (p. 308). However, according to the 1990 *Dictionary of Christianity in America*, Miller only published eight articles in the *Vermont Telegraph* (p. 740). The discrepancy may be the result of how the editors of these two reference volumes count the various parts of the Miller's articles.

19.   Miller, quoted in Devens, 308–309.

20.   Melton, 113.

21. Melton, 113.

22. W. J. Fisher, *The Telescope* (Cambridge, MA: Bond Astronomical Club, 1934), quoted in Jordan, 30.

23. R. M. Devens, *Our First Century* (Springfield, MA: C. A. Nichols & Co., 1876), 329–330.

24. George Constable ed., *Forces of Nature* (Alexandria, VA: Time-Life Books, 1990), 44.

25. Colonel Abraham Davenport, quoted in Constable, 44.

26. Jordan, 31.

27. Emma Howell Cooper, *The Great Advent Movement* (Washington, D. C.: Review & Herald Publishing Assn., 1968), 31.

28. S. Bliss, "Memoirs of Willliam Miller," 250–252, quoted in White, 387.

29. William Miller, *Signs of the Times*, January 25, 1843, 147, quoted in Francis D. Nichol, *The Midnight Cry* (Washington, D.C.: Review and Herald Publishing, 1945), 126; cf. Arthur Spalding, *Origin and History of Seventh-day Adventists*, 4 vols. (Washington, D. C.: Review & Herald Publishing Assn., 1961), 1:88 and Melton, 113.

30. William Miller, quoted in Samples et. al., 106.

31. Devens, *American Progress*, 305.

32. Devens, *American Progress*, 301–302, 305.

33. Eva Shaw, *Eve of Destruction* (Chicago: Contemporary Books, 1995), 65.

34. Quoted in Shaw, 65.

35. William Miller, quoted in Shaw, 65.

36. C. E. Sears, quoted in Shaw, 65–66.

37. William Miller, *Midnight Cry*, February 15, 1843, 237, quoted in Nichol, 163; cf. C. Marvin Pate and Calvin B. Haines, *Doomsday Delusions* (Downers Grove: InterVarsity Press, 1995), 119.

38. William Miller, *Advent Herald*, March 6, 1844. n.p, quoted in Nichol, 162; cf. Pate and Haines, 119.

39. *Midnight Cry*, quoted in Shaw, 67.

40. Noah Webster, quoted in Spalding, 53.

41. Shaw, 68.

42. Cohen, 25.

43. William Miller, quoted in Nichol, 170–171; cf. Sylvester Bliss, *Memoirs of William Miller* (Boston: J. V. Himes, 1853), 256, quoted in Nichol, 171.

44. Cohen, 28–29.

45. Quoted in Cohen, 29–30.

46. Quoted in Devens, 312.

47. Sears, quoted in Cohen, 31.

48. Devens, *American Progress*, 312.

49. Spalding, 94–95.

50. Joseph Bates, quoted in Samples et. al., 108.

51. Hiram Edson, undated manuscript fragment, Heritage Room, Andrews University Library, quoted in Ronald L. Numbers and Jonathan M. Butler, eds., *The Disappointed: Millerism and Millenarianism in the Nineteenth Century* (Bloomington: Indiana University Press, 1987), 215.

52. Luther Boutelle, *Sketch of the Life and Religious Experience of Eld. Luther Boutelle* (Boston: Advent Christian Publication Society, 1891), 62–72, quoted in Numbers and Butler, 211.

53. Devens, *American Progress*, 307.

CHAPTER 8

1. *The Watchtower* (Brooklyn: Watchtower Bible & Tract Society), April 1, 1972, 197.

2. The tragic consequences of the Jehovah's Witnesses ban on blood has been reported countless times in various newspapers. American Red Cross figures published in 1980 reveal that approximately 100 people per 1,000 need a blood transfusion every year. The JWs 1997 average membership totaled 5,353,078 (for source, see endnote #3), which means that every year approximately 535,307 need blood. No one has kept statistics on JW deaths due to the Watch Tower's ban on blood, but the numbers must be staggering. Even if only one out of every ten JW who needs a transfusion dies, this would add up to 53,530 deaths a year. Consider the following JW-related news story headlines: "Boy Dies as Family Refuses Medical Aid" (1961), "Pregnant Woman Dies After Refusing Transfusion" (1986), J. W. Woman Dies Refusing Transfusion" (1989), "Man Refuses Blood for 4 Days, Dies" (1989), "Witness Wins in Court, Dies in Hospital" (1990). These headlines were taken from David Reed, *Comments from the Friends*, Fall 1991 and Duane Magnani, *Danger At Your Door* (Clayton, CA: Witness, Inc., 1987).

3. *The Watchtower*, "1997 Service year Report of Jehovah's Witnesses Worldwide," January 1, 1998, 21.

4. David A. Reed, *Jehovah's Witness Literature* (Grand Rapids: Baker Books, 1993), 155.

5. *Awake*, December 22, 1997, 2 and *The Watchtower*, January 1, 1998, 2.

6. The lengthy list of scholars that have criticized the *New World Translation* (NWT) as biased and unreliable includes Dr. Bruce Metzger, professor of New Testament at Princeton University; British scholar H.H. Rowley and the late Dr. Julius Mantey, author of A Manual Grammar of the Greek New Testament. Metzger called the NWT "a frightful mistranslation," "erroneous," "pernicious," and "reprehensible." Mantey labeled the NWT "a shocking mistranslation." In reference to the NWT, Rowley commented: "From beginning to end this volume is a shining example of how the Bible should not be translated." For references, see Ron Rhodes, *Reasoning from the Scriptures with the Jehovah's Wintesses* (Eugene, OR: Harvest House, 1993), 97.

7. Greta Hawkins (Public Affairs Representative for the Watch Tower), author's October 29, 1997 interview with Hawkins.

8. *The Watchtower*, October 1, 1967, 587.

9. *The Watchtower*, July 1, 1973, 402.

10. In reference to Russell's *Studies in the Scriptures* series of books, the September 15, 1910 issue of *Zion's Watch Tower & Herald of Christ's Presence* stated: "[N]ot only do we find that people cannot see the divine plan in studying the Bible by itself, but we see, also, that if anyone lays the SCRIPTURE STUDIES aside, even after he has used them, after he has become familiar with them, after he has read them for ten years — if he then lays them aside and ignores them and goes to the Bible alone, though he has understood his Bible for ten years, our experience shows that within two years he goes into darkness. On the other hand, if he had merely read the SCRIPTURE STUDIES with their references, and had not read a page of the Bible, as such, he would be in the light at the end of two years, because he would have the light of the Scriptures." *Zion's Watch Tower & Herald of Christ's Presence*, September 15, 1910, 298- 299, as reprinted in the Watch Tower reprints, vol. 5 (Pittsburgh: Watch Tower Bible & Tract Society, 1919), 4685.

11. *Zion's Watch Tower & Herald of Christ's Presence*, February 1881, 3, as reprinted in the Watch Tower reprints, vol. 1 (Pittsburgh: Watch Tower Bible & Tract Society, 1919), 188; *Zion's Watch Tower & Herald of Christ's Presence*, August 1883, 1, as

reprinted in the Watch Tower reprints, vol. 1 (Pittsburgh: Watchtower Bible & Tract Society, 1919), 513; *Zion's Watch Tower & Herald of Christ's Presence*, July 15, 1906, 230–231, as reprinted in the Watch Tower reprints, vol. 5 (Pittsburgh: Watch Tower Bible & Tract Society, 1919), 3822.

12. After Russell's death, the WTBTS released a seventh volume of *Studies in the Scriptures* (1917), which was purportedly a "posthumous work of Pastor Russell." In reality, it was written by Clayton J. Woodwoorth and George Fisher, two loyal followers of Russell's successor, J. F. Rutherford.

13. Charles Taze Russell, *The Time Is At Hand*, vol. 2 of *Studies in the Scriptures*, 1906 edition (Allegheny, PA: Watch Tower Bible & Tract Society, 1889), 76–77.

14. Russell, 101.

15. Russell, 98–99; cf. Charles Taze Russell, *Thy Kingdom Come*, vol. 3 of *Studies in the Scriptures*, 1908 edition (Allegheny, PA: Watch Tower Bible & Tract Society, 1891), 126.

16. In 1892, Russell stated: "The date of the close of that 'battle' [of Armageddon] is definitely marked in Scripture as October, 1914. It is already in progress, its beginning dating from October, 1874." *Zion's Watchtower & Herald of Christ's Presence*, January 15, 1892, 21–23 as reprinted in the Watch Tower reprints, vol. 2 (Pittsburgh, PA: Watch Tower Bible & Tract Society, 1919), 1355; cf. "We see no reason for changing the figures. . . . They are, we believe, God's dates, not ours. But bear in mind that the end of 1914 is not the date for the *beginning*, but for the *end* of the time of trouble." *Zion's Watchtower & Herald of Christ's Presence*, July 15, 1894, 226–231, as reprinted in the Watch Tower reprints, vol. 2, 1677.

17. Charles Taze Russell, *Pastor Russell's Sermons* (Brooklyn: People's Pulpit Association, 1917), 676.

18. Russell, *Thy Kingdom Come*, 341.

19. J. F. Rutherford, *Millions Now Living Will Never Die* (Brooklyn: Watch Tower Bible & Tract Society, 1920), 89–90, 97.

20. Even before Rutherford made his 1918 speech, the Watch Tower was presenting 1925 as a probable date for the world's end. *The Finished Mystery* (Brooklyn: Watch Tower Bible & Tract Society, 1917) stated: "[T]here is evidence that the establishment of the Kingdom in Palestine will probably be in 1925, ten years later than we once calculated" (p. 128). Well into 1925, the Society was still printing literature declaring that the establishment of God's kingdom on earth would occur near 1925. The following excerpt is taken from *The Way to Paradise* (Brooklyn: Watch Tower Bible & Tract Society, 1925), written by W. E. Van Amburgh, the Society's corporate secretary and treasurer: "We should, therefore, expect shortly after 1925 to see the awakening of Abel, Enoch, Noah, Abraham, Isaac, Jacob . . . . These will form the nucleus of the new kingdom on earth. . . . No doubt many boys and girls who read this book will live to see Abraham . . . and those other fanciful men of old. . . . Of course, it will take some time to get things in smoothly running order after the great stress between now and 1926" (pp. 224–228).

21. *The Watchtower*, October 15, 1917, 317–318, as reprinted in the Watch Tower reprints, vol. 7 (Brooklyn: Watch Tower Bible & Tract Society, 1919), 6157.

22. *The Watchtower*, September 1, 1922, 262.

23. *The Watchtower*, March 15, 1923, 86.

24. Rutherford, 97.

25. *The Watchtower*, July 15, 1924, 211.

26. *The Watchtower*, January 1, 1925, 3.

27.   J. F. Rutherford, *Comfort for the Jews* (Brooklyn: Watch Tower Bible & Tract Society, 1925), 86, 88.

28.   J. F. Rutherford, *Comfort for the People* (Brooklyn: Watch Tower Bible & Tract Society, 1925), 9.

29.   *The Watchtower*, September 1, 1925, 262.

30.   *The Watchtower*, August 1, 1926, 232.

31.   *The Watchtower*, July 15, 1922, 217.

32.   *The 1980 Yearbook of Jehovah's Witnesses* (Brooklyn: Watch Tower Bible & Tract Society, 1979), 62.

33.   Rutherford, *Millions*, 89–90.

34.   Rutherford, *Millions*, 97.

35.   *The Watchtower*, October 1, 1929, 302.

36.   *The New World* (Brooklyn: Watch Tower Bible & Tract Society, 1942), 104.

37.   *Consolation*, May 27, 1942, 13.

38.   *Consolation*, October 29, 1941, 11.

39.   *Informant*, May 1940, 1.

40.   *The Messenger*, September 1, 1940, 6.

41.   *The Watchtower*, September 15, 1941, 288.

42.   J. F. Rutherford, *Face Facts* (Brooklyn: Watch Tower Bible & Tract Society, 1938), 46.

43.   *The Watchtower*, November 1, 1938, 323.

44.   J. F. Rutherford, *Salvation* (Brooklyn: Watch Tower Bible & Tract Society, 1939), 325.

45.   *God's Kingdom of A Thousand Years Has Approached* (Brooklyn: Watch Tower Bible & Tract Society, 1973), 209–210. In reality, the date 1914 quietly replaced the 1874 date in a 1930 *Golden Age* magazine, which read in part: "In Matthew 24, Jesus gives His disciples some proofs that He would be present . . . If it is true that Jesus has been present since the year 1914, then it must be admitted that nobody has seen Him with natural eyes." *Golden Age*, c. 1930, 503.

46.   *Life Everlasting — In Freedom of the Sons of God* (Brooklyn: Watch Tower Bible & Tract Society, 1966), 29, 35; cf. *The Watchtower*, May 1, 68, 271.

47.   *Awake!*, October 8, 1966, 18.

48.   The October 8, 1966 issue of *Awake!* reads: "In what year, then, would the first 6,000 years of man's existence and also the first 6,000 years of God's rest day come to an end? The year 1975" (p. 19).

49.   *Awake!*, October 8, 1966, 20.

50.   *The Watchtower*, August 15, 1968, 494, 499.

51.   *Kingdom Ministry*, May 1974, 3.

52.   *Awake!*, November 8, 1974, 11.

53.   *Kingdom Ministry*, June 1969, 3.

54.   *Kingdom Ministry*, January 1968, 5.

55.   Raymond Franz, *Crisis of Conscience* (Atlanta: Commentary Press, 1983), 199.

56.   *The Watchtower*, July 16, 1976, 440.

57.   *Awake!*, October 8, 1968, 13.

58.   *The Watchtower*, October 1, 1978, 31.

59.   "[T]he babies of that generation are now 70 years old or older. And others alive in 1914 are in their 80's or 90's, a few even having reached a hundred. There are still many millions of that generation alive. Some of them 'will by no mean pass away until all think occur.'" *The Watchtower*, May 15, 1984, 5.

60.   Jehovah's Witnesses use the term "New Light" to describe the various changes that are continually made to the set of doctrines that they must believe.

61.   *The Watchtower*, November 1, 1995, 19.

62.   *Awake!*, October 8, 1973, 19.

63.   *The Watchtower*, October 15, 1980, 31.

64. *The Watchtower*, May 1, 1985, 4).
65. *The Watchtower*, November 1, 1995, 17.
66. *The Watchtower*, June, 1, 1997, 28.
67. *The Watchtower*, May 1, 1938, 143.
68. *The Watchtower*, July 1, 1943, 203.
69. *The Watchtower*, January 15, 1959, 40–41.
70. *The Watchtower*, January 1, 1942, 5.
71. *The Watchtower*, February 1, 1938, 35.
72. *The Watchtower*, May 15, 1984, 6–7.
73. *Awake!*, January 8, 1982, 2.
74. *Awake!*, March 8, 1988, 2.
75. *Awake!*, October 8, 1968, 23.
76. The following charts present a few of the doctrines on which the WTBS has contradicted itself:

College Education

1969	1992- Present
"Many schools now have student counselors who encourage one to pursue higher education . . . . Do not be influenced by them. Do not let them 'brain- wash' you with the Devil's propaganda to ,. get ahead, to make something of yourself in this world. The world has very little time left! Any "future" this world offers is no future! . . . Make pioneer service, the full- time ministry, with the possibility of Bethel or missionary service your goal." *Awake!*. March 15, 1969, 171.	[T]he general trend in many lands is that the level of schooling required to earn decent wages is now higher than it was a few years ago. . So no hard- and- fast rules should be made either for or against extra education. . . . If Christian parents responsibly decide to provide their children with further education after high school, that is their prerogative." *The Watchtower*, November 1, 1992, 18- 20.

The Great Pyramid

Pre- 1928	Post- 1928
"THE TESTIMONY OF GOD'S STONE WITNESS AND PROPHET, THE GREAT PYRAMID IN EGYPT. . . [T] he Great Pyramid . . . acquires new interest to every Christian advanced in the study of God's Word; for it seems in a remarkable manner to teach, in harmony with all the prophets, and outline of the plan of God, past, present and future." Russell, *Thy Kingdom Come*, 313- 314. "The great Pyramid of Egypt, standing as a silent and inanimate witness of the Lord, is a messenger; and its testimony speaks with great eloquence concerning the divine plan." *The Watchtower*, May 15, 1925, 148.	"[N]owhere in the Word of God is the pyramid of Gizeh either directly or indirectly mentioned . . . . [T] o teach it in the church is a waste of time, to say the least of it. It is more than a waste of time. It is diverting the mind away from the Word of God and from his service. If the pyramid is not mentioned in the Bible, then following its teachings is being led by vain philosophy and false science and not following after Christ. . . [T] he great pyramid of Gizeh, as well as the other pyramids thereabout, also the sphinx, were built by the rulers of Egypt under the direction of Satan the Devil . . Satan put his knowledge in dead stone, which may be called Satan's Bible, and not God's stone witness." *The Watchtower*, November 15, 1928, 341, 344.

Organ Transplants

1967	1980- Present
"When there is a diseased or defective organ, the usual way health is restored is by taking in nutrients. . . . When men of science conclude that this normal process will no longer work and they suggest removing the organ and replacing it directly with an organ from another human, this is simply a shortcut. Those who submit to such . . operations are thus living off the flesh of another human. That is cannibalistic. . . . Jehovah God did not grant permission for humans to try to perpetuate their lives by cannibalistically taking into their bodies human flesh, whether chewed or in the form of whole organs or body parts taken from others." *The Watchtower*, November 15, 1967 702; cf. *Awake!*, June 8, 1968: "There are those, such as the Christian witnesses of Jehovah, who consider all transplants between humans as cannibalism" (p. 21).	"Regarding the transplantation of human tissue or bone from one human to another, this is a matter for conscientious decision by each one of Jehovah's Witnesses. Some Christians might feel that taking into their bodies any tissue or body part from another human is cannibalistic. . Other sincere Christians today may feel that the Bible does not definitely rule out medical transplants of human organs. . . . It may be argued, too, that organ transplants are different from cannibalism since the 'donor' is not killed to supply food. . . Clearly, personal views and conscientious feelings vary on this issue of transplantation. . [T]here is no Biblical command pointedly forbidding the taking in of other human tissue." *The Watchtower*, March15, 1980, 31.

77.   The following are a few of the many doctrinal positions on which the WTBTS has reversed itself, each time demanding that members of the organization change their beliefs accordingly, or else face expulsion from the group and the loss of salvation: *Who are the "higher powers" mentioned in Romans 13?*: In 1886, the WTBTS claimed that Romans 13 referred to earthly governments, stating: "Evil as these Gentile governments have been, they were permitted or 'ordained of God' for a wise purpose (Rom. 13:1)." Charles Taze Russell, *The Divine Plan of the Ages*, vol. 1 of *Studies in the Scriptures*, 1908 edition (Allegheny, PA: Watch Tower Bible & Tract Society, 1886), 250; cf. *Zion's Watch Tower & Herald Of Christ's Presence*, July 1/15, 1893, 214–216, as reprinted in the Watch Tower reprints, vol. 1 (Pittsburgh: Watch Tower Bible & Tract Society, 1919), 1555. From 1929–1959, however, the WTBTS taught that Romans 13 did *not* apply to earthly governments, but to Jesus Christ and Jehovah God: "THE HIGHER POWERS — Rom. 13:1. . . . These scriptures prove that Christ Jesus is the 'higher power' and that Jehovah is the highest or supreme power. 'The higher powers' may therefore be applied to both Jehovah and Jesus, because Christ Jesus always carries out the order of his Father." *The Watch Tower*, June 1, 1929, 163, 165; cf. *Let God Be True* (Brooklyn: Watch Tower Bible & Tract Society, 1946), 248 and *Jehovah's Witnesses in the Divine Purpose* (Brooklyn: Watch Tower Bible & Tract Society, 1959), 91). By 1980, the WTBTS had reverted back to its 1886 position, declaring: "At Romans 13:1 we read: 'Let every soul be in subjection to the superior authorities,' that is, to governments." *The Watchtower*, May 15, 1980, 4. *Is every Jehovah's Witness a minister?*: This important question has been a constant source of confusion for rank-and-file JWs because their leaders continue changing the official

position of the WTBTS: Yes (*The Watchtower*, April 15, 1970, 250); No (*The Watchtower*, December 1, 1975, 733); Yes (*The Watchtower*, March 15, 1981, 14–17). *Will the men destroyed at Sodom be resurrected at the end of the world?*: Again, this question has been answered and contradicted by WTBTS leaders on numerous occasions: Yes (*The Watchtower*, July 1879 , 7–8, as reprinted in the Watch Tower reprints, vol. 1, 7); NO (*The Watchtower*, June 1, 1952, 338); Yes (*The Watchtower*, August 1, 1965, 479); No (*The Watchtower*, June 1, 1988, 31); Yes (*Insight on the Scriptures*, vol. 2 [Brooklyn: Watch Tower Bible & Tract Society, 1988], 985); No (*Revelation: It's Grand Climax At Hand* [Brooklyn: Watch Tower Bible & Tract Society, 1988], 273).

78.   *The Watchtower*, December 1, 1991, 7.

79.   *Golden Age*, February 4, 1931, 293.

80.   *Consolation*, May 31, 1939, 8.

81.   *Awake!*, August 8 , 1993, 25. The change to the JW position on vaccinations occurred in 1952, with the following pronouncement: "Is vaccination a violation of God's law . . . ? The matter of vaccination is one for the individual that has to face it to decide for himself. . . . [I]t does not appear to us to be in violation of the everlasting covenant made with Noah." *The Watchtower*, December 15, 1952, 764.

82.   *Zion's Watch Tower & Herald of Christ's Presence*, August 1879, 5, as reprinted in the Watch Tower reprints, vol. 1, 24.

83.   *Zion's Watch Tower & Herald of Christ's Presence*, November 1, 1914, 325–326, as reprinted in the Watch Tower reprints, vol. 6 (Pittsburgh: Watch Tower Bible & Tract Society, 1919), 5565.

84.   J. F. Rutherford, *Creation* (Brooklyn: Watch Tower Bible & Tract Society, 1927), 315.

85.   *The Watchtower*, August 15, 1993, 9.

86.   *Zion's Watch Tower & Herald of Christ's Presence*, October/November 1881, 3., as reprinted in the Watch Tower reprints, vol. 1, 289.

87.   Charles Taze Russell, *The Battle of Armageddon*, vol. 4 of *Studies in the Scriptures*, 1913 edition (Allegheny, PA: Watch Tower Bible & Tract Society, 1897), 621.

88.   J. F. Rutherford, *Prophecy* (Brooklyn: Watch Tower Bible & Tract Society, 1929), 65.

89.   *The Watchtower*, January 15, 1993, 5.

90.   Ishii's testimony: "[A]t the back of our house on Tojo-cho, Osaka, there was a house with a sign: 'Osaka Branch of the International Bible Students Association' . . . I visited the house. 'Do you believe in the second advent of our Lord?' I asked the young man who answered the door. 'Christ's second advent was realized in 1914,' he answered. In astonishment, I told him that was impossible. 'You should read this book,' he said, handing me *The Harp of God*. . . . Eventually, my husband found out I was reading a Christian book. . . . he began wondering whether something very important was involved and so read *The Harp of God* himself. I was baptized the following year, March 23, 1929." *The Watchtower*, May 1, 1988, 22.

91.   J. F Rutherford, *The Harp of God*, 1928 edition (Brooklyn: Watch Tower Bible & Tract Society, 1921), 235–236.

92.   Nathan's testimony: "After the war ended in 1918 . . . I rejoined the army and went off to India...In May 1920 the malaria flared up again, and I was sent up into the foothills to recuperate . . . Months later, down in Kanpur, I started a Bible study group hoping to learn more about the Lord's return. It was there that I met Frederick James...a zealous Bible student. He explained to me that Jesus had been present since 1914, invisible to man. . . . I read *Studies in the Scriptures*, by Charles Taze Russell, and became even more convinced than ever that I should respond to the call to preach." *The Watchtower*, September 1, 1990, 11.

93. Rutherford, *Creation*, 289, 306 and *Prophecy*, 65.

94. Russell, *Thy Kingdom Come*, 234, 235.

95. Russell, *The Time is at Hand*, (1923 edition), 11.

96. Russell, *The Battle of Armageddon*, (1923 edition), 621.

97. *The Watchtower*, September 15, 1990, 17.

98. *Is This Life All There Is?*, (Brooklyn: Watch Tower Bible & Tract Society, 1974), 46.

CHAPTER 9

1. Ronald Reagan, quoted in James Mills (former president of the California State Senate), *San Diego Magazine*, 1985, cited in Simon Dwyer, "The Plague Yard: An American Travelogue," in *Rapid Eye 2*, Simon Dwyer, ed. (London: Creation Books, 1995), 232–233. According to Mills, Reagan made this statement to him during a 1971 political banquet.

2. Dave Hunt, *Global Peace and the Rise of the Antichrist* (Eugene, OR: Harvest House, 1990), 42–43.

3. Dave Hunt, *Countdown to the Second Coming* (Eugene, OR: Harvest House, 1991), 35.

4. Jack Van Impe, *2001: The Edge of Eternity* (Dallas: Word, 1996), 5–6, 10, 112, 152, 204.

5. Cyprian, Treatise 5, "An Address to Demetrianus," quoted in Randy Waters, "The Lure of the Apocalypse," *Free Minds Journal*, vol. 11(6), November/December, 1992, 9.

6. Pope Gregory, quoted in T. Francis Glasson, *His Appearing and His Kingdom* (London: The Epworth Press, 1953), 45; cf. Waters, 9.

7. David Allen Lewis, "Signs of His Coming," *Prophecy Watch International*, July 1997, 2.

8. Jack Van Impe, "A Prophetic Overview: 2001 — Countdown to Eternity," *Perhaps Today*, Jan./Feb. 1995, Internet edition at http://www.jvim.com/PerhapsToday/JanFeb97/2001.htm.

9. A 1992 *New York Times Magazine* article noted: "Throughout the 90's, many people have shared an eerie sense that the number and severity of natural disasters is increasing ("Does God Play Hardball?," *New York Times Magazine*, June 15, 1992, 13).

10. Phillip Hoag, "No Such Thing As Doomsday?," *Preparedness Journal*, Winter 1996/1997, 5.

11. Hal Lindsey, *1980s — Countdown to Armageddon* (New York: Bantam, 1981 paperback edition), 30.

12. Peter LaLonde, *Why We Believe We're Living In THE LAST DAYS* (Niagara Falls: The Christian World Report, n.d.), 12.

13. David Allen Lewis, *Signs of His Coming* (Green Forest, AR: New Leaf Press, 1997), 24.

14. Michael D. Evans, *Seven Years of Shaking: A Vision* (Euless, TX: Mike Evans Ministry, 1994),188.

15. Dave Brodie, Internet post to alt.talk.calvary.chapel, July 12, 1997, Subject: End Times Armageddon Scenario: An Overview of Events to Come.

16. Jack Van Impe, "News About Natural Phenomena: Killer Earthquakes On the Rise," *Intelligence Briefing*, Internet edition at http://www.jvim.com/IntelligenceBriefing/May1997/nature.html.

17. The "killer earthquake" statistics quoted by Brodie and Van Impe (i.e., 1950s = 9, 1960s = 13, 1970s = 51, 1980s = 86, 1990–1996 = 150) were apparently taken from

a U.S. Geological Survey Earthquake Report (Boulder, Colorado). These same figures appeared in Grant Jeffrey's 1994 prophecy book *Prince of Darkness: Antichrist and the New World Order* (Toronto, Canada: Frontier Research Publications, 1994), 311.

18.   Charles F. Richter, *Natural History*, December 1969, 44, quoted in Carl Olof Jonsson and Wolfgang Herbst, *The Sign of the Last Days: When?* (Atlanta: Commentary Press, 1987), 51. Richter stated the following: "One notices with some amusement that certain religious groups have picked this rather unfortunate time to insist that the number of earthquakes is increasing. In part they are misled by the increasing number of small earthquakes that are being catalogued and listed by newer, more sensitive stations throughout the world."

19.   Susan Hickman, letter to members of the International Association of Near Death Studies, received by author in 1997, 1.

20.   Sun Bear and Wabun Wind, *Black Dawn, Bright Day* (New York: Simon & Schuster, 1992), 75.

21.   Norman L. Shoaf, *The Good News of the World Tomorrow*, 7, quoted in Jonsson and Herbst, 50–51.

22.   Seweryn J. Duda, letter to Carl Jonsson and Wolfgang Herbst, July 7, 1986. Photostatic copy available in Jonsson and Wolfgang Herbst, 247.

23.   Wilbur Rinehart, letter to Jonsson and Herbst, August 8, 1985, 2; Keiiti Aki, letter to Jonsson and Herbst, September 5, 1985, 1; Waverly J. Person, letter to Jonsson and Herbst, October 8, 1985, 1. Photostatic copies of these letters are available in Jonsson and Herbst, 240, 242, 245.

24.   *Seneca Ad Lucilium Epistulae Morales*, trans., Richard M. Gummere, vol. 2 (London: 1920), 437.

25.   E. A. Thompson, *A History of Attila and the Huns*, 91, quoted in Jonsson and Herbst, 76.

26.   Jonsson and Herbst, 76–78.

27.   John Milne and A. W. Lee, *Earthquakes and Other Earth Movements* (London, 1939), 134, quoted in Jonsson and Herbst, 74–75. Milne and Lee write: "The information available for examination of the distribution of earthquakes in different parts of the world throughout historic times has been collected in many catalogues. The older catalogues, which were prepared from reports found in the histories of various countries, are necessarily incomplete, and do not give a fair representation of the distribution of seismic phenomena over the entire globe. . . . There are numerous inaccurate or obscure references in the original writings, and the data are frequently given according to some little known system of reckoning. The entries for that ancient shocks refer, for the most part, to widespread disasters."

28.   Peter Matthews, ed., *The Guinness Book of Records: 1996* (New York: Bantam, 1996), 144.

29.   Hal Lindsey, *The 1980s: Countdown to Armageddon* (King of Prussia, PA: Westgate Press, 1980), 30; cf. Hal Lindsey, *Apocalypse Planet Earth* videotape (Hal Lindsey Ministries, Inc., 1990).

30.   *You Can Live Forever In Paradise On Earth* (Brooklyn, NY: Watch Tower Bible & Tract Society, 1982), 151.

31.   Douglas T. Harris, "The Signs of the Times," Bethel Ministries Newsletter, Jan./Feb. 1986, reprint, 1. Available from Free Minds, Inc., Box 3818, Manhattan Beach, CA 90266

32.   B. J. Oropeza, *99 Reasons Why No One Knows When Christ Will Return* (Downers Grove: InterVarsity Press, 1994), 78.

33. James Cornell, *The Great International Disaster Book* (New York: Pocket Books, 1979), 131.

34. This earthquake chart, which is by no means exhaustive, is taken from Jonsson and Herbst, 80. It was compiled using several different sources that Jonsson and Herbst list as follows: Robert A. Ganse and John B. Nelson, *Catalog of Significant Earthquakes 2000 B.C. – 1979* (Boulder, Colorado: 1981, 3–33, [Report SE-27 of the World Data Center A for Solid Earth Geophysics]); On the Messina/Reggio quake, see A. Imamura, *Theoretical and Applied Seismology* (Tokyo, 1937), 140, 202, and 204, which says that some 83,000 died in Messina and c. 20,000 in Reggio. Other sources used are: N. N. Ambraseys in *Revue pour l'étude des calamités*, No. 37 (Geneve, Switzerland: December 1961), 18f; J. H. Latter, "Natural Disasters," *Advancement of Science*, June 1969, 363, 370; N. N. Ambraseys & C. P. Melville, *A History of Persian Earthquakes* (Cambridge: 1982); R. A. Daly, *Our Mobile Earth* (New York & London, 1926); A. T. Wilson, "Earthquakes in Persia," *Bulletin of the School of Oriental Studies*, London Institution, Vol. VI (1930-32); Dr. A. Sieberg in *Handbuch der Geophysik*, Prof. B. Gutenberg, ed., Vol. IV, Leipzig 1932; and James Cornell, *The Great International Disaster Book*. Death figures vary, and in several cases some sources give considerably higher figures than shown in the table. The new catalog of *Strong Earthquakes in the U.S.S.R. From Ancient Times Through 1977* (Report SE-31 of the World Data Center A, July 1982) gives 200,000-300,000 deaths for the earthquake in Gansana, Iran, in 1139. Cornell (p. 153) sets the death figure for the 1693 quake in Sicily at 153,000, and Sieberg (in Gutenberg, p. 854) has 150,000 for the Japanese earthquake in 1703. For the two earthquakes that hit Tabriz in Iran in 1721 and 1780, estimates range up to 250,000 and 205,000 respectively. (Ambraseys/Melville, pp. 54, 184, 186). Two other relatively recent quakes that may have been "superearthquakes" are the earthquake in Japan in 1855, which may have claimed 106,000 lives (Sieberg in Gutenberg, p. 854), and the earthquake in Kangra, India, in 1905, of which Cornell (p. 139) says that "some other reports claim nearly 370,000 people were killed in Central India when several villages were completely destroyed." Neither of these have been included in the table.

35. *Survival into a New Earth* (Watch Tower Bible & Tract Society, 1984), 23.

36. Jonsson and Herbst, 47. In *The Earthquake Handbook* (1979), Peter Varney traces modern seismology back to Robert Mallet in the 1850s. Professor N. N. Ambraseys, however, considers John Michell (1724–93) to be the first *true* seismologist (Ambraseys, *Engineering Seismology*, University of London, Inaugural lecture, November 18, 1975, 54).

37. Jonsson and Herbst, 47. The seismograph was invented by John Milne, who has been called the father of English seismology.

38. John Hagee, *Beginning of the End* (Nashville: Thomas Nelson, 1996), 98.

39. This statement, although it is not included in Hagee's main text, is buried in the endnotes of *Beginning of the End* (p. 193).

40. Hagee, 194.

41. J. R. Church, "Riders of Revelation 6, Mount Up," in William T. James, ed., *Foreshocks of Antichrist* (Eugene, OR: Harvest House, 1997), 337.

42. Church, 337.

43. Mattys Levy and Mario Salvadori, *Why the Earth Quakes* (New York: W. W. Norton, 1995), 77.

44. Levy and Salvadori, 77–78.

45. Jack Van Impe, "Signs of the Times," *Intelligence Briefing*, 1996 special edition, Internet edition at http://www.jvim.com/PerhapsToday/Special1996/signs.html

46. *Ancient Prophecies I* (The Learning Channel), December 31, 1996.

47. Hal Lindsey, interview on *This Week In Bible Prophecy*, transcript available on the Internet at http://www.twibp.com/interviews/teachers/lindsey/lindsey.003.html.

48. National Hurricane Center, "The Most Intense Hurricanes In The United States: 1900-1996" (statistical table), available through the National Hurricane Center's World Wide Web Internet home page.

49. The National Climatic Data Center maintains "the world's largest active archive of weather data." Its vast storehouse of information may be accessed through the Internet at http://www.ncdc.noaa.gov/.

50. National Climatic Data Center, "Hurricanes in the 19th Century: Putting the Present in Longer-Term Perspective," 1997, Internet edition at http://www.ncdc.noaa.gov/ol/climate/research/ogp/papers/diazhur.html.

51. National Climatic Data Center.

52. National Climatic Data Center.

53. Frank E. Bair, ed., *The Weather Almanac* (Detroit: Gale Research, 1992), 85.

54. Elizabeth Clare Prophet, interview on *Ancient Prophecies I*.

55. Hal Lindsey, *The Promise* (1982), 198, quoted in Jonsson and Herbst, 88.

56. J. R. Church, *Hidden Prophecies in the Song of Moses* (Oklahoma City: Prophecy Publications, 1991), 106, cited in Oropeza, 77.

57. Hal Lindsey, interview on *This Week In Bible Prophecy* (hosted by Peter and Paul LaLonde), transcripts available on the Internet at http://www.twibp.com/interviews/teachers/lindsey.076.html.

58. Noah Hutchings (Southwest Radio Church), appeal letter, n.d, quoted in Oropeza, 77.

59. Jack Van Impe, *The AIDS Cover-Up*, TV Soundtrack, 1986, quoted in Russell Chandler, *Doomsday* (Ann Arbor: Servant Publications, 1993),157.

60. Van Impe, *Perhaps Today*, "A Prophetic Overview."

61. This information on AIDS was obtained by the author during a telephone interview with the U. S. Center for Disease Control HIV/AIDS Hotline, September 10, 1997.

62. Jack Van Impe, "The Age Of Plagues," *Intelligence Briefing*, Internet edition at http://www.jvim.com/PerhapsToday/Special1996/plagues.html.

63. Mark Caldwell, "Blessed With Resistance," *Discover*, January 1994, 46.

64. World Health Organization, 1996 Executive Summary, available from the World Health Organization's World Wide Web homepage at http://www.who.ch/whr/1996/exsume.htm.

65. Jonsson and Herbst, 97–98.

66. Barbara Tuchman, *A Distant Mirror: The Calamitous 14th Century* (London: 1979), xiii, quoted in Gary DeMar, *Last Days Madness* (Atlanta, GA: American Vision, Inc., 1994), 249.

67. Isaac Asimov, *A Choice of Catastrophes* (London, 1980), 242, quoted in Jonsson and Herbst, 101.

68. George Deaux, *The Black Death 1347* (London, 1969), 143, 144, quoted in Jonsson and Herbst, 101.

69. Michael W. Dols, *The Black Death in the Middle East* (Princeton, New Jersey, 1977), vii, quoted in Jonsson and Herbst, 101.

70. Emmanuel Le Roy Ladurie, *The Mind and Method of the Historian* (Brighton, Sussex, England, 1981), 71, quoted in Jonsson and Herbst, 101.

71. Robert S. Gottfried, *The Black Death* (London, 1983), 163, quoted in Jonsson and Herbst, 101.

72. *Funk & Wagnalls Standard Dictionary* (New York: Harper Collins, 1983), 258.

73. Adam Jasser, "Globalisation Poses Threat to Human Health," November 19, 1997, America Online.

74. Sten Iwarson, interview in *Göteborgs-Posten*, June 2, 1985, quoted in Jonsson and Herbst, 120.

75. Jonsson and Herbst, 104–105.

76. According to the World Health Organization (WHO), epidemics continue to breakout periodically. Poverty, inadequate health care systems, and poor social conditions are the cause of these plagues. The WHO's 1996 summary of the state of the world explains: "More than 1,000 million people [1 billion] live in extreme poverty. Half the world's population lacks regular access to the most needed essential drugs. Continuing global population growth and rapid urbanization force many millions of city dwellers to live in overcrowded and unhygienic conditions, where lack of clean water and adequate sanitation are breeding grounds for infectious disease. Migration and the mass movement of many millions of refugees or displaced persons from one country to another as a result of wars, civil turmoil or natural disasters, also contribute to the spread of infectious diseases. As a result of the economic and social crises still affecting many countries, health systems which should offer protection against disease have, in extreme cases, either collapsed or not even been built. The result is a resurgence of diseases that were once under control or should be controllable, given adequate resources. . . . Some countries impose unjustified restrictions on travelers coming from infected countries; others are tempted to conceal information about infections within their own borders. The result is a fragmented, uncoordinated approach to infectious disease control and inadequate global information to allow worldwide monitoring. Changes in global food trade create new opportunities for infections to flourish. They include the shipment of livestock; new methods of food production, storage and marketing; and altered eating habits.

77. Famine chart adapted from *Compton's Living Encyclopedia*, America Online.

78. *The Watchtower*, October 15, 1975, 634.

79. *Let Your Kingdom Come* (Brooklyn: Watch Tower Bible and tract Society, 1981), 122; cf. *You Can Live Forever In Paradise On Earth*, 150.

80. Jack Van Impe, "Beyond 2000 — World Without End, Amen," *Perhaps Today*, November/December 1995, Internet edition at http://www.jvim.com/PerhapsToday/NovDec95/Beyond2000.html

81. Jonsson and Herbst, 20–25.

82. Hal Lindsey, *The Late Great Planet Earth* (Grand Rapids: Zondervan, 1970), 147.

83. R. R. Palmer and Joel Colton, *A History of the Modern World to 1815* (New York), quoted in Jonsson, and Herbst, 137.

84. According to Jonsson and Herbst, "Prussia, Austria, Britain, France, Russia, Sweden, Spain and most of the German States of the Holy Roman Empire became embroiled in the struggle. Issues included control of North America and India. It was this war that brought Britain to its position as the leading imperial power of the world" (p. 137).

85. Jonsson and Herbst, 145–147.

86. Jonsson and Herbst, 144–147

87. Tim LaHaye, "Twelve Reasons Why This Could Be The Terminal Generation," in *When the Trumpet Sounds* (Eugene, OR: Harvest House, 1995), 430.

88. Jonsson and Herbst, 147.

89. J. David Singer and Melvin Small, *The Wages of War 1816–1965* (New York: John Wiley & Sons, 1972), 201.

CHAPTER 10

1. Tim Weber, quoted in Steve Rabey, "Warning: The End Is Near, Again," *Gazette Telegraph*, December 28, 1991, D2.

2. Eklal Kueshana (a.k.a. Richard Kieninger), *The Ultimate Frontier* (Stelle, IL: The Stelle Group, 1963), quoted in advertisement for *Future Fate* videotape, transcript of Kieninger's comment is available through the Internet at http://www.future-fate.com/graphic/predict/mecpred.shtml

3. Nathan Cohen Beskin, transcribed text of a sermon delivered on April 14, 1931, reprinted in Robert W. Smith, *The "Last Days"* (Pyramid Press: Salt Lake City, 1932), 42–43.

4. Gus McKey, *Time Cycles in the Bible* (Los Angeles: Los Angeles Free Tract Society, n.d.), reprinted in Smith, 51.

5. J. D. Douglas gen. ed., *The New International Dictionary of the Christian Church* (Grand Rapids: Zondervan, 1974; 1878 edition), 1005.

6. James Horvath, *He's Coming Soon* (Lake Mary, FL: Creation House, 1995), 20–21.

7. Gordon Lindsay, *The World: 2000 A.D.* (Dallas: Christ for the Nations, 1968), 90–92, quoted in Horvath, 21.

8. Jack Van Impe, *Jack Van Impe Presents* television program, Trinity Broadcasting Network, July 2, 1997. Ironically, Van Impe steadfastly maintains that "[t]he world is not coming to an end — not now, not in the year 2000" (Jack Van Impe, "Beyond 2000 — World Without End, Amen," *Perhaps Today* newsletter, November/December 1995, Internet edition at http://www.jvim.com/PerhapsToday/NovDec95/Beyond2000.html). How can Van Impe make such a statement given his propensity for date-suggesting? Apparently, he feels that because he sees Christ's 1,000-year reign beginning near the year 2000, then the world is not *technically* going to end. It will continue under the reign of Jesus Christ for another 1,000 years. But, of course, the Christian view of Christ's earthly reign certainly involves the end of the world *as we know it*. Consequently, Van Impe is doing little more than playing word games. In the field of logic, he is committing the logical fallacy know as "making a distinction without a difference."

9. Jack Van Impe, "A Prophetic Overview: 2001 — Countdown to Eternity," *Perhaps Today* newsletter, January / February 1995. Internet edition at http://www.jvim.com/PerhapsToday/JanuaryFebruary1995/Countdown.html

10. Jack Van Impe, "Beyond 2000 — World Without End, Amen."

11. Van Impe, *Jack Van Impe Presents*.

12. Richard Landes, "While God Tarried: Disappointed Millennialism and the Making Of the Modern West," *Deolog*, 4:1 (1997): 6–9, 22–27, 41, 45, Internet edition at http:// www.mille.org/wgt-prec.html.

13. John Cumming, *The End: Or the Proximate Signs of the Close of This Dispensation*, 95– 96, cited in Dwight Wilson, *Apocalypse Now* (Tyler, TX: Institute for Christian Economics, 1991), 25. Cumming wrote: "Just as the six days have their seventh, the 6,000 years will have their seventh thousand, or what we call the millennium."

14. McKey, reprinted in Smith, 54.

15. Salem Kirban, *Guide to Survival* (Huntington Valley, PA: Salem Kirban, 1972), 126.

16. Ron Reese, *The Midnight Hour Approaches! Your Time Is Almost Over* (tract printed in Brooklyn, MI: n.d.), quoted in B. J. Oropeza, *99 Reasons Why No One Knows When Christ Will Return* (Downers Grove: InterVarsity Press, 1994), 65.

17. Oropeza, 67.

18.   Michael Green, "The Second Epistle of Peter and the Epistle of Jude," vol. 18 of *The Tyndale New Testament Commentaries*, 1980 edition, (Grand Rapids: William B. Eerdmans, 1968), 20 volumes, 133.

19.   John Calvin, quoted in Green, 134.

20.   John Mueller, "Depressed by Politics? Some Words of Cheer," *Los Angeles Times*, October 31, 1996, B11.

21.   Mueller, B11.

22.   Ralph Woodrow, *His Truth Is Marching On: Advanced Studies of Prophecy in the Light of History* (Riverside, CA: Ralph Woodrow Evangelistic Association, 1977), 22.

23.   The *Epistle of Barnabus* was written c. 130 A.D., which means that it could not have been authored by the Barnabus mentioned in the Bible as being Paul's companion. Paul's associate would have been long deceased by the year 130.

24.   William Alnor, *Soothsayers of the Second Advent* (Old Tappan, NJ: Fleming H. Revell, 1989), 106.

25.   Rexella Van Impe, *Jack Van Impe Presents*, Trinity Broadcasting Network, July 2, 1997. During this television program, Jack Van Impe agreed with his wife's assertion that it was indeed Paul's traveling companion who had written the *Epistle of Barnabas*.

26.   The *Epistle of Barnabas* is available on the Internet at http://wesley.nnc.edu/noncanon/fathers/ante-nic/barnabus.htm.

27.   Tim LaHaye, "Will God Destroy Russia?" in *Storming Toward Armageddon: Essays in Apocalypse*, William T. James ed. (Green Forest, AK: New Leaf Press, 1992), 259.

28.   Hal Lindsey, "Strategic Forecasts," *International Intelligence Briefing*, April 1994, 7, cited in William T. James, "Wars, Rumors of Wars, Raging Human Seas of Hatred" in *Earth's Final Days: Essays in Apocalypse III*, William T. James ed. (Green Forest, AK: New Leaf Press, 1994), 52.

29.   Hal Lindsey, *International Intelligence Briefing* television program, Trinity Broadcasting Network, September 25, 1997.

30.   John Walvoord, *Armageddon, Oil and the Middle East Crisis* (Grand Rapids: Zondervan, 1974; 1990 edition), 141.

31.   Dave Breese, "The Soviet Phoenix Rises," in *Foreshocks of Antichrist*, William T. James ed. (Eugene, OR: Harvest House, 1997), 246.

32.   David Allen Lewis, *Prophecy 2000* (Green Forest, AK: New Leaf Press, 1990; 1995 edition), 389, 395.

33.   Dave Breese, "Planet Earth in Crisis: Overview and Update" in *Earth's Final Days*, 310–311.

34.   Wilbur Glen Voliva, quoted in Associated Press, "Voliva Gives World Only Four More Years," reprinted in Robert W. Smith, *The "Last Days"* (Salt Lake City: Pyramid Press, 1932), 23.

35.   Charles Taylor, *Watch 1988 — The Year of Climax* (Huntington Beach, CA: Today in Bible Prophecy, 1988), 84.

36.   Charles Taylor, *Bible Prophecy News 17*, no. 3 (July–August–September, 1988), 8.

37.   Alexander Bobilev, interview with William Alnor, March 28, 1989, quoted in William Alnor, 141.

38.   Walter A. Elwell ed., *Baker Encyclopedia of the Bible*, vol. 2 (Grand Rapids: Baker Books, 1988; 1995 edition), 1377.

39.   Wilson, 24.

40.   Richard Landes, *The Apocalyptic Dossier: 967-1033*, Internet edition at http://www.mille.org/1000-dos.htm.

41. Oropeza, 99.
42. Peter LaLonde, *One World Under Anti-Christ* (Eugene, OR: Harvest House, 1991), 215–216, 221.
43. Hal Lindsey, *The 1980s: Countdown to Armageddon* (New York: Bantam, 1980), 68.
44. Hal Lindsey, "The Armageddon Scenario" in *Steeling the Mind of America*, compiled by Bill Perkins (Green Forest, AK: New Leaf press, 1995), 121–122.
45. Pat Robertson, quoted in *Christian Life, November* 1984; also quoted in Wilson, xxx.
46. Pat Robertson, *The Secret Kingdom: Your Path to Peace, Love, and Financial Security* (Dallas: Word, 1992), 255, quoted in Gary DeMar, *Last Days Madness* (Atlanta: American Vision, Inc.), 271.
47. Wilson, 59. A 1928 edition of *The Pentecostal Evangel*: "Here you have read that Russia is going to war with Palestine. That is coming. . . . There is where we are to-day. Therefore, we may expect very shortly that this conflict will take place" (*The Pentecostal Evangel*, 13, quoted in Wilson, 59).
48. William R. Goetz, *Apocalypse Next* (Camp Hill, PA: Horizon Publishers, 1980), 123.
49. Goetz, 131–132.
50. Goetz, 149–150.
51. William R. Goetz, *Apocalypse Next*, 1996 edition (Camp Hill, PA: Horizon Books, 1980), 135–136.
52. Goetz (1996 edition), 143, 145, 149.
53. Goetz (1996 edition), 183, 184.
54. C. F. Keil and F. Delitzsch, *Commentary on the Old Testament*, 10 vols. (Peabody, MA: Hendrickson Publishers, 1996), transl. James Martin and M. G. Easton, originally published in 1866–1891 by T. & T. Clark (Edinburgh, England), 9:330.
55. Josephus, quoted in Geoffrey W. Bromiley, *The International Standard Bible Encyclopedia*, 4 vols. (Grand Rapids: William B. Eerdmans, 1986; 1990 edition), 3:222.
56. Barry J. Beitzel, *The Moody Atlas of Bible Lands* (Chicago: Moody Press, 1985), 5.
57. C. Marvin Pate and Calvin B. Haines, *Doomsday Delusions* (Downers Grove: InterVarsity Press, 1995), 163.
58. Rob Linsted, *The Next Move: Current Events in Bible Prophecy* (Wichita, KS: Bible Truth, n.d.), quoted in DeMar, 270.
59. Hal Lindsey, radio interview, August 20, 1991, KKLA, cited in Tim Callahan, "The Fall of the Soviet Union & the Changing Game of Prophecy," *Skeptic*, vol. 3(2),1995, 96.
60. Hal Lindsey, radio interview, September 15, 1992, KKLA, cited in Callahan, 95.
61. *Encyclopedia Britannica* and *Great Soviet Encyclopedia*, quoted in Callahan, 96.
62. Callahan, 96.
63. Charles F. Pfeiffer and Everett F. Harrison eds., *The Wycliffe Bible Commentary* (Chicago: Moody Press, 1962 756.
64. Pfeiffer and Harrison, 756.
65. Dave Hunt, *How Close Are We?* (Eugene, OR: Harvest House, 1993), 27.
66. D. A. Carson, quoted in Wendy Murray Zoba, "Future Tense," *Christianity Today*, October 2, 1995, 21. Carson received his Ph.D. from Cambridge University.
67. William T. James, "Israel: The Clear Signal," in *Storming Toward Armageddon*, 60, 162.
68. Tim LaHaye, "Twelve Reasons Why This Could Be The Terminal Generation," in *When the Trumpet Sounds* (Eugene, OR: Harvest House, 1995), 430.
69. Tim LaHaye, *The Beginning of the End* (Wheaton, IL: Tyndale House, 1972), 165.
70. LaHaye, 165–168.

71.   Tim LaHaye, *The Beginning of the End* (Wheaton, IL: Tyndale House, 1972; 1991 edition), 192–193.

72.   LaHaye, (1991 edition), 193.

73.   John Cumming, *The End*, 260–262, quoted in Wilson, 27. An even earlier work that cited the restoration of Jews to Palestine as a sign of the end was *A Dissertation on Prophecies, That Have Been Fulfilled, Are Now Fulfilling, or Will Hereafter Be Fulfilled, Relative to the Great Period of 1260 years; The Papal and Mohammedan Apostacies; the Tyrannical Reign of Antichrist, or the Infidel Power; and the Restoration of the Jews* written by George Stanley Faber and published in 1804 (see Wilson, 20).

74.   Wilson, 27.

75.   LaHaye (1972 edition), 168.

76.   LaHaye, (1972 edition), 168–169.

77.   LaHaye, (1991 edition), 193.

78.   LaHaye, (1991 edition), 194.

79.   Wilson, 40–41,

80.   *The Weekly Evangel*, January 5 1918, 5, quoted in Wilson 42.

81.   W. W. Fereday, "After the Great War," *Our Hope*, XXVI (1919–1920), 34, quoted in Wilson, 43.

82.   Oropeza, 89–90.

83.   Gary DeMar, another evangelical writer, notes in *Last Days Madness* that Israel is often compared to a vine, pomegranate, olive, palm, and cedar (Ps. 92:12; Ezek. 17:22– 23; Hosea 9:10). According to DeMar, the Bible's preferred symbols of Israel seem to be the vine (John 15:1–11), olive tree (Rom. 11:16–24), and flock of sheep (Is. 40:11; Jer. 23:2; Matt. 26:31; Luke 12:32; John 10:16; 1 Peter 5:2).

84.   Oropeza, 90–93.

85.   Ron Rhodes, author's September 29, 1997 interview with Rhodes.

86.   Rhodes. Author's September 29, 1997 interview with Rhodes.

87.   Zoba, 22.

88.   F. F. Bruce, foreword to Carl E. Armerding and W. Ward Gasque eds., *A Guide to Biblical Prophecy* (Peabody, MA: Hendrickson Publishers, 1989), 7, originally published by Baker Books, 1977.

89.   D. Brent Sandy, "Did Daniel See Mussolini?," *Christianity Today*, February 8, 1993, 34.

CHAPTER 11

1.   Charles Strozier, interview on *Ancient Prophecies I* (The Learning Channel), December 31, 1996.

2.   All quoted segments of Orson Welles's radio adaptation of H. G. Wells's *The War of the Worlds* were taken from "real audio" sound clips currently on the Internet. Although I have tried to transcribe the dialogue as accurately as possible, there may be minor errors in the transcript due to the poor sound quality of the recordings. I am, however, unaware of any such errors. Internet sound clips are available at http:// earthstation1.simplenet.com/War_of_the_Worlds_Broadcast/ War_of_the_Worlds.ram.

3.   Gordon Stein, *Encyclopedia of Hoaxes* (Detroit: Gale Research, 1993), 100; cf. "Radio Listeners in Panic, Taking War Drama as Fact," *New York Times*, October 31, 1938, 1, 4.

4. Stein, 101; cf. "Martian Invasion Terrorizes Chile," *New York Times*, November 14, 1944, 1 and "Mars Raiders' Cause Quito Panic; Mob Burns Radio Plant; Kills 15," *New York Times*, February 14, 1949, 1, 7.

5. Louis Farrakhan, speech, January 14, 1991, cited in "So You Think," 1991, quoted in Mattias Gardell, *In the Name of Elijah Muhammad* (Duke University Press, 1996), 162.

6. Sun Bear, quoted in Scott Peterson, *Native American Prophecies* (St. Paul, MN: Paragon House, 1990), 195. Sun Bear states: "From now until the year 2000, and beyond that a bit, we're going to be seeing major changes. . . . They [humans] have to make a change of consciousness and perspective . . . . Otherwise, they aren't going to survive and the planet may not either."

7. Stephen Sorenson, "Industry Insiders Track Book Trends," *Bookstore Journal*, December 1996, 17.

8. *CBA Marketplace*, May 1997, 94. In his book *Beginning of the End* (Nashville: Thomas Nelson, 1996), John Hagee declares: "The literal, physical appearance of Jesus Christ will come soon. . . . [P]lease grasp with your head and your heart this overpowering truth from the Word of God — we are the terminal generation" (pp. 116, 187). Hagee made a similar statement during and interview with Ministries Today magazine ("Taking the Lead," *Ministries Today,* July/August 1996, 46), stating: "We are living in the closing moments of the Dispensation of grace. . . . We are, beyond all doubt, the terminal generation."

9. *CBA Marketplace*, July 1997, 224.

10. *CBA Marketplace*, December 1997, 84.

11. Drosnin's 1997 book presents several possible end of the world dates including 2012 and 2113.

12. *Christian Book Distributors Catalogue*, December 1997, 43.

13. *Christian Book Distributors Catalogue*, December 1997, 42.

14. *"Apocalypse* Film in Production," *CBA Marketplace*, November 1997, 99.

15. *Preparedness Expo 1995* brochure, 1995, 6–9.

16. *Preparedness Expo 1995*, 15–18.

17. Don McAlvany, "Conclusion and Recommendation," *McAlvany Intelligence Advisor,* August 1993, 19.

18. As of 1997, the annual subscription rate for the *McAlvany Intelligence Advisor* (12 issues) was $115.

19. Charles Taylor, *Bible Prophecy News 16* (October, November, December, 1987), 2, quoted in William Alnor, *Soothsayers of the Second Advent* (Old Tappan, NJ: Fleming H. Revell, 1989), 91.

20. Texe Marrs, "Night Cometh!" in *Storming Toward Armageddon: Essays in Apocalypse*, William T. James, ed. (Green Forest, AR: New Leaf Press, 1992), 130.

21. Texe Marrs, mass mailing appeal letter, c. 1995.

22. Norman Cohn, quoted in "Millenarianism," November 17, 1995, Internet article at http://www.physics.wisc.edu/~shalizi/notebooks/millenarianism.html.

23. Reuters, "Americans Believe They're in Trouble," January 20, 1996, text from America Online.

24. Harold Meyerson. "State of Hatred," *LA Weekly,* April 28, 1995, reprinted in Don Hazen, Larry Smith and Christine Triano, eds. *Militias in America 1995* (San Francisco: Institute for Alternative Journalism, 1995), 58.

25. Russ Bellant, "The Paranoid and the Paramilitary," *Detroit Metro Times*, Internet edition available AlterNet BBS gopher site, pathway begins at gopher://

gopher.igc.apc.org:70/1, to Progressive Gophers folder, to AlterNet folder, to Militias in America folder, to Additional Articles on Militias folder.

26.   Chip Berlet, quoted in Susan Ladd and Stan Swofford, "Discontent Feeds Movement, Observers Say," *News & Record* (Greensboro, NC), June 27, 1995, Internet edition at http://www.infi.net/nr/extra/militias/m-discon.htm; cf. "Women Who Love to Hate," *Mademoiselle*, August 1994, 186.

27.   "Baby-Faced Killers," *Newsweek*, May 5, 1997, 14.

28.   John J. DiIulio Jr, quoted in David G. Savage, "Strict Florida Stand On Teen 'Thugs' Fuels Policy Debate," *Los Angeles Times*, July 11, 1996, A20; cf. Laura Myers, "Report: Children More Violent, Victimized," *Orange County Register*, 3 (news section).

29.   James Alan Fox, quoted in Robert Lee Hortz, "Experts Warn of New Generation of Killers," *Los Angeles Times*, February 18, 1995, A41.

30.   William R. Macklin, "Christian Broadcaster Changes Mind, Says World Will End Sunday," *Knight-Ridder / Tribune News Service*, October 1, 1994 (Orange County California Public Library Online).

31.   Mircea Eliade ed., *Encyclopedia of Religion*, 16 volumes in 8 volumes (New York: Macmillan, 1987), 9-10:527

32.   Carl Holland, quoted in Ken Baker, "End of the World is Rapidly Approaching, Say Those with Apocalyptic Fervor," *Knight-Ridder Tribune Service* (originally appeared in the *Newport [Virginia] News Daily*), January 11, 1995 (Orange County California Public Library Online System).

33.   Randall Watters, "The Lure of the Apocalypse," *Free Minds Journal*, November/December 1992, vol. 11(6), 9.

34.   David Allen Lewis, "Signs of His Coming," *Prophecy Watch International*, July 1997, 2.

35.   Carl Olof Jonsson and Wolfgang Herbst, *The Sign of the Last Days: When?* (Atlanta: Commentary Press, 1987), x.

36.   Grant Jeffrey, *Prince of Darkness: Antichrist and the New World Order* (Toronto, Canada: Frontier Research Publications, 1994), 312.

37.   Jack Van Impe, "Beyond 2000 — World Without End, Amen," *Perhaps Today*, November/December 1995, Internet edition at http://www.jvim.com/PerhapsToday/NovDec95/Beyond2000.html

38.   Hal Lindsey, interview on *This Week in Bible Prophecy*, transcripts available on the Internet at http://www.twibp.com/interviews/teachers/lindsey/lindsey.001.html

39.   "Michigan Issues Warrant for Mark Koernke," *Patriot Report*, October 1994, 3.

40.   Mark Koernke, *America in Peril* (Real World Productions, 1993).

41.   Morris Wilson, quoted in James Risen, "Militia Networks Boast An Alternate Take On Reality," *Los Angeles Times*, April 30, 1995, A30.

42.   George Eaton, "Mark Koernke Draws Crowds Across U.S.," *Patriot Report*, February 1995, 3.

43.   Richard Abanes, *American Militias* (Downers Grove, IL: InterVarsity Press, 1996,) photo section. This volume included a photo reproduction of two segments of Koernke's military file (obtained through the Freedom of Information Act), both of which contradict his claims to have been an Army Intelligence Analyst who once commanded a full brigade.

44.   Department of the Army, "Current and Previous Assignments," Mark Koernke, Section VII.

45.   James McQuaid, "Mark From Michigan," *Soldier of Fortune*, August 1995, 46.

46. Department of the Army, "Current and Previous Assignments," Mark Koernke, Section VII.

47. Department of the Army, Personnel Information on Mark Koernke.

48. When I told Sgt. 1st Class (E-7) Larry Rapoza of the Mission Viejo, California, U.S. Army Recruiting Station about Koernke's claims, he could not help but chuckle, commenting: "A sergeant doesn't command a second and third Brigade."

"Fairly ridiculous?" I asked.

"Yeah," answered Rapoza, who then gave his impressions of what might have occurred: "It's feasible that he [Koernke] was attached to a [reserve] division, and would have advised a division commander, or a brigade commander, on areas of his expertise . . . (i.e., the military intelligence field). . . . That's feasible that he was an advisor. To actually say he *commanded* a brigade—that he had command and control, was the final decision maker—I don't see how that's feasible. . . . I can probably put my stripes on the line and safely say that as a Spec. 5, I don't think he would have commanded— and that's the key word, "commanded"—had command and control over a brigade. He could have been an *advisor* to a brigade commander. Larry Rapoza, author's January 5, 1995 interview with Rapoza.

49. Kenneth Klenk, author's February 12, 1996 interview with Klenk. Commissioned officers begin their ranking at O-1 (Second Lieutenant). A full Colonel is an O-6 grade.

50. Koernke.

51. Mark Koernke, *A Call to Arms* (Real World Productions, 1993).

52. David Van Biema, "Mark Koernke," *Time*, June 26, 1995, 57.

53. Jeffrey Kaplan, "A Guide to the Radical Right," *Christian Century*, August 2–9, 1995, 741.

54. Linda Thompson, "02/NWO Recap," BBS message #14009 (Fr: Linda Thompson, To: All), February 8, 1994, *AEN News*-FidoNet.

55. Thompson, Linda, "ALERT," BBS message #14290 (Fr: Linda Thompson, To: All), March 27, 1994, *AEN News*-FidoNet; cf. R. Joseph Gelarden, "Lawyer Urges Nation to Join Against Feds At Waco Site," *Indianapolis Star*, March 31, 93, E1.

56. Department of the Army, "SPECIAL ORDER NUMBER 249 EXTRACT," 19 December 1974.

57. Department of the Army, Special Orders, February 10, 1975, 1; cf. Department of the Army, Personnel Qualification Record, Part 2, Section II-Current and Previous Assignments, #35.

58. *Channel 6 News* (Indianapolis, IN), July 4, 1994.

59. Department of the Army, Personnel Qualification.

60. Department of the Army, Personnel Qualification.

61. Linda Thompson, ATTACKS.ZIP file, *AEN News*-Fidonet BBS.

62. Klenk.

63. Linda Thompson, *Curriculum Vitae*.

64. Thomas A. Pyrz, letter from Thomas A. Pyrz to Mr. John Reynolds, August 16, 1994.

65. American Justice Federation recorded telephone message, February 18, 1994.

66. John Baskette, "A Review of Chuck Missler's Beyond Coincidence," *Answers in Action Journal*, vol. 1(3), Summer 1997, 11. This journal is a small publication available exclusively through Answers in Action, a countercult Christian organization that may be reached by writing to: PO Box 2067, Costa Mesa, CA 92628.

67. I have psersonally spoken with numerous Christians—e.g., evangelical pastors, sounter-cult ministers, and Christian scholars—who have voiced criticisms to me regarding Missler's habit of bending the truth."

68.   Chuck Missler, 1994 Prophecy Update lecture (tape #CC262), April 9, 1994.

69.   Loren Ellis, author's November 1, 1997 interview with Ellis.

70.   Eloise Fisher, author's November 1, 1997 interview with Fisher.

71.   Dick Cooke, author's November 1, 1997 interview with Cooke.

72.   Missler.

73.   Maastricht Treaty, text and listing of European Union members is available on the Internet at http://www.altairiv.demon.co.uk/maastricht/heads.html.

74.   See biography of chuck Missler in William T. James gen. ed., *Foreshocks of Antichrist* (Eugene, OR: Harvest House, 1997), 407.

75.   Steve Atkin, author's November 28, 1997 interview with Atkin. The group's membership also includes extremist radio talk show hosts such as Jeffrey Baker (see Chapter 4), a right-wing conspiracy theorist who broadcasts his program on short-wave channels. Baker, although he is not a racist, builds his New World Order conspiracies around the fraudulent and anti-Semitic book *The Protocols of the Learned Elders of Zion.*

76.   Atkin, author's November 28, 1997 interview with Atkin.

77.   David Allen Lewis., quoted in Dawn Peterson, "Churches Vary On Importance of Bible Prophecy, Apocalypse," *Springfield (Missouri) News Leader,* June 29, 1997, reprinted in *Prophecy Watch International,* July 1997, 4.

78.   Peterson, 4.

79.   Chuck Missler, "Russia's Fatal Thrust to the South," in *Raging into Apocalypse: Essays in Apocalypse IV* (Green Forest, AK: New Leaf Press, 1995), 174.

80.   Peter Lalonde and Paul LaLonde, *The Mark of the Beast* (Eugene, OR: Harvest House, 1994), 187, 189, 193.

81.   Chuck Smith — founder of the worldwide Calvary Chapel system of churches, which as of 1992 had an estimated attendance of 230,000 conservative Christians (*National and International Religion Report,* 1992, 8) — was one of the most influential Christian leaders to have propagated Lindsey's 1981 timetable. His 1976 booklet entitled *Snatched Away* (Costa Mesa, CA: Maranatha Evangelical Association of Calvary Chapel, 1976), mirrored the views expressed in *The Late Great Planet Earth*:

        "Jesus said, 'This generation shall not pass away, till all these things be fulfilled.' What generation? . . . *That generation* which sees the fig tree bud forth [i.e., Israel] . . . . That generation that was living in May 1948 shall not pass away until the second coming of Jesus Christ takes place and the kingdom of God established upon the earth. How long is a generation? Forty years on average in the Bible. . . . Where does that put us? It puts us right out at the end. We're coming down to the wire" (p. 21.).

        Although Smith casually remarked in his 1978 booklet *Future Survival* (Costa Mesa, CA: Calvary Chapel, 1978) that he "could be wrong" about 1981, he went on to reiterate that the date was his "deep conviction" and that all of his plans were "predicated upon that belief" (p. 20). The year 1980 found Smith continuing to promote Lindsey's timetable in his booklet *End Times* (Costa Mesa, CA: The Word for Today, 1978): "I believe that the generation of 1948 is the last generation. Since a generation of judgment is forty years and the Tribulation period lasts seven years, I believe the Lord should come back for His Church any time before the Tribulation starts, which would mean anytime before 1981. (1948 + 40 − 7 = 1981)" (1980 edition, p. 35–36).

        As late as December 31, 1981, Smith continued to hold out for the rapture. During a special New Year's Eve church service packed with trusting followers, he proclaimed: "If we're here at this time next year, I will be very surprised." Chuck Smith, quoted in Steve Rabey, "Warning: The End Is Near, Again," *Gazette Telegraph*, December 28, 1991, D1.

When the rapture did not occur, Smith and his congregation were quite surprised, as were a vast numbers of other Christians who had bought into Lindsey's calculations. During a 1989 interview with William Alnor (Alnor, pp. 41–42), Smith would only admit to having come "close to" date-setting, maintaining that he had not taught it "as scriptural dogma." It was merely his "personal conviction that Christ was coming before 1982." Then, during a December 27, 1996 talk-radio program (Chuck Smith, *To Every Man An Answer*, KWVE, December 27, 1996). Smith distanced himself even further from the situation by claiming that he had *never* named a rapture date! A listener who called the show asked Smith if either he or Calvary Chapel had ever made a "prediction of Christ's return." The response was less than accurate: "No, uh, never, we all, we do believe he's going to return soon, and, uh, but, never any date. No. No. No. Never any date because no man knows the day or the hour."

Despite Smith's embarrassing promotion of Lindsey's 1981 date, subsequent years found him continuing to steadfastly preach a Jesus-is-just-around-the-corner message (minus a definitive date). For example, in 1989 Smith authored *Dateline Earth: Countdown to Eternity* (Old Tappan, NJ: Fleming H. Revell, 1989). On page 49 of this volume he suggested a 2014 date for the end by declaring: "I believe the scene of redemption as previewed by the apostle John [i.e., Book of Revelation] will be occurring very soon — within the next 25 years *at the maximum* (emphasis added). Such statements have made some persons in Smith's congregation confused about how they should live on a day-to-day basis, which is one of the inherent dangers to end-time extremism. Consider the following statement from an October 21, 1992 letter written by a Kelly K. to the Christian Research Institute (America's largest counter-cult ministry). The woman attends Smith's Calvary Chapel of Costa Mesa:

[T]here is sooo much talk & teaching of this being the end times from my Pastor (Chuck Smith) whom I esteem highly & many others, that I'm confused about planning for my childrens' (& my husband and I) future, as far as our goals & dreams for our family if the Lord tarries . . . . [O]n the one hand I'm very anxious awaiting to see Jesus & on the other what's the use in planning ahead? Is it all in vain?

Documentation supporting Kelly's comments can be found in sermon after sermon by Smith, as well as in his 1991 booklet *The Final Curtain* (Eugene, OR: Harvest House, 1991). Although this more recent end-time volume does not set dates, it does say that the signs of Jesus' return are everywhere and that Christians may have to wait only "a little while longer" for the rapture: "[B]efore our very eyes God is positioning nations and current events," wrote Smith. "God is orchestrating the final events prior to the return of Jesus Christ" (pp. 4, 42).

82.   Smith, *Future Survival*, 17, 20.

83.   David Hocking, a "Real Audio" recording of Hocking's statement can be obtained through the Internet at http://village.ios.com/~dougg/calvary/cc2ndcom.htm#members.

84.   Holland, see endnote #32.

APPENDIX A

1. James Mauro, "Bright Lights, Big Mystery," *Psychology Today*, July/August 1992, 56.

2. Timothy Ferris, *The Mind's Sky: Human Intelligence in a Cosmic Context* (New York: Bantam Books, 1991), quoted in Timothy Ferris, "A Cosmological Event," *New York Times Magazine*, December 15, 1991, 44.

3. Carol Zaleski, *Otherworld Journeys* (New York: Oxford University Press, 1987), 134.

4. Mauro, 57.

5. Mauro, 57.

6. James H. Lindley, Sethyn Bryan, and Bob Conley, "Near-Death Experiences in a Pacific Northwest American Population: The Evergreen Study," *Anabiosis—The Journal for Near-Death Studies*, vol. 1(2), December 1981, 110.

7. William J. Serdahely, "Variations from the Prototypic Near-Death Experience: The 'Individually Tailored' Hypothesis," *Journal of Near-Death Studies*, vol. 13(3), Spring 1995, 189.

8. Melvin Morse, author's July 29, 1994 interview with Morse.

9. Morse.

10. Beth Ann Krier, "Near-Death Visions," *Los Angeles Times*, September 18, 1990, E6.

11. Mauro, 56.

12. Glen Gabbard and Stuart Twemlow, "Do 'Near-Death Experiences' Occur Only Near-Death?—Revisited," *Journal of Near-Death Studies*, vol. 10(1), Fall 1991, 46.

13. Michael Sabom, *Recollections of Death* (New York: Harper & Row, 1982), 173.

14. Susan Blackmore, *Dying to Live*, Prometheus Books edition (London: Grafton, 1993), reprinted in America by Prometheus Books, (Buffalo: Prometheus Books, 1993), 211.

15. Sabom, 173–174.

16. Wilder Penfield, *The Mystery of the Mind* (Princeton: Princeton University Press, 1975), 21–22, quoted in Blackmore, 212.

17. Wilder Penfield, "The Role of the Temporal Cortex in Certain Psychical Phenomena," *The Journal of Mental Science*, 101:458, quoted in Blackmore, 212.

18. Blackmore, 213; cf. Stuart W. Twemlow, "Clinical Approaches to the Out-of-Body Experience" *Journal of Near-Death Studies*, vol. 8(1), Fall 1989, 37 and J. R. Stevens, "Sleep is for Seizures: A New Interpretation of the Role of Phasic Events in Sleep and Wakefulness," in *Sleep in Epileptics* (New York: Academic Press, 1982), M. B. Sternman, M. N. Shouse and P. Passouant eds., 249–264.

19. Kenneth Ring, "Amazing Grace: The Near-Death Experience As A Compensatory Gift," *Journal of Near-Death Studies*, vol. 10(1), Fall 1991, 36.

20. Jill Neimark, "It's Magical, It's Malleable, It's Memory," *Psychology Today*, January/February 1995, 45.

21. Neimark, 80.

22. Neimark, 45.

23. Ring, 212–213.

APPENDIX B

1. "I Didn't Know That . . .," *Los Angeles Times*, June 16, 1997, B2; cf. Marvin D. Mayer, "Awaiting the End of Millennium Malarkey," *Los Angeles Times*, January 1, 1997, B7.

2.   Kenneth L. Woodward, "Uh-Oh, Maybe We Missed the Big Day," *Newsweek*, August 11, 1997, 15; cf. "Some Care, Some Don't," *U.S. News & World Report*, March 10, 1997, 12.

3.   Burt Wolf, *Gatherings & Celebrations* (New York: Doubleday, 1996), 5–6.

4.   Wolf, 6.

5.   Joseph Gallagher, "Don't Count On Millennium to Be the End," *National Catholic Reporter*, August 11, 1995, 21.

6.   William David Spencer, "Does Anybody Really Know What Time It Is?," *Christianity Today*, July 17, 1995, 29.

Index

Soviet Union, dissolution of, 87-88, 288-89

Spain
    doomsday movements, 168-69
    flagellants, 179
    tensions between Christians and Muslims, 169

Spangler, Lee T., 44

Sparks, Joyce, 144

SRC. *See* Southwest Radio Church

Stearns, Peter, 171

Stern, Kenneth, 129

Stewart, Basil, 71

Stiles, Orvil, 322

Stoeffler, Johannes, 60

Stoics, 160

Strozier, Charles, 303

suicides. *See* mass suicides

Sumrall, Lester, 99

Sun Bear, 260, 307

survivalists, 83, 146, 152, 309-10

Switzerland, Order of the Solar Temple, 22-25

Taborites, 181

Tate, David, 131

Taylor, Charles, 99, 102, 287, 310-11

Taylor, John, 69-70

T.E.L.A.H. *See* Heaven's Gate

Tertullian, 165

Tetzel, Johann, 182

Teutons, 160-61

Thibodeau, David, 309

Thomas, Harold, 322

Thomas, Joi, 77

Thompson, E. A., 262

Thompson, Linda D., 117, 317, 320-21

Tokyo, nerve gas attack in subway, 25

Toole, Ken, 132

tornadoes, 269-70

Torpo, Serghei (Vissarion), 15-16

tribulation, 6, 7

See also premillennialism

Trochmann, John, 113, 115, 152-53, 309

Troeltsch, Ernst, 3

Tsvygun, Maria (Maria Devi Khristos), 16-21

Tzadok, Ariel, 78

UFOs, 32-41, 45-46, 141-42

United Nations, New World Order theories, 116-18, 128, 140-41, 151-52, 318

United States
    Branch Davidians, 9-14
    colonial period, 209-10
    Heaven's Gate, 31-41
    Jehovah's Witnesses, 229-51
    Millerites, 210-27

U.S. Army, 318-19, 320-21

U.S. Geological Survey, National Earthquake Information Center, 266

U.S. National Hurricane Center, 268

Ussher, James, 71, 281, 283, 284

Van Auken, John, 57

Vance, Dan, 151

Van Impe, Jack, 108, 125-26, 149-52, 285, 309, 316
    signs of end-times seen by, 256, 258, 259, 267, 271, 272, 276
    time calculations, 6, 282

Viega, Poia, 14

Vikings, 160-61

VISA, 125-26

Vissarion (Serghei Torpo), 15-16

Vitalis, Orderic, 285

Voliva, Wilbur Glen, 287

Vuarnet, Alain, 25

Vuarnet, Patrick, 25

Wabun Wind, 260

Waco (Texas). *See* Branch Davidians

Walvoord, John, 286

Warfield, Benjamin, 120